Charles Storrs Halsey

An Etymology of Latin and Greek

Charles Storrs Halsey
An Etymology of Latin and Greek
ISBN/EAN: 9783743394278
Manufactured in Europe, USA, Canada, Australia, Japa
Cover: Foto ©Thomas Meinert / pixelio.de

Manufactured and distributed by brebook publishing software (www.brebook.com)

Charles Storrs Halsey

An Etymology of Latin and Greek

AN ETYMOLOGY

OF

LATIN AND GREEK.

BY

CHARLES S. HALSEY, A.M.

BOSTON:
PUBLISHED BY GINN, HEATH, & CO.
1882.

PREFACE.

THE following work had its origin in a felt want. Many students of the classical languages, all along the early part of their course, use text-books provided with vocabularies. These vocabularies, from the necessity of their limits, are brief and imperfect, and they enter but little into the subject of etymology. Even when afterwards the lexicon is used, the etymology is often studied only for separate words as they occur in reading; and the scattered and fragmentary information given in the lexicons produces a corresponding state of knowledge in the mind even of a diligent student. No connected, systematic, or thorough knowledge of etymology is thus acquired. In the grammar something may be done for historical etymology; but the requirements of other topics in a school grammar must always prevent this subject from receiving there the full treatment which its importance demands.

There remain the larger works expressly devoted to the subject, nearly all of them in German, excellent when one gets to them and is prepared for them, but by their style and fulness, as well as size and cost, not adapted to the wants of an American school-room or of the ordinary student. They will be studied only by the few, and the benefit to be derived from them will generally come only when the student is far advanced in his course, and after years of study of other works.

But historical etymology, that gives the original and central meaning of related words, and, gathering the words themselves together, unites them by the natural bond of their common origin, should not be so long deferred, nor should it be pursued only as a higher range of study. Itself the historical foundation of all the structure of language, certainly it should form a prominent part in the foundation of the course of study. Presented in a simple form, it can be made to furnish a large vocabulary of the most practical words, and these not arranged for comparison in the separate language merely, Greek with Greek, Latin with Latin, but placed side by side, each language throwing light upon the other. A wider comparison enriches with knowledge and enlarges the mind; a deeper comprehension of the laws of progress in language reveals new and interesting truth, arousing curiosity and stimulating to further investigations.

It has been urged against the study of etymology that we have not within our reach sufficient material to furnish the basis of the science, and that etymologists, proceeding often not upon any well-ascertained general principles, but upon superficial resemblance of words, and even roaming off in wild excursions of fanciful associations, have produced such results as to bring the study into deserved condemnation. We must always bear in mind that historical etymology is not specially concerned with the absolute origin of language. It is concerned to ascertain the early forms, wherever they are traceable. True, there are many words which we cannot trace to their early forms; but there are also very many words, and these the most important, that we can trace, and of their etymology our knowledge is as reliable as any in the whole range of language. It must be acknowledged, too, that the work of many professed etymologists did in former times bring discredit upon the study. But the case is now widely different. The general principles and methods according to which all scientific etymological research must proceed, are now thoroughly established and recognized. The application of these principles requires a wide and careful comparison of kindred words. As this comparison is always going on and becoming still wider and more discriminating, the special results attained, relating either to single words or to the rules deduced, must always be held as open to any modification which may be reasonably required by continued investigation.

For a long period of time, extending to the year 1876, the views of etymologists in regard to the rules of Indo-European phonetics were in substantial agreement. Beginning with that year, certain important modifications were proposed in some of the rules of the Indo-European phonetic system; and these modifications are now generally accepted among the German philologists. These views will be found stated and explained in Part I., Chap. VI., and Part IV., Chaps. I.-III. In presenting them I am much indebted to Prof. Maurice Bloomfield, with whose cordial approval I have given the statement of those chapters condensed mainly from his paper on the Greek Ablaut, published in the "American Journal of Philology" for September, 1880. The Preliminary Statement of the same views is condensed from his article in the Journal of December, 1881. The roots, arranged in accordance with this system, are given by themselves near the close of the volume, so that the use of them will not lead to any confusion.

In the preparation of the present work, the author has endeavored to conform to the latest investigations of the highest authorities. In general, doubtful or disputed etymologies have been omitted, or, in the few cases given, they are marked doubtful. The table of vowel-scales is from Schleicher's "Comparative Grammar." It is assumed that any student who may use this Etymology is already provided with a suitable grammar of Latin or Greek; and, therefore, this work does not state in full the prefixes and suffixes which are given in the grammars. Neither does it aim to present in full the processes of inflection, which would require a larger treatise upon comparative grammar.

The object of this work is to present, within the limits of a school-book, the most needful etymological information that is not adequately furnished by the grammar or the lexicon. Even within these limits, some things are stated that are not intended to be learned in the early part of a student's course, *e.g.*, the Sanskrit forms. They are given because they illustrate the subject, and may be used for later reference. Great prominence has been given to the derivation of English words. Many of the cognate words here treated have descended to us through the French, or through the Teutonic family. A complete index is furnished for the Latin, the Greek, and the cognate English words.

The study of etymology, as here presented, may advantageously begin at an early stage in the study of Latin; and it should continue, in some form, throughout the course of classical education. The present work may be used for regular daily lessons in connection with the study of the classical text, and may also, with equal advantage and facility, be employed for reference on individual words.

C. S. HALSEY.

SCHENECTADY: April, 1882.

PRELIMINARY STATEMENT OF THE NEW SYSTEM OF INDO-EUROPEAN PHONETICS.

The changes proposed by the new system have reference chiefly to the vowels. It is held that the European vowels, $\breve{a}$, $\breve{e}$, $\breve{o}$, are not, as had been previously supposed, later modifications of an original Indo-European $\dot{\breve{a}}$, but are themselves original Indo-European vowels. The theory of vowel-increase has been abandoned; the consequence is roots of the form $a^e s$, $a^e i$, $sra^e u$, $bha^e r$, $ma^e n$, $da^e ik$, $da^e rk$, $bha^e ndh$, (ἐσ, εἰ, σρευ, φερ, μεν, δεικ, δερκ, πενθ). Formerly the roots were inconsistently set down as εσ, φερ, μεν, δερκ, πενθ, but ἰ, σρυ, and δικ, thus allowing the e a function in the one case and denying it the same in another which is perfectly parallel. These roots have in addition to the form with ablaut a^o (Greek o: οι, δορκ, πονθ, etc.) a weak form, which differs from the strong by the lack of this e (o): σ, ἰ, σρυ, φρ, μν, δικ, δρκ, πνθ. This reduced form may safely be assumed to have stood originally only in formations which had the word-tone on some non-radical syllable, — thus naturally bringing about a less distinct pronunciation of the root-syllable. The graphical representation of this weakened utterance is *root minus the e-o vowel.*

The recognition of these weak root-forms leads irresistibly to the assumption of *Indo-European lingual and nasal vowels;* Indo-European $\underset{\sim}{r}$, ($\underset{\sim}{l}$), $\underset{\sim}{n}$, $\underset{\sim}{m}$, represented in Greek by αρ or ρα (αλ or λα) for the lingual, and α and αν, α and αμ, for the nasal vowels.

Strange in external appearance are the Indo-European and Greek groundforms or explanatory symbols which are the result: *τ$\underset{\sim}{n}$-νυμαι for τάνυμαι; *β$\underset{\sim}{n}$-ϳω for βαίνω = venio. The

Greek groundform for ἐφθάρατο would be *ἐ-φθρ-ντο. It certainly does not seem as if one of the acquisitions of the grammatical science of to-day were simplicity of method in representing its processes. We will, however, gladly put up with a cumbrous system of symbols, if we are compensated for it by exactness — if such symbols help to convey to the reader the exact meaning of the writer. This quality the signs, which may be gleaned from the examples above, in general possess to a high degree. $i̯$ is the designation for semivocalic or semiconsonantal y in distinction from the full consonant (spirant) y; the same is true for $u̯$. When we examine the symbol-group *$n̥sma^e$, there can be no doubt as to the exact value represented by it: $n̥s$- is a syllable in which the element that carries the syllable tone is in the main nasal (a nasal vowel). The vocalic color of this nasal vowel the symbol does not undertake to express, and it is indeed unknown. The representations of it in the various languages of the family diverge widely: Greek and Sanskrit a and an; but German un, Latin en, Lithuanian in. In the same way $r̥$ is an element mainly of a lingual character, bearing the tone of the syllable; in the rendering of it the Sanskrit at least coincides with the symbol (Sanskrit $r̥$); the other languages again vary greatly: Zend $ĕrĕ$; Greek $αρ$ and $αλ$; Latin and German or (ur); Lithuanian ir. The remainder ma^e is practically identical with Greek $με$. The symbol does not, however, profess to define the value of the Indo-European vowel, which it renders, quite so closely; a^e expresses a vowel sound lying somewhere between e and a, but without quite reaching a; in the same way a^o is a sound between o and a which does not quite reach a. Nevertheless it is becoming more and more common to write simply e and o for a^e and a^o even at the expense of perfect exactness; and in the present work the more simple forms are preferred, so that in Indo-European roots and words e may be found where a^e could also be written, and o where a^o could also be written.

· The writers of the new school treat the vowel-phenomena in 'reihen,' 'vocalreihen,' an expression which, like many German grammatical terms, can be rendered but inadequately into English by 'vowel series.' Parallel with the three vocalic forms presented in the a^e-reihe (form with a^e, form with a^o, and form without this a^e-a^o) there appear three other series —the ē-series: ē, ō, ĕ, the ā-series: ā, ō, ă, and the ō-series: ō, ō, ŏ, justifying the following proportion for the Greek:

TABLE I.

ε-series : ε : o : — =
η-series : η : ω : ε =
ā-series : ā : ω : ă =
ω-series : ω : ω : o

An example of the η-series is presented by: τί-θη-μι, θω-μό-ς, τί-θε-μαι; of the ā-series by φη-μί, φω-νή, φα-μέν; of the ω-series by δί-δω-μι, δέ-δω-κα, δο-τός.

In order to understand the origin of these series, i.e., the method which led to their recognition, it will be necessary to refer to the 'Theory of Sonant Coefficients.' This theory assumes that all Indo-European roots can have but one vowel, a^e (e) varying with a^o (o); all other seemingly vocalic elements are in reality semiconsonants, which assume the function of vowels only when this e-o has for some reason been lost; this semiconsonant is called 'sonant coefficient.' In cases where the root does not possess such a sonant coefficient, it remains vowelless (πέτ-ομαι, ἐ-πτ-όμην). This agrees incontrovertibly with all the facts in the case of roots of the a^e-series; πετ, δει, χευ, δερ, στελ, μεν, λειπ, ἐλευθ, δερκ, πενθ, etc., can interchange with ποτ, δοι, etc., but only upon the loss of this ε or o do the semiconsonantal elements contained in these roots assume the function of vowels: δι, χυ, δρ, στλ, μγ, λιπ, ἐλυθ, δρκ, πγθ, etc. The possible sonant coefficients of roots of the a^e-series are accordingly: i, u, r, (l), n, m; and if we add these to the real vowels of the a^e-series, we obtain the following five (or six) series within the a^e-series:

TABLE II.

$\epsilon\iota : o\iota : \iota =$ $(\epsilon\lambda : o\lambda : \lambda) =$

$\epsilon\upsilon : o\upsilon : \upsilon =$ $\epsilon\nu : o\nu : \underset{.}{\nu} =$

$\epsilon\rho : o\rho : \underset{.}{\rho} =$ $\epsilon\mu : o\mu : \underset{.}{\mu}$

In Greek the roots made according to these models are about 250, and it is probable that more than one-half of the roots which occur in verbal formations are of this class. In the other languages also these roots are preponderatingly represented (e.g., Sanskrit and Gothic). The thought, then, that the remaining roots also may be found constructed on the same plan does not lie far removed, and the attempt has been boldly made. As in Table II., ι, υ, ρ, (λ), ν, μ are the sonant coefficients to ϵ-o; as these are forced in the reduced root-form to play the part of vowels (ι, υ, $\underset{.}{\rho}$, $(\underset{.}{\lambda})$, $\underset{.}{\nu}$, $\underset{.}{\mu}$), so in Table I. ϵ of the η-series is a sonant coefficient ($\underset{.}{\epsilon}$), which is performing the function of a vowel, because the real root-vowel ϵ-o has been lost; i.e., η stands for $\epsilon\epsilon$; ω for $o\epsilon$; in the same way the vocalism of the $\bar{a}$-series goes back to $\epsilon\breve{a}$ for $\bar{a}$; $o\breve{a}$ for ω, and $\breve{a}$ is the sonant coefficient; so also the ω-series is to be resolved into ϵo, oo, and o. We could then add to Table II. three perfectly parallel series:

TABLE III.

$\epsilon\epsilon : o\epsilon : \epsilon =$

$\epsilon a : oa : a =$

$\epsilon o : oo : o$

From the standpoint of the phonetist it is believed that no objection can be urged; ϵ, a, and o can be '*consonans*' as well as ι and υ (Sievers, Phonetik, p. 123): the contractions with the root-vowels into the vowel-forms actually occurring would also pass criticism, though it is to be noted that in the first perpendicular column of Table III. the *semiconsonantal* elements impress their vocalic color on the result (εε, εα, εο : η, ā, ω), while in the second perpendicular column the semiconsonantal element succumbs, and the result of the contraction (ω) has the *vocalic color of the real root-vowel* (o).

From the standpoint, however, of the history of the Indo-European languages, we are not at present warranted in accepting these results (shown in immediate connection with Table III.). No one language shows even a single instance in which the elements supposed to underlie the contraction occur uncontracted. This, to be sure, is no final condemnation; we are becoming accustomed more and more to view the immediate historic background of the separate Indo-European languages, — the Indo-European parent language, as a real language devoid of unnatural regularity, presenting in many respects phenomena of a very secondary nature, — phenomena which had a long history before them; and the possibility of these contractions must not be absolutely denied. Practically, however, they cannot *as yet be recognized in that form*. This theory has, nevertheless, yielded one result that we may safely adopt, namely, the recognition of the fact that the η and ā of the η- and ā- series vary with ω under the same circumstances under which ε varies with o.

It will be interesting now to see what vocalic and semivocalic material is furnished for the Indo-European parent speech.

The a^s-series yields two real vowels: a^e and a^o (*e* and *o*) and the following sounds wavering between consonantal and vocalic function: *y* and *i*; *v* and *u*; *r* and *ṛ* (*l* and *ḷ*); *n* and *ṇ*, *m* and *ṃ*; perhaps also the nasals corresponding to the two Indo-European guttural series, which could be designated by *ñ* and *ṋ*, and *n̄* and *n̳*. Its diphthongs would be *ei, oi, eu, ou*, (in a wider sense of the term also *er, or* (*el, ol*); *en, on*; *em, om*, and even *eñ, oñ*; *en̄, on̄*).

The $\bar{e}$-series yields: $\bar{e}$ and $\bar{o}^1$ (so designated to differentiate it from the $\bar{o}$'s of the two following series) and e.

The $\bar{a}$-series yields: $\bar{a}$ and $\bar{o}^2$; and a.

The $\bar{o}$-series yields: $\bar{o}^3$ and $\bar{o}^4$ and o. Of diphthongal material in which the first part is a long vowel there appears certainly at least: $\bar{a}u$ in the stem $n\bar{a}u$-; Ionic (not pan-hellenic) νηῦ-ς; Sanskrit $n\bar{a}\acute{u}$-s; Latin $n\bar{a}v$-is.

We subjoin a provisional scheme of Indo-European vowels and semivowels, claiming neither absolute correctness nor scientific symmetry in the symbols employed. It will, however, suffice to give a fair idea of what is supposed to be the material contained by the immediate predecessor of the separate languages of the Indo-European family.

Pure short vowels: $\breve{e}$ —— $\breve{o}$; $\breve{a}$
Their diphthongs: ei —— oi; ai
                    eu —— ou; au
Long vowels: $\bar{e}$ —— $\bar{o}^1$
                $\bar{a}$ —— $\bar{o}^2$
                $\bar{o}^3$ ——($\bar{o}^4$)

Short vowels or semivowels corresponding to these: e, a, o.

One diphthong: $\bar{a}u$

Semiconsonants: y-i; v-u; r-$\d{r}$; (l-$\d{l}$); m-$\d{m}$; n-$\d{n}$ ($\tilde{n}$-$\d{\tilde{n}}$; $\bar{n}$-$\d{\bar{n}}$).

SUGGESTIONS IN REGARD TO THE STUDY OF ETYMOLOGY.

As this subject, in its systematic form, has not been commonly taught in the schools, it seems appropriate to offer some suggestions, in general for the study of Etymology, and in particular for the use of the present work.

1. We must bear in mind that the most important and practical facts may be clearly ascertained without determining all their theoretical and antecedent conditions. Thus, to establish the important fact that certain words are etymologically related to each other, it is not necessary to establish the roots of the words themselves. E.g., there is an undoubted etymological connection between the verb φέρω, to bear, and the adjective φορός, bearing; and this connection remains conclusively established whether we assign for the word-group three root-forms, φερ, φορ, φρ, or two root-forms, φερ, φορ, or one root-form, φερ, or even if we say that no root-form can be assigned at all. So, also, the verb *tendo*, to stretch, is to be connected with the noun *tŏnus*, a stretching, sound, tone; and this connection remains conclusively established whether we assign two root-forms, *ten, ton*, or only one root-form, *ten*, or even if we say that no root-form can be assigned at all.

At the present time, there is a great deal of movement of opinion in the etymological field. Various innovations are proposed, prominent among them that of bi-syllabic roots. In view of all the proposed changes, it is well to be cautious about accepting any roots without reserve. From the nature of the case, roots cannot be known by direct or positive evidence. They can be laid down only with various degrees of probability in their favor; yet, at all events, they may serve a practical purpose as convenient labels to aid us in associating related words.

2. In accordance with this principle, it is held that the word-groups, or sets, numbered in this work 1–528 belong etymologically as thus arranged. These words furnish an orderly and practical vocabulary; and they may become fixed in the memory by the very association that binds the words themselves together, namely, their etymological relation to each other.

3. Careful discrimination is needed in adapting the different parts of this study to the wants of the student in the different stages of his progress. A younger student, in the early part of a classical course, may advantageously learn some roots, and how to form from them stems and words, and may thus acquire a useful vocabulary; but to master fully the principles involved in the theoretical views will require a mind more mature, and a higher and wider range of study. Therefore, at first and with younger pupils, the application should receive the greater attention, and the theory should be presented only in its most prominent and practical features.

4. While it is desirable that the scholar should be acquainted with the leading principles of both the older and the later system, in practice one must be preferred to the other. In general, where the later views conflict with the earlier, the author would recommend the later views, as more likely to prove correct; and especially would advise that the *roots* should be taken *as arranged in Part IV., Chap. IV.*

5. It is, of course, in itself undesirable to present conflicting views, even if they are only theoretical, in a work designed for school use. One system, uniform, consistent, and commanding the assent of the etymological world, would be a great desideratum. But certainly such a system cannot be presented now. No one can prophesy how far distant the day may be when theoretical views shall be harmonized; and

it is not wise to defer to that uncertain day the acquisition of practical knowledge.

In the present work, an effort is made to avoid as far as possible the confusion liable to arise from a statement of opposing theoretical views. For this purpose, in the body of the work, the principles of the older school are first clearly set forth. As these principles commanded until very recently an assent almost universal, they should be stated fully; and any part of them that may be modified or even overthrown by later investigation deserves to be stated, at least as a part of the history of the progress of the science. The principles of the new school are then given in Part I., Ch. VI., and their application in Part IV., Ch. I.–IV.

It has been thought advisable to present at the very outset of the work a brief statement of the new-school system, with an explanation of the symbols which it employs. This preliminary statement has therefore been given in the preceding pages.

6. This work can be intelligently studied by one who has no knowledge of the Greek language; but it would be advantageous for a Latin scholar to learn the Greek alphabet and the sounds of the letters, as it would require but little time, and the additional benefit would be very great.

7. A simple illustration is here presented to show one method in which the subject may be taught. Let us examine first the Latin words under set No. 142. In all these words we find a common syllable *fŭg;* and in *fūgi,* the perfect of *fŭgio,* we find the same syllable with a long quantity, *fūg.* Here, then, we have a root in its two forms, *fŭg, fūg.* We observe in these Latin words one meaning that is general in its character and common to all the words. This meaning is expressed in English by the word 'flee.' The syllable *fŭg, fūg,* is a simple, primitive form, expressing only the general meaning of these words. As such, it is called their root.

By joining to this root significant elements, we may render

its meaning more limited, and so form stems and then words. Thus, by adding *a* to the root *fŭg*, we form *fŭga*, the stem of the noun *fŭga*, flight. By adding to this stem the various case-suffixes, we may inflect the noun through all its variations of case and number. By adding to the root *fŭg* the suffix *ā*, we form *fŭgā*, the stem of the verb *fŭgāre*, to put to flight. By adding to this stem the various suffixes that make up the verbal endings, we may inflect the verb through all its variations of voice, mood, tense, person, and number. The root *fŭg*, with the termination *ax*, forms the adjective *fŭgax*, apt to flee. Strictly speaking, we should say that the suffix added to the root is only that which with the root forms the stem of the word; but it is often more simple and convenient, as well as customary in grammars, to state at once for nouns and adjectives the ending of the nominative singular, and for verbs the ending of the first person singular of the present indicative active. The other process, though accurate, may sometimes prove rather complicated. In this instance, in the termination *ax*, *x* is for *c-s*, of which the *s* is the case-suffix of the nominative singular; *c-s* is for *co-s;* and the *ā* was originally the stem-vowel of an *ā*-verb; so that the entire process might be represented by *fŭg-ā-co-s, fŭg-ā-c-s, fŭg-āx, fŭgāx.*

A process similar in general to that illustrated with the Latin words may be applied to the Greek words in set No. 142. We find the root in two forms, φευγ, φὔγ. From this root stems may be formed, and then words. Thus, by adding the suffix *a* to the root φὔγ, we form φὔγα, the (original) stem of the noun φὔγή, flight.

The various prefixes and suffixes used in word-formation, together with their significations and application, are given in the grammars; and it is not thought best to enlarge the present work by a re-statement of what is already well stated in the grammars.

CONTENTS.

PART I.

Principles of Etymology.

	Page
PROVINCE OF THE SCIENCE	1
CLASSIFICATION OF INDO-EUROPEAN LANGUAGES	1–3
GROWTH OF LANGUAGE	3, 4
ROOTS	4–7
ROOTS CLASSIFIED BY THEIR FORM	6
ROOTS CLASSIFIED BY THEIR SIGNIFICATION	6, 7
CLASSIFICATION OF ALPHABETIC SOUNDS	7
SOUNDS OF THE ENGLISH ALPHABET	8
SOUNDS OF THE INDO-EUROPEAN ALPHABET	10
SOUNDS OF THE SANSKRIT ALPHABET	11
SOUNDS OF THE GREEK ALPHABET	11, 12
SOUNDS OF THE LATIN ALPHABET	12–14
PHONETIC CHANGE	14–20
GRIMM'S LAW	14, 15
GENERAL PRINCIPLE OF PHONETIC CHANGE	16
GENERAL RESULTS OF PHONETIC CHANGE	16–19
I. WEAK ARTICULATION	16–18
Vowel Change	16, 17
1. Substitution	16
2. Loss	16
3. Assimilation	17
4. Dissimilation	17

xviii CONTENTS.

	Page
Consonant Change	17, 18
1. Substitution	17
2. Loss	17, 18
3. Assimilation	18
4. Dissimilation	18
II. INDISTINCT ARTICULATION	18, 19
1. Labialism	18
2. Dentalism	18
3. Parasitic Sound	18
4. Aspiration	19
VOWEL-INCREASE	19, 20
THE VIEWS OF THE NEW SCHOOL	21–40

PART II.

Regular Substitution of Sounds.

	Page
TABLE OF REGULAR SUBSTITUTION OF SOUNDS	41, 42
Κ	43–64
Γ	64–74
Χ	75–80
Τ	80–91
Δ	92–102
Θ	102–109
Π	109–123
Β	124
Φ	124–131
Ν	131–138
Μ	138–146
Ρ	146–152
Λ	152–160
Σ	161–164
Ξ	164
F	165–167

	Page
SPIRITUS ASPER FOR INITIAL *s*	167, 168
SPIRITUS ASPER FOR *j*	168
VOWELS	168–170

PART III.

Irregular Substitution of Sounds.

LABIALISM	171–177
DENTALISM	177, 178
PHONETIC WEAKENING	178, 179
SPORADIC CHANGE OF LIQUIDS	179, 180

PART IV.

Application of the Principles of the New School.

ABLAUT I.	181–185
ABLAUT II.	186–188
ABLAUT III.	189–194
ARRANGEMENT OF THE ROOTS	194–201
GREEK INDEX	203–220
LATIN INDEX	221–238
ENGLISH INDEX OF COGNATE WORDS	239–252

EXPLANATIONS.

In Part II. and Part III. the words are arranged in sets, numbered from 1 to 528. In general, at the beginning of each set, five things are stated in the following order: 1. The Indo-European root; 2. The Sanskrit root; 3. The Greek root; 4. The Latin root; 5. The meaning of the roots. Each of the first four particulars is separated from the following by a semicolon, and a dash is used to show that a root is wanting. If a root appears in one language under more than one form, the forms are separated from each other by a comma. In these sets the sign √ is not needed and not used; elsewhere it is used to denote a root, and Indo-European roots are printed in capitals. If any form, however placed or marked, contains more than one syllable, it may not be called strictly a root; also, if inclosed in parenthesis, it may not be a root.

At the beginning of each great division of the sets, the corresponding letters of Indo-European, Sanskrit, Greek, and Latin, for that division are shown by the same method of representation. A cognate English word is printed in italics; and, if not a definition, it is also enclosed in brackets. In the separate indexes of Greek, Latin, and English, the figures refer to the number of the set of words.

* denotes a theoretical form, i.e., a form which, though not actually occurring, may be supposed to have preceded the existing form to which it is attached. A theoretical form is also sometimes denoted by being enclosed in parenthesis and following the sign =.

† denotes that a word is borrowed from Greek.

‡ denotes that a word is found only in inscriptions, or in the old grammarians or lexicographers.

Other signs and abbreviations are employed with the significations usual in grammars and lexicons.

PART I.

Principles of Etymology.

CHAPTER I.

CLASSIFICATION OF INDO-EUROPEAN LANGUAGES.

ETYMOLOGY treats of individual words, with reference to their origin and development. Its methods of investigation are historical, aiming to ascertain the forms which were earliest, with their corresponding meanings, and the form and meaning of each subsequent modification.

Nearly all the languages of Europe, and two at least of those of Asia, the Sanskrit and the Zend, are found by comparison to have such resemblances to one another as to prove that they are descended from a common stock. They constitute a very large and important class, and as they have been spoken by nations living throughout a region that extended from India on the east to the western boundaries of Europe, they are called the Indo-European languages. They are also known by other names, — Aryan, Indo-Germanic, Japhetic.

The common stock from which they spring is called the Indo-European original-language. The words of this original language are not known to us by the direct evidence of any records, but from an extended comparison of the later existing forms in the derived languages we infer the forms of the original language. Neither do we know where or when the people lived who spoke this original language. It seems probable that their home was somewhere in south-western Asia, and the time of their dispersion not less than three thousand years before Christ. From their successive and continued migrations, chiefly toward the west, arose the most important nations and languages of the civilized world.

Indo-European languages may be divided into three principal groups or divisions. These are: —

I. The *Aryan* division, comprising the Indian and the Eranian (or Iranian) family of language. Of the Indian family, that of which we have the oldest record is the Old-Indian, which is the language of the oldest portion of the Vedas. At a later time, when it had become fixed in a more simple form and subject to certain grammatical rules as a written literary language, and thus distinguished from the popular dialects, it was called Sanskrit. The Eranian family includes the Zend, the Old-Persian, and the Armenian.

II. The *South-Western European* division. This includes:—

1. The Greek. The ancient Greek is represented now by the Romaic or modern Greek.

2. The Latin, akin to which were the Oscan and the Umbrian of central Italy. The chief modern representatives of Latin are Italian, Spanish, Portuguese, and French.

3. The Keltic, the language of the tribes found by the Romans in Spain, Gaul, Britain, and Ireland.

III. The *Northern European* division. This includes: —

1. The Sclavonic family, comprising numerous languages; among them Russian, Bulgarian, Polish, Bohemian, Lithuanian, and Old-Prussian.

2. The Teutonic family. Of this family the oldest member is the Gothic, which became extinct in the ninth century. The modern Teutonic languages are divided into two distinct groups, the Scandinavian and the Germanic. The Scandinavian includes the Danish, Swedish, Norwegian, and Icelandic. The Germanic is subdivided into two branches, the High Germanic and the Low Germanic. The Low Germanic includes: (1) The Friesic, (2) The Anglo-Saxon, (3) The Old

Saxon, (4) The Dutch, (5) The Low German. The English language is descended from the Anglo-Saxon; but it has also received large additions from other sources, especially from Latin through the French.

CHAPTER II.

GROWTH OF LANGUAGE.

THE various forms of inflected words have been constructed by joining together elements that were originally independent words. To illustrate the process, let us compare the expression *he did love* with the expression *he loved*. Of the form *loved*, let us examine the suffix -*d*. In Anglo-Saxon it is -*de*, which is derived from *dide*, the imperfect of *dŏn*, 'do.' A similar form appears also in Gothic. From the Anglo-Saxon word *dide* comes the English *did*. Thus the suffix -*d* and the auxiliary verb *did* have the same origin; they have also the same effect on the meaning of the verb, so that, in regard to origin and meaning, *loved* = *did love*. The difference between the two expressions lies in the manner of applying the auxiliary. In the form *did love*, the auxiliary appears before the principal verb, not united in one word with the verb, and not abbreviated in its English form. In the word *loved*, the auxiliary appears after the principal verb, joined in one word with it, and abbreviated to -*d*, which we then call a suffix. In the word *godly*, the suffix *ly* is derived from an independent word, the same word from which we get the English *like; godly* = *god-like*. This suffix *ly* is the one used in forming most of our English adverbs. So also the French adverbial ending *ment* is derived from the Latin ablative *mente; grandement*, 'grandly,' was originally *grandi mente*, 'with great mind.' In the Latin verb *vŏcābam*, the suffix *bam* was originally an independent word, the imperfect from the root BHU (No. 348).

The process here illustrated is of very great importance and wide application. In the Indo-European languages, *all form-making which we can trace within the historical period is by this same method, namely, by external accretion.* We may logically conclude that this was the only method in the more ancient times, and therefore that it is sufficient to account for the whole structure of Indo-European language. Wherever we find in any word a subordinate part, indicating some modification or relation of the main radical idea, there we find what remains of a formerly independent word, which has ceased to be independent, and has become an affix. The Indo-European original-language in its earliest stage *consisted entirely of monosyllabic words.*

Entire words in a language may pass out of use, and so be lost. This may occur from various causes, as when the idea is no longer sufficiently important to the community to call for any word as its exponent, or when a given word is crowded out of use by another word coming in to take its place, or when, from no assignable cause other than mere chance, a word becomes obsolete. Still more important in the history of language is the loss of forms of grammatical inflection. Of this, the English language furnishes the most striking illustrations. Many of its suffixes have disappeared from their combination; but their place has been supplied by separate and auxiliary words.

CHAPTER III.

ROOTS.

A ROOT is a simple, primitive form, expressing only the general meaning of a word. Such a form, within the boundaries of any one of the Indo-European languages, we may properly describe by the name of the language in which it occurs; the corresponding root in the Indo-European original-language we call the Indo-European root. Thus, the Greek ἄκων, a javelin, and the Latin ăcus, a needle, are kindred in etymology. The Indo-European root from which they come is *ak*, the Greek root is ἀκ, the Latin root *ac*. So the Greek φεύγω and the Latin *fŭgio* are kindred; their Indo-European root is *bhugh*, the Greek root is φυγ, the Latin root *fŭg*. Of an inflected word the fundamental part, to which the terminations are appended, is called the stem.

By taking from a word everything that is formative or accidental, we obtain the root. In the verb *vŏcābam*, the last four letters are strictly formative. The root is *vŏc*, which means simply 'call.' The suffix *a* forms with the root *vŏc* the stem *vŏcā*; the suffix *bam* was originally a separate word, the imperfect from the root BHU (No. 348), containing already the personal ending *m*, which marks the first person singular in the active voice. This *m* is from the pronominal root shown in the pronoun *me* (No. 385). In the word *vocabam*, the suffix *bam* performs the office of an auxiliary; *ba* is called the sign of the imperf. ind., and *m* is called the personal ending. In the verb ἐτίθετο, the parts ε, τι, and το are formative, ε denoting past time, τι denoting duration, and το denoting the person, number, and voice. The root is θε. In the verb ἐγίγνετο, the parts ε, γι, ε, and το are known to be formative, and when they are taken away, the remaining part γν might seem to be the root; but the root is really the syllable γεν, of which the ε has in some forms of the verb been dropped. The full root γεν is seen in other forms of the verb and in the cognate noun γένος.

Neither roots nor stems are to be regarded as mere abstractions obtained by any mechanical process of separating a word into its parts. In the earliest history of the Indo-European original-language, the roots were capable of independent use; they were themselves the monosyllabic words of the language. They form, therefore, the groundwork upon which is built the structure of stems and words, — the process of building being one of composition, or joining one root to another. Of an inflected word, the root which conveys the general and principal meaning is called the root of the word, or the principal root. The roots joined to this, and serving to define, restrict, or vary its application, are called affixes. An affix placed before a principal root is called a prefix; placed after a principal root it is called a suffix.

Every root is a monosyllable, and of every unmodified root the vowel is short. A root containing a long vowel is a modified root. A root may sometimes vary in its form, and yet retain its meaning unchanged or but slightly changed. In such case we may place the forms side by side, generally giving that one first which has the widest use. Examples are καλ, κελ; στελ, σταλ; βαλ, βελ; τρεπ, τραπ; ὀκ, ὀπ. Whenever we have evidence that one form of the root existed before another or others, we may call that which was historically first the unmodified root, and every later form a modified root. We find a considerable number of roots existing in double forms, of which one is longer than the other by a final consonant. In such cases, the shorter form is believed to be the original one, and it is called a primary root; the longer form is called a secondary root; and the process of adding is called expansion. Example: primary root (Indo-Eur.), *bha;* secondary root, *bhan.*

Roots are divided according to their signification into two classes: I. *Verbal roots* (called also *predicative* and *notional*); II. *Pronominal roots* (called also *demonstrative* or *relational,* and sometimes called *radicals*).

I. VERBAL ROOTS. These express action, condition, or quality. From them are formed verbs, nouns, and adjectives. They constitute by far the more numerous class, being numbered by hundreds. They are also more complicated in their structure.

II. PRONOMINAL ROOTS. These indicate simply relation, especially the relation of place. From them are formed pronouns, adverbs, conjunctions, and all original prepositions. The pronominal roots are very few in number. They are of the simplest structure. Examples (Indo-Eur.) are *a, i, ma, na, tu, ka.*

CHAPTER IV.

ALPHABETIC SOUNDS.

THE sound of *a*, as heard in the word *far*, is the fundamental tone of the human voice, the tone naturally produced when the mouth is most fully open and the current of breath entirely unmodified. It is appropriately called a completely open sound, and the vowel representing it a completely open vowel. The opposite extreme is shown in the sounds of *k* as in *keel*, *t* as in *tan*, *p* as in *pan*. Here, some of the organs of speech having been entirely closed, the sounds are heard only upon the breaking of the contact; they are appropriately called completely close sounds, and are represented by the completely close mutes. Between these two extremes belong all the other alphabetic sounds, and they are properly arranged according to their relative degrees of closure. The principal mute-closures are three: one made by lip against lip, the labial closure, giving the sound represented by *p*; one made by the front of the tongue against the roof of the mouth, near the front teeth, the lingual closure, giving the sound represented by *t*; one, in the back of the mouth, made against the soft palate by the rear upper surface of the tongue, the palatal closure, giving the sound represented by *k*. The other classes of sounds may also be arranged in three corresponding lines of gradual closure, proceeding from the completely open *a* to the completely close mutes, *k, t, p*. This method of arrangement has been applied (Whitney's "Life and Growth of Language," p. 62) in the following scheme to represent the alphabetic sounds of the English language: —

		a		
Sonant.	æ	A		Vowels.
	e		o	
		ə		
	i		u	
	y	r l	w	Semivowels.
	ng	n	m	Nasals.
Surd.	h			Aspiration.
Sonant.	zh	z		Sibilants.
Surd.	sh	s		
Sonant.		dh	v	Spirants.
Surd.		th	f	
Sonant.	g	d	b	Mutes.
Surd.	k	t	p	
	Palatal Series.	Lingual Series.	Labial Series.	

(Sibilants and Spirants grouped as Fricatives; all lower rows grouped as Consonants.)

As it is very important to observe the exact sound represented by each character in this alphabetic scheme, illustrative words are here given. Beginning with *a*, and going downward at the left, we have *a* as in *far;* œ, *pan;* e, *fate, they;* i, *mete, pique;* y, *yet;* ng, *ring;* zh, *azure;* sh, *shall;* g, *get;* k, *keel:* going downward centrally, we have *a* as in *far;* ə (inverted *e*), *but;* r, *ran;* l, *land;* n, *no;* z, *zeal;* s, *so;* dh, *then;* th, *thin;* d, *do;* t, *tan:* going downward at the right, we have *a* as in *far;* A, *war;* o, *note;* u, *tool, rule;* w, *wall;* m, *may;* v, *vain;* f, *fame;* b, *ban;* p, *pan*. *H* is sounded as in *hale*.

Let us first compare *k, t, p* with *g, d, b,* their corresponding sonants. In the former series there is no sound while the organs of speech are closed; in the latter there is, even during the continuance of the closure, a tone produced by the vibration of the vocal chords. Herein lies the fundamental distinction of 'surd' and 'sonant' sounds. The former are produced by unintonated breath; the latter by intonated breath. Surd sounds have sometimes been called by other names, as 'strong,' 'hard,' 'sharp'; and sonant sounds have been called by other corresponding names, as 'weak,' 'soft,' 'flat'; but these names should be rejected, and the terms 'surd' and 'sonant' should be employed, because they express the true distinction. In Greek and Latin the surd aspirated mutes are often, and with sufficient propriety, called simply aspirates. Next to the mutes come the fricatives, divided into two sub-classes, spirants and sibilants. Then come the nasals (sometimes called resonants).

Beginning now at the other extreme with the open vowel a, we form by successive degrees of approach of the tongue to the palate the series of palatal sounds represented in the scheme by $a, œ, e, i$. By contraction with the lips, we form the labial series represented by a, A, o, u. The semivowels stand nearly on the dividing line between vowels and consonants. The closest of the vowels are i and u. By abbreviating their sounds sufficiently before another vowel-sound, we should change them into the consonantal sounds of y and w. With them belong r and l, which are in many languages used also as vowels. The distinctions of long and short vowel, and the three compound vowel-sounds, or diphthongs, ai (*aisle, isle*), au (*out, how*), and Ai (*oil, boy*), are for the sake of simplicity omitted in the scheme. The method of arrangement thus employed for the English alphabet may with equal advantage be applied to the alphabet of any language, to exhibit its internal relations or to compare it with other alphabets. It is in this work employed to illustrate the alphabetic sounds of Indo-European, Greek, and Latin.

Sounds of the Indo-European Alphabet.

		Palatal Series.	Lingual Series.	Labial Series.		
Sonant.	{		a		} Vowels.	
		i		u		
		y	r l	v	Semivowels.	
			n	m	Nasals.	
Surd.	h				Aspiration.	Consonants.
Surd.			s		Sibilant.	
Surd.	kh		th	ph	} Aspirated Mutes.	
Sonant.	gh		dh	bh		
Sonant.	g		d	b	} Mutes.	
Surd.	k		t	p		

The Indo-European original-language had three vowels,— *a, i, u;* three diphthongs,— *aa, ai, au;* and thirteen consonants, — *k, t, p, g, d, b, y, r, l, v, m, n, s.* A was sounded as in *far, i* as in *machine, u* as in *rule, tool.* Every short vowel had the same kind of sound as its corresponding long vowel, but less prolonged in time of utterance. In the pronunciation of a diphthong, each vowel received its own proper sound,— the sound of the second following that of the first without any interruption. The diphthongs were sounded approximately as follows: *aa* as in *far; ai* as in *aisle; au* as *ou* in *house.* The consonants, *k, t, p, d, b, r, l, m, n, h* were sounded as in English; *g* as in *get; y* as in *yet; s* as in *so; v* as *w* in *wait; kh, th, ph* were pronounced almost as in *inkhorn, hothouse, topheavy; gh, dh, bh* as in *loghouse, madhouse, Hobhouse.*

The aspiration *h* is found only in close combination with the mutes. All the aspirated mutes, and the letters, *y*, *l*, and *v*, were wanting in the earliest stage of the language.

Sounds of the Sanskrit Alphabet.

Short *a* as in *vocal, cedar, organ*, or *u*-short in *but;* long *a* as in *father;* short *i* as in *pin;* long *i* as in *pique;* short *u* as in *pull, push;* long *u* as in *rule, rude;* the vowel ṛ represents simply a smooth or untrilled *r*-sound, assuming a vocalic office in syllable-making; the vowel ḷ represents an *l*-sound similarly uttered — like the English *l*-vowel in *able, angle, addle; e* is sounded as in *prey;* ai as in *aisle; o* as in *so;* au as *au* in German *Haus* or *ou* in Eng. *house; n = ng* in *king; k' = ch* in *church; g' = j* in *judge;* ñ = *gn* in *Campagna; j = y* in *yes;* ç = *sh* in *shall;* ṭ, ḍ, ṇ are commonly pronounced as *t, d, n,* but they were produced originally by the influence of a neighboring *r*, the lower surface of the tongue being brought against the palate in pronouncing them; *v* = probably the Eng. *w; kh, th, ph* are pronounced almost as in *inkhorn, hothouse, topheavy; gh, dh, bh* as in *loghouse, madhouse, Hobhouse.*

Sounds of the Greek Alphabet.

For etymological purposes the following pronunciation is to be employed: α as *a* in *far;* η as *e* in *fête;* ῑ as *i* in *machine;* ω as *o* in *note;* υ was sounded originally as *u* in *rule* or *oo* in *tool*, later as French *u*. Every short vowel has the same kind of sound as its corresponding long vowel, but less prolonged in time of utterance. In the pronunciation of a diphthong, each vowel has its own proper sound, the sound of the second following that of the first without any interruption. The diphthongs are sounded approximately as follows: αι as *ai* in *aisle;* ει as *ei* in *eight;* οι as *oi* in *oil;* υι as *uee* in *queen* or as *ui* in *quit;* αυ as *ou* in *house;* ευ as *eu* in *feud;* ου as *ou* in *group;* ᾳ, ῃ, ῳ like α, η, ω. Of the consonants, β, δ, κ, π, τ, ρ, λ, μ, ν, ψ are sounded like their corresponding letters in English; γ before κ, γ, ξ, and χ has the sound of *n* in *anger* (= *ng* in *ring*), and in any other position it has the sound of *g* in *get;*

Sonant.		α			Vowels.
		ε	ο		
		η	ω		
		ι	υ		
		ρ	λ		Semivowels.
	γ (= *Eng.* ng)	ν		μ	Nasals.
Surd.	‘				Aspiration.
Surd.		σ			Sibilant (*fricative*).
Surd.	χ	θ		φ	Aspirated Mutes.
Sonant.	γ	δ		β	Mutes.
Surd.	κ	τ		π	
Sonant.		ζ			Double Consonants.
Surd.	ξ			ψ	
	Palatal Series.	Lingual Series.		Labial Series.	

σ has the sound of *s* in *so*. The letters φ, θ, χ probably had at first the sounds of *ph, th, ch,* in Eng. *uphill, hothouse, blockhead;* afterwards they were sounded as in Eng. *graphic, pathos,* and German *machen*. The letter ξ is sounded as *x* in *mix;* ζ may be sounded like *dz* in *adze* or like *z* in *zone*.

Sounds of the Latin Alphabet.

For etymological purposes, the Roman (or Phonetic) method of pronunciation is to be employed. According to this method, ā is pronounced as in *far;* ē as in *they;* ī as in *machine;* ō as in *holy;* *ū* as *u* in *rule* or *oo* in *tool.* Every short vowel has the same kind of sound as its corresponding long vowel, but less prolonged in time of utterance. In the pronunciation of a diphthong, each vowel receives its own proper sound, the sound of the second following that of the first without any

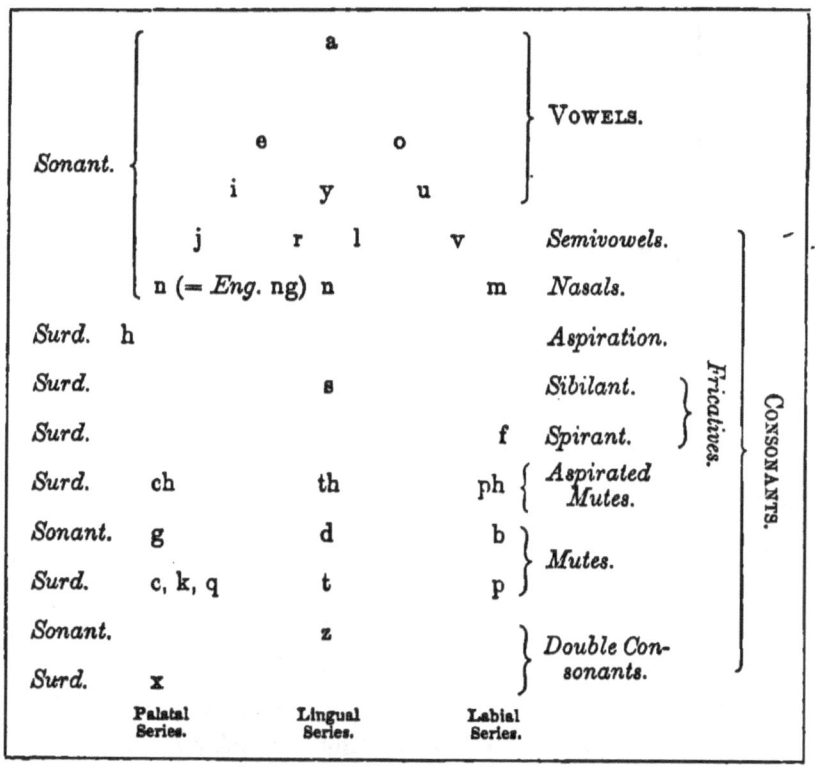

interruption. The diphthongs are (*ai*), *ae, ei,* (*oi*), *oe, ui, au, eu,* (*ou*); the forms inclosed in parenthesis being found only in early Latin. The diphthongs are sounded approximately as follows: *ai* as *ai* in *aisle; ae* originally sounded as (Roman) *ăē'*, later as (Roman) *ē; ei* as *ei* in *eight; oi* as *oi* in *oil; oe* nearly as German *oe* in *Oel,* or Eng. *o* in *world; ui* as *uee* in *queen; au* as *ou* in *house; eu* as *eu* in *feud; ou* as *ou* in *group.* Of the consonants, *b, d, p, t, r, l, m, n, h* are sounded as in

English; *j* as *y* in *yes;* *s* as in *so;* *v* like *w* in *wait;* *f* as in *fate;* *g* as in *get;* *c, k, q* as *c* in *can;* *ch, th, ph*, as *c, t, p*, with the slight addition of *h*-sound, as in the words, *blockhead, hothouse, uphill;* *x* as in *mix*. The letters *y* and *z* were introduced into the Latin language after the time of Cicero, and were used only in words taken from Greek, *y* being employed to represent the Greek *v*, and *z* to represent the Greek ζ. Latin *y* has the sound of French *u*, and for this reason its position in the scheme is between *u* and *i*; *z* may be sounded like *dz* in *adze* or like *z* in *zone*.

CHAPTER V.

PHONETIC CHANGE.

Throughout the history of language, changes of sound are going on. In comparing one language with any of its kindred, we must first ascertain to what sounds of the latter the sounds of the former regularly correspond. We then have a guide for the regular etymological comparison of words. An illustration of this appears in what is called (from its discoverer) "Grimm's Law of Permutation of Consonants," which exhibits, with some exceptions not necessary here to be shown, the regular interchange between (1) Sanskrit, Greek, and Latin, taken as one group; (2) Gothic and Low German dialects (including English); (3) High German and its stock (including modern German). This law may be expressed by the following formula: —

(1) Sanskrit, Greek, Latin	Aspirate	Sonant	Surd
(2) Gothic and Low German (including English)	Sonant	Surd	Aspirate
(3) High German	Surd	Aspirate	Sonant

PHONETIC CHANGE.

It may be illustrated by the following table:—

I.						
1.	Greek θ	θυγάτηρ	θῆρ	θύρα	μέθυ	
	Latin f		fera	fores		
2.	English d	daughter	deer	door	mead	
3.	German t or th = t	tochter	thier	thor	meth	
II.						
1.	Greek δ	ὀδούς	δαμᾶν	δύο	ἔδειν	ὕδωρ
	Latin d	dens	domare	duo	edere	unda
2.	English t	tooth	tame	two	eat	water
3.	German z or s	zahn	zähmen	zwei	essen	wasser
III.						
1.	Greek τ	τύ (σύ)	τρεῖς		τό	
	Latin t	tu	tres	tenuis	is-tud	frater
2.	English th	thou	three	thin	that	brother
3.	German d	du	drei	dünn	das	bruder

General Table of Grimm's Law.

Original Sounds.		A			B	C
		Sanskrit.	Greek.	Latin.	Gothic and Low Germ.	High Germ.
Aspirates	KH	gh (h)	χ	h, f (g, v)	g	k
	TH	dh (h)	θ	f (d, b)	d	t
	PH	bh (h)	φ	f (b)	b	p
Sonants	G	g (j)	γ	g	k	ch
	D	d	δ	d	t	zz
	B	b	β	b	p	f, ph
Surds	K	k	κ	c, q	h, g (f)	h, g, k
	T	t	τ	t	th, d	d
	P	p	π	p	f, v	f, v

PRINCIPLE OF PHONETIC CHANGE.

The principle which underlies the greater part of phonetic change is the *tendency to ease of utterance*. In using the organs of speech, we naturally tend to economize or diminish effort, to reduce the distance between one sound and another, and so to make each necessary step in utterance as short and easy as possible. Accordingly, *the general direction of phonetic change is from the extremes toward the middle of the alphabetic scheme*, movement in the opposite direction being only exceptional or from special causes.

RESULTS OF PHONETIC CHANGE.

The results of phonetic change appear chiefly under two forms: I. *Weak Articulation;* II. *Indistinct Articulation.*

I. WEAK ARTICULATION.

Weak Articulation appears under four forms: I. *Substitution;* II. *Loss;* III. *Assimilation;* IV. *Dissimilation.* These four forms are applied to vowels and to consonants.

Vowel-Change.

I. SUBSTITUTION. By substitution the following changes may be made. Original *a* may be changed, —

1. In Greek and Latin to ε, e: √SAD, ἔδος, sedes. This change was very extensive even in the Graeco-Italic period.
2. In Greek and Latin, to o, o: √DAM, δόμος, dŏmus.
3. In Greek, to ι: Indo-Eur., dá-dhā-mi; Greek, τί-θη-μι.
4. In Latin, to *i*, — a very frequent change, especially in the second member of a compound word: √KAP, capio, accipio.

II. LOSS. In the following examples, the vowel lost is enclosed in parenthesis. Greek: γίγ(ε)νομαι, ἔσ(ε)χον, πατ(ε)ρός. Latin: (e)sum, gig(e)no, discip(u)lina.

III. ASSIMILATION. When a vowel closely connected with a consonant has its utterance thereby made difficult, it may be changed to a vowel, having for that position an easier utterance. This is one form of assimilation. The resulting vowel is *u* in *flagro, fulgor; pello, pulsus:* *e* in *genosis, genoris, generis* (from *genus*). Two vowels in contact may approximate each other: *(*e*)*syam,* **siam,* **siem.* Two vowels separated from each other only by a consonant sometimes assimilate: *bone, bene.*

IV. DISSIMILATION. The object of dissimilation is to prevent repetition of the same vowel. Thus, *sequontur* was a form retained instead of *sequuntur; aliinus* became *alienus.*

Consonant-Change.

I. SUBSTITUTION.

1. In Greek and Latin we have a change from original surd to sonant; *e.g.*, orig. *k* to γ, *g*: √PAK, πήγνυμι, *pagus.*

2. Greek shows an aversion to the original letters, *y, s,* and *v*; orig. *y* disappears, or is seen only in its effects; *v* appears as *F*; *s* is retained at the end of roots and words, but initial *s* before a vowel is generally changed to the rough breathing.

3. In Latin, the original letters *y, s, v* are generally retained, but often *s* passes into *r*, and *y* and *v* are interchanged with *i* and *u*.

II. LOSS. This may be initial, medial, or final. In Greek and Latin an original initial *s* or *v* is sometimes lost: √SMI, μειδάω, *mīror;* √VARK, VALK, VLAK, ῥάκος, *lacer.* Medial loss is not so frequent, very rare in Greek: φέρε(τ)ι, μείζο(ν)α, μείζω. In Latin, it occurs most frequently before *y, s,* and *v*: *di*(*c*)*sco, ma*(*g*)*ior, sua*(*d*)*vis.* It occurs also before nasals: *lu*(*c*)*na, lu*(*c*)*men;* and before *t* and *d*: *tor*(*c*)*tus, i*(*s*)*dem.* Loss at the end of a word affects single consonants or combinations of consonants. In Greek, when several consonants end a word, they are sometimes all dropped, as in γάλα(κτ); but generally the last only is retained, and the preceding vowel is then lengthened; as, τιθέ(ντ)s, τιθείς. In Latin, a combination of several consonants may end a word, as in *ferunt, urbs;* but in the older Latin, final consonants, especially *s, m, t,* were frequently dropped.

III. ASSIMILATION. The most important rules for assimilation of consonants in Greek and Latin are given in the grammars.

IV. DISSIMILATION. The rules are given in the grammars. Examples are ἀδτέον, ἀστέον; ἐ-θύ-θην, ἐτύθην; θί-θη-μι, τίθημι; *claudtrum, claustrum.*

II. INDISTINCT ARTICULATION.

In general, the immediate cause of indistinct articulation is an excessive tendency to ease of utterance. A part of the needful sound of a word is slurred or omitted; then some indistinct or indefinite sound is added on; and this, afterwards becoming more definite, may lead to the utterance of a sound even more difficult than the original one which had thus suffered. Indistinct articulation appears under the following forms: I. *Labialism;* II. *Dentalism;* III. *Parasitic Sound;* IV. *Aspiration.*

I. LABIALISM. This is a change from *k* to π and *p*, or from *g* to β and *b*. If the *k* is pronounced lazily, a slight *w*-sound is apt to be produced immediately after it; and then, if the lips be nearly closed, an indistinct labial sound is produced. For examples, see Nos. 496–515.

II. DENTALISM. This is a change from *k* to τ, or from *gh* to θ. For examples, see Nos. 516–520.

III. PARASITIC SOUND. In Greek, δy may regularly become ζ. Initial *y*, if uttered lazily, may have a slight sound of δ (here called parasitic) uttered before it, and then the δy may become ζ. Thus, for original *y* in √YUG, we find ζ in √ζυγ, ζύγον.

IV. ASPIRATION. Examples are φρουρός, for προορός; ἐπίβαθρον, for ἐπίβατρον; ὕδωρ from √UD.

VOWEL-INCREASE.

An important kind of phonetic change is what is called *vowel-increase* ('intensification,' 'strengthening,' 'raising'). The vowels, arranged in the order of their strength, and beginning with the weakest, are in Greek, ι, υ, ε, ο, α; in Latin, i, u, e, o, a. Change of any vowel into one farther to the right, or into a long vowel or diphthong, is *vowel-increase*. Change in the opposite direction is *vowel-decrease* ('weakening,' 'lowering'). Vowel-increase is extensively employed in forming stems from roots. The following arrangement of the different vowel-scales will illustrate the successive steps of vowel-increase. Reckoning from the fundamental-vowel toward the right, we have vowel-increase shown in two successive steps. The change from the fundamental-vowel as shown toward the left is vowel-decrease, which appears as either 'weakening' or 'loss.'

Vowels of the Indo-European Language.

	Fund.-Vowel.	First Step.	Second Step.
a-scale	ă	a + a = aa = ā	a + aa = āa = ā
i-scale	ĭ	a + i = ai	a + ai = āi
u-scale	ŭ	a + u = au	a + au = āu

Vowels of Sanskrit.

		Weakening.	Fund.-Vowel.	First Step.	Second Step.
a-scale	loss	i, u; ī, ū	ă	ā	ā
i-scale			ĭ	ē	āi
u-scale			ŭ	ō	āu

Vowels of Greek.

		Weakening.	Fund.-Vowel.	First Step.	Second Step.
a-scale	loss	ι, υ	ε, ο, ᾰ	ο, ᾱ, η	ω
i-scale			ῐ	ει (αι)	οι
u-scale			ῠ	ευ (αυ)	ου (αυ)

Vowels of Latin.

(Old-Latin in heavy type.)

		Weakening.	Fund.-Vowel.	First Step.	Second Step.
a-scale	loss	i, u	ĕ, ŏ, ă	o, ē, ā	ō
i-scale			ĭ	e**i**, ī, ē, a**i**, ae	o**i**, oe, ū
u-scale			ŭ	e**u**, au, ō	o**u**, ū

The following rules and examples illustrate some applications of vowel-increase:

In Greek,—
1. Radical ε is raised to ο: √φερ, φόρος; √γεν, γέγονα.
2. " α " ᾱ, η: √λᾰκ, λέ-ληκ-α, λε-λᾱκ-α.
3. " ι " ει: √ῐ, εῖ-μι; √πιθ, πείθω.
4. " ι " οι: √ῐ, οῖ-μος; √πιθ, πέποιθα.
5. " υ " ευ: √φῠγ, φεύγ-ω.

In Latin,—
1. Radical a is raised to ā, ē: √ag, amb-āg-es, ēg-i.
2. " e " o: √mĕn, mŏn-eo.
3. " e " ē: √tĕg, tēg-ula.
4. " i " ī, oe: √fĭd, fīd-us, foed-us.
5. " u " ū: √dŭc, dūc-o.

CHAPTER VI.

THE VIEWS OF THE NEW SCHOOL.

The researches of comparative philologists have for the past few years been directed very largely to a closer study of the vocalism of the Indo-European languages. The final opinions on vocalism of Schleicher, as laid down in the third edition of his "Compendium," 1870 (p. 10, ff.), and of Curtius in the fifth edition of his "Grundzüge der Etymologie," 1879 (Bk. I. § 7), may be regarded as the ripest expressions of the views of the old school.

The treatises of Verner, Brugman, Fick, Collitz, De Saussure, Johannes Schmidt, etc., contain more or less directly and explicitly the opinions of the new school, and these opinions are now generally accepted in Germany.

1. The brilliant discovery of Verner, in which he successfully explained almost the last remaining exception to the first "rotation of mutes" of Grimm's law, was not of merely local importance. In explaining the exception, he proved indirectly that *the accent of the Rig Veda, in its broad outlines, was once the accent of every Indo-European language;* that, therefore, it is a correct method to search for the effects of this accent where tradition has failed to bring it down to historical times (as in the German languages), or where it has been driven out by a new system (as in Greek).

2. The accentuation of the Veda is wedded to a phenomenon which penetrates the entire language. The syllable upon which the tone rests has a fuller vocalization than the others, especially those immediately preceding the tone. This causes the so-called strong and weak forms *é-mi* and *i-más, ta-nó-mi* and *ta-nu-más, påd-am* and *pad-å*, etc. Tracing these weak forms,

and distinguishing them from the strong ones, not only on Indian ground but also in the European languages (a process rendered safe by Verner), led Brugman to *the discovery of lingual and nasal vowels* on a level with Indian r and l, occurring in every language of the family in parallel and identical formations, and manifesting, therefore, a phenomenon of the original Indo-European language. Excepting r and l, in India the lingual and nasal vowels lack separate alphabetic signs, and are expressed by certain fixed groups of letters. So Greek αρ and ρα represent Indian r, Gr. αλ and λα = Ind. l; so Sk. *a* and *an*, Gr. *a* and *αν*, are the expedients by which nasal vowels (n, v) are rendered.

3. The time-honored opinion, which explained the European vowels ă, ĕ, ŏ (*a*, *ε*, *o*) as later modifications of an original Indo-European ă which had been preserved intact in the Indo-Iranian languages, thus received its first shock; for it appeared that Sanskrit ă, when in connection with nasals it represented a nasal vowel, was a sound historically different from ă in other connections; while Greek *a*, in connection with linguals as well as nasals, was not the residue of the assumed original Indo-European ă. This led Brugman to characterize *European* ă, ĕ, ŏ as *Indo-European*, an assumption which was destined to be verified from a totally different direction.

4. *This proof came from the Indo-Iranian palatal series:* Sk. *c, j, jh;* Zd. *c* (*sh*), *j* (*zh*), which is a modification of the first Indo-European guttural series k^1, g^1, gh^1. The close study of these, inaugurated by Ascoli, Fick, and Hübschmann, led at last to a recognition (simultaneous, as it seems, in various quarters) of the fact that they owe their origin, not as had been previously assumed, to parasitic palatal vowels sounded after them, but simply to the fact that a palatal vowel actually following the guttural changed it to a palatal, and that this palatal vowel was often in Indo-Iranian written ă, corresponding to European *e*; that therefore *this Indo-Iranian* ă *had, at the period in which the palatals originated, still a physiological*

value, which is best expressed by a°. So Brugman's assumption, that the European triad ă, ĕ, ŏ was more original than the Indo-Iranian ă, became an assured fact of science.

I.

The vowel variation of the couplets λειπ-λοιπ, ἐλευθ-ἐλουθ, γεν-γον, etc., reaches back to the earliest period of our family of languages, as far as the deepest investigation of scholars has pierced. It is the key-note, the starting-point from which the vocalism of every Indo-European language must be investigated. Whenever the question of priority arises between a root-form λιπ on the one hand, and λειπ-λοιπ on the other, the weak form must be regarded as a reduction. λειπ as well as λοιπ, if occasion for reduction or weakening should present itself, would both naturally reduce to λιπ, while there is no reason to assume that λιπ can be heightened by the effect of accent into both λειπ and λοιπ. It is, therefore, the converse of *guna* which grammar must see in verbal formations when strong and weak root-forms alternate with one another.

If, then, the root is to be looked for in the strong forms, the result is a double root where there exist two strong forms, a single root where there is but one. We should arrive then at such roots for the Greek: πετ-ποτ, δει-δοι [in δε(γ)ος and δε-δοι-κα]; χευ, χου [in χέ(ϝ)ω and χο(ϝ)εύς]; λειπ-λοιπ; ελευθ-ελουθ; μεν-μον; στελ-στολ, πενθ-πονθ, etc.; single roots λᾱθ, λᾱβ, φᾱ, στᾱ, etc. The *weakest* form πτ, δι, κλι, λιπ, ἐλυθ, μν, στλ, πνθ, λᾰθ, φᾰ, στᾰ, etc., has provisionally been termed a *reduced* form. It will not require very keen perception or close scrutiny to perceive that the term '*reduced*' is false. We must here watch lest grammatical method and terminology obscure the facts of language. In ἴ-μεν : εἶ-μι, ι is no more a reduction from εἰ than εἰ the *guna* of ι; they are forms as perfectly independent of one another as λείπω and λέλοιπα, as βέλος and βολή. When the form ἴ-μεν (originally ἰ-μέν) came into existence, *it did not start from an accented base* εἴ, which lost its accent, with it an ε, and became ι; all that can be said is, that words of this group, when they have the accent on formative elements, appear with the radical or significant element ι; when they have the accent on the root, with one of the two radical elements εἰ or οἰ.

If what we have stated is in accordance with the facts, the idea of a single root falls to the ground. We have in word-groups which show the variation between ε and o a root-system consisting of three forms, two strong ones and one weak one; in all other word-groups a root-system of two forms, a weak one and a strong one. Designating the first class by AA, the second by BB, we have:—

Class AA.		Class BB.	
Strong Forms.	*Weak Forms.*	*Strong Forms.*	*Weak Forms.*
I. μεν II. μον	III. μν	I. and II. στᾰ	III. στᾰ
I. πειθ II. ποιθ	III. πιθ	I. and II. θη	III. θε
I. πετ II. ποτ etc.	III. πτ etc.	I. and II. λᾱθ etc.	III. λᾰθ etc.

All other root-forms are modifications of these ground-forms; *e.g.*, μα in με-μα-τον and μαν in μαίνομαι (= μαν-yομαι) are but modifications of μν, having their cause in the character of the inflectional elements which appear in connection with the root; in the same way τραφ and ταρφ, in ἔ-τραφ-ον and ταρφ-ύς, are but graphical expedients for rendering the sound-group τρφ (τρφ) in the root-system τρεφ, τροφ, τρφ, etc. Hereafter we will designate a root-form like μεν, χευ or χε(F), πει, πετ, etc., as ablaut I.; μον, χο(F), ποιθ, ποτ, etc., as ablaut II.; μν (μα, μαν), χυ, πιθ, πτ, etc., as ablaut III.

II.

From the first days of the comparative study of the Indo-European family of languages, up to the year 1876, it was held almost without a dissenting voice that the body of short vowels which the so-called original Indo-European language possessed consisted of a, i, u. Of these a was supposed to have remained unchanged in the Asiatic division of the family, the Indian and Iranian languages; while in the European languages it had in a large proportion of cases been weakened into e and o, the sounds holding physiologically a middle position respectively between a and i, and a and u. An exhaustive investigation of this supposed breaking up of Indo-European a on European ground was made by Curtius in 1864. It resulted in establishing the fact that the deviation of a into e occurred on the whole in the same words and formations in all of the European languages; that it could not have taken place in each one of them independently of the others; that, therefore, a common European language must be assumed; from this the several European languages had separated, as the Iranian and Indian languages had done from a common Indo-Iranian language. On the other hand, the coloring of a into o had taken place later and separately in the several European branches, because the o of one branch does not accord with the o of another.

Fick, in his book "Die Spracheinheit der Indo-Germanen Europas," makes use of Curtius' results in the same direction; he also holds to an Indo-European a which in Europe divided itself into a and e; of these two, a again was resolved, in the separate European branches, into a and o. The vowel system of Schleicher, which on the whole is artificial, does not deviate in any material respects from those above mentioned, as far as the short vowels are concerned.

Two points, which are the result of this system of short vowels, are to be carefully noted:—

1. In Sanskrit *a* is throughout the language one and the same vowel, being everywhere the direct descendant of the original Indo-European *a*.

2. Greek ă represents throughout the language what has been left undisturbed of the original Indo-European *a*, a large part of this latter having been changed to ε and ο.

The first serious attack upon this system of short vowels struck at the two rules which have been deduced. In vol. ix. of Curtius' "Studien" there appeared the famous article by Karl Brugman, entitled "Nasalis Sonans," etc., which for the first time definitely proved the negative of these two rules. It will not be necessary to go through Brugman's proofs. Though his article furnished the key to the understanding of the Indo-European linguals and nasals, and more or less directly has formed the basis for most of the successful investigations on vocalism since that day, principles which are laid down there can now be presented in a more comprehensive fashion, owing to further investigations by Brugman himself and by others.

Brugman starts with the discussion of an interesting fact which Sievers teaches in his "Lautphysiologie," p. 26 ff. He observes that in the usual pronounciation of words containing nasals (*n*, *m*) and liquids (*r*, *l*), these are pronounced both as vowels and as consonants. As vowels, they form in connection with one or more consonants a distinct syllable, just as any other vowel. So in 'sieben mal acht' (*sie-bn̥*), 'wir ritten nach hause' (*rit-tn̥*), 'tändeln' (*tän-dl̥n*), 'wandern' (*wan-dr̥n*). English examples would be: 'the father is' (*fa-thr̥*), 'ankle' (*an-kl̥*), 'heaven' (*hea-vn̥*), 'handsome' (*han-sm̥*), etc. On the other hand, the consonantal pronunciation of linguals and nasals is seen in '*beritt-ne*': 'beritten' (*berit-tn*); '*ath-me*': 'a-them' (*a-thm*); Eng. '*ank-let*': 'ankle' (*an-kl*), etc. The alphabets of these languages fail to furnish separate characters for these two classes of sounds, — a fact which of course in nowise throws a doubt on their existence.

The Vedic and Sanskrit, as is well known, do possess distinct characters for lingual vowels, which are transcribed in the manner in which we have differentiated them in German and English from their corresponding consonants; viz.: *ṛ* and *ḷ*.

The change between the lingual consonants and lingual vowels is quite analogous to that between *y* and *i*, and *v* and *u*; before vowels there always appears the consonantal pronunciation *r* and *l*, *y* and *v*; before consonants the treatment of the linguals, though in principle the same as that of the dental and labial vowels, is characterized by a smaller degree of sensitiveness than these. While the latter always appear as *i* and *u* before consonants, *r* and *l* are changed to their corresponding vowels only when preceded as well as followed by consonants, or in the beginning of a word when followed by a consonant. A few examples will suffice. As the weak forms of the perfect of the verb *nī*, 'to lead,' appear as *ni-ny-* before endings beginning with a vowel, so do the weak forms of the verb *kar* appear as *ca-kr-* in the same connections: *ni-ny-á, ni-ny-ús, ni-ny-é,—ca-kr-á, ca-kr-ús, ca-kr-é*. But between consonants the semi-consonantal elements of these roots appear as vowels: *nī-tá-s, kṛ-tá-s, çru-tá-s*. So also the same change is seen in *i-más* : *y-anti;* in *ca-kṛ-má* : *ca-kr-ús;* in *tu-ṣṭu-má* : *tu-ṣṭuv-ús* (for *tu-ṣṭv-ús*); cf. *cā-klp-ré*.

The Sanskrit does not possess distinct characters to express nasals between two consonants (nasal vowels); these, however, indicate their presence by very distinct and peculiar phenomena. As we have *y* : *i*, *v* : *u*, *r* : *ṛ*, and *l* : *ḷ*, we have also *n* : *ṇ* and *m* : *ṃ*. *ṇ* and *ṃ* appear almost always as simple *ă*, sometimes as *ăn* (*ăm*); this *an*, which is the phonetic equivalent of *ṇ*, can be differentiated from $an = a + n$ by the aid of the Greek. While the latter *an* corresponds to Gr. εν or ον, the former appears in Greek also as αν, occurring there, as well as in Sanskrit, only in formations which require the weak form of the root (ablaut III.). So *mán-as* ($an = a + n$) = μέν-ος;

ma-mán-tha (*an* = *a* + *n*) = Gr. μέ-μον-α; but *mán-ye* for *mṇ-ye* corresponds to Gr. μαίνομαι for μαν-γομαι for μν-γομαι.

There appear, then, in Sanskrit, instead of merely the sounds *y–i*, *v–u*, as mediators between vowels and consonants, the very considerable body which is made up by these and the linguals and nasals in addition. The Sanskrit system of semi-consonants is as follows:—

Consonants:	y	v	r	l	n	m
Vowels:	i	u	ṛ	ḷ	a, an	a, am

This proves that *Sanskrit* a *is not everywhere the same sound, and not everywhere the direct representative of Indo-European* a. The Indo-European *a* will suffer further infringements in the course of our discussion, until it will have shrunk into comparative insignificance.

This variable function of semi-consonants is by no means restricted to Sanskrit. In every language of the family these sounds occur, but with still less perfect systems of expression. In Sanskrit there are at least distinct characters for lingual vowels; in the other languages these, as well as the nasal vowels, lack single characters, and are everywhere expressed by combinations similar to those which are found for nasal vowels even in Sanskrit. The following is the system for the Greek:—

Consonants:	(y)	(F)	ρ	λ	ν	μ
Vowels:	ι	υ	αρ, ρα	αλ, λα	α, αν	α, αμ

Consonant *y* is shown in δέ(y)ος; cf. δέ-δοι-κα : κέ(y)-ομαι; cf. κεῖ-μαι. F is shown in χέ(F)-ω; cf. χεύ-ω : κλέ(F)-ος = Sk. *çráv-as*. The consonants ρ, λ, ν, and μ are occasionally split into αρ, αλ, αν, and αμ; a phenomenon quite parallel with the breaking up of *y* and *v* in Sanskrit into *iy* and *uv*.

The following is the system for Gothic and High German:—

Consonants:	j	v	r		l	n	m
Vowels:	i	u	Goth. *aúr*	Goth. *ul*	*un*	*um*
			H. G. *or*	H. G. *ol*		

The following is the system for Latin : —

    Consonants: *j*   *v*   *r*   *l*   *n*   *m*
    Vowels: *i*   *u*   *or* (*ur*) *ul* (*ol*)   *en*   *em*

The extent to which Greek a *and Sanskrit* a *do not represent Indo-European* a *is very considerable.* In Greek the great mass of a's that appear in the vicinity of liquids and nasals are but defective (or rather excessive) graphic representations of the weakest imaginable vocalic element (sh'va).

The discovery of the preceding facts was soon employed as the entering wedge for a series of attacks upon Indo-European *a*, which have by this time resulted in a very serious curtailment of it, and by consequence in an almost totally changed system of Indo-European vowels. The first step was here again taken by Brugman (Curtius' Studien, ix. 367, ff.; Kuhn's Zeitschrift, xxiv. 1, ff.), successful at least in that it pointed the right way for further examination. He there assumes for Greek ε, ο, α, three different Indo-European sounds, which he indicates by a^1, a^2, and a^3; a^3 he regards as an original short *a*, which appears in Europe as *a*; in Sanskrit sometimes as *a*, sometimes as *i* (examples: Gr. στα-τό-ς, Lat. *sta-tu-s*, Sk. *sthi-tá-s*); a^1 corresponds to European and Armenian *e* and Sk. Zend *a*; a^2 corresponds to Greek, Italic, Celtic, and Slavic *o*, German and Lithuanian *a*, also to Sk. *a* in a closed syllable; but in an open syllable, in cases represented by *bhár-ā-mas* (φέρ-ο-μεν), *pād-am* (πόδ-α), *dātár-am* (δώτορ-α), *ushás-am* (ἠό-α), *jānu* (γόνυ), δᾶρυ (δόρυ), a^2 is, according to Brugman, represented by Sk. *ā*. That, however, the lengthening of the *ā* in these cases is accidental or owing to special Sanskrit laws, was shown (in the main successfully) by Collitz and J. Schmidt. Aside from this, Brugman had intuitively seen the truth, though the more concrete proofs of his system came from a totally different direction, as will be shown in the next section. It will be seen that European and Armenian *e*'s were *e* from all time; that the Sanskrit and Iranian *a*, which correspond to it, are either special deviations dating from a comparatively late period in the co-existence of these languages; or, what is even more probable, that this *a* in these languages is but an insufficient sign for a sound which would be best indicated by *ae* (a^e); as yet there has been no proof that the Sanskrit *a* which corresponds to Greek *o* is a sound which is colored by *o* (a^o); it is enough to know that the Greek ablaut ε : *o* exists in every language of the family.

III.

The fact that the Indo-European languages have two series of guttural consonants was discovered and settled by Ascoli, and has become one of the best-known laws of Indo-European phonetics. They are generally differentiated by the designations k^1, g^1, gh^1, and k^2, g^2, gh^2, for the common Indo-European period. In Sanskrit the first series is left in part as *k*, *g*, *gh* (Zend *k*, *g*); it also appears palatalized as *c*, *j*, *h* (Zend *c* and and *sh*, *j* and *zh*). In Greek this series appears partly as κ, γ, χ, partly as π, β, φ; these latter interchange in a few instances with τ, δ, θ, under circumstances which are in principle the same as those in which Sk. *k*, *g*, *gh*, interchange with *c*, *j*, and *h*. The second Indo-European series k^2, g^2, gh^2, shows in Sanskrit a sign devoted solely to itself only for k^2, namely ç; while the sounds g^2 and gh^2 share the signs *j* and *h* with the palatals of the series *k*, *g*, *gh*. In Zend k^2 is ç; g^2 and gh^2 are *z*. In Greek k^2, g^2, and gh^2 appear regularly as gutturals: κ, γ, χ.

The following scheme will illustrate the subject: —

Indo-European.			Sanskrit.			Zend.	
k^1	g^1	gh^1	*k*	*g*	*gh*	*k* (*kh*)	*g* (*gh*)
k^2	g^2	gh^2	*c* } ç	*j*	*jh*	*c* (*sh*)	*j* (*zh*)

Indo-European.			Greek.					
k^1	g^1	gh^1	κ	γ	χ	π	β	φ
						τ	δ	θ
k^2	g^2	gh^2				κ	γ	χ

It is the palatal series which has branched off from the first guttural series — Sk. c, j, h; Zd. c, j; Gr. τ, δ, θ — which concerns the subject here treated. The true cause of this division remained unrecognized up to the time of Ascoli; he was the first to get some inkling of the way to a legitimate explanation. He states that in Zend the change from a guttural to a palatal in the three degrees of the adjective, *aka-*, *ashyô*, and *acista-* [$k : c\ (sh)$], is due to the change of the vowel following the guttural, and also notes that there is no root of the form *gi* either in Sanskrit or Zend, but that they show *ji*. This is really a recognition, fragmentary as it may be, of the principle that palatalization is due to the influence of palatal vowels actually occurring after gutturals. According to J. Schmidt, Dr. Vilhelm Thomsen was the first to hint that the *European* languages, with their supposed secondary vocalization, might be drawn in as auxiliaries in such a way that Sanskrit and Zend syllables *ca* and *ka* should be explained from κε and κα as European equivalents, and that thus the palatals before a written *a* owe their origin to the fact that this *a* was in such connections originally sounded as *ae* (a^e). The full principle was recognized, as it seems, nearly simultaneously by Collitz, Karl Verner, Saussure, and J. Schmidt.

If we formulate the principles which are laid down by these writers, there result the following rules: —

1. The Indo-Iranian palatals — Sk. c, j, h; Zend $c\,(sh), j\,(zh)$ — are a modification of the first guttural series (k^1, g^1, gh^1) before palatal vowels, — $i\,(y)$, a^e ($a^e i, a^e u$), — and can originally have stood only before these vowels.

2. The vowel signs *a*, *ai*, and *au*, in the Indo-Iranian languages, actually represent two series of vowels at least (more if more can be proved); namely: a^e, $a^e i$, $a^e u$, and *a, ai, au*, — the former corresponding to *e, ei, eu* (Gr. ε, ει, ευ) in the European languages.

The last rule bears upon the correct understanding of Greek ablaut in three vital points.

(a) In the ablaut series the ε which appears in the row marked I. (ablaut I.) is not the result of the weakening of Indo-European a, but represents an original sound, which is clearly expressed in the European branches of the family, and

I.	πετ	στελ	περθ	πενθ	ρευ (ρεϝ)	πειθ, etc.
II.	ποτ	στολ	πορθ	πονθ	ρου (ροϝ)	ποιθ, etc.
III.	πτ	σταλ	πραθ	παθ	ρυ	πιθ, etc.

which is not expressed by a distinct sign in the Indo-Aryan languages, but there manifests itself in the palatals of the Indo-European series k^1, g^1, gh^1; namely, c, j, h.

(b) Again looking at the series of roots laid down under (a), it will appear that all the forms under I. are on the same level as far as the root vowel is concerned; so also the forms under II. From necessity, the forms under III. are also on a level; one of these holds the same grammatical position as the other; one is used in the same kinds of formations, verbal and nominal, as the other.

(c) The sound a appears in III. only in connection with linguals and nasals; it is something special.

The following examples illustrate the origin of palatalization, and the Sanskrit sound a^e:—

Variation between k and c: Sk. cuk-rá-s : çóc-iṣṭa-s; çak-rá-s : çac-iṣṭa-s; Zend aka- : acista-; Sk. ark-á-s : arc-í-s.

Variation between g and j: tig-má-s : téj-iṣṭa-s; tyag-á-s : tyáj-as, etc.

The facts and principles illustrated by these examples for the Indo-Iranian languages are represented in Greek also. The variation takes place here between *labials* (which represent original gutturals) and the *dentals* of Curtius' dentalism, which take the place of palatals. Not indeed in so widely diffused a manner has the original difference between the labials (= gutturals) and dentals (= palatals) been held fast; it has been wiped out very largely at the expense of the palatals; but there are still enough data left to show that the Greek started with the same differences, and that these differences were based upon the same cause, the character of the following sound. As in Sk. a palatal before i (y), a^e $(a^e i, a^e u)$ corresponds to a guttural before other sounds, so in Greek there is still a respectable body of forms which show dentals before ι and ε (ει, ευ) which vary with labials according to the proportion:—

$$\tau, \delta, \theta : \pi, \beta, \phi = \text{Sk. } c, j, h : k, g, gh.$$

Greek palatalization appears in the following cases:—
1. τίς, gen. τε(σ)ο, τε: πό-τερος = Zend *cis, cahyā, ca* : Sk. *ka-tarás*.
2. πέντ-ε : πέμπ-τος = Sk. *páñc-a : pank-ti-s*.
3. τρι-οττίς, ὄσσε, ὄσσομαι : ὄψομαι.
4. ὀδελός : ὀβολός.

The vocalism of the Greek has the largest claim to being a correct, undisturbed reflex of that of the corresponding roots in all the languages of the family. Sanskrit and Zend in reality possess the root-triad (πετ, ποτ, πτ; λειπ, λοιπ, λιπ) to even a larger extent than the Greek; but the first two ablauts have fallen together, at least graphically.

Surprising is the non-sensitiveness of the Latin to variations of root-vowels, especially if its otherwise close kinship with Greek is kept in view. It everywhere evinces the tendency to urge some one of the root-vowels through the entire group of formations belonging to the root. To a large extent this is the vowel of the root-form (ablaut I.). So the vowel of *lego, clepo, tremo, pe(r)do, serpo*, etc., fails to vary with ablaut II. (*o*) in the perfect. On the other hand, the Indo-European perfect vowel (ablaut II.) is contained in *to-tond-i, spo-pond-i*, and *mo-mord-i;* but the radical vowels of these words have spread over their entire respective word-groups, either assimilating the vowel, or suppressing forms which show another root-vowel, and placing such as had *o* in their place. Such are the presents of these words: *tondeo, spondeo, mordeo*, which legitimately show *o*, but are in reality causative formations, such as Gr. φορ-έω to φέρω. The weakest root-form (ablaut III.) is retained to the exclusion of the other two in the groups of which *sci-n-d-o, fi-n-d-o, ju-n-g-o* are presents, *e.g., jungo, junxi, junctus, jugum, conjux*, etc. Still enough has been left of a Latin ablaut to show that it once coincided with the Greek, though there is no one case in which all three forms have been preserved. Examples of roots which show the first and second forms of the root are: *nex : noc-eo; teg-o : tog-a; sequi : socius*. Of groups which show ablauts I. and III., examples are *fer-o : for-(ti)s* = Sk. *bhṛ-t-is; dīc-o* (= *deic-o*) : *causi-dĭc-us; dūc-o* (= *deuc-o*) : *duc-em; ūr-o* (= *eus-o*) : *ŭs-tus*. Of groups which show ablauts II. and III., an example is *mon-eo : men-(ti)-s* = Sk. *ma-ti-s*.

The triple form of the root is not an accidental modification on European ground of a *simplex* primitive form, but it belongs to our family of languages as a whole; it is Indo-European. It is a fact which has until lately not been sufficiently emphasized that *each one of the three root-forms is restricted to a certain number of formations, nominal and verbal;* this fact alone, if reflected on consistently, is enough to establish the root-triad as Indo-European.

IV.

A closer look at the physiological construction of the roots which show the variation between ε and ο (Class AA) yields the following results: These roots have in their strong forms, as purely vocalic element, this ε varying with ο and nothing else. The remaining elements have never the character of pure vowels, but are either full consonants or semi-consonants, or both. Of the first category there is but one type, that exhibited in roots like πετ, ἐς, etc.; the root-vowel is preceded and followed by a consonant (spiritus lenis in ἐς, ἐδ, etc.).

This we name type A. The rest arrange themselves best according to the following scheme: Type B, those which end in a semi-consonant; type C, those which contain a semi-consonant preceded and followed by other consonants:—

A.	B.	C.
πετ, ποτ	δε(y), δοι	λειπ, λοιπ
ἰδ, (ὀδ) in the	χευ, χο(ϝ)	ἐλευθ, ἐλουτθ
Goth. perf.	δερ, δορ	δερκ, δορκ
αἱ, etc.	στελ, στολ	κλεπ, κλοπ
	μεν, μον	πενθ, πονθ
	τεμ, τομ	ρεμφ, ρομφ
	etc.	etc.

This classification has especial value for understanding ablaut III., — the weakest, the accentless form of the root. This differs from the two strong ones in no particular, except that it does not possess the purely vocalic element (ε or ο) which appears in the strong forms. The root-forms which lie at the base of ablaut III. are, therefore:—

A.	B.	C.
πτ	δι	λιπ
σ	χυ	ἐλυθ
etc.	δρ	δρκ
	στλ	κλπ
	μν	πνθ
	τμ, etc.	ρμφ, etc.

It is evident that some of these last groups are unpronounceable in certain connections; *e.g.*, according to type A we have ἔ-σχ-ον, the second aorist, which legitimately shows the weakest form; so also ἐκ-τός for σχ-τός, the verbal adjective, is made from the same degree of the root (cf. ἔ-πιθ-ον and πισ-τός); but the difficult group of consonants σχτ- necessitated the insertion of a short vowel. It is not to be supposed, however, that the ε in ἐκ-τός possessed in speaking the same value as that of ἔχ-ω, as long as the position of the accent was not disregarded in pronunciation. In weak forms of the types στλ, δρκ, πνθ, ῥμφ, etc., the lingual and nasal consonants were changed to lingual and nasal vowels; λ, when vocalized, appears as αλ, λα; ρ as αρ, ρα; ν and μ appear as α, αν, and α (αμ).

It has appeared sufficiently that the assumption of a root λιπ or φυγ by the side of πετ is inconsistent, because the two root-forms have totally different functions in their respective groups of words; the above schemes will furnish a purely physiological reason. Roots which contain an ι or υ are never followed by another semi-consonant (ρ, λ, μ, ν); there are no roots of a type μιν, διρ, πινθ, διρκ, etc., as there are μεν, δερ, πενθ, δερκ, etc. Nasals do, indeed, occur after ι and υ in certain formations, generally the present, as πυ-ν-θ-άνομαι, Lat. sci-n-d-o, etc.; but a look at some other formation from the same root will quickly teach that the nasal does not belong to the root [πεύ(θ)σομαι, Sk. *chi-chéd-a*]. On the other hand, when a nasal or lingual is preceded by ε, it belongs to the root, and appears, or must be accounted for, in all formations; so πένθ-ος, πέ-πονθ-α, πείσο-μαι (= πένθ-σομαι), Sk. *ta-sthámb-a*, *ba-bándh-a*, etc. The morphological function of nasals and linguals, which belong to the root, is therefore precisely the same as that of ι (*y*), υ (*F*) belonging to the root. Both waver between a vocalic and a consonantal condition, according to their surroundings; both are totally different from the ε and ο which appear in the root. These are the root-vowels proper, and about these the semi-consonantal and consonantal elements of the root are grouped.

The triple root (Class AA) runs through nearly 250 groups of Greek words, is preponderant in Teutonic and Sanskrit, and is really the phenomenon from a discussion of which any treatise on ablaut must start. It is not, however, the only kind of root which appears either in Greek or in the kindred languages; there are considerable numbers of roots which show but two forms, differing from one another merely in the quantity of the root-vowel, Class BB, and that in such a way that the form with the long vowel occurs in precisely those formations in which Class AA shows the forms with ε and ο. The form with the short vowel occurs in those formations in which Class AA shows the weak form (ablaut III.) as the following scheme will show:—

	I.		II.	III.	
AA	πείθ-ω, φεύγ-ω, μέν-ω,	τεῖχ-ος ζεῦγ-ος μέν-ος	πέ-ποιθ-α ἐλ-ήλουθ-α μέ-μον-α	ἐ-πέ-πιθ-μεν, ἐλ-ἠλυθ-μεν, μέ-μα-μεν,	πισ-τός φυκ-τός -μά-τος
BB	λάθ-ω, ἵ-στη-μι, τί-θη-μι, δί-δω-μι,	λᾶθ-ος στή-μων θή-μων δώ-τωρ	λέ-λᾱθ-α ἕ-στη-κα ἕ-θη-κα δέ-δω-κα	λέ-λασ-μαι, ἕ-στᾰ-μεν, τέ-θε-μαι, δέ-δο-μαι,	-λασ-τος στᾰ-τός θε-τός δο-τός

The Latin exhibits ablaut consisting in variation between long and short vowels in *scāb-i* : *scăb-o* ; *fōd-i* : *fŏd-io* ; *ōd-i* : *ŏd-ium*, etc. Sanskrit has not often kept this kind of formation undisturbed; it appears in *ça-çād-a* : *çā-çăd-ús* ; *á-sthā-t* : *sthi-tá-s*, etc.

The question now fairly presents itself: What are the causes of these phenomena which penetrate the vocalism of our languages with such far-reaching regularity; what is the cause that sets δέ-δο-μαι against δέ-δω-κα; φυκ-τός against φεύγ-ω; πείθ-ω against πέ-ποιθ-α, and both against πισ-τός? The question naturally falls into two distinct parts: (1) What is the relation, in both AA and BB of the scheme above, of

the forms in column III. to those in columns I. and II.?
(2) In Class AA what causes the difference in the root-vowels of columns I. and II.?

Surprising as it may seem, this *latter* question remains as yet unanswered. In spite of the large extent of the material which is accessible, there has not been found anything upon which an explanation of the ablaut ε : ο can be rested with safety. That it is not accidental and inorganic, as it was formerly regarded, is clear from the regularity of its distribution, and not the less clear because the reason of it has not been as yet discovered. It is to be noted that it is not restricted to the *root* of words; it occurs as well in formative elements.

Very different is the state of our knowledge with regard to the *former* question. The cause whose workings we see in the difference between πισ-τός, and πείθ-ω and πέ-ποιθ-α, is perfectly well known. It is the varying position of the accent which creates the difference between strong and weak forms. The languages which have preserved this ablaut best, have fortunately also with it preserved a sufficient amount of data for its explanation.

The Vedic texts which are accented show that, as a rule, the strong form of the root occurs when the tone rests on the root; the weak form, when the tone rests on inflectional elements; so *é-mi* (*aⁱi-mi*) : *i-más; da-dárç-a : da-dṛç-ús; vác-as : uk-tás*, etc.

The Greek originally possessed the law of accentuation indicated by these examples to much the same extent as the old Aryan language of India. But in the historical period of the language a new principle, the recessive accentuation, has usurped its place, leaving but a few fossilized remnants of the old method. In θρασ-ύς, πισ-τός, λε-λασ-μένος, λιπ-έ-σθαι, etc., we have survivals of the older accentuation, accompanied by the weak form of the root. Generally the accent has been subjected to the new law; usually, however, without disturbing the form of the root which had accompanied the old accent.

So ἴ-μεν, πέ-φα-ται, ἔ-φθαρ-μαι, κάρ-σις, were once oxytone, for they contain the weakest form of their roots: ι, φα (φν), φθαρ (φθρ), καρ (κρ).

The German shows the traces of the old tone system in two ways:—

(1) In the ablaut. This coincides in its leading traits with the ablaut of the Greek and Vedic. The two strong forms (ablauts I. and II.), as *steig* and *staig*, *bind* and *band*, occur in those formations in which Vedic words present the strong form of the root accompanied by the accent; the weak forms of the root, as *stig*, *bund* (= *bṇd*), in those in which the Vedic shows weak forms, and the accent on a formative element.

(2) An exception to the first German rotation of mutes (*Grimm's Law*) is due to this method of accentuation. In a considerable number of cases Indo-European surd mutes do not, as the law demands, appear in the Germanic languages as *surd spirants*, but as *sonant spirants;* this irregularity takes place only in the middle of a word between two sonants. The irregular Teutonic sound to a considerable extent alternates with the regular one in inflected words belonging to the same root. In the inflection of verbs the Germanic languages, with the exception of Gothic, show this alternation in such a way that the irregular sound appears in precisely those forms which contain the weakest form of the root (ablaut III.); while the regular consonant appears in the two strong forms of the root (ablaut I. and II.). The entire phenomenon lives to-day in High German in such changes as *ziehe* : *gezogen ; kiese* : *erkoren ;* Eng. *lose* : *forlorn*. The cause of it was discovered by Karl Verner. He saw that there was a living remnant of Vedic and Indo-European accentuation preserved in this alternation of consonants. *The forms with irregular consonant and weakest root-form* (ablaut III.) *originally had the tone on their inflectional elements* (zig-úm *and* zig-a-ná) *in Indo-European times, and have it in the accented Vedic texts which have come down to us* (e.g., bi-bhid-imá *and* bhin-ná) ; *the forms with regular*

consonant were accented on the root (zí'h-a *and* zê'h); Ved. *bhár-ā-mi* and *ja-bhár-a.* Verner's law formed one of the most important factors in establishing the truth that the broad facts of Vedic accentuation once ruled in all Indo-European languages; it is the strongest justification of the method of accounting for variations of root-vowels which is now universally practised; in fact, it has been seen that, so far, ablaut, wherever it is explainable, is so on the basis of this law of accent. Wherever this fails, there is as yet no other known fact or principle which furnishes additional light. Explanation must be held in abeyance until further investigation or new material shows the way.

PART II.

Regular Substitution of Sounds.

Indo-European.	Sanskrit.	Greek.	Latin.
a	a	ă ϵ o	a e o
			i u
â	â	ā η ω	â ê ô
i	i	ῐ	i
			e
î ?	î	ī	i
u	u	ῠ	u
			o
û ?	û	ῡ	u
ai	ê	αι ϵι οι	ai ê oi
			ae oe î û
âi	âi	ᾳ ῃ ῳ	
au	ô	αυ ϵυ ου	au o
			u
âu	âu	αυ ηυ	au
k	k kh k' ç	κ	c q
g	g g'	γ	g

Indo-European.	Sanskrit.	Greek.	Latin.
gh	gh h	χ	*init.* h, *med.* g
t	t th	τ	t
d	d	δ	d
dh	dh	θ	*init.* f, *med.* d, b
p	p ph	π	p
b	b	β	b
bh	bh	φ	*init.* f, *med.* b
ṅ	ṅ ñ	γ *before gutt.*	n
n	n ṇ	ν	n
m	m	μ	m
r	r	ρ	r
l	l	λ	l
j	j	*init. spir. asp.*	j
s	s sh	σ, *spir. asp.*	s (r)
v	v	F	v

K

k; k, kh, k', ç; κ; c, k, q, (seldom g).

1. ak, ank; ak'; ἀγκ; anc, unc; bend, curve.

ἀγκ-ών, a bend; ἄγκ-ος, a bend, hollow, valley; ὄγκ-ος, a bend, hook, barb; ἀγκ-ύλος, crooked; ἄγκ-ῡρα, an *anchor*.

anc-īle, a small, oval shield; anc-ŭlus (dim.), a man-servant; anc-ŭla (dim.), a maid-servant; anc-illa (dim.), a maid-servant, female slave; anc-illāris, relating to maid-servants, [*ancillary*]; ang-ŭlus, an *angle*, a corner; unc-us, a hook; unc-us (adj.), hooked, curved; ad-unc-us, bent in, hooked, curved; ung-ŭlus, a ring; †anc-ŏra, an *anchor*.

2. ak; aç; ακ; ac; sharp, pointed, swift.

ἄκ-ων, a javelin; ἄκ-ανος, ἄκ-αινα, a thorn; ἄκ-ρος, at the point or end, highest, outermost; ἄκ-ρις, ὄκ-ρις, a mountain-peak; ὠκ-ύς, swift; ὀξ-ύς, sharp, keen, swift, [*oxide, oxygen, oxytone*].

ăc-er, sharp, acute, [*acrid, crabbed, eager*]; ăc-rimōnia, sharpness, *acrimony*; ăc-erbus, harsh; ăc-erbitas, harshness, *acerbity*; ăc-ervus, a heap; ăc-eo, to be sour; ăc-esco (inch.), to become sour; ăc-ētum, sour wine, vinegar, [*acetic*]; ăc-ĭdus, sour, *acid*; ăc-ies, *edge*, keen look, sight, army in battle-array; ăc-uo, to sharpen; ăc-ūtus (part.), sharpened; ăc-ūtus (adj.), sharp, pointed, *acute*; ăc-ūmen, a point, acuteness, *acumen*; ăc-us, a needle, [to *egg*, to *edge* = to urge on or incite]; ōc-ior, swifter; ōc-ĭter, swiftly.

3. ark; —; ἀλκ, ἀρκ; arc; keep off, hold good. In the root ἀρκ the more prominent meaning is the positive one, to hold good; in ἀλκ, the negative meaning, to keep off.

ἀλ-αλκ-εῖν, to keep off; ἀλκ-ή, strength, courage, defence; ἀρκ-έω, to keep off, to suffice; ἄρκ-ιος, certain, sufficient.

arc-eo, to shut up, to keep off; co-erc-eo, to enclose something on all sides or wholly, to restrain, confine, *coerce;* ex-erc-eo (lit. to thrust or drive out of an inclosure), to drive on, keep at work, to *exercise;* ex-erc-itium, *exercise;* ex-erc-ĭtus, a trained or disciplined body of men, an army; arx, a citadel, height, defence; arc-a, a chest, [*ark*]; arc-ānus, trusty, secret; arc-ānum, a secret, a mystery.

4. ἄρκτος, a bear.

Arctos, the Great and the Lesser Bear (Ursa Major et Minor); ursus (for urcsus), a bear; ursa, a she-bear.

5. —; daç; δακ; —; bite.

δάκ-νω, to bite; δάκ-ος, an animal of which the bite is dangerous; δῆγ-μα, a bite.

6. δάκρυ, δάκρυον, a tear; δακρύω, to weep.

lacrĭma, lacrŭma (old form dacrima, dacruma), a tear, [*lachrymal*]; lacrĭmo, lacrŭmo, to weep. The root is perhaps the same as of No. 5.

7. δάκτυλος, finger, [*dactyl*]. The root is probably δεκ (δεχ) in δέκομαι (δέχομαι), to take. By some authorities the root is referred to No. 10.

dĭgĭtus, finger, [*digit*]. The root of this word is by some authorities referred to No. 10.

8. δέκα, ten.

dĕcem, *ten;* Dĕcember (decem and -ber = fer, Sanskrit bhar, to carry, bear), *December,* the tenth month of the Roman year (reckoned from March); dĕcĭmus, dĕcŭmus, the tenth, [*decimal*].

9. —; darç; δερκ, δρακ; —; see.

δέρκ-ομαι, to look, to see; δέργ-μα, a look; δράκ-ων, a *dragon;* δορκ-άς, a gazelle.

10. dak; dic; δικ, δεικ; dic; show.

δείκ-νυμι, to show, to point out; δεῖξ-ις, a pointing out; δεῖγμα, something pointed out; δίκ-η, right, justice (orig. sense, custom, usage).

dīc-o (vb. conj. 1), to proclaim, to devote; **ab-dīc-o** (to proclaim one's self removed from a thing), to disown, renounce, *abdicate;* **dē-dīc-o** (to adjudge a thing from one's self to a deity), to *dedicate;* **in-dīc-o,** to point out, to *indicate;* **prae-dīc-o,** to cry in public, to proclaim, declare, [*predicate*]; dīc-o (vb. 3), to say, (compd. w. ab, ad, com, contra, e, in, inter, prae), [*contradict, edict, interdict, predict, verdict*]; **dic-tio,** a saying, *diction,* [*dictionary*]; dic-to (freq.), to say often, prescribe, *dictate;* **dic-tātor,** a *dictator;* **dic-tĭto** (intens.), to say often or emphatically.

11. dak; (dac-as, fame); **δοκ; dic;** be esteemed, esteem.

δοκ-έω, to think, seem; δόξ-α, opinion.

dĕc-et, it is proper, it is fitting, (compd. w. ad, com, de); **dĕc-ens,** becoming, fit, *decent;* **dĕc-or (ŏris),** what is seemly or becoming, elegance, grace; **dĕc-ōrus,** becoming, suitable, *decorous;* **dĕc-ōrum,** propriety, *decorum;* **dĕc-us (ŏris),** ornament, honor, glory; **dĕc-ŏro,** to *decorate,* adorn, (compd. w. com, de); **dig-nus** (= dic-nus), worthy; **dig-nitas,** worthiness, *dignity;* **dig-nor,** to deem worthy, to regard as worthy of one's self, to *deign;* **de-dig-nor,** to *disdain;* **in-dig-nor,** to consider unworthy, to be *indignant.*

12. du, du-k; duh; δυκ; dūc; draw, lead.

δα-δύσσε-σθαι, to draw.

dūc-o, to lead, conduct, draw, (compd. w. ab, ad, circum, com, de, di, e, in, intro, ob, per, prae, praeter, pro, re, retro, se, sub, subter, super, trans), [*abduce, abduction, adduce, adduction, circumduct, circumduction, condúce, condúct, conduction, cónduct, deduce, deduction, diduction, educe, eduction, induce, induct, induction, introduce, introduction, prodúce, próduce, próduct, production, reduce, reduction, retroduction, seduce, seduction, subduce, subduct, subduction, superinduce, superinduction, traduce, traduction*]; **ē-dŭc-o** (conj. 1), to bring up a child physically or mentally, to rear, to *educate;* **dux,** a leader; **duc-to** (freq.), to lead, conduct; **duc-tĭlis,** that may be led or drawn, *ductile.*

13. εἴκοσι, Bœot. Ϝίκατι, twenty.

vīginti, twenty; **vīcesĭmus, vīcensĭmus, vīgesĭmus,** the twentieth.

14. vik; vik´; Ϝικ, ικ; vic; yield, give way.

εἴκ-ω, to yield.

vī-to (= **vic-i-to),** to shun, avoid, (compd. w. de, ; **vĭc-is,** change, alternation, *vicissitude;* **vĭc-issim,** in turn.

15. ἑκατόν, a hundred. Sk. **çata-m.**

centum, a hundred, [*cent*]; **centesĭmus,** the hundredth; **centŭria,** an assemblage or a division consisting of a hundred, a *century;* **centŭrio,** a commander of a hundred men, a *centurion.*

16. vak; vaç; Ϝεκ, ἐκ; vic; will, desire.

ἑκ-ών, willing; ἕκ-ητι, by means of, for the sake of; ἕκ-ηλος, at rest, at one's ease.

in-vī-tus (= in-vic-i-tus), unwilling.

17. ἑκυρός, a father-in-law; ἑκυρά, a mother-in-law. Sk. **çvaçuras.**

sŏcer, a father-in-law; **socrus,** a mother-in-law.

18. vark, vrak, valk, vlak, lak; —; **Ϝελκ; lac;** draw, drag, allure.

ἕλκ-ω, to draw; ὁλκ-ή, a drawing; ὁλκ-ός, that which draws, that which is made by drawing, a furrow.

†**lăc-io,** to entice, allure, (compd. w. ad, e, in, per, pro), [*elicit*]; **de-lec-to** (intens.), to allure, delight, [*delectable*]; **delĭcātus,** alluring, *delicate;* **deliciōsus,** *delicious;* **lăqu-eus,** a snare; **il-lĕc-ĕbra,** enticement.

19. ἕλκος, a wound, an ulcer.
ulcus, a sore, an *ulcer;* ulcĕro, to make sore, to cause to *ulcerate;* ulcerātio, *ulceration.*

20. Sk. rt. ark', beam.
ἠλέκτωρ, the beaming sun; ἤλεκτρον, amber, a shining metal [*electricity*]; Ἠλέκτρα, Electra.

21. Greek rt. ἰκ.
ἰκ-μάς, moisture; ἰκ-μαίνω, to moisten.

22. Greek rt. Ϝικ, ἰκ, come.
ἴκ-ω, ἰκ-νέομαι, ἰκ-άνω, to come, reach; ἰκ-έτης, ἰκ-τήρ, a suppliant; ἰκ-ανός, coming far enough, sufficient; ἴκ-μενος, following, favorable.

23. κάδος, a jar or vessel for water or wine.
cădus, a large vessel for containing liquids.

24. καθ-ἄρός, clean, clear, pure; καθ-αίρω, to purify; κάθαρσις, purification, [*cathartic*].
cas-tus (= cad-tus), pure, *chaste;* in-ces-tus, impure, unchaste; in-ces-tum, in-ces-tus, unchastity, *incest;* cas-tīgo (castum-ago), to set right, to correct, *chastise, chasten, castigate.*

25. Pronominal stems, ka, ki; —; κα, κο; —.
καί, and. From the same stem comes τε with τ for κ.
que, and.

26. Greek rt. κακ.
κακ-ός, bad; κακ-όω, to maltreat; κακ-ύνω, to damage; κάκ-η, wickedness.

27. κάλαμος, a reed, a fishing-rod; καλάμη, a stalk; καλαμεύς, a reaper, an angler.
Sk. kalamas, a kind of rice, a writing-reed. călămus, a reed; culmus, a stalk, *culm.*

28. kar, kal, kla, kla-m; —; καλ; kal, cal, cla; call.
κἄλ-έω, to call; κλη-τήρ, κλή-τωρ, one who calls or summons; κλῆ-σις, a calling, call; κλη-τεύω, to cite, to summon.

căl-o, kăl-o, to call, call together, summon; **inter-călo,** to *intercalate;* **Căl-endae, Kăl-endae,** (the day when the order of days was proclaimed), the first day of the Roman month, the Calends; **Căl-endārius, Kăl-endārius,** of or pertaining to the Calends; **Căl-endārium, Kăl-endārium,** the interest-book of a money-lender, [*calendar*]; **inter-căl-āris,** *intercalar, intercalary;* **con-cĭl-ium,** an assembly, a *council;* **nomen-clā-tor,** one who calls by name; **nomen-clā-tūra,** a calling by name, *nomenclature;* **clas-sis** (= cla-t-ti-s, or = κλᾶ-σις = κλῆ-σις), (a mustering, a summons), a *class*, an army, a fleet; **classĭcus,** (of or belonging to a classis), belonging to a class of the Roman people, belonging to the first class, of the highest rank, *classical;* **clā-mo,** to call, cry out, shout, [*claim*], (compd. w. ad, com, de, ex, in, pro, re, sub), [*acclaim, acclamation, declaim, declamation, exclaim, exclamation, proclaim, proclamation, reclaim, reclamation*]; **clā-mĭto** (freq.), to cry out violently, to vociferate; **clā-mor,** a loud call, a shout, a cry, *clamor.*

29. kal; (stem-form **kala**); **καλ; cal, cel;** cover.

καλ-ία, a wooden dwelling, hut, barn, granary; καλ-ιός, καλ-ιάς, a hut, a cabin. An expansion of the root **καλ** is found in the stem καλυβ of καλύβ-η, hut, and καλύπ-τω, to cover. Another expansion is probably the root **κλεπ,** No. 55.

†**căl-ix,** a cup; †**căl-yx,** the bud, cup, or *calyx* of a flower; **căl-īgo,** a thick atmosphere, mist, fog; **cel-la** (prob. a dim. form for **cel-ula**), a store-room, granary, chamber, [*cell*]; **cel-larium,** a receptacle for food, a pantry, [*cellar*]; **cel-lŭla** (dim.), a small store-room or apartment, [*cellule, cellular, cellulose*]; **cĕl-o,** to conceal; **con-cēl-o,** to *conceal* carefully; **oc-cŭl-o,** to cover, cover up, hide, [*occult, occultation*]; **ŏc-cul-lus,** a covering, a cap, a hood; **cŏl-or,** *color;* **cŏl-ōro,** to color; **de-cŏl-ōro,** to discolor; **clam** (old access. form **cal-lim**), secretly; **clan-destīnus,** (for **clam-dies-tinus**), secret, *clandestine;* **gal-ea,** a helmet; **gal-ērum, gal-ērus, gal-ēra,** a covering for the head, a cap; **clip-eus, clypeus, clupeus, clipeum,** a shield. From the root **cel** come the O. H. Ger. **helan,** to conceal, and **hella,** hell; A.-S. hell; Eng. *hell.*

30. καλός, beautiful; καλλίων, more beautiful; κάλλος, καλλονή, beauty; καλλύνω, to beautify. The λλ of these words is produced by assimilation from *lj*. Kindred with these words are the following: Sk. **kal-jas,** healthy, pleasant; Goth. **hail-s,** sound, healthy; Ger. **heil,** sound, whole; A.-S. **hal,** sound, whole; O. Eng. *hale, hole;* Eng. *hale* (written also *hail*), *whole, heal, health.*

31. Sk. rt. **kmar,** be crooked.

καμάρα, anything with an arched cover, a vault, a covered wagon.

cămur, cămŭrus, crooked, turned inwards; † camĕra, † camăra, a vault, an arched roof, an arch, [*chamber*].

32. **kan; (kan-kaṅ-i,** bell); **καν; can;** sound.

καν-άσσω, καν-άζω, to sound; καν-αχή, a sharp sound; κόναβος, a ringing, clashing; κύ-κν-ος, a swan.

căn-o, to sing (compd. w. com, in, ob, prae, re, sub); cănōrus, melodious; can-to (freq.), to sing, (compd. w. de, ex, in, re), [*chant, cant, chanticleer, enchant, incantation, recant*]; can-tor, a singer; can-trix, a songstress; prae-cen-tor (fr. prae-cĭn-o), a leader in music, a *precentor;* in-cen-tor (fr. in-cĭn-o), a precentor, an inciter; in-cen-tīvus (adj.), that strikes up or sets the tune, that provokes or incites; in-cen-tīvum, an *incentive;* can-tŭs, song, music; can-tillo (dim. fr. can-to), to sing low, to hum, [*cantillate*]; can-tĭcum, a song, a solo; can-ticŭlum (dim.), a little song, a *canticle;* ac-cen-tus (fr. accĭno), a blast, signal, *accent*, tone; con-cen-tus, harmony, *concént*.

33. **kap; —; καπ; cap;** take hold of, seize.

κώπ-η, any handle, the handle of an oar, handle of a sword.

căp-io, to take hold of, (compd. w. ad, ante, com, de, ex, in, inter, ob, per, prae, re, sub), [*conceive, conception, conceit, deceive, deception, deceit, except, incipient, inceptive, inception, intercept, interception, perceive, perception, receive, receipt, reception, susceptible*]; cap-to (freq.), to strive to seize, (comp.w. com, dis, ex, in, ob, re); cap-esso (desid.), to take or catch at eagerly; **anti-cĭp-o,** to take before, to *anticipate;* **oc-cŭp-o,** to take possession of, to *occupy,* [*occupation*]; **prae-oc-cŭp-o,** to *preoccupy;* **căp-ax,** *capacious;* **căp-acitas,** *capacity;* **căp-istrum,** a halter; **cap-tor,** a hunter, a *captor;* **captīvus,** a *captive;* **căp-ŭlus, căp-ŭlum,** a tomb, a handle, a hilt; **manceps** (**mănus, căpio**), a purchaser, contractor; **man-cĭp-o, man-cŭp-o,** to make over as property, to transfer; **eman-cĭp-o,** to *emancipate;* **muni-cĭp-ium** (**munia, capio**), a free town; **municipālis,** *municipal;* **princeps** (**primus, capio**), first, chief; **principālis,** first, *principal;* **prae-ceptor,** one who takes beforehand, a ruler, *preceptor;* **re-cep-tācŭlum,** a *receptacle.*

34. κάπ-ηλος, a peddler; καπ-ηλεύω, to be a κάπ-ηλος, or retail dealer; κᾰπ-ηλεία, retail trade, tavern-keeping.

caupo, a petty tradesman, an innkeeper; **caupōna,** a landlady, an inn.

35. kvap; (kap-is, kap-ilas, incense); **καπ; vap** (for **cvap**); breathe forth.

κᾰπ-ύω, to breathe forth; κε-καφ-ηώς, gasping; καπ-νός, smoke.

văp-or (for **cvapor**), exhalation, *vapor;* **văp-ōro,** to emit steam or vapor; **e-văp-ōro,** to *evaporate;* **vap-ĭdus,** that has emitted steam or vapor, *i.e.* that has lost its life and spirit, spoiled, *vapid;* **vap-pa,** wine that has lost its spirit and flavor, vapid wine.

36. κάπ-ρος, a boar.

căp-er, a he-goat, [*caper, caprice, capricious*]; **cap-ra,** a she-goat; **Cap-ricornus** (**caper, cornu**), *Capricorn.*

37. κάρα, κάρηνον, the head; κρανίον, the skull, [*cranial,* N. Lat. *cranium*]; κάρανος, a head, chief; καρανόω, to achieve; κορῠφή, the head; κρήνη, a spring.

cĕrĕbrum, the brain, [*cerebral*].

38. κῆρ, κέαρ, καρδ-ία, κραδ-ίη, *heart.*

cor (st. **cord**), heart, [*cordial*]; **cordātus,** wise; **vēcors,** senseless.

39. καρκίνος, a crab.
cancer, a crab [*cancer*].

40. Greek rt. **καρπ, κραπ.**
καρπ-άλιμος, swift; κραιπ-νός, swift; κραιπ-άλη, a drunken headache; κάλπη, a gallop.

41. καρπός, fruit, [*harvest*]; κάρπιμος, fruitful; καρπόω, to bear fruit, (mid.) to get fruit for one's self; κρώπιον, a sickle.
Latin rt. **carp.**
carp-o, to pick, pluck, gather, to *carp* at, (compd. w. com, de, dis, ex, prae); carptim, by detached parts, separately.

42. Indo-Eur. rt. **kar,** hard.
κάρ-υον, a nut, the stone in stone-fruit; καρύα, the walnut-tree.
car-īna, the keel of a ship, a nut-shell, (cf. Eng. naut. terms, hull, shell); calx, a small stone, limestone; cal-cŭlus (dim. fr. calx), a small stone (used in playing draughts, in reckoning or in voting), [*calculus*]; cal-cŭlo, to *calculate*.

43. Greek rt. **καυ, καϝ.**
κα-ί-ω, to burn; καῦ-μα, burning heat; καυ-στός, burnt, capable of being burnt; καυ-στικός, capable of burning, *caustic*.

44. ki; çi; κει (stem); qui, ci; lie (recline).
κεῖ-μαι, to be laid, to lie; κοί-τη, a bed, a couch; κοι-μάω, to put to sleep; κῶ-μος, a jovial festivity, a revel; κώ-μη, a village, [*home*]; κω-μῳδός (κῶμος, ἀείδω), a comedian; κω-μῳδία, a comedy.
quī-es, rest, *quiet;* rĕ-quī-es (re, quies), after-rest, *i.e.* rest from labor, suffering, care, etc., [*requiem*]; qui-esco, to rest, to keep quiet, (compd. w. ad, com, re), [*quiescent, acquiesce*]; cī-vis, a citizen; cī-vīlis, of citizens, *civil;* cī-vīcus, of citizens, *civic;* cī-vītas, citizenship, the state, a *city*.

45. sak, ska, ski; k'hâ; σκι, σκα; sci, sec, sac; split, cleave, sever, distinguish, decide.
κεί-ω, κε-άζω, to split; κέ-αρνον, a carpenter's axe.
scī-o, (prop. to distinguish, discern), to know, (compd. w.

com, ne); **sci-entia,** knowledge, *science;* **con-sci-entia,** joint knowledge, consciousness, *conscience;* **con-sci-us,** knowing with others or by one's self, *conscious;* **sci-sco** (inch.), to seek to know, to inquire, to decree; **a-sci-sco, ad-sci-sco,** to receive as true, to receive in some capacity; **con-sci-sco,** to approve, to decree a thing together or in common; **de-sci-sco,** to set one's self loose, to free one's self from (this compound brings out most clearly the meaning of the root); **prae-sci-sco,** to find out beforehand; **re-sci-sco,** to find out, ascertain a thing (bringing it again to light from concealment); **scī-tus,** knowing, wise; **scī-tum,** a decree; **sĕc-o,** to cut, to cut off, (compd. w. circum, com, de, dis, ex, in, inter, per, prae, pro, re, sub), [*secant, dissect, intersect*]; **sec-ta,** a path, way, *sect;* **sec-tio,** a cutting, cutting off, *section;* **sec-ūris,** an axe; **serra** (?) (perhaps = sec-ra), a saw; **serrātus** (?), *serrated;* **seg-mentum,** a piece cut off, a *segment;* **sīc-a** (?), a dagger; **sax-um,** any large, rough stone, a detached fragment of rock; **sex-us,** (prop. a division), a *sex*.

46. Indo-Eur. rt. **skal,** be rough, be harsh.

κελ-αινός, black; κελαι-νεφής, black with clouds, cloud-wrapt, black.

squāl-eo, to be stiff or rough, to be filthy or squalid; **squāl-or,** stiffness, roughness, filthiness, *squalor;* **squāl-ĭdus,** stiff with dirt, filthy, *squalid*.

47. κέλ-ευ-θος, a way; ἀκόλου-θος, following; ἀκόλου-θος (subst.), a follower; ἀκολου-θέω, to follow, [*anacoluthon*].

cal-lis, a path.

48. **kal; kal;** κελ**; cel;** urge on, drive.

κέλ-λω, to drive on; κελ-εύω, κέλ-ομαι, to urge or drive on, exhort, command; κέλ-ης, a courser; βου-κόλ-ος, a herdsman, [*bucolic*].

cel-lo (found only in compounds); **per-cel-lo** (lit. to impel greatly), to beat, strike, beat down, urge on; **prō-cel-lo,** to drive or urge forward; **prŏ-cul,** afar off; **cĕl-er,** swift; **cĕl-ĕrĭtas,** swiftness, *celerity;* **cĕl-ĕro,** to quicken, hasten, be quick; **ac-cĕl-**

ĕro, to hasten, *accelerate*, make haste; cĕl-ox, swift; cĕl-ox, a swift-sailing ship, a yacht; prŏ-cel-la, a violent wind, a storm.

49. κέρας, horn; κερāός, horned, of horn; κρῑός (?), a ram; ῥινόκερως (ῥίς, κέρας), the *rhinoceros*.

cornu, *horn*, [*corn* (on the foot), *corner, cornet, cornucopia, unicorn*].

50. κερ-ᾰσός, the cherry-tree (κερασός is to κέρας as cornus to cornu); κρᾰ-νον, κρά-νεια, the cornel-tree.

cornus, a cornel-cherry tree, a javelin made of cornel-wood.

51. skar; çar; κερ; —; cut off, damage.

κείρ-ω, to cut short, cut off, ravage, destroy; κορ-μός, the trunk of a tree; κέρ-μα, anything cut small, small coin; κουρ-ά, a shearing; κουρ-εύς, a barber; κερ-αΐζω, to destroy, to plunder; κηρ-αίνω, to destroy; Κήρ, the goddess of death or doom; κήρ, death, doom; κόρ-ος, κοῦρ-ος, a boy, a youth (from the custom of cutting the hair at the time of puberty); κόρ-η, κούρ-η, a maiden, a bride; κουρ-ίδιος, wedded.

cur-tus, shortened, short, [*curt, curtail*].

52. Indo-Eur. rt. kap, grasp, have. (This No. is probably connected with No. 33.)

κεφαλή, the head; κεφάλαιος, of the head; ἀκέφαλος, without head, *acephalous*.

căp-ut, the head, [*cap, cape, captain*]; căp-ĭtālis, relating to or belonging to the head, relating to life, *capital;* Căp-ĭtōlĭum, the Capitol (at Rome), [*a capitol*]; căp-ĭtŭlum, (dim.), a small head, (in architecture) the capital of a column, (in late Latin) a *chapter*, section, [*capitulate*]; căp-illus, the hair of the head, the hair; căp-illāris, of or pertaining to the hair, [*capillary*]; anceps, [an, caput], (lit. two-headed), double, that extends on two opposite sides, wavering, doubtful; bĭceps (bis, caput), two-headed, divided into two parts; praeceps (prae, căput), headlong, (of places) steep, *precipitous;* praeceps (subst.), a steep place, a *precipice;* praecĭpĭto, to throw down headlong, to *precipitate*.

53. skap; —; σκαπ; —; dig.

κῆπ-ος, a garden.

camp-us, a plain, a field, [*camp*, n. and v., *encamp*].

54. ki; çi; κι; ci; rouse, excite, go.

κί-ω, to go; κί-νυμαι, to move one's self, to go; κῑ-νέω, to move, to set in motion.

cĭ-ĕo (fr. the primitive form cĭo prevailing in the compounds, accio, excio, etc.), to put in motion, to move, disturb; ac-cĭ-o, to summon; ex-cĭ-o, to call out; cĭ-tus, put in motion, swift; cĭ-to, quickly; cĭ-to (freq.), to put into quick motion, rouse, summon, *cite*; ex-cĭ-to, to call out or forth, to *excite*; in-cĭ-to, to urge forward, to *incite*; solli-cĭ-tus, solī-cĭ-tus (sollus, [old word meaning 'entire'] cieo), wholly, *i.e.* violently moved, disturbed, *solicitous*; sollī-cĭ-to, solī-cĭ-to, to disturb, urge, *solicit*.

55. klap; —; κλεπ; clep; steal. (This No. is probably connected with No. 29.)

κλέπ-τω, to steal; κλώψ, κλοπ-εύς, κλέπ-της, a thief; κλοπ-ή, theft, [*klopemania*, *kleptomania*].

clĕp-o, to steal.

56. sklu; —; κλει, κλειδ; clu; shut, close, fasten.

κλη-ί-ς, κλείς, a key; κλεί-ω, to shut.

clāv-i-s, a key; clāv-icŭla (dim.), a small key, [*clavicle*]; clāv-us, a nail; clau-d-o (in compounds cludo), to shut, *close*, (compd. w. circum, com, dis, ex, in, inter, ob, prae, re, se), [*conclude, disclose, exclude, include, inclose, interclude, preclude, recluse, seclude*]; claus-tra (in sing. claustrum, rare), a lock, door, defence; claudus, lame.

57. kli; —; κλι; cli; lean (incline).

κλί-ν-ω, to make to bend, to lean, to incline, [*enclitic*]; κλί-νη, that on which one lies, a couch; κλῐ-μα, inclination (of ground), region, *clime, climate;* κλῖ-μαξ, a ladder, a *climax;* κλῐ-σία, a place for lying down, or reclining, a hut, a couch; κλῑ-τύς, a slope, hill-side.

clī-vus, a gently-sloping height, a hill; clī-no (found only in participle clinatus, inclined), [*lean*]; ac-clī-no, to lean on or against; dē-clī-no, to turn aside or away, to *decline*, [*declination, declension*]; in-clī-no, to bend in any direction, to *incline*, [*inclination*]; re-clī-no, to bend or lean back, to *recline*.

58. kru, klu; çru; κλυ; clu; hear.

κλύ-ω, to hear; κλυ-τός, heard of, renowned, [*loud*]; κλέ-ος, report, fame; κλε-ίω (poet. for κλέ-ω), to make famous, celebrate; κλει-νός, κλει-τός, renowned.

clu-ŏo, clŭ-o, to hear one's self called in some way, to be called; cli-ens, clu-ens, (one who hears), a *client*, dependant, retainer; in-clŭ-tus, in-clĭ-tus, celebrated, famous; glō-ria, *glory*, fame; glo-rior, to glory, to boast; glo-riōsus, *glorious*, famous; clā-rus, (prop. well audible), *clear*, loud, brilliant, illustrious; clā-ro, to make clear; de-clā-ro, to make clear, to manifest, *declare*; clā-rĭfĭco (clarus, facio), to make illustrious, [*clarify*]; laus (for claus), praise, glory, [*laud*]; lau-do, to praise; lau-dā-bĭlis, praiseworthy, *laudable*.

59. klu; —; κλυ; —; wash, cleanse.

κλύ-ζω, to wash; κλύ-δων, a wave.

‡clu-o (= purgo), to cleanse; clŏ-āca, a sewer, a drain.

60. sku, skav; kav; koF; cav; look, observe.

κο-έ-ω, to perceive, to hear; θυο-σκόος, one who looks on at a sacrifice, a sacrificing priest; ἀκού-ω, to hear, [*acoustic*]; ἀκου-ή, ἀκο-ή, hearing, a sound.

căv-ĕo, to be on one's guard, to take care; cau-tus, careful, wary, *cautious*; cau-tio, *caution*; cu-ra, care, [*cure*]; cū-ro, to care for, [*curate, curator*]; se-cū-rus (se = sine, cura), free from care, free from danger, *secure*, [*sure*]; cū-riōsus, careful, inquiring eagerly or anxiously about a thing, *curious*; cu-riosĭtas, curiosity; cau-sa, caussa, a *cause*, [*causal, because*]; ac-cū-so (orig. = ad causam provocare), to call one to account, to *accuse*; ex-cū-so (prop. to release from a charge), to *excuse*; in-cū-so, to accuse, to complain of; rĕ-cū-so, to make an objection against, to refuse, [*recusant*].

61. κόγχη, κόγχος, a bivalve shell-fish, mussel (muscle).
concha, a bivalve shell-fish, mussel (muscle), mussel-shell, snail-shell, trumpet, [*conch, conchology*].

62. ku; kû; —; —; scream.
κόκκυξ, a *cuckoo;* κόκκū, the cuckoo's cry; κυκκύζω, to cry like a cuckoo, to crow.
cŭcŭlus, a cuckoo.

63. κολ-ωνός, κολ-ωνή, a hill; κολ-οφών, a summit.
cel-sus, high, lofty; ante-cel-lo, to surpass; ex-cel-lo, to raise, to rise, to *excel;* prae-cel-lo, to distinguish one's self, to excel; cŏl-ŭmen, cul-men, the summit, [*culminate*]; cŏl-umna, a *column*, a pillar; col-lis, a hill.

64. skap; —; κοπ; —; cut, strike.
κόπ-τω, to strike, to cut, [*apocope, syncope*]; κόμ-μα, that which is struck, that which is knocked off, a piece, a short clause of a sentence, [*comma*]; κοπ-ή, a striking, a cutting in pieces; κοπ-εύς, a chisel; κοπ-ίς, a broad, curved knife; κόπ-ις, a prater, a wrangler; κόπ-ος, a striking, suffering, weariness; κοπ-ιάω, to be tired; κοπ-άζω, to grow tired or weary; κωφ-ός, blunt, dumb, deaf.

65. kar; —; —; —; croak.
κόρ-αξ, a raven; κορ-ώνη, a *crow*.
These words are probably akin to the onomatop. words κράζω [rt. κραγ], to *croak* [like the raven]; κρώζω, to cry like a crow, to caw.
cor-vus, a raven; cor-nix, a crow.

66. skar, skar-d, skra-d; (kûrd, a spring, a leap); κραδ; card; swing.
κράδ-η, the quivering twig at the end of a branch, a branch; κραδ-άω, κραδ-αίνω, to swing.
card-o, a hinge; card-ĭnālis, of a door-hinge, on which something turns or depends, principal, *cardinal*.

67. kar; kar; κρα, κραν; cer, cre; do, make.

κραίν-ω, to accomplish, fulfil; κράν-τωρ, κρεί-ων, κρέ-ων, a ruler; Κρόνος, Cronos (identified with the Latin Saturnus), son of Uranus and Gaia; κρᾰ-τύς, strong; κρᾰ-τύνω, to strengthen; κρά-τος, κάρ-τος, strength; κρα-τέω, to be strong, to rule; κάρ-τερος, κρα-ταιός, strong, mighty; ἀριστοκρατία (ἄριστος, best), the rule of the best-born, an *aristocracy;* αὐτο-κρᾰτής, (αὐτός, self), ruling by one's self, having full power, [*autocrat*]; δημο-κρατία (δῆμος, the people), *democracy,* popular government.

Cĕr-ēs, Ceres (prob. the goddess of creation), the goddess of agriculture; Cĕr-eālis, pertaining to Ceres, pertaining to grain or agriculture, *cereal;* prō-cĕr-us, high; crĕ-o (old form cer-eo), to bring forth, produce, make, *create,* beget, [*creator, creature*]; prō-cre-o, to bring forth, beget, *procreate;* re-cre-o, to make or create anew, to restore to a good condition, *rĕ-create, rĕcreate,* [*rĕ-creation, rĕcreation*]; cre-sco (inch.), to come forth, appear, grow up, increase, [*crescent*], (compd. w. ad, com, de, in, pro, re, sub), [*accretion, concrete, concretion, decrease, decrement, increase, increment*]; crē-ber (lit. made to increase), frequent, numerous; cor-pus, a body (whether living or lifeless), a *corpse,* [*corps, corporal, corporeal, corpulent*]; cor-pŏro, to make or fashion into a body, (compd. w. ad, com, in), [*corporate, incorporate, corporation, incorporation*]; caer-ĭmōnĭa, cĕr-ĭmōnĭa (sacred work, divine rite), sanctity, veneration, a religious *ceremony.*

68. kru, krav, karv; —; —; —; be hard, curdle.

κρέ-ας, flesh; κρεῖ-ον, a meat-tray.

crŭ-or, blood; cru-entus, bloody; căr-o, flesh; car-nālis, fleshly, *carnal.*

69. skar; kar; κρι; cer, car (for **skar**); separate.

κρῑ-νω, to separate, judge, decide; κρί-μνον, coarse ground barley; κρῐ-τής, a judge; κρί-σις, decision, trial, *crisis;* κρῐ-τῐκός, critical, [*critic, criticise*]; κρῐ-τήριον, a test, a *criterion.*

cer-n-o, to separate, distinguish, perceive, decide, (compd. w. com, de, dis, ex, in, se, sub, super), [*concern, decrec, discern, discreet, secern, secrete, secret, secretary*]; **cer-tus** (part.), determined; **cer-tus** (adj.), established, *certain;* **cer-tō, cer-tē,** certainly; **cer-to** (freq.), to decide something by a contest, to fight; **con-cer-to,** to contend zealously, [*concért, cóncert*]; **de-cer-to,** to fight earnestly, to fight it out; **crī-brum,** a sieve; **crī-men** [contr. from **cernimen,** (lit. a judicial decision)], a charge, a *crime;* **criminālis,** *criminal;* **crimino,** to accuse, *to criminate;* **dis-crī-men,** separation, distinction; **dis-crī-mĭno,** to separate, distinguish, *discriminate.*

70. kru; (krû-ras, sore); κρυ; **cru;** be hard. (This root is probably connected with Nos. 42 and 68.)

κρύ-ος, κρυ-μός, icy-cold, frost; κρυό-ομαι, to be icy-cold; κρυό-εις, chilling; κρυ-σταίνομαι, to be congealed; κρύ-σταλλος, ice, *crystal.*

. **cru-sta,** the hard surface of a body, shell, *crust;* **cru-sto,** to cover with a rind, shell, etc.; **in-cru-sto,** to *incrust;* **cru-dus,** bloody, raw, unripe, *crude;* **cru-dēlis,** *cruel,* fierce.

71. Greek rt. κτα, κταν, κτεν.

κτείν-ω, to kill; κτόν-ος, murder; καίν-ω, to kill.

72. Greek rt. κτι.

ἐΰ-κτί-μενος, well-built; περι-κτί-ονες, ἀμφι-κτί-ονες, the dwellers around, neighbors; κτί-ζω, to settle, found, build; κτί-σις, a founding, a settling.

73. ku; çvi; κυ, κοι; —; swell, be hollow.

κυ-έω, to be pregnant; κύ-ος, κύ-ημα, κῦ-μα, a foetus; κῦ-μα, the swell of the sea, wave; κύ-αρ, κύ-τος, a hollow; κοῖ-λος, hollow; κοι-λία, a belly; καυ-λός, a stalk.

in-cĭ-ens, pregnant; **căv-us,** hollow, [*cave, cavity*]; **căv-erna,** a hollow, a *cavern;* **cau-lis,** a stalk; **cau-lae,** an opening, a hollow; **cae-lum, coe-lum** (for **cav-ilum**), the sky; **cae-lestis,** *celestial.*

74. kar, kvar, kur; (k'a-kr-a-s for ka-kra-s, wheel); κυρ, κυλ; —; curved.

κυρ-τός, curved, [*crook*]; κίρ-κος, a circle, a kind of hawk which flies in a circle; κυλ-λός, crooked; κύ-κλος, a circle, [*cycle, cycloid, cyclone, cyclopedia, or cyclopaedia* (παιδεία, education)]; κυλ-ίω (κυλ-ίνδω), to roll along; κορ-ώνη, anything curved, e.g., the curved stem of a ship; κορ-ωνός, κορ-ωνίς, curved.

cir-cus, a circular line, a circle; cir-cŭlus (contr. circlus), a circular figure, a *circle;* cir-cŭlor, to form a circle, [*circulate, circulation*]; cir-cum, cir-cā, around; cŏr-ōna, a garland, a crown, a circle of men, a *corona*, [*coronal, coronation, coronel, colonel* (prob.), *coroner, coronet*]; cur-vus, curved.

75. κύ-ων, a dog, [*cynic, cynosure*].

căn-is (for cvan-is), a dog, [*hound*]; căn-īnus, *canine*. These words are by some considered to be akin to those under No. 73.

76. κῶ-νος, a pine-cone, a *cone*, [*conic, conical, hone*].

cŭneus, a wedge, [*cuneiform, cuniform*]; cos, a whetstone, a hone; cau-tes, a rough, pointed rock; că-tus, sharp to the hearing, clear-sighted, intelligent. Of these words the meaning of the root is "pointed, sharp." Cf. No. 2.

77. ra, rak, lak; lap; λακ; **loqu, loc;** sound, speak.

ἔ-λακ-ον, λέ-λᾱκ-α, λά-σκω, to sound, shriek, shout; λακ-ερός, talkative.

lŏqu-or, to speak, (compd. w. ad, com, e, inter, ob, prae, pro, re), [*allocution, colloquy, colloquial, eloquent, interlocution, obloquy, prolocutor*]; lŏqu-ax, *loquacious;* loqu-ēla, speech.

78. vark, valk, vlak, lak; (vrac̦k', scindere); Fρακ, Fλακ, λακ; lac; tear.

ῥᾰ-κ-ος, a ragged garment, a *rag;* λάκ-ος, λακ-ίς, a rent; λακ-ερός, torn; λάκ-κος, a hole.

lăc-er, mangled, lacerated, torn to pieces; lăc-ĕro, to tear to pieces, *lacerate;* lac-inia, the lappet, edge or corner of a garment, a small piece; **lăc-us** (anything hollow), a tank, a reservoir, a *lake;* **lăc-ūna,** a cavity, a gap, a defect.

79. λεύσσ-ω, to *look.* (Connected, though not directly, with No. 80.)

80. ruk, luk; (ruk´, appear, shine); **λυκ; luc;** light, shine.

ἀμφι-λύκ-η, morning twilight; λύχ-νος, a lamp; λευκ-ός (adj.), light, white.

lūc-eo, to be light or clear, to shine, (compd. w. di, e, inter, re, sub, trans), [*look, translucent*]; **lūc-esco** (inch.), to begin to shine, to grow light, (compd. w. in, re); **lūc-erna,** a lamp; **lux, lū-men** (for *luc-men*), *light;* **lū-mĭ-no,** to light up; **il-lū-mĭno,** to light up, to *illuminate;* **lū-mĭnōsus,** full of light, *luminous;* **lūcĭdus,** shining, clear, *lucid;* **lū-na** (for *luc-na*), the moon, [*lune, lunar, lunatic*]; **il-lus-tris,** lighted up, clear, *illustrious;* **il-lustro,** to light up, make clear, *illustrate,* render famous.

81. λύκος, a wolf.
lupus, a *wolf.*

82. mak; makara-s; μακ; mac; extend, make large.

μάκ-αρ, blessed; μᾱκ-ρός, long; μῆκος, length.

mac-to (lit. to make large), to worship, honor, (*macto* is best referred to No. 320, when it means to kill, slaughter, destroy); **mac-tus,** venerated, honored. It is probable that there were three related roots existing side by side, *mak* (No. 82), *mag*, and *magh*, all three perhaps to be traced back to the root *ma*, and all with the meaning of extension.

83. nak; naç; νεκ; nec, noc; perish, destroy, injure.

νέκ-υς, corpse; νεκ-ρός (noun), corpse; νεκ-ρός (adj.), dead. **nĕc-o,** to kill; **per-nĕc-o,** to kill utterly or completely; **nex,** a violent death, murder, slaughter; **inter-nĕc-io, inter-nĭc-io,** a massacre, a general slaughter, a destruction; **inter-nĕcĭnus, inter-nĕc-īvus,** deadly, destructive, *internecine;* **per-nĭc-ies,** destruction, calamity; **per-nĭc-iōsus,** destructive, *pernicious;* **nŏc-eo,** to do harm, to injure; **noxa** (= *noc-sa*), harm, injury; **nox-ius,** injurious, *noxious,* guilty.

REGULAR SUBSTITUTION OF SOUNDS. 61

84. nak; nak; (st. νυκτ); (st. **nocti**); perish, destroy, injure.

The root is the same as of No. 83, since night is said to be "no man's friend."

νύξ, night; νύκ-τωρ (adv.), by night, nightly; νύκ-τερος, νυκ-τερινός (adj.), by night, nightly; νυκ-τερίς, a bat.

nox, *night*, [*fortnight*]; **noctu, nocte, nox** (adv'ly), in the night; **noc-turnus**, *nocturnal;* **noc-tua**, a night-owl; an owl.

85. vik; viç; Fικ; vic; come, enter, settle.

οἶκος (Ϝοῖκος), οἰκία, house; οἰκέτης, an inmate of one's house; οἰκέ-ω, to inhabit, dwell.

vic-us, a village, [*-wick, -wich*, as in *Berwick, Norwich*]; **vic-inus** (adj.), near, neighboring; **vic-inus** (subst.), a neighbor; **vic-initas**, neighborhood, *vicinity;* **villa** (most probably for *vicula*, from *vicus*), a country-house, country-seat, farm, *villa*, [*vill, village, villain*].

86. ὀκτώ, eight; ὄγδοος, eighth.

octo, *eight;* **octāvus**, eighth, [*octave*].

87. pak; —; πεκ; **pec;** comb.

πέκ-ω, πείκ-ω, πεκ-τέ-ω, to comb, to shear; πέκ-ος, πόκ-ος, wool, fleece.

pec-to, to comb; **pec-ten**, a comb.

88. πεύκ-η, the fir; πευκ-ών, a fir-wood; πεύκ-ινος, of or made of fir.

89. Greek rt. πικ.

πικ-ρός, πευκ-εδανός, bitter, sharp; ἐχε-πευκ-ές (βέλος), sharp. Connection of this root with No. 88 is probable.

90. pik, pig; piç; πικ; pic, pig, pi-n-g; prick, prick with a needle, embroider, color, paint. (Connection of this root with Nos. 89 and 88 is probable).

ποικ-ίλος, many-colored.

ping-o, to *paint*, embroider, (compd. w. ad, de, ex, sub), [*depict*]; **pic-tor**, a painter; **pic-tūra**, painting, a painting, a *picture;* **pig-mentum**, paint, *pigment*.

91. plak, pla-n-k; —; (st. πλακ); plac; spread out.

πλάξ, anything flat and broad; πλάκ-ινος, made of boards; πλακ-οῦς, a flat cake.

planc-a, a board, a *plank;* plā-nus (for *plac-nus*), even, level, flat, *plane.*

92. park, plak, plag; park'; πλεκ; plag, plec, plic; braid, plait, entwine.

πλέκ-ω, to plait, weave; πλέγ-μα, anything twined or plaited; πλοκ-ή, a twining, plaiting, anything plaited or woven; πλόκ-αμος, a lock of hair.

pleo-to, to plait, interweave; am-pleo-tor, to wind or twine around, to encircle, embrace; com-plec-tor, to entwine around, [*complex, complexion*]; plĭc-o, to fold, to wind together, (compd. w. ad, circum, com, ex, in, re), [*applicant, application, complicate, complication, explication, explicit, implicate, implication, implicit, replication*]; sup-plĭc-o, to kneel down or humble one's self, to *supplicate;* sup-plic-atio, a public prayer or *supplication;* plăg-a, a hunting-net; plăg-ĭum, man-stealing, kidnapping, [*plagiarist, plagiarism, plagiarize*].

93. πόρκος, a swine, hog, pig.

porcus, a swine, hog, pig, [*pork, porcupine,* (fr. *porcus,* swine, and *spina,* thorn)].

94. σκαιός, left, on the left hand or side, [*skew, askew*]; σκαιότης, left-handedness, awkwardness.

scaevus, left, toward the left side, awkward; scaevĭtas, awkwardness, misfortune.

95. —; —; (st. σκαλπ); scalp; cut, scratch.

σκάλοψ, σπάλαξ, ἀσπάλαξ, the mole.

scalp-o, to cut, scratch, engrave, [*scalp*]; scalp-rum, a sharp, cutting instrument, a knife; scalp-ellum (dim.), a small surgical knife, a *scalpel;* talp-a (= *stalp-a* = *scalp-a*), a mole.

96. skand; skand; σκαδ; scad; move swiftly.

σκάνδ-αλον, σκανδ-άληθρον, a trap-spring, a snare, stumbling-block, *scandal;* σκανδ-αλίζω, to make to stumble, to give offence or scandal to any one, to *scandalize*.

scand-o, to climb, to ascend, (compd. w. ad, com, de, e, in, super, trans), [*ascend, descend, transcend*]; **scā-la** (for *scand-la*) (mostly in pl. **scālae**), a flight of steps, a staircase, a ladder, [*scale*, a series of steps, a graduated instrument for measuring; *scale*, to climb].

97. skap; —; σκαπ, σκιπ, σκιμπ; scap; support.

σκήπ-τω, to support, to press against, to let fall upon; Dor. σκᾶπ-ος, σκῆπ-τρον, σκήπ-ων, a staff; σκηπ-τός, a gust of wind, a thunderbolt; σκίμπ-τω, collateral form of σκήπτω; σκίπ-ων, collateral form of σκήπ-ων.

†**scăp-us,** a *shaft;* **scip-io,** a staff; **scōp-ae,** twigs; **scŏp-io,** a stalk; **scam-num** (for *scap-num*), a bench.

98. Greek rt. σκαπ.

σκάπ-τω, to dig; σκαπ-άνη, a spade; σκάπ-ετος, κάπ-ετος, a ditch.

99. spak; spaç; σκεπ; spec; spy.

σκέπ-τομαι, to look carefully, spy, examine, consider; σκεπ-τικός, thoughtful, reflective, [*skeptic*]; σκοπ-έω, to look at; σκοπ-ή, σκοπ-ιά, a lookout-place; σκόπ-ελος, a lookout-place, a high rock; σκοπ-ός, a watchman, a mark, [*scope*].

spĕc-io, to look, to look at, (compd. w. ad, circum, com, de, di, in, intro, per, pro, re, sub), [*aspect* (noun), *circumspect* (adj.), *conspicuous* (adj.), *inspect, introspect, perspective, perspicuous, prŏspect, prospectus, respect, respite, suspect*]; **spec-to** (freq.), to look at, (compd. w. ad, circum, de, ex, in, per, pro, re, sub); **ex-spec-to, expecto,** to look out for, to *expect;* **spĕc-ŭla,** a watch-tower; **spĕc-ŭlum,** a mirror; **spec-trum,** an appearance, image, *spectre*, [*spectrum*]; **spĕc-ies,** a seeing, sight, appearance, kind, *species;* **spĕc-ĭmen,** that by which a thing is seen or recognized, an example, a *specimen;* **spĕc-ŭlor,** to spy out, to watch, [*speculate*].

100. ska, skad; —; —; —; cover.

σκι-ά, a shadow, shade; σκια-ρός, σκιε-ρός, shady; σκιά-ω, to overshadow; σκη-νή, a tent or booth; σκότ-ος, darkness.

cae-cus (= sca-i-cus), blind; că-sa (= scad-ta), a cottage or cabin; cas-sis, a helmet; cas-trum, a castle, fortress, (cas-tra, pl., a camp); scaena, scena, the stage, a *scene*.

101. sku; sku; σκυ; scu; cover.

σκευ-ή, equipment, dress; σκεῦ-ος (mostly in pl. σκεύ-η), furniture; σκευ-άζω, to prepare; σκῦ-τος, κύ-τος, a skin, hide; ἐπι-σκύ-νιον, the skin of the brows; σκῦ-λον (mostly in pl. σκῦ-λα), the arms stripped off from a slain enemy, spoils.

ob-scu-rus, dark, *obscure;* scū-tum, an oblong shield; cŭ-tis, the skin, the *hide;* spŏ-lium, the skin or hide of an animal; spŏ-lium (usu. in pl. spolia), the arms or armor stripped from a defeated enemy, booty, *spoil*.

102. Greek rt. σκυλ.

σκύλ-λω, to skin, flay, mangle.

103. φάλκ-ης, a crooked piece of ship-timber, rib of a ship.

falx, a sickle, [*falcon*]; flec-t-o, to bend, curve, turn, (compd. w. circum, de, in, re), [*deflect, inflect, reflect, flexible*].

Γ

g; g, g'; γ; g.

104. ag; ag; ἀγ; ag; drive, move, convey, lead, weigh, consider.

ἄγ-ω, ἀγ-ινέω, to lead, drive, hold, account; ἀγ-ός, ἄκ-τωρ, a leader; ἀγ-ών, an assembly, a contest; ἀγ-υιά, a street; ὄγ-μος, a straight line, a furrow; ἄγ-ρα, the chase, the prey; ἀγ-ρεύω, ἀγ-ρέω, to hunt, to catch; ἡγ-έομαι, to go before, to lead, believe, suppose, hold; ἄξ-ιος, weighing as much, worth as much, worthy; ἀξ-ιόω, to think or deem worthy of, to demand; ἄγα-ν (lit. drawing), very; ἀγ-ήνωρ (ἄγαν, ἀνήρ), manly, proud, stately.

ăg-o, to put in motion, lead, drive, (compd. w. ab, ad, amb, circum, com, de, ex, in, per, praeter, pro, re, retro, sub, subter, trans), [*agent, act, cogent, re-act, transact*]; **ag-men,** a course, line, troop, army; **ăg-ĭlis,** easily moved or moving, *agile,* [*agility*]; **ac-tor,** a doer, agent, *actor;* **ac-tus,** the moving, driving, doing, *act* (subst.); **ac-tio,** a doing, an *action;* **ăg-ĭto** (freq.), to put in motion, *agitate;* **amb-ĭg-uus,** drifting or moving to both sides, uncertain, *ambiguous.*

105. Greek rt. **ἀγ.**

ἄζ-ομαι, to stand in awe of, to dread, to reverence; ἀγ-νός, pure; ἄγ-ιος, devoted to the gods, sacred, accursed; ἀγ-ίζω, to hallow, make sacred; ἐν-αγ-ίζω, to offer sacrifice to the dead; ἄγ-ος, consecration, sacrifice,

106. ἀγρό-ς (stem ἀγρο), a field; ἄγριος, living in the fields, wild; ἀγριόω, to make wild.

ăger (stem *agro*), a territory, a field, [*acre*]; **agricultūra** (better separately **agri cultūra**), *agriculture;* **agrārius,** pertaining to land, *agrarian;* **pĕrăgro** (*per, ager*), to travel through or over, to traverse; **pĕrĕgrīnor,** to live in foreign parts, to travel about, *peregrinate.* These words are perhaps all to be traced to the same root as under No. 104, ἀγρός and **ager** being so named "a pecore agendo," like the German *trift,* pasturage, from *treiben,* to drive.

107. arg; arg', rag'; ἀργ; arg; shine, be light or bright.

ἀργ-ός, ἀργ-ής, ἀργ-εννός, ἀργ-ινόεις, bright, white, shining; ἄργ-υρος (subst.), silver; ἄργ-ιλλος, ἄργ-ιλος, white clay.

arg-entum, silver, [*argent*]; †**arg-illa,** white clay, [*argil, argillaceous*]; **arg-uo,** to make clear, prove, assert, accuse, [*argue*]; **arg-ūtus,** clear, bright, clear-sounding; **arg-ūmentum,** proof, *argument.*

108. gau; —; γαυ, γαϝ; gau; be glad.

γαῦ-ρος, exulting, haughty; γα-ί-ω, to exult; γη-θέω, to rejoice; γῆ-θος, γη-θοσύνη, joy; γη-θόσυνος, glad; γά-νυμαι, to be glad; γά-νος, brightness, gladness.

gau-deo, to rejoice (inwardly); **gau-dium,** (inward) joy.

109. St. γαλακτ (nom. γάλἄ), milk.
Latin stem, lact (nom. lac), milk, [*lacteal, lactation*].

110. γαστήρ (St. γαστερ), belly, [*gastric*].
venter (perh. for *gventer*), belly, [*ventricle, ventriloquist*]. Original initial *g* became *gv*, of which Latin retained *v*. Cf. No. 509 and 514.

111. gam; —; γεμ; gem; be full.
γέμ-ω, to be full; γεμ-ίζω, to fill; γόμ-ος, freight; γομ-όω, to load.
gĕm-o, to sigh, to groan; gĕm-ĭtus, a sighing, sigh, groan; in-gĕm-o, in-gem-isco, to groan or sigh over a thing.

112. ga, gan, gna; g'an; γεν, γα; gen, gna; beget, bring forth, produce, come into being, become.
γί-γν-ομαι (for γι-γέν-ομαι), to come into a new state of being, to come into being, to be born, to become; γείν-ομαι, to beget, bring forth, be born; γέν-ος, race; γεν-εά, race, family, [*genealogy*]; γεν-έτηρ, γεν-έτης, father, son; γεν-έτειρα, mother, daughter; γέν-εσις, origin, [*genesis*]; γυν-ή, woman; γνή-σιος, legitimate, genuine.
gi-gn-o (for *gi-gen-o*), to beget, bring forth, (compd. w. e, in, pro, re); gen-ĭtor, father; pro-gen-ĭtor, ancestor, *progenitor;* gĕn-etrix (less freq. gen-itrix) mother; gen-s, a clan, house, race, nation; in-gens (*in, gens*, that goes beyond its kind), vast, great; gen-tīlis, of or belonging to the same clan or race, national, foreign, [*gentile, genteel, gentle, gentleman, gentry*]; gĕn-us, birth, race, *genus*, [*generic*]; in-gĕn-ium, innate quality, natural disposition; in-gĕn-iōsus, of good natural abilities, *ingenious;* in-gĕn-uus, native, free-born, worthy of a freeman, frank, *ingenuous;* prō-gĕn-ies, descent, descendants, offspring, *progeny;* gĕn-er, son-in-law; gĕn-ius (the innate superior nature, the spirit), the tutelar deity of a person, place, etc., *genius;* indi-gĕn-a, native, *indigenous;* gĕn-ŭīnus, innate, *genuine;* gĕn-erōsus, of noble birth, noble-minded, *generous;* gĕn-ĕro, to beget, produce, *generate*, (compd. w. de, in, pro, re),

[*degenerate, regenerate*]; gĕmĭnus, twin-born, twin-; gemini, twins; gĕn-ĕtīvus, of or belonging to birth; gĕn-ĕtīvus casus, the *genitive* case; gĕn-ĭtālis, of or belonging to generation or birth, *genital;* na-scor (for *gna-scor*), to be born, to be begotten, (compd. w. circum, e, in, inter, re, sub), [*nascent, natal, cognate, innate*]; prae-gna-ns, *pregnant;* na-tūra, *nature;* nā-tio, birth, a race, a *nation*.

113. γέρ-ανος, a crane.
gr-us, a crane.
The Indo-Eur. rt. is perhaps *gar*, be old.

114. γέρ-ων, an old man; γραῦ-s, an old woman; γῆρ-ας, old age. The Ind-Eur. rt. is *gar*, be old, become infirm.

115. gus; gush; γευ; gus; taste, try.
γεύ-ω, to give a taste of; γεύ-ομαι, to taste; γεῦ-σις, a tasting, taste; γεῦ-μα, a taste, food.
gus-tus, a tasting, taste, [*gust*]; gus-to, to taste, [*gustatory, disgust*].

116. γῆ (contr. from γέα), γα-ῖ-α, Earth, land, the earth, [*geode, geodesy, geography, geology, geometry*]; γεί-των, a neighbor. The Indo-Eur. rt. is probably *ga*, go (No. 509) or No. 112.

117. gar; gar; γαρ; gar; sound, call.
γῆρ-υς, speech, voice; γηρ-ύω, to speak.
gar-rio (for *gar-sio*), to chatter, prate, chat, [*call*]; gar-rŭlus, talkative, *garrulous;* gal-lus (for *gar-lus*), a cock; gal-līna, a hen; gal-līnāceus, of or belonging to domestic fowls, *gallinaceous*.

118. Greek rt. γλαφ.
γλάφ-ω, to hew, dig, hollow out; γλάφ-ῠ, a hollow; γλαφ-υρός, hollow, smooth.
glăb-er, smooth, bald.

119. Greek rt. **γλυφ.**

γλύφ-ω, to carve, engrave, [*glyphic, hieroglyphic*]; γλύφ-ανος, a carving-tool; γλύπ-της, a carver, a sculptor.

†glūb-o, to deprive of the bark, to peel; **glū-ma,** a hull or husk.

120. gan, gna; ģnâ; γνο, γνω; gna, gno; perceive, know.

γι-γνώ-σκω, to learn to know, to perceive, to *know,* to *ken,* [*can, con*]; γνῶ-σις, a seeking to know, knowledge; γνώ-μη, a means of knowing, mind, opinion; γνω-στός, γνω-τός, known; γνω-ρίζω, to make known; νόος, mind; νοέω, to perceive, to think.

gnā-rus, gna-ruris, ‡**na-rus,** knowing, skilful; **i-gnā-rus** (*in, gnarus*), ignorant; **i-gnō-ro,** not to know, [*ignore, ignorant*]; **nar-ro,** to make known, tell, *narrate,* (compd. w. e, prae, re); **nā-vus** (*gnā-vus*), diligent, active; **i-gnā-vus,** inactive, slothful; **no-sco** (= *gno-sco*), to get a knowledge of, to come to know; **i-gno-sco,** not know, to pardon, overlook; **a-gno-sco,** to know, to recognize (an object already known); **co-gno-sco,** to become acquainted with, to learn, [*cognition, cognizant, connoisseur*]; **re-co-gno-sco,** to know again, to *recognize,* [*recognition*]; **no-tio,** an examination, an idea, a *notion;* **no-bĭlis** (= *gno-bilis*), that can be known or is known, famous, *noble;* **nŏ-ta,** a mark, sign, *note;* **nŏ-to,** to mark, to *note,* (compd. w. ad, de, e, prae, sub), [*notation, annotation, denote*]; **nor-ma** (= *gnor-ima*), a square, a rule; **nor-mālis,** made according to the square, [*normal*]; **ē-nor-mis** (out of rule), irregular, immoderate, *enormous;* **ē-nor-mĭtas,** irregularity, vastness, *enormity.*

There is a relationship between the root γνο, perceive, and the root γεν, produce. The connecting link is probably the idea of coming contained in the root *ga, gam.*

121. γόνυ, knee; γουν-όομαι, γουν-άζομαι, to clasp another's knees, to implore; γνύξ, with bent knee; πρό-χνυ, with the knees forward, on one's knees.

gĕnu, the *knee,* [*genuflection*].

122. skrabh; —; γραφ; scrib, scrob, scrof; dig, grave.

γράφ-ω, to *grave*, scratch, write, [*-graph*]; γραφ-ή, writing; γραφ-ίς, a style for writing; γραφ-ικός, of or for writing, *graphic;* γραμ-μή, a line; γράμ-μα, a letter, [*grammar*].

scrōf-a, a sow, [*scrofula*]; scrŏb-is, a ditch; scrīb-o, to write, (compd. w. ad, circum, com, de, ex, in, inter, per, post, prae, pro, re, sub, super, trans), [*ascribe, circumscribe, cónscript, describe, inscribe, postscript, prescribe, proscribe, rescript, subscribe, superscribe, transcribe*]; scrīb-a, a public writer, a secretary, *scribe*.

123. Greek rt. Ϝεργ.

ἔρδ-ω, ῥέζω, to do; ἔργ-ον, *work;* ἐργ-άζομαι, to work; ὄργ-ανον, an instrument, an *organ;* ὄργ-ια, secret rites, *orgies*.

124. varg; varg'; Ϝεργ, Ϝειργ; urg; press, turn, urge.

ἔργ-ω, εἴργ-ω, εἴργ-ω, to shut in, to shut out, to hinder; εἰργ-μος, a shutting in or up, a prison; εἰρκ-τή, an inclosure, a prison. urg-eo, to press, to *urge*, (compd. w. ex, per, sub).

125. ju, yu, yu-g, yu-dh; jug'; ζυγ; Jug; bind, join.

ζεύγ-νυμι, to join, yoke; ζεῦγ-μα, a band, bond, *zeugma;* ζεῦγ-ος, a team; ὁμό-ζυγ-ος, yoked together; ζυγ-όν, ζυγ-ός, a yoke.

jus (that which joins together, that which is binding in its tendency or character), right, law, justice, [*jurist*]; jus-tus, *just;* jus-titia, *justice;* jū-dex, a *judge;* ju-dĭco, to judge, (compd. w. ab, ad, di, prae), [*adjudge, adjudicate, prejudge, prejudicate*]; jū-dĭcium, a judgment; ju-diciālis, *judicial;* prae-jū-dicium, a preceding judgment, a *prejudice;* jū-ro, to swear, to take an oath, (compd. w. ab, e, com, de, ex), [*abjure, conjure*]; per-jū-ro, per-jŭ-ro, pē-jŭ-ro, (*per, juro*), to swear falsely, to *perjure* one's self; per-jū-rium, *perjury;* jur-go (*jus, ago*), to quarrel, to proceed at law; in-ju-ria, anything that is done contrary to justice, *injury;* ju-n-go, to *join*, yoke, (compd. w. ab, ad, com, dis, in, inter, se, sub), [*adjoin, adjunct, conjoin, conjunctive, conjunction, disjoin, disjunct, disjunctive, subjoin, subjunctive*];

jŭg-um, a *yoke;* jū-mentum (for *jugimentum*), a draught-animal; con-junx, con-jux, husband, wife; con-jŭg-ālis, relating to marriage, *conjugal;* jŭg-o, to bind, join, marry; con-jŭgo, to join together, unite, *conjugate;* sub-jŭg-o, to bring under the yoke, to *subjugate;* bī-gae, bī-ga, (for *bijugae*), a pair of horses yoked together, a car or chariot drawn by two horses; jūg-ĕrum, an acre (or, rather, a *juger*) of land; jux-ta (superlative form from *jugis*), near to, nigh, [*juxtaposition*]; cunctus (contr. from *conjunctus*) [more freq. in pl. cuncti], all together, all; jŭg-ŭlum, (the joining thing), the collar-bone, the throat, [*jugular*]; jŭg-ŭlo, to cut the throat, to kill; jŭ-beo, (perhaps from *jus, habeo*), to order, to command.

126. dhigh; dih; θιγ; fig, fi-n-g; touch, feel, knead.

θιγ-γάν-ω, to touch; ἔ-θιγ-ον, I touched; θίγ-ημα, a torch.

fi-n-g-o, to shape, form, contrive, *feign,* [*feint*]; fic-tio, a forming, *fiction;* fig-men, fig-mentum, formation, figure, production, fiction, *figment;* fig-ŭlus, a potter; fĭg-ūra, form, *figure;* fĭg-ūro, to form, to shape; trans-fig-ūro, to transform, *transfigure;* ef-fĭg-ies, an imitation, image, *effigy.*

127. lang, lag; —; λαγ; lag; be slack, lax.

λαγ-αρός, slack, thin; λάγ-νος, lewd.

langu-eo, to be weak or languid; langu-esco (inch.), to become weak or languid; langu-ĭdus, faint, weak, *languid;* langu-or, weakness, *languor;* lax-us, wide, loose, *lax;* lax-o, to make wide or roomy, to unloose, slacken; rĕ-lax-o, to stretch out or widen again, to unloose, *relax;* prō-lix-us (*pro, laxus*), stretched far out, long, *prolix.*

128. Connection of this number with 127 is probable.

λαγγάζω, λογγάζω, to slacken, to give up, *linger,* [*lag, laggard*].

longu-s, *long;* longĭ-tūdo, length, [*longitude*]; longinquus, long, distant, prolonged.

129. rug; rug'; λυγ; lug; be grieved.

λυγ-ρός, sad, baneful; λευγ-αλέο-ς, wretched; λοιγός, ruin; λοίγ-ιο-ς, ruinous, deadly.

lūg-eo, to lament, mourn; **lūg-ŭbris,** of or belonging to mourning, *lugubrious;* **luc-tus,** sorrow, mourning.

130. lig; —; (st. λυγ); **lig;** join closely, bind.

λύγ-ος, a pliant twig; λυγ-όω, to bend; λυγ-ισμός, a bending.

lĭg-o, to bind, (compd. w. ad, circum, com, de, in, ob, prae, re, sub), [*alligation, oblige, obligate, obligation, liable, league*]; **lĭg-āmen, lĭg-āmentum,** a band, [*ligament*]; **lic-tor,** (he who binds or ties the rods or culprits), a lictor; **lex** (perh. fr. rt. λεχ, [No. 150], denoting something laid down; perh. fr. rt. *leg,* of *lego,* to read [No. 440], denoting that which is read, i.e., a proposition or motion reduced to writing and read to the people with a view of their passing it into a law), a law, [*legal, legislate, legitimate*].

131. mark, marg; marg'; μελγ; mulg; come into contact with, rub away, strip off.

ἀ-μέλγ-ω, to *milk;* ἀ-μελξ-ις, a milking; ἀ-μολγ-εύς, a milk-pail; ἀ-μολγ-αῖος, of milk.

mulg-eo, to milk; **mulc-tus,** a milking; **mulc-tra, mulc-trum,** a milking-pail.

132. mark, marg; marg'; μεργ; merg; come into contact with, rub away, strip off.

ἀ-μέργ-ω, to pluck off; ἀ-μοργ-ός, a squeezing out; ὀ-μόργ-νυμι, to wipe away; ὀ-μοργ-μα, that which is wiped off, a spot.

merg-ae, a two-pronged pitchfork; **merg-es,** a sheaf, a two-pronged pitchfork.

133. varg; ûrg'; ὀργ; vĭrg; swell.

ὀργ-άω, to swell, to be eager or excited; ὀργ-ή, impulse, passion, anger; ὀργ-άς, a fertile spot of land; ὀργ-άς (fem. adj.), marriageable.

vĭrg-a, a green branch, rod, wand; **vĭrg-o,** a maiden, a *virgin.*

134. arg, rag; arg; ὀργ, ὀρεγ; reg; stretch, extend.

ὀρέγ-ω, ὀρέγνυμι, to stretch out; ὀριγ-νάομαι, to stretch one's self, reach after, reach; ὄρεγ-μα, a stretching out; ὄρεξ-ις, a longing after; ὀρεχ-θέω, to stretch one's self; ὄργ-υιἄ, ὀργ-υιά, the length of the outstretched arms, a fathom.

rĕg-o, to keep straight or from going wrong, to lead straight, direct, rule, (compd. w. ad, com, di, e, per, pro, sub), [*regent, correct, direct, erect*]; **por-rĭg-o** (*por = pro, rego*), to stretch or spread out before one's self, to extend; **pergo** (*per, rego*), to go on, proceed, pursue with energy, arouse; **surgo, surrigo** (*sub, rego*), to raise, to rise, (compd. w. ad, com, ex, re), [*surge*]; **resurrectio** (in eccl. Latin), a rising again from the dead, *resurrection;* **rec-tus** (led straight along), straight, correct, *right;* **rex,** a ruler, a king; **reg-ālis,** royal, *regal;* **regnum,** kingly government, kingdom, dominion; **reg-ŭla,** a *rule,* [*regular*]; **rĕg-io,** a direction, line, boundary-line, portion (of the earth or the heavens), *region;* **erga** (syncop. for *e-rega,* from *ex* and the root *reg,* to reach upward, be upright), over against, opposite, toward; **ergo** (for *e-rego,* from *ex* and the root *reg,* to extend upward), proceeding from or out of, in consequence of, because of, consequently, therefore.

135. stag; sthag; στεγ; steg, teg; cover.

στέγ-ω, to cover; στέγ-η, τέγ-η, στέγ-ος, τέγ-ος, a roof, a house; στεγ-ανός, στεγ-νός, closely covered.

steg-a, the deck of a ship; **tĕg-o,** to cover, (compd. w. circum, com, de, in, ob, per, prae, pro, re, super), [*thatch, deck, protect*]; **tĕg-ĭ-men, tĕg-ŭ-men, teg-men,** a covering, [*integument*]; **tĕg-ŭ-lae,** tiles, roof-tiles; **tec-tum,** a roof; **tŏg-a,** a garment, the toga; **tŭg-urium (teg-urium, tig-urium),** a hut, a cottage.

136. σφίγγ-ω, bind tight or fast; σφιγκ-τός, tight-bound; σφίξ-ις, σφιγ-μός, a binding tight; φῑ-μός, a muzzle.

fīg-o, to *fix,* fasten, (compd. w. ad, circum, com, de, in, ob, prae, re, sub, trans), [*affix, infix, prefix, suffix, transfix*]; **fībŭla** (contr. fr. *figĭbŭla*), that which serves to fasten two things together, a clasp.

137. ὑγ-ρός, wet, moist, [*hygrometer*]; ὑγρό-της, moisture; ὑγρ-αίνω, to wet.

ūv-esco, to become moist; **ūv-or**, moisture; **ū-mor** (not *humor*), a liquid, moisture, *humor;* **ūv-ĭdus, ū-mĭdus** (less correctly **hūmĭdus**), moist, wet, *humid;* **ū-meo** (less correctly **hūmeo**), to be moist or wet; **ū-mecto** (less correctly **humecto**), to moisten, to wet; **ū-līgo**, moisture.

138. **vag, ug, aug; vag, ug; ὑγ; veg, vĭg, aug;** be active, awake, strong.

ὑγι-ής, sound, healthy; ὑγι-ηρός, ὑγι-εινός, healthy, [*hygiene*]; ὑγ-ίεια, health; ὑγι-αίνω, to be sound or in health; ὑγι-άζω, to make sound or healthy.

vĕg-eo, to move, excite; **vĕg-ĕto**, to arouse, enliven, quicken, [*vegetate, vegetable, vegetation*]; **vĭg-eo**, to be lively or vigorous, to flourish; **vĭg-esco**, to become lively or vigorous; **vĭg-or**, liveliness, *vigor;* **vĭg-il**, awake, alert, [*vigil*]; **vĭg-il**, a watchman; **vĭg-ĭlo**, to watch, [*vigilant*]; **aug-eo**, to increase; **aug-mentum**, an increase, [*augment, augmentation*]; **auc-tio**, an increase, a sale by increase of bids, an *auction;* **auc-tor** (incorrectly written *autor* or *author*), a maker, producer, *author;* **auc-toritas**, a producing, *authority;* **aug-ustus**, majestic, *august;* **Aug-ustus,** *Augustus,* [*August*]; **aux-ilium, aid; aux-iliāris**, aiding, *auxiliary.*

139. φηγό-s, oak; φηγ-ών, an oak-grove; φήγ-ινος, φηγ-ινέος, oaken.

†**fāg-us**, a beech tree; **fāg-ĭnus**, beechen. These words may perhaps be traced to the root φαγ (No. 340), thus referring originally to a tree with edible fruit.

140. **bhrag, bharg; bhrâg'; φλεγ; flag, fulg;** burn, shine.

φλέγ-ω, φλεγ-έθω, to burn, blaze, [*blink, bright*]; φλέγ-μα, a flame, inflammation; φλεγ-υρός, burning; φλόξ, a flame.

flăg-ro, to blaze, burn, (compd. w. com, de), [*flagrant*]; flam-ma (= *flag-ma*), a blazing fire, *flame;* flam-mo, to flame, blaze; in-flam-mo, to set on fire, light up, *inflame;* in-flammatio, a setting on fire, conflagration, *inflammation;* flā-men (= *flag-men*), (lit. he who burns, sc. offerings), a priest; flagĭto, to demand anything fiercely or violently, to press earnestly, importune; flăg-ĭtium, an eager or furious demand, a disgraceful act done in the heat of passion, a disgraceful act; flăgĭtiōsus, infamous, *flagitious;* fulg-eo, to flash, to shine, (compd. w. ad, circum, ex, ob, prae, re, trans), [*effulgent, refulgent*]; fulg-or, lightning, brightness; fulg-ur, lightning, a thunderbolt; ful-men, a thunderbolt; ful-mĭno, to hurl lightning, [*fulminate*]; ful-vus, deep yellow, tawny.

141. bhrag, bharg; bharg'; φργ; frig; burn.

φρύγ-ω, to roast; φρύγ-ανον, dry wood; φρύγ-ετρον, a vessel for roasting barley; φρυκ-τός, roasted; φρυκ-τός, a fire-brand, signal-fire.

frīg-o, to roast. The words under No. 141 probably have some connection with those under No. 140.

142. bhugh, bhug; bhug'; φυγ; fug; bend out, bend around, turn one's self, flee.

φεύγ-ω, to flee, [*bow*]; φῠγ-ή, flight; φύζα, flight, fright; φῠγ-άς, a fugitive, an exile; φύξ-ις (φεῦξ-ις), flight, refuge; φύξ-ιμος (φεύξ-ιμος), adj., whither one can flee.

fŭg-io, to flee, (compd. w. ab, com, de, di, ex, per, pro, re, sub, subter, trans); fŭg-o, to cause to flee, to put to flight; fŭg-ĭto (freq.), to flee eagerly or in haste, to shun; fŭg-a, flight, [*fugue*]; per-fŭg-a, trans-fŭg-a, a deserter; fŭg-ĭtīvus (adj.), fleeing away, *fugitive;* fŭg-ĭtīvus (subst.), a fugitive; rĕ-fŭg-ium, a fleeing back, a place of refuge, a *refuge;* subterfug-ium, a *subterfuge;* fŭg-ax, apt to flee, fleet, *fugacious.*

X

gh; gh, h; χ; h, (in the middle of a word) g.

143. —; arh; ἀρχ; —; worth.

ἄρχ-ω, to be first, begin, lead, rule; ἀρχ-ός, a leader; ἀρχ-ή, beginning, the first place or power, sovereignty; ἄρχ-ων, a ruler; ὀρχ-αμος, the first, a leader; ἀν-αρχ-ία, want of government, *anarchy;* μόν-αρχ-ος, μον-άρχ-ης, ruling alone, *monarch;* ἱερ-άρχ-ης, a high-priest, *hierarch.*

144. agh, angh; ah; ἀχ, ἀγχ; ang; squeeze, press tight, cause pain or anguish.

ἄγχ-ω, to press tight, to strangle; ἀγχ-όνη, a strangling; ἄγχ-ι, ἀγχ-οῦ, near; ἄχ-νυμι, ἄχ-ομαι, ἀχ-εύω, ἀχ-έω, to be in grief, be troubled; ἄχ-ος, pain, distress; ἄχ-θος, a burden; ἄχ-θομαι, to be loaded, weighed down, grieved.

ang-o, to press tight, to cause pain; ang-or, a compression of the throat, strangling, *anguish,* [*anger*]; ang-ustus, narrow, close; ang-īna, the quinsy; anx-ius, distressed, troubled, *anxious.*

145. vragh; —; βρεχ, βροχ; rĭg; wet.

βρέχ-ω, to wet; βροχ-ετός, a wetting.

rĭg-o, to wet; ir-rĭg-o, to lead or conduct water or other liquids to a place, to *irrigate;* ir-rĭg-uus, well-watered, watering.

146. ragh, lagh; rah; λαχ; lev for legv; flow, run, hasten.

ἐ-λαχ-ύς, small.

lĕv-is, *light* (in weight), light (in motion), swift; lĕv-ĭtas, lightness, easiness or rapidity of motion, *levity;* lĕv-o, to lift up, lighten, relieve, (comp. w. ad, e, re, sub), [*alleviate, relieve*]; lĕv-āmentum, an *alleviation.*

147. vagh; vah; ἐχ, Fεχ; veh; move (tran

ὄχ-ος, a carriage; ὀχ-έομαι, to be borne; ὄχ-ημα, a vehicle; ὄχ-λος, a crowd; ὀχ-λέω, to move, disturb; ὀχ-ετός, a water-pipe.

věh-o, to bear, carry [*wag* (vb. and noun), *weigh*, *wave* (vb. and noun)], (compd. w. ad, circum, com, de, e, in, per, prae, praeter, pro, re, sub, super, trans); věh-es, a carriage loaded, a wagon-load; věh-icŭlum, a carriage, a *vehicle*, a *wagon*, a *wain;* vec-to (freq.), to bear, (compd. w. ad, com, sub, trans); vec-tor, a bearer, a rider, passenger; vec-tūra, a bearing; vec-tīgal, a payment for carrying, impost, revenue; vē-lum (= *veh-lum* or *veg-lum*), a sail, a cloth, covering; vē-lo, to cover, (comp. w. ad, de, re); vexillum (dim. of *vēlum*), a military ensign, a standard, a flag; vex-o (freq.), to move violently, to trouble, *vex;* via (= *veh-ia*), a *way;* vīo, to go, travel; dē-vio, to turn from the straight road, to *deviate;* ob-vio, to meet, prevent, *obviate;* de-vius, lying off the high-road, out of the way, *devious;* ob-vius, in the way so as to meet, [*obvious*]; ob-vīam (*ob*, *viam*) (adv.), in the way, towards, to meet.

148. sagh; sah; σεχ, ἐχ, ἐχ; —; hold on, be strong.

ἔχ-ω, to have, to hold; ἔχ-ομαι, to hold one's self fast, to cling closely; σχέ-σις, a state, condition; σχῆ-μα, a form; σχο-λή, leisure (holding up); ἑξῆς, ἐξείης, holding on to each other, one after another; σχε-δόν, near; ἴσχ-ω (= σι-σεχ-ω), to hold on, restrain; ἰσχάν-ω, ἰσχανάω, to hold back, to check; ἐχ-ῠρός, ὀχ-ῠρός, firm.

†schŏla, (spare time, leisure; hence in partic.) leisure given to learning, a place of learning, a *school*, [*scholar*].

149. Greek rt. ἀχ, ἀγχ, same as No. 144.

ἔχι-ς, ἔχι-δνα, an adder; ἔγχελυ-ς, an eel.

angui-s, a serpent.

150. lagh; —; λεχ; lec; lie (recline).

λέχ-ος, a bed; λέκ-τρον, a couch, bed; ἄ-λοχ-ος, the partner of one's bed; λοχ-εύω, to bring forth; λοχ-εία, birth; λόχ-ος, an ambush; λόχ-μη, a thicket.

lec-tus, a couch, bed; lec-tīca, a litter, a sedan.

151. righ; ligh; lih, rih; λιχ; lĭg, lĭ-n-g; lick.

λείχ-ω, λιχ-μάω, λιχ-μάζω, to lick, lick over; λιχ-ανό-s, the forefinger; λίχ-νος, greedy.

li-n-g-o, to *lick*, lick up; **lĭg-urio**, to lick, to be dainty, fond of good things.

152. stigh; stĭgh; στιχ; stig?; stride, step, stalk.

στείχ-ω, to walk, march, [*stile, stirrup*]; στίχο-s, στοῖχο-s, a row, rank, line; στιχά-ομαι, to march in rank.

ve-stīg-o? [etym. dub.; perh. Sk. *vahis* (*bahis*) out, and rt. *stigh*], to track, trace out; **ve-stig-ium?** a footstep, trace, *vestige*.

153. Greek rt. **τρεχ.**

τρέχ-ω, to run; τρόχ-os, a running, a course; τροχ-ós, a wheel; τρόχ-ις, a runner, footman.

154. gha, ghī; —; χα, χαν; hī; yawn, gape, separate.

χαίν-ω, χά-σκ-ω, to *yawn*, gape; χά-σμα, a yawning, hollow, *chasm*; χά-os, *chaos*, space, a vast gulf or chasm; χαῦ-νos, gaping, loose; χε-ιά, a hole; χή-μη, a gaping.

hī-o, to open, open the mouth, be eager; **hī-sc-o** (inch.), to open, open the mouth, speak; **hī-ātus**, an opening, eager desire, *hiatus*.

155. gadh, ghad; —; χαδ; hend; seize, take.

χα-ν-δ-άνω, to take in, hold, be able, [*get*].

pre-hend-o, prae-hend-o, prend-o, to seize, grasp, (compd. w. ad, com, de, re) [*apprehend, comprehend, reprehend, apprehension, comprehension, reprehension*]; **praed-a** (= *prae-hend-a* = *prae-hid-a*), booty, *prey;* **praed-atorius,** plundering, *predatory;* **praed-o,** a robber; **praed-or,** to plunder; **depraedatio** (late Lat.), a plundering, *depredation;* **praed-ium,** a farm, estate.

156. ghar, ghar-d, ghra-d; hråd, ghrad; χλαδ; grad, gra-n-d; sound, rattle.

χάλαζᾰ, a hail-storm; χαλαζ-άω, to hail.

grand-o, hail, a hail-storm; **grand-ĭnat,** it hails; **sug-grund-a** (*sub-grund-a*), the eaves.

157. χαμα-ί, on the ground; χᾰμᾶ-ζε, χαμά-δις, to the ground; χᾰμᾶ-θεν, from the ground; χαμ-ηλό-s, χθαμ-αλός, near the ground, low.

hŭm-us, the earth, the ground; hŭm-i, on the ground or to the ground; hŭm-o, to cover with earth; in-hŭm-o, to bury in the ground, *inhume, inhumate,* [*exhume*]; hŭm-ĭlis, low, *humble;* hŭm-ĭlĭtas, lowness, *humility;* hŏm-o (ancient form hemo), a human being, a man, [*homicide*]; nē-mo (= *ne-hemo* = *nehomo*), no person, no one; hŭm-ānus, of or belonging to man, *human, humane;* hŭm-anĭtas, *humanity.*

158. ghar, ghra; har; χαρ; gra; shine, be glad, glow, desire enthusiastically.

χαίρ-ω, to rejoice, [*yearn*]; χαρ-ά, joy; χάρ-μα, a source of joy, a joy; χάρ-ις, grace, favor; χαρ-ίζομαι, to favor; χαρ-ίεις, graceful.

grā-tus, beloved, grateful, *agreeable,* [*agree*]; grā-tia, favor, gratitude, *grace;* grā-tiis, grā-tis, out of favor, for nothing, *gratis;* grā-tuitus, that is done without pay, *gratuitous;* grā-tŭlor, to rejoice, to congratulate; con-grā-tŭlor, to wish joy, to *congratulate;* ardeo, to be on fire, burn, glow, [*ardent, arson*].

159. ghar; har; χερ; hir, her; take, grasp.

χείρ, hand, [*chirography*]; εὐ-χερ-ής, easy to handle; δυσ-χερ-ής, difficult to handle or manage; χέρ-ης (adj.), subject, in hand; χείρ-ων (= χερ-ίων), worse, inferior; χόρ-τος, an inclosed place, a feeding-place, fodder, a *yard,* [*garden*].

hir, ir (old Latin), hand; ĕrus, hĕrus, a master; ĕra, hĕra, mistress; hēr-es, an *heir;* hēr-edĭtas, heirship, *inheritance,* [*hereditary*]; hor-tus (an enclosure for plants), a *garden;* co-hors, a place enclosed, an enclosure, the multitude enclosed, a company of soldiers, a *cohort,* [*court*].

160. ghjas, —, —, —, yesterday.

χθές, ἐχθές, *yesterday;* χθιζό-s, χθιζ-ινός, χθεσ-ινός, of yesterday. hĕri or hĕre (for *hesi,* orig. *hes*), yesterday; hes-ternus, of yesterday.

161. ghi; (hi-ma-s, snow); χι; **hi;** winter.

χι-ών, snow; χεῖ-μα, winter-weather, storm; χει-μάζω, to expose to the winter-cold, to raise a storm; χει-μαίνω, to raise a storm; χί-μετλον, a chilblain; χει-μών, winter; χει-μέρινος, of or in winter.

hi-ems, winter; **hi-ĕmo,** to pass the winter, to be stormy; **hī-bernus,** of winter, wintry, stormy; **hī-berna,** winter-quarters; **hī-berno,** to pass the winter, [*hibernate*].

162. χόλο-s, χολή, *gall*, anger; χολ-ικό-s, bilious; χολ-άω, to be full of black bile, to be angry; χολ-όω, to make bilious, to enrage; μελαγ-χολ-ία, a depraved state of the bile in which it grows very black, a melancholic temperament, [*melancholy*].

fel, the gall-bladder, gall, poison.

163. Greek rt. **χρεμ.**

χρεμ-ίζω, χρεμ-ετίζω (onomatop.), to neigh, whinny, [*grim, grum*]; χρόμ-η, χρόμ-os, a crashing sound, a neighing; χρόμ-αδος, a crashing sound, a creaking.

164. ghar; ghar; χρι; fri, fric; grate, rub.

χρί-ω, to touch the surface of a body lightly, to graze, rub, anoint; χρῖ-σις, an anointing; χρῖ-μα, χρῖ-σ-μα, unguent, oil; χρι-στός, used as ointment, (of persons) anointed; Χριστός, the Anointed One, the *Christ*.

fri-o, to rub, break into small pieces; **frī-ăbĭlis,** easily broken or crumbled to pieces, *friable;* **frĭ-c-o,** to rub, [*fricative*]; **fric-tio,** a rubbing, *friction;* **denti-fric-ium,** a tooth-powder, *dentifrice*.

165. ghu; —; **χυ, χεϝ, χευ; fu, fud;** pour.

χέ(ϝ)ω, (fut. χεύ-σω), to pour, [*gush, gutter*]; χύ-μα, χεῦ-μα, a liquid; χύ-σις, χο-ή, a pouring, a stream; χοῦς (χό-ος), a liquid measure, a heap of earth; χῡ-μός, juice, liquid; χυ-λός, juice, moisture.

fo-n-s, a spring, *fountain, fount* [*font*]; ‡ **fu-tis,** a water-vessel; **ef-fū-tio,** to babble forth, to chatter; **con-fū-to,** to cool anything by pouring water into it or upon it, to repress, to *confute;*

rĕ-fū-to, to check, repel, *refute*, [*refuse*]; fu-n-d-o, to pour, (compd. w. circum, com, di, ex, in, inter, ob, per, pro, re, sub, super, trans), [*fuse, confuse, diffuse, effuse, infuse, interfused, suffuse, transfuse*]; prŏ-fū-sus (part.), poured forth; prŏ-fū-sus (adj.), lavish, *profuse;* fu-sio, a pouring forth, a melting [*fusion*]; fut-tĭlis (= *fud-tilis*), (less correctly fū-tilis), that easily pours out, untrustworthy, worthless, *futile.*

T
t; t, th; τ; t.

166. ἀντ-ί, over against, instead of, [*answer*, fr. A.-S. *and* (against) and *swaran* (to swear); *anti-*, a prefix signifying against, opposed to, contrary to, in place of]; ἀντ-α, ἄντη-ν, ἀντί-κρύ, (advbs.), over against; ἀντί-ος, ἐν-αντί-ος, opposite, contrary to; ἄντ-ομαι, ἀντ-άω, ἀντ-ιάω, to meet.

ante (for *anted*, old form *anti*. The form *ante-d* is preserved in *antid-ea, anteid-ea*, and is to be regarded as an ablative, while ἀντί and *anti* are locative in form, and ἄντα is instrumental), before, [used as a prefix in forming many English words (e.g., *antedate), ancient*]; **antĕā** (old form **antid-ĕā, anteid-ĕā**; antea = *ante, ea;* cf. *antehac, postea, posthac*), adv., before, formerly; **an-tĕrior**, adj. comp., that is before, former, *anterior;* **ant-īquus**, ancient, [*antique*]; **ant-īquo**, to leave in its ancient state, (of a bill) to reject; **ant-īquĭtas**, age, *antiquity.*

167. star; star; ἀστρ**; astr, ster;** strew (cf. No. 185).

ἀστήρ, a *star* (the stars may have been so called from their being "strewn over the vault of heaven"); ἀστερόεις, starry; ἄστρον, a star.

stella (for *ster-ula*), a star, [*stellar, stellated, constellation*]; **astru-m**, a star, a constellation, [*astral*].

168. ἔτι, still, longer, further, moreover; προσέτι, over and above.

et, and; **et-iam,** and also, and even; **at, ast,** but, moreover;

atqui, but, and yet; atque, ac, and also, and even, and; **ăt-ăvus**, a great-great-great-grandfather, an ancestor.

169. ἔτος, a year; ἐτήσιος, lasting a year; ἐτησίαι, periodical winds; τῆτες (σῆτες), of this year; νέωτα, next year.
vĕtus, old; **vĕtĕrānus**, old, *veteran;* **veterasco** (inch.), to grow old; **vetustus**, old, ancient; **vetulus** (dim.), little old.

170. ἰταλός, a bull [from ἰταλός is derived *Italia*].
vitŭlus, vitŭla, a calf.

171. μετά, in the middle, in the midst of, among, *with*, after, (μετά in form is instrumental and has perhaps no direct relationship to μέσος, though both words may possibly be derived from the root *ma*, No. 386); μέταζε, (adv.) afterwards; μετα-ξύ, (adv.) between.

172. ὀστέον, a bone; ὀστέϊνος, ὄστινος, of bone, bony.
os, a bone, [*ossify*]; **oss-ĕus**, of or like bone, *osseous*.

173. pat; pat; πετ**; pet;** move quickly, (in Sk. and Gr.) fly, fall.
πέτ-ομαι, to fly; ὠκυ-πέτ-ης, swift-flying; ποτ-άομαι (poet. freq. of πέτομαι), to fly about; πτέ-ρον, a feather, a wing; πί-πτ-ω (Dor. aor. ἔ-πετ-ον), to fall; πτῶ-σις, a falling, fall; πότ-μος, that which befalls one, one's lot, destiny.
pĕt-o, to fall upon, attack, seek, (compd. w. ad, com, ex, in, ob, re, sub), [*appetence, appetite, compete, competent, competence, repeat*]; **im-pĕt-us**, an attack, impulse, [*impetuous*]; **perpes** (gen. *per-pĕt-is*), **per-pĕt-uus**, continuous, *perpetual;* **prae-pes** (gen. *prae-pĕt-is*), flying forwards, swift of flight; **acci-pit-er** (from root *ac* and root *pet;* cf. ὠκύπτερος, swift-winged), a bird of prey, the hawk; **penna** (= *pet-na, pes-na*), **pinna**, *a feather*, a wing, [*pen*]; **pin-nātus**, feathered, *pinnate, pinnated;* **pinnaculum**, a peak, *pinnacle* (being in appearance like a feather).

174. St. πετα. πετά-ννυ-μι, πίτ-νημι, to spread out; πέτ-ασμα, anything spread out, (pl.) hangings, carpets; πέτ-ασος, a broad-brimmed hat; πέτ-αλον, a leaf, a plate (of metal), [*petal*]; πέταλος, outspread, flat; πατ-άνη, a kind of flat dish.

păt-eo, to lie open, to be open, [*patent, fathom*]; pat-esco (inch.), to be laid open, to become visible; păte-făcio (*pateo, facio*), to make or lay open; păt-ŭlus, open, spread out, wide; păt-ĕra, a broad, flat dish, a libation-saucer or bowl; pat-ĭna, a broad, shallow dish, a *pan* (fr. L. Lat. *panna*); pat-ella (dim.), a small pan or dish, the knee-pan, patella.

175. sta; stha; στα; sta; stand.

ἔ-στη-ν, I placed myself, I stood; ἵ-στη-μι, to make to stand, to place, to weigh; στά-σις, a placing, a standing, a party, sedition; στα-μίν, anything that stands up, (pl.) the ribs of a ship standing up from the keel; στά-μνος, an earthen jar or bottle; ἱστός, anything set upright, a ship's mast, the beam of a loom, the loom; στή-μων, the warp; στα-τήρ, a weight.

sto, to stand, [*stay*], (compd. w. ab, ante, anti, circum, com, di, ex, in, ob, per, prae, pro, re, sub, super), [*circumstance, constant, distant, extant, instant, obstacle, obstetrical*]; stă-tus, a standing, a position; stă-tim, steadily, immediately; stăbĭlis, that stands firm, *stable*, [*stability*]; stă-tio, a standing, a *station*, [*stead, steady, steadfast, bedstead, homestead*]; stă-tor (fr. *sto*), a magistrate's attendant; Stator (an epithet of Jupiter), the stayer, the supporter; stă-tuo, to cause to stand, to set up, establish, (compd. w. ad, com, de, in, prae, pro, re, sub), [*statute, constitute, destitute, institute, prostitute, restitution, substitute*]; stă-bŭlum, a standing-place, a dwelling, a *stable;* si-st-o, to cause to stand, to place, to stand, to be placed, (compd. w. ad, circum, com, de, ex, in, inter, ob, per, re, sub, super), [*assist, consist, desist, insist, persist, resist, subsist*]; inter-sti-tium, a space between, *interstice;* sol-stĭ-tium, the time when the sun seems to stand still, the *solstice;* super-sti-tio (orig. a standing still over or by a thing; hence, amazement, dread, esp. of the divine or supernatural), excessive fear of the gods, *superstition;* de-stĭ-no (*de* and obs. *stano*), to make to stand fast, to establish, *destine*, [*destination*]; ob-stĭ-no (lengthened from *obsto*), to set about a thing with firmness or resolution, to persist in ; ob-stĭ-natus, determined, *obstinate*.

176. stal; —; σταλ, στελ; stol; set, place.

στέλ-λω, to set, place, despatch, send ; στόλ-ος, an expedition ; στάλ-ιξ, a prop ; στή-λη, a post, a monument ; ἀπό-στολ-ος, a messenger, an *apostle*.

prae-stōl-or, to stand ready for, to wait for ; stol-ĭdus ? (standing still), dull, obtuse, *stolid*; stul-tus ?, foolish.

177. Greek rt. στεμφ, στεμβ, prop, stamp.

στέμφ-ῠλον, pressed olives or grapes ; ἀ-στεμφ-ής, unmoved, unshaken ; στέμβ-ω, to shake, to misuse, [*stamp*]; στοβ-έω, στοβ-άζω, to scold.

178. Greek rt. στεν.

στέν-ω, στεν-άχω, to groan, sigh ; στόν-ος, a sighing or groaning ; στείν-ω (Ep. form of στένω), to straiten ; στείν-ομαι, to be straitened or confined ; στεν-ός, στειν-ός, narrow, confined, [*stenography* fr. στενός, γράφω] ; στεῖνος, a narrow space, pressure, straits, distress. The meaning "groan" arises from that of "confinement" or "pressure." Cf. No. 188.

179. Greek rt. στερ.

στέρ-ομαι, to be without, to lack ; στερ-έω, στερ-ίσκω, to deprive of.

180. στερ-εός, στερρός, στέρ-ιφος, hard, firm ; στεῖρ-α, keel-beam ; στερ-ίφη, στεῖρ-α, barren ; στήρ-ιγξ, a prop ; στηρ-ίζω, to set fast, to prop.

stĕr-ĭlis, barren, *sterile*.

181. stap, stip; stha; στεφ (for στεπ); stip; cause to stand, support, make thick, firm, full.

στέφ-ω, to surround, crown ; στέμ-μα, στέφ-ος, στέφ-ανος, a garland, [*stem*] ; στεφ-άνη, an encircling or surrounding.

stīp-o, to crowd together, surround closely, surround, (compd. w. circum, com), [*constipate*]; stīp-ator, an attendant ; stīp-es (collat. form **stips,** gen. *stĭpis*), a log, a post, a trunk of a tree; **stĭp-is** (a genitive from an assumed nom. *stips,* meaning originally small coin in heaps), a gift, a contribution; **stĭp-endium** (*stips, pendo*), a tax, tribute, income, *stipend;* **stĭp-ŭla** (dim.), a stalk; **stĭp-ŭlor,** (prob. from an unused adj. *stĭpŭlus,* firm; or perhaps from *stips*), to bargain, *stipulate.*

182. στί-α, *stone.*

183. stig; tĭg'; στιγ; stig, sting; prick, puncture.

στί-ζω, to prick, [*sting, stick*]; στίγ-μα, στιγ-μή, prick, mark, spot, a mark burnt in, a brand, [*stigma*]; στικ-τός, pricked, spotted.

†**stĭ-lus,** a pointed instrument, a style (for writing); **stĭ-mŭlus** (for *stig-mŭlus*), a goad, incentive, *stimŭlus;* **stĭ-mŭlo,** to urge onward, goad, *stimulate;* **in-stĭg-o,** to urge, incite, *instigate;* **sting-uo** (lit. to prick or scratch out, poet. and rare for *exstinguo*), to quench, extinguish; **ex-sting-uo,** to quench, *extinguish,* destroy; **in-sting-uo,** to instigate; **in-stinc-tus** (part.), instigated; **in-stinc-tus** (subst.), instigation, impulse, [*instinct*]; **di-sting-uo,** (prop. to separate by points), to separate, *distinguish.*

184. στό-μα, mouth; στό-μαχος, mouth, opening, the throat, the orifice of the stomach, the *stomach;* στω-μύλος, mouthy, wordy, talkative.

185. star; star; στορ; ster, stra; strew.

στορ-έ-ννυ-μι, στόρ-νυ-μι, στρώ-ννυ-μι, to spread out, *strew;* στρῶ-μα, a mattress; στρω-μνή, a bed; στρα-τός, an encamped army.

ster-no, to spread out, (compd. w. com, in, per, prae, pro, sub, super), [*prostrate*]; **con-ster-no** (conj. 3), to strew over, to throw down, to prostrate; **con-ster-no** (conj. 1), to overcome, bring into confusion, to alarm; **con-ster-natio,** confusion, *consternation;* **strā-ta,** a paved road, a *street;* **strā-tus,** spread out; **strā-tum,** a bed-covering, bed, couch, [*stratum, substratum*]; **strā-men, strā-mentum,** *straw,* litter; **strā-ges,** an overthrow, slaughter; lā-tus (old Latin, *stla-tus*), broad, wide, [*latitude*]; stru-o, to place one thing by or upon another, to build, (compd. w. ad, circum, com, de, ex, in, ob, prae, sub, super), [*construe, construct, destroy, destruction, instruct, obstruct, substructure, superstructure*]; strŭ-es, a heap; in-strū-mentum, an implement, *instrument*.

186. Greek rt. στυ.

στύ-ω, to set up, erect; στῦ-λος, a pillar, post; στο-ά, a colonnade, piazza, portico; ἡ στο-ά ἡ ποικίλη, the Poecile, or great hall at Athens (Zeno taught his doctrines here, whence he was called the Stoic); Στωϊκός, a *Stoic*.

187. στύπ-ος, a stem, *stump;* στύπ-η, tow.

stup-pa (less correctly stūp-a, stīp-a), tow; stŭp-eo, to be struck senseless, to be amazed [*stupefy*]; stŭp-ĭdus, amazed, dull, *stupid*.

188. ta, tan; tan; τα, ταν, τεν; ten; stretch.

τᾰ-νύω, to stretch; τα-νύομαι, τᾰ-νύ-μαι, to stretch one's self, to be stretched; τείν-ω, (tr. or int.), to stretch; τι-ταίν-ω (Ep.), to stretch; τά-σις, a stretching; τό-νος, a cord, tension, *tone;* τανυ-, τα-ναός, extended, long; ἀ-τεν-ής, stretched, tight, stiff; τέ-ταν-ος, stretched, rigid; τέ-τᾰν-ος, a stretching, convulsive tension; τέν-ων, a sinew; ταιν-ία, a band.

ten-do, to stretch (compd. w. ad, circum, com, de, dis, ex, in, ob, obs, per, por, prae, pro, re, sub), [*tend, tender* (vb.), *tension, tent, attend, contend, distend, extend, intend, ostensible, portend, pretend, subtend*]; ten-to or temp-to (freq.), to handle, try, prove (compd. w. ad, ex, in, obs, per, prae, re, sub), [*ostentation, sustentation, tentative, tempt, attempt*]; těn-ěo, to hold, to keep (compd. w. ab, ad, com, de, dis, ob, per, re, sub), [*tenant, tenable, tenement, tenure, tenet, abstain, attain, contain, content, detain, obtain, pertain, retain, sustain*]; těn-ax, holding fast, *tenacious;* per-tĭn-ax, that holds very fast, that continues very long, persevering, *pertinacious;* těn-us (prop. lengthwise, to the end), as far as, to; prō-tĭn-us, forward, further on, continuously, forthwith; **tĕn-uis** (prop. stretched out), *thin*, fine, delicate, [*tenuous, tenuity*]; **tĕn-uo,** to make thin, to rarefy (compd. w. ad, ex), [*attenuate, extenuate*]; **tĕn-or,** a holding fast, an uninterrupted course, *tenor;* **tŏn-o,** to thunder (compd. w. ad, circum, com, de, in, re), [*detonate, intone, intonate*]; **tŏn-itrus,** *thunder;* **tŏn-us,** a stretching, a sound, *tone* [*tonic*]; **con-tĭn-uus,** connected with something, *continuous;* **tĕn-er,** soft, delicate, *tender*.

The root of these words has the primary meaning "stretch." From this, three special meanings have been developed, viz.: 1. thin, tender; 2. "that which is stretched out" (hence), string, sinew; 3. tension, tone, noise.

189. stag; —; ταγ; **tag;** touch.

τε-ταγ-ών, taking, grasping.

ta-n-g-o (old collat. form *tago*), to *touch*, [*tag, tack, take, tangent*]; **at-ting-o,** to touch, attack, come to; **con-ting-o,** to touch on all sides, to touch, to take hold of, to happen, [*contingent*]; **tăg-ax,** apt to touch, light-fingered, thievish; **tac-tus, tac-tio,** touch, [*tact*]; **con-tac-tus, con-tăg-io, con-tăg-ium, con-tā-men,** touch, *contact, contagion;* **con-tam-ĭno** (= *con-tag-mĭno*), to touch, defile, *contaminate;* **taxo** (= *tag-so*), (freq.), to touch sharply, to reproach, estimate, rate, [*tax*]; **in-tĕg-er,** untouched, whole, entire, blameless, [*integer*]; **in-teg-rĭtas,** completeness, blamelessness, *integrity*.

190. ta; —; τακ; **ta;** flow, die away, decay.

τήκ-ω (ἐ-τάκ-ην), to melt; τακ-ερός, melting; τηκ-εδών, a melting away, wasting away, decline; τάγ-ηνον, τήγ-ᾰνον, a saucepan.

tā-bes, a wasting away, corruption; **tā-beo,** to melt away, waste away; **tā-besco** (inch.), to melt gradually, waste away; **tā-bum,** corrupt moisture, corruption.

191. ταῦρος, a bull.

taurus, a bull, a steer. The etymology of these words is to be found in the adjectival use of the Sk. *sthŭras*, firm, strong. (Nos. 175, 186.)

192. Pronominal stems: **tu, tva, tava; tva;** τε (for τϜε); **te, tu.**
σύ (softened in ordinary Greek from τύ), *thou;* τεός (for the ordinary σός), *thy.*
tu, thou; **tuus,** thy.

193. τέγγ-ω, to wet, moisten; τέγξι-ς, a wetting.
ting-o, to wet, moisten, soak in color, color, *tinge;* **tinc-tūra,** a dyeing, [*tincture*].

194. tak, tuk; tak; τακ, τεκ, τοκ, τυκ, τυχ; **tec;** form, generate, hit, prepare.
τίκ-τω (aor. ἔ-τεκ-ον), to beget, to bring forth; τέκ-ος, τέκ-νον, child; τοκ-εύς, a parent; τόκ-ος, birth, interest; τέκ-μαρ, a goal, an end; τεκ-μήρ-ιον, a token; τόξ-ον, a bow; τοξ-ικός (adj.), of or for the bow; τὸ τοξ-ικόν (sc. φάρμακον), poison for smearing arrows with, [*toxicology*]; τέχ-νη, art; τεχ-νικός, artistic, *technical;* τέκ-των, a carpenter; τυγχ-άνω (2 aor. ἔ-τυχ-ον), to hit, happen; τύχ-η, success, fortune, chance; τεύχ-ω, to make ready, make, produce; τύκ-ος, a mason's hammer.
tig-num (= *tec-num*), building materials, a stick of timber, a beam; **tē-lum** (= *tec-lum*), a weapon, a missile; **tex-o,** to weave, fit together, construct, (compd. w. ad, circum, com, de, in, ob, per, prae, re, sub); **tex-tus,** texture, construction, *text;* **con-tex-tus,** a connection, [*context*]; **prae-tex-tus,** (a weaving in front), outward appearance, *pretext;* **tex-tilis,** woven, *textile;* **tex-tor,** a weaver; **tē-la** (prob. = *tex-la*), a web, the warp; **sub-tē-men** (= *sub-teg-men,* contr. fr. *subteximen*), the woof; **sub-tī-lis** (*sub, tēla,* prop. woven fine), fine, delicate, precise, *subtile, subtle;* **sub-tī-lĭtas,** fineness, keenness, *subtlety.*

195. tal; tul; τελ, ταλ; **tol, tul;** lift, bear.
τλῆ-ναι, to bear, endure; τάλ-ας, ταλᾱός, τλή-μων, wretched, suffering; τάλ-αντον, a balance, a thing weighed, a *talent;* ἀ-τάλ-αντος, equal in weight, equivalent; τάλ-αρος, a basket; τελ-αμών, a broad strap or band, a pillar (in architecture); τόλ-μα, courage; τολ-μάω, to bear, to dare.

tŭl-o (perf. tĕ-tŭl-i; ante-class. collat. form of *fero*), to bring, bear; tŭl-i (used as perf. of *fero*), to move, carry, bear, endure; tol-lo, to lift up, raise, to carry away; lā-tus (*tlā-tus*), having been borne; il-lāt-īvus, inferential, *illative;* pro-lāt-o, to extend, to delay; tŏl-ĕro, to bear, support, *tolerate;* tŏl-ĕrābilis, that may be borne, *tolerable.*

196. tam; —; τεμ, ταμ; tem; cut.

τέμ-νω (2 aor. ἔ-ταμ-ον), to cut; τμή-γω, to cut, cleave; τομ-ή, the end left after cutting, a stump; τμῆ-μα, τέμ-αχος, a slice cut off; τομ-εύς, one that cuts, a knife; ταμ-ίας, a dispenser, a steward; ταμ-ία, a housekeeper; τέμ-ενος, a piece of land cut or marked off, a piece of land cut or marked off from common uses and dedicated to a god.

tem-plum, a space marked out, a consecrated place, a *temple;* tem-pus(?), (prop. a section; hence, in partic., of time), a portion or period of time, a time, [*tense, time, temporal, temporary, temporize, contemporary, extempore, extemporaneous, extemporize*]; tem-pestas, a portion of time, a time, time (with respect to its physical qualities), weather (good or bad), a storm, *tempest;* con-tem-plor (fr. *templum;* orig. pertaining to the language of augury), to view attentively, observe, *contemplate;* ton-deo, to shear, clip; ton-sor, a barber, [*tonsorial, tonsure*].

197. tar; tar; τερ; ter, tra; step over or across.

τέρ-μα, a boundary, goal; τέρ-μων, boundary, end; τέρ-θρον, an end; τέρ-μιος, at the end, last; τερ-μιόεις, going even to the end.

ter-mĭnus (collat. forms ter-mo, ter-men), a boundary-line, a limit, a *term;* ter-mĭno, to set bounds to, limit, *terminate;* de-ter-mĭno, to limit, to *determine,* [*determination*]; ex-ter-mĭno, (to drive out from the boundaries), to drive away, banish, remove, destroy, *exterminate;* in-tra-re, to step or go into, to enter; tra-ns, across, *through;* tra-nstrum, a cross-beam, *transom,* a cross-bank for rowers.

198. tar; tar; τερ; ter, tor, tri, tru; rub, bore.

τείρ-ω, τρύ-ω, τρί-βω, to rub, [*drill, throw, thread*]; τρύ-χω, to wear out, consume; τέρ-ην, smooth, delicate, tender; τε-τραίν-ω (τι-τραίν-ω, τι-τρά-ω), to bore through; τερ-έω, to bore through, to turn on a lathe; τέρ-ετρον, a gimlet; τερ-ηδών, a worm that gnaws wood, etc.; τόρ-ος, a borer; τορ-ός, piercing; τόρ-νος, a pair of compasses, a turner's chisel; τορ-ύνη, a stirrer, a ladle; τορ-εύω, to bore through, to work figures in relief, to chase; τορ-έω, to bore; τρῦ-μα, a hole.

těr-o, to rub (compd. w. ad, com, de, ex, in, ob, per, prae, pro, sub), [*trite, attrition, contrite, contrition, detriment*]; těr-es, (rubbed off), rounded off, smooth; těr-ĕbra, a borer; těr-ĕbro, to bore, bore through; †těr-ēdo, a worm that gnaws wood, etc.; †tor-nus, a turner's wheel, lathe; tor-no, to turn in a lathe, fashion, *turn;* tri-o, (the crusher, or the one that rubs to pieces, hence) an ox (as employed in tilling the ground); septentriōnes, septemtriōnes, (prop. the seven plough-oxen, hence) as a constellation, the seven stars near the north pole (called also the Wain, and the Great or Little Bear); trī-tor, a rubber, a grinder; trī-tura, a rubbing, threshing; trī-tūro, to thresh; trī-tĭcum, wheat; trī-bŭlum, trī-bŭla, a threshing-sledge; trī-bŭlo, to press, oppress, afflict, [*tribulation*]; trŭ-a, a ladle.

199. —; tarp; τερπ, τραπ, θρεφ, τρεφ, θραφ, τραφ; —; fill, delight, comfort.

τέρπ-ω (τραπ-εί-ομεν), to satisfy, to delight; τέρψις, τερπ-ωλή, full enjoyment, delight; τερπ-νός, delightful; τρέφ-ω, to make firm, thick, or solid, to make fat, to feed, rear; τροφ-ή, nourishment, food; ἀ-τροφ-ία, want of food or nourishment, *atrophy*.

200. tars; tarsh; τερσ; tors; be dry.

τέρσ-ομαι, to be or become dry; τερσ-αίνω, to make dry; τρασ-ιά, ταρσ-ιά, a place for drying things; ταρσ-ός, a frame of wicker-work.

torr-eo (for *tors-eo*), to dry or burn; torrens (part. adj.), burning, (of streams) rushing, roaring, rapid; torrens (subst.), a *torrent;* torr-is, a firebrand; tes-ta (*tosta* fr. *torreo*), a piece of burned clay, a brick, a piece of earthenware, the shell of shell-fish; **testāceus,** consisting of bricks, covered with a shell, *testaceous;* **tes-tu, tes-tum,** the lid of an earthenware vessel; **tes-tūdo,** a tortoise, tortoise-shell, tortoise (milit. term); **terr-a?** (prop. the dry land), the earth, [*terrestrial, subterranean, inter, terrier, terrace*].

201. tata; tatâ-s; τέττα; tăta; (Eng. papa), a name by which young children speaking imperfectly call their father. Cf. Eng. dad, daddy.

202. tras; tras; τρεσ; ters; tremble.

τρέ-ω (Homeric aor. τρέσσα), to tremble, to run trembling, to flee; τρή-ρων, fearful, timorous.

terr-eo (*ters-eo*), to make to tremble, to frighten; **terr-ĭfĭco,** to *terrify;* **terr-ibĭlis,** frightful, *terrible;* **terr-or,** great fear, dread, *terror.*

203. tram; —; τρεμ; trem; tremble.

τρέμ-ω, to tremble; τρόμος, a trembling; τρομ-ερός, trembling; τε-τρεμ-αίνω, τρομ-έω, to tremble; ἀ-τρέμ-ᾰς, without trembling, unmoved.

trĕm-o, to shake, to *tremble;* **trĕm-esco, trĕm-isco** (inch.), to begin to shake or tremble; **trĕmĕ-făcio,** to cause to shake or tremble; **trĕm-endus,** (to be trembled at), formidable, *tremendous;* **trĕm-or,** a trembling, *tremor;* **trem-ŭlus,** shaking, trembling, *tremulous.*

204. Stems, **tri; trĭ; τρι; trĭ, tre, ter;** three.

τρεῖς, τρί-α, three; τρῐ-τος, the third; τρί-ς, thrice; τρισσός, threefold.

tre-s, tri-a, *three;* **ter-tius,** the *third,* [*tertiary*]; **ter,** three times; **ter-ni,** three each; **tri-plex** (*ter, plico*), threefold, *triple,* [*treble*]; **tri-ens,** a third part; **trĭ-ārii,** a class of Roman soldiers who formed the third rank from the front; **trĭ-bus,** (orig. a third part of the Roman people), a division of the people, a *tribe;* **trĭ-būnus** (prop. the chief of a tribe), a chieftain, a *tribune;* **trĭ-būnal,** a judgment-seat, *tribunal;* **trĭ-buo,** (to assign or give to a tribe), to assign, to give, (compd. w. ad, com, dis, in, re), [*attribute, contribute, distribute, retribution*]; **trĭ-būtum,** a *tribute;* **tri-vium** (*tres, via*), a place where three roads meet, a fork in the road, a cross-road; **tri-viālis,** (prop. that is in or belongs to the cross-roads or public streets; hence, transf.) that may be found everywhere, common, ordinary, *trivial.*

205. tu; tu; τυ; tu; swell, grow, be large.

τύ-λος, τύ-λη, any swelling or lump, a knot (in wood), [*thumb*]; τυ-λόω, to make callous.

tū-ber, a swelling, *protuberance,* [*tuber*]; **tŭ-mor,** a swelling, *tumor;* **tŭ-meo,** to swell; **tŭ-mesco** (inch.), to begin to swell; **tŭmĕ-făcio,** to cause to swell; **tum-ĭdus,** swollen, *tumid;* **tum-ŭlus,** a mound, a hill, *tomb.*

206. stud; tud; τυδ; tud; thrust, hit, strike.

Τυδ-εύς, Τύδ-ας, Τυνδ-άρης, Τυνδ-άρεος, proper names signifying "Striker, Beater."

tu-n-d-o (pf. tŭ-tŭd-i), to beat, strike, (compd. w. com, ex, ob, per, re), [*thud*]; **con-tū-sio,** a bruising, a bruise, *contusion;* **ob-tū-sus,** blunt, dull, *obtuse;* **tŭd-es,** a hammer.

207. —; tup; τυπ; —; strike.

τύπ-τ-ω, to strike, [*thump, stump, stub, stubble, stubborn*]; τύπος, τυπή, τύμ-μα, a blow; τῠπ-άς, a hammer; τύμπ-ανον, a drum.

†**tymp-ănum,** a drum, *tympanum.*

208. stvar, stur; tvar; —; —; make a noise, make confusion.

τύρ-βη, disorder, throng; τύρ-βᾰ, pell-mell; τυρ-βάζω, to trouble, stir up; τυρ-βασία, revelry.

†**tur-ba,** uproar, confusion, a crowd; **tur-bo,** to disturb, *trouble,* (compd. w. com, dis, de, ex, inter, ob, per, pro), [*disturb, perturb*]; **tur-bĭdus,** disordered, disturbed, *turbid;* **turbulentus,** restless, *turbulent;* **tur-bo,** a whirlwind; **tur-ma,** a troop, a throng.

Δ

d; d; δ; d.

209. svad; svad; ἁδ (σϜαδ); suad; taste good, please.

ἀνδ-άνω (ἕ-αδ-ον), to please; ἥδ-ομαι, to enjoy one's self, to take pleasure; ἥδ-ος, ἡδ-ονή, pleasure; ἡδ-ύς, ἥδ-υμος, sweet, pleasant; ἅσ-μενος, well-pleased, glad; ἐδ-ανός, sweet.

suā-vis (for *suadvis*), *sweet*, pleasant; suā-vĭtas, sweetness, agreeableness, [*suavity*]; suā-vium, (the sweet or delightful thing), a kiss; suād-eo, to advise, to persuade, (compd. w. com, dis, per), [*dissuade, persuade*]; suād-ēla, persuasion; suā-sio, *suasion;* suā-sor, an adviser.

210. da, da-k; —; δα; doc; learn, teach.

δέ-δα-ε (2 aor.), he taught; δε-δα-ώς (2d pf. part.), having learned, acquainted with; δε-δά-ασθαι (for δε-δά-εσθαι, 2 aor. m. inf.), to search out; ἐ-δά-ην (2 aor. pass.), I learned; δι-δάσκ-ω, to teach; ἐδί-δαξ-α (1 aor.), I taught.

dŏc-eo, to teach, to show, (compd. w. com, de, e, per, prae, pro, sub); dŏc-ĭlis, easily taught, *docile;* doc-tor, a teacher, [*doctor*]; doc-trīna, instruction, learning, [*doctrine*]; dŏc-ŭmentum, a lesson, a specimen, [*document*]; disco, to learn, (compd. w. ad, com, de, e, per, prae); disc-ĭpŭlus (fr. *disco* and the root of *puer, pupilla*), a pupil, a *disciple;* disc-ĭplīna, instruction, *discipline.*

211. —; daj; δα; —; distribute.

δα-ί-ω, to divide; δα-ίς, δαι-τύς, δαί-τη, a meal, a feast; δαιτρός, a carver; δαί-νῡ-μι, to give a banquet or feast; δαί-νυ-μαι, to feast; δαι-τυ-μών, a guest; δαίζ-ω, to cleave asunder, to rend; δα-τέ-ομαι, to divide among themselves; δα-σ-μός, a division, a tribute.

212. —; du; δαF; —.

δα-ί-ω, to kindle; δα-ί-ς, a fire-brand, torch; δᾱ-λό-ς, a fire-brand.

213. dam; dam; δαμ; dom; tame, subdue.

δαμ-άζ-ω, δαμ-ά-ω, δαμ-νά-ω, δάμ-νη-μι, to overpower, *tame*, subdue; δάμ-αρ, a wife; δαμ-άλης, a subduer, a young steer; -δαμος, (in compounds), taming; ἄ-δμη-τος, ἄ-δμη-ς, ἀ-δάμ-ατος, ἀ-δάμ-αστος, unconquered, untamed; δμώ-ς, a slave.

dŏm-o, to tame, subdue, [*daunt*]; dŏm-ĭtor, a tamer, conqueror; dŏm-ĭnus, a master, [*dominie*]; dŏm-ĭna, a mistress, lady, wife, *dame*, [*madame*]; dŏm-inium, a feast, ownership, lordship, [*dominion, domain*]; dŏm-ĭnor, to be lord and master, to have dominion, [*dominate, domineer, dominant, predominant*].

214. dap; dap; δαπ, δεπ; dap; distribute.

The modified root *dap* is derived from the shorter root *da* (as given in No. 211), and possibly it is connected with the root *da* (as given in No. 225).

δάπ-τ-ω, to devour, to rend; δαπ-άνη, expense; δαπ-ἄνηρός, δάπ-ἄνος, extravagant; δαψιλής, abundant, liberal; δεῖπ-νον, a meal.

dap-s, a sacrificial feast, a banquet; dap-ĭno, to serve up as food.

215. dar; drâ; δαρθ; dorm; sleep.

δαρθ-άν-ω, to sleep.

dorm-io, to sleep; [*dormant, dormer, dormouse*]; dorm-ĭto (freq.), to be sleepy; dorm-ĭtorium, a sleeping-room, *dormitory*.

216. δασύ-ς, thick (with hair, with leaves, etc.), rough; δαυ-λός, thick, shaggy; δάσος, a thicket; δασύνω, to make rough or thick.

densus, thick, *dense;* denso, denseo, to make dense or thick, (compd. w. ad, com), [*condense*]; dū-mus (old form *dusmus* for *densĭmus*), a thorn-bush, a bramble; dūmōsus (dummōsus, dusmosus), full of thorn-bushes, bushy.

217. -δε, toward; οἰκόνδε, homeward.
-do (du) in en-do, in-du; A. S. tô; Eng. *to*.

218. —; dâ; δε; —; bind.
δέ-ω, δί-δη-μι, to bind; δέ-σις, a binding; δε-τή, sticks bound up, a fagot; δε-σ-μός, a band, a fetter; κρή-δε-μνον, (κράς, δέω), part of a woman's head-dress, a veil; δια-δέω, to bind around; δία-δη-μα, a band or fillet, a *diadem*.

219. dam; dam; δεμ; dom; build.
δέμ-ω, to build; δέμ-ας, build, form, body; δόμ-ος, a building, a room, [*timber*]; δῶμα, δῶ, a house.
dŏm-us, a house, [*dome*]; dŏm-estĭcus, of or belonging to one's house or family, *domestic*, private; dŏm-icilium (*domus* and *cel-*, root of *celare*, to conceal), a dwelling, *domicile*.

220. dak; daksh; δεξ; dex; take hold of, seize. The root is the same as No. 7, with the addition here of an *s*.
δεξιό-ς, δεξι-τερό-ς, on the right hand or side; περι-δέξιος, ἀμφι-δέξιος, with two right hands, i.e., using both hands alike.
dex-ter, on the right hand or side, right, *dexterous* (*dextrous*).

221. —; dar; δερ; —.
δέρ-ω (δείρ-ω, δαίρ-ω), to skin, to flay; δέρ-ος, δορ-ά, δέρ-μα, skin, [*derm*, *dermatology*]; δέῤῥις, a leathern covering.

222. δειρή, Att. δέρη, the neck, throat; δειρά-ς, the ridge of a chain of hills (like αὐχήν and λόφος).
dorsum, dorsus, the back, a ridge or summit of a hill; dorsŭālis, of or on the back, *dorsal*.

223. dî; dî, ḍî; δι; dî; be afraid, frightened, restless.
δί-ω, to flee, to be afraid; δί-ομαι, δί-εμαι, to put to flight, to flee; δεί-δ-ω, to fear; δέος, fear; δει-λό-ς, cowardly; δει-νό-ς, fearful, terrible; δει-μός, fear; δῖ-νος, a whirling, dizziness, a threshing-floor; δῖ-νω, δι-νεύω, δῖ-νέω, to thresh out.
dī-rus, ill-omened, dreadful, *dire, direful*.

224. di, div, dyu; di, div, dju; δι, διF; di, div; be bright, shine, gleam, play.

δέ-α-το, δο-ά-σσατο, seemed; δῆ-λος, clear, evident; Ζεύς (st. ΔιF, gen. Διός), Zeus; δῖ-ος, divine, noble; ἔν-διος, at midday; εὐ-δί-α, fair weather, calm; Διώνη, Dione.

die-s, a *day*, [*dial, dismal* (*dies, malus*)]; **prī-die** (fr. the obs. *pri* [whence *prior, primus, pridem*] and *dies*), the day before; **postri-die** (loc. form fr. *posterus* and *dies*), on the day after; **cottī-die, cŏtī-die** (less correctly **quŏtī-die**) (*quot, dies*), daily; **prŏpĕ-diem** (also separately **prope diem**), at an early day, very soon; **dīū** (old acc. form of duration of time), by day (very rare), a long time; **inter-dīū,** by day; **diur-nus** (for *dius-nus*), of or belonging to the day, daily; ‡**diur-nālis,** *diurnal,* [*journal, journey*]; **du-dum** (diu-dum), a short time ago, formerly; **nŭdius** (*num* [i.e. *nunc*] and *dius* = *dies,* always used in connection with ordinal numbers), it is now the ... day since; **nŭdius tertius,** three days ago, the day before yesterday; **dīv-us, di-us,** divine; **dīvīnus,** *divine;* **dīv-us,** a god; **dīv-a,** a goddess; **dĕu-s,** a god, a *deity;* **dĕa,** a goddess; **Dĭŏv-is** or **Dĭjŏvis** (collat. form of **Jovis,** old nom. for later **Juppiter),** the old Italian name for Juppiter; **Juppĭter, Jupĭter** (*Jovis, pāter;* Jovis for Djovis), Jupiter or Jove, [A. S. Tives-däg, Eng. *Tuesday*]; **Dĭāna** (for *Divana*), Diana; **jŭv-o?,** to help, to please; **jŭv-ĕnis,** *young;* **jŭv-ĕnis,** a young person; **juv-enīlis,** youthful, *juvenile;* **jŭv-encus** (contr. fr. *juvenicus*), a young bullock; **jŭv-enca,** a young cow, a heifer.

225. da, do, du; da; δο; da, do, du; give.

δί-δω-μι, to give; δο-τήρ, δω-τήρ, a giver; δό-σις, δώς, a giving, a gift; δω-τίνη, δω-τύς, δῶ-τις, a gift; δῶ-ρον, a gift, a present.

do (inf. *dăre*), to give, [*date*, n. and vb.]; **circum-do,** to put around; **pessum-do,** to press or dash to the ground, to destroy; **addo,** to put to or near, to *add;* **de-do,** to put away, give up, surrender, devote; **di-do,** to give out, distribute; **ē-do,** to put forth, produce, [*edit*]; **per-do,** to put through, put entirely away, destroy, waste, lose, [*perdition*]; **disperdo,** to destroy, waste; **prō-do,** to put or give forth, produce, publish, disclose, betray; **red-do,** to give back, give up, [*render, rendition*]; **trā-do** (*trans, do*), to give up or over, to surrender, to transmit, to relate; **traditio,** a giving up, a saying handed down from former times, a *tradition;* **ven-do** (contr. fr. *venum, do*), to sell, *vend;* **dă-tor,** a giver; **dă-tīvus,** of or belonging to giving, (**dativus casus,** the *dative* case); **prō-dĭ-tor,** a traitor; **de-dĭ-tio,** a surrender; **dē-dĭ-tīcius,** one who has surrendered; **dō-num,** a gift; **dō-no,** to give one something as a present, *donate,* [*donor*]; **con-dōno,** to give up, pardon, *condone;* **rĕ-dōno,** to give back again, restore, forgive; **dō-natio,** a presenting, donation; **dōs,** a dowry, a gift; **dō-to,** to endow, provide, [subst. *dower, dowry*]; **dō-tālis,** of or belonging to a dowry; **du-im,** pres. sub., old Lat. for *dem;* **damnum** (for *daminum,* neut. of old part. of *dăre* = τὸ διδόμενον), injury, *damage;* **dam-no,** to damage, condemn, *damn;* **con-demno,** to *condemn;* **indemnis** (*in, damnum*), uninjured; **indemnĭtas,** security from damage or loss, *indemnity.*

226. δόλο-ς, cunning; δέλεαρ, a bait.

† **dŏlus,** guile, deceit; **dŏlōsus,** cunning, deceitful.

227. —; **dra;** δρα; —; run.

ἀπο-δρᾶ-ναι, to run away; δι-δρά-σκω, to run; δρα-σ-μός, flight; ἀ-δρα-στος, not running away, not to be escaped.

228. Greek rt. δρα, do. (This root is possibly to be joined with No. 227. Πράσσω is originally a verb of motion; the Skt. *k'ar,* run, and *kar,* do (No. 67), *tar,* pass over, and τέλος, τελεῖν (No. 197) are of the same origin.)

δρά-ω, to do; δρᾶ-μα, a deed, act, *drama;* δρη-στήρ, a laborer; δρα-στοσύνη, δρη-στοσύνη, service; δρᾶ-νος, a deed.

229. —; **dram;** δραμ; —; run. (This root is made from the shorter root δρα, No. 227.)

ἔ-δραμ-ον, I ran; δρόμ-ος, a running; ἱππό-δρομ-ος, a chariot-road, race-course, *hippodrome;* δρομ-εύς, a runner.

230. δρῦ-ς, a *tree*, an oak, [*Druid*]; δρυ-μός, a coppice, a wood; δρῦ-τόμος, δρυοτόμος, a wood-cutter; δένδρον, δένδρεον, a tree, [*dendriform, dendrology, dendrometer*]; δόρυ, a stem, tree, spear-shaft, spear; δούρειος, δουράτεος, wooden.

231. δύο, δύω, δοιοί, *two;* δίς (for δϝις), twice; δεύ-τερος, the second; Δευ-τερο-νόμιον (δεύτερος, νόμος), *Deuteronomy* (= the second or repeated law); δοιή, doubt; διά, through, apart (in compos.); δί-χα, δι-χθά, in two, asunder, two ways; δί-σσος, double; δυώ-δεκα, δώ-δεκα, twelve.

dŭo, *two,* [*deuce* (in gaming)]; **duālis,** that contains two, *dual;* **du-plex** (*duo, plico*), two-fold, *double,* [*duplicity*]; **dŭ-plĭco,** to double, [*duplicate*]; **du-plus** (*duo, pleo*), double, twice as large, twice as much; **bis** (for *duis,* fr. *duo*), twice; **bī-ni** (= *bis-ni*), two distributively, two for each; **bi-nārius,** containing or consisting of two, [*binary*]; **com-bī-no** (*com, bīni*), to unite, *combine;* **bī-vīra** (*bis, vir*), a woman married to a second husband; **dis-** (in compos.), apart, asunder, away; **dŭ-bius** (for *duhibius, duo, habeo,* held as two or double, i.e., doubtful), moving in two directions alternately, wavering, uncertain, doubtful, *dubious;* **dŭ-bĭto** (for *duhĭbĭto,* freq. fr. *duhibeo,* i.e., *duo, habeo*), to move in two directions alternately, waver, *doubt;* **bellum** (ante-class. and poet. duellum), war, hostilities between two nations, [*duel, belligerent*]; **Bellōna,** the goddess of war; **per-duellio,** treason, a public enemy; **bello,** to wage war; **de-bello,** to finish a war, to subdue; **re-bello,** to wage war again (said of the conquered), to *rebel;* **im-bellis,** unwarlike, weak.

232. δυσ-, insep. prefix opp. to εὖ, and, like the Eng. un- or mis-, always with the notion of hard, bad, unlucky, *dys-;* δυσ-μενής, ill-disposed, hostile; δυσ-εντερία (δυσ-, ἔντερον), *dysentery;* δυσ-πεψία (δυσ-, πέπτω, πέσσω), *dyspepsia, dyspepsy.*

233. ad; ad; ἔδ; ad, ed; eat.
ἔδ-ω, ἐσ-θί-ω, ἔσ-θω, to *eat;* ἐδ-ωδή, ἐδ-ητύς, ἔδ-εσμα, εἶδ-αρ, food.

ad-or (this word may belong to No. 251), a kind of grain, spelt, [*oats*]; ad-ōreus, pertaining to spelt; ad-ōrea, a reward of valor (in early ages this consisted of grain), glory, fame; ĕd-o, to eat, [*edible*], (compd. w. ad, com, ex, sub, super); ĕd-ax, voracious, *edacious;* in-ĕd-ia, fasting; ē-sŭrio (desid.), to desire to eat, to hunger; es-ca (for *ed-ca*), food; ves-cor (*vē* [here a strengthening prefix] and the root *ed*), to fill one's self with food, to take food, to eat; vescus (contr. fr. *ve* [here a negative prefix] and *esca*), small, feeble.

234. sad; sad; ἑδ; sed, sol; sit.

ἕζ-ομαι, to seat one's self, to sit; εἷ-σα, to make to sit, to seat; ἕδ-ος, ἕδ-ρα, a seat; ἱδ-ρύω, to make to sit down, to found. sĕd-eo, to sit, (compd. w. ad, circum, de, dis, in, ob, per, port [No. 317], prae, re, super), [*set, settle, seat, sedentary, assess, assize, assiduous, possess, preside, reside, supersede*]; sĕd-es, a seat; sel-la (for *sed-la*), a seat, a chair; sol-ium (from root *sol*, kindred with *sed*), a chair of state, a throne; sessio, a sitting, *session;* dē-ses, idle; dē-sid-ia, idleness; in-sid-iae, an ambush, plot, snare; in-sid-iosus, deceitful, *insidious;* ob-sid-io, ob-sid-ium, a siege; prae-ses, sitting before a thing to guard it, protecting, presiding; prae-ses, a protector, ruler, president; prae-sĭd-ens, a *president;* praesidium, a defence, a garrison; subsidium, aid, support, [*subsidy, subsidiary*]; sĭd-o, to sit down, settle, (compd. w. ad, circum, com, de, in, ob, per, port [No. 317], re, sub), [*subside*]; sēd-o, to allay, calm, check; sēd-ātus, calm, *sedate,* [*sedative*]; sēd-atio, an allaying.

235. sad; sad; ἑδ; sed, sol; go.

ὁδ-ός, way; ὁδ-ίτης, a traveller; ὁδ-εύω, to travel; ὁδ-ός, οὐδ-ός, threshold; οὖδ-ας, the ground; ἔδ-αφος, foundation, ground; περί-οδος, a going round, circuit, *period.* sēd-ŭlus, busy, *sedulous;* sŏl-um, the floor, the ground, *soil;* sŏl-ea, a covering for the foot, a *sole,* a sandal; ex-sul?, ex-ul?, an exile; ex-sŭlo?, ex-ŭlo? (also ancient form exsolo), to be an exile, to exile; exsilium, exilium, *exile.* *Sedŭlus, sŏlum, sŏlea, exsul, exsŭlo, exsilium* are all referred by some authorities to No. 234; and by others, *exsul, exsŭlo, exsilium*, together with *praesul* and *consul*, are referred to No. 523.

236. vid; vid; ἰδ, Fιδ; vid; see.

εἶδ-ον (Ep. ἔFιδον, ἴδ-ον, Fίδον), I saw; εἶδ-ομαι, to appear; οἶδ-α, I know (have seen); εἶδος, form, species; εἴδ-ωλον, an image, [*idol*]; 'Α-ΐδ-ης, Α-ΐδ-ης, ᾅδης, the god of the lower world, the lower world; ἴσ-τωρ, ἴσ-τωρ, knowing, skilful; ἰσ-τορέω, to inquire; ἰσ-τορία, *history, story;* ἴδ-ρις, knowing, experienced; ἰνδ-άλλομαι, to appear.

vĭd-eo, to see, (compd. w. in, per, prae, pro, re), [*vision, visible, invisible, prevision, provide, provision, revise, revision*]; **vĭdēlĭcet** (contr. fr. *videre licet*), it is permitted (or easy) to see, evidently, namely; **ē-vĭd-ens,** *evident,* manifest; **in-vid-ia,** *envy,* hatred; **in-vĭd-us,** envious; **in-vid-iōsus,** *invidious, envious;* **prō-vĭd-entia,** foresight, *providence;* **prō-vĭd-us, prō-vĭd-ens,** foreseeing, *provident,* prudent; **prūdens** (= *prōvidens*), foreseeing, *prudent;* **vĭtrum** (root in *video*, to see, as transparent), glass; **vitreus,** of glass, glassy, *vitreous;* **vīso** (freq.), to look at attentively, to go in order to look at, to *visit,* (compd. w. in, pro, re), [*revisit*]; **vĭsĭto,** to see, to visit; **vĭsĭtatio,** an appearance, *visitation.*

237. svid; svid; ἰδ, σFιδ; sud (for svid); sweat.

ἰδ-ίω, ἰδ-ρόω, to sweat; ἴδ-ος, ἰδ-ρώς, sweat.

sūd-o, to sweat, (compd. w. de, ex, in, re), [*exude*]; **sūd-or,** sweat, [*sudorific*].

238. mad, med; mâ (No. 386); **μεδ; mod;** measure, place a measure or limit to. These roots are apparently derived from the shorter roots shown under No. 386.

μέδ-ω, to protect, rule over; μέδ-ομαι, to provide for, think on; μήδ-ομαι, to resolve, contrive; μέδ-οντες, guardians; μηστωρ, a counsellor; μῆδ-ος, counsel; μέδ-ιμνος, a measure.

mŏd-us, measure, manner, *mode,* [*mood*]; **mŏdo** (orig. abl. of *modus*), only, merely, (of time) just now, lately; **mŏd-ernus**

(fr. *modo*), *modern;* **com-mŏd-us,** that has a due or proper measure, complete, suitable, convenient, *commodious*, [*commode, commodity*]; **com-mŏd-um,** convenience, advantage; **mŏd-ĭcus,** having or keeping a proper measure, moderate; **mŏd-ulus** (dim.), a small measure, a measure, [*model*]; **mŏd-ŭlor,** to measure, *modulate;* **mŏd-estus,** keeping due measure, moderate, *modest;* **mŏd-ĕror,** to fix a measure, set bounds, *moderate*, regulate; **mŏd-ius, mŏd-ium,** a measure, a peck; **mŏd-ĭfĭco** (*modus, facio*), to limit, regulate, [*modify*].

239. Greek rt. μελδ.

μέλδ-ω, to *melt*, make liquid, [*smelt*]; μέλδ-ομαι, to melt, grow liquid.

240. ad; —; ŏδ; od, ol; smell.

ὄζ-ω (pf. ὄδ-ωδ-α), to smell (intrans.); ὀδ-μή (ὀσ-μή), a smell, odor; δυσ-ώδ-ης, ill-smelling.

ŏd-or, a smell, *odor;* **ŏd-ōro,** to give a smell or fragrance to, to perfume; **ŏd-ōror,** to smell at, to smell out, search out, investigate; **ŏd-ōrārius,** of or for perfuming; **ŏd-ōrātus,** sweet-smelling; **ŏd-ōrus,** *odorous*, keen-scented; **ŏl-eo** (**ŏl-o**), to smell (intr. or tr.), (compd. w. ad, ob, per, re, sub), [*redolent*]; **ŏl-ĭdus,** emitting a smell; **ŏl-or,** a smell; **ol-făcio** (uncontracted collat. form, *ŏlĕfăcio*), to cause to smell of, to smell, [*olfactory*].

241. ὀδούς, a tooth.

den-s (st. *dent*), a *tooth*, [*dentist*]; **dent-io,** to get or cut teeth; **dent-itio,** teething, *dentition;* **dent-ātus,** toothed, *dentated;* **bĭ-dens** (old form *duidens*), an animal for sacrifice (having two rows of teeth complete), a sheep.

242. pad; pad; πεδ, ποδ; ped; tread, go.

πέδ-ον, the ground; πεδ-ίον, a plain; πέδ-η, a fetter; πέδ-ιλον (mostly in pl.), sandals; πεζ-ός, on foot; πέζ-α, the instep; πούς, foot; τρί-πους, three-footed, a *tripod*.

pes, a *foot*, [*biped, quadruped, centiped, centipede*]; **pĕd-ālis,** of or belonging to the foot, of or belonging to a foot (in length), [*pĕdal, pĭdal*]; **pĕd-es,** one that is or goes on foot, a foot-soldier; **pĕd-ester** (adj.), on foot, *pedestrian;* **pĕd-ĭca,** a *fetter* (for the feet); **com-pes,** a fetter or shackle for the feet; **com-pĕd-io,** to fetter; **ex-pĕd-io,** to extricate, disengage, [*expedient, expedite, expedition*]; **im-pĕd-io,** to entangle, *impede;* **prae-pedio,** to shackle; **pĕd-um,** a shepherd's crook; †**trĭpus,** a tripod; **pessum** (prob. contracted from *pedis-versum*, toward the feet), to the ground, down; **pessum ire,** to fall to the ground, to perish; **pessum dăre** (less correctly in one word **pessumdăre** or **pessundăre**), to press or dash to the ground, to destroy.

243. sak, ska, ski, ska-n, skan-d, ski-d; skhad; σκεδ, σχεδ, κεδ; scand; cut, cleave, separate.

σκεδ-άννῡ-μι, to scatter; σκίδ-να-μαι, to be spread or scattered; σκέδ-ᾰσις, a scattering; σχέδ-η, a tablet, a leaf; σχεδ-ία, a raft.

scand-ŭla (scind-ŭla), a shingle.

244. skidh?; k'hid; σκιδ, σχιδ; scid, cid, caed; cut, cleave, separate.

σχίζ-ω, to split; σχίζ-α, a piece of wood cleft off, (in pl.) firewood; σχίσ-μα, a cleft, division, *schism*.

scind-o (pf. **scĭd-i**), to cut, to split, (compd. w. ab, circum, com, de, di, ex, inter, per, prae, pro, re), [*scissors, exscind, rescind*]; **caed-o,** to cut, strike, kill, (compd. w. ad, com, de, dis, ex, in, inter, ob, prae, re, sub, trans), [*concise, decide, incise, incisive, incision, precise*]; **cae-mentum** (contr. fr. *caedimentum*, fr. *caedo*), stone as hewn from the quarry, [*cement*]; **cae-lum,** a chisel.

245. spad, spand; spand; σφαδ; fund; move violently, reel, swing.

σφαδ-άζω, to toss the body about, struggle, struggle spasmodically; σφαδ-ασμός, a spasm, convulsion; σφεδ-ανός, eager, violent; σφοδ-ρός, vehement, violent, excessive; σφόδ-ρα, exceedingly, violently; σφενδ-όνη, a sling; σφενδ-ονάω, to sling.

fund-a, a sling, a casting-net, a money-bag, [*fund*, n. and vb.]; fūsus?, spindle.

246. ὕδρα, ὕδρος, a water-serpent, *hydra*, [*otter*].

247. vad, ud, und; ud; ὑδ; und; wet, moisten.

ὑδ-ωρ (st. ὑδαρτ), *water*, [*hydraulic* (αὐλός, a pipe), *hydrate, hydrogen* (rt. γεν), *hydrometer* (μέτρον, measure), *hydrophobia* (φόβος, fear)]; ὑδ-ρία, a water-pitcher; ὑδ-ρεύω, to draw or carry water; ὑδ-ραίνω, to water, [*hydrant*]; ἄν-υδ-ρος, wanting water, waterless; ὑδ-αρής, ὑδ-αρός, watery; ὑδ-ερος, ὑδ-ρωψ, *dropsy* (abbreviated from *hydropsy*).

und-a, a wave, water; und-o, to rise in waves, to surge, (compd. w. ab, ex, in), [*undulate, abound, abundant, inundate, redound, redundant*].

Θ

dh; dh; θ; sometimes **f** at the beginning of a word, usually **d** in the middle of a word.

248. vadh; —; Fεθ; vad; wager, pledge, bail.

ἄ-εθ-λον, ἆθ-λον, ἀ-έθ-λιον, the prize of a contest; ἆθ-λος, a contest; ἀθ-λέω, ἀθ-λεύω, to contend for a prize; ἀθ-λητής, ἀθ-λητήρ, a combatant, prize-fighter, *athlete*, [*athletic*].

văs (gen. văd-is), bail, security, *gage*, [A. S. *wedd* = pledge, promise, Eng. *wedlock*]; văd-ĭmōnium, a promise secured by bail, security; văd-or, to bind over by bail; praes (*prae, vas*), a surety, bondsman (in money matters).

249. idh; indh, idh; αιθ; aed; burn, shine.

αἴθ-ω, to light up, burn; αἴθ-ος, a burning heat, fire; αἰθ-ός, burnt, fiery; αἴθ-ων, fiery, burning; αἰθ-ήρ, *ether*, the upper air; αἴθ-ρη, αἴθ-ρα, clear sky, fair weather; αἴθ-οψ (αἰθός, ὄψ), fiery-looking, fiery; Αἰ-θίοψ, an Ethiop, Ethiopian.

aed-es (originally fire-place, hearth, altar), a temple, (plur.) a house; **aedi-fĭco,** to build; **aedĭ-fĭcĭum,** a building, an *edifice;* **aed-ĭlis,** an *aedile;* **aedĭlicius,** pertaining to an aedile; **aeditŭus** (*aedes, tueor*), a keeper of a temple, temple-warden; **aes-tas,** the summer; **aes-tīvus,** of summer; **aes-tīvo,** to pass the summer; **aes-tus,** heat; **aes-tuo,** to be warm, to burn; **aes-tuosus,** full of heat, very hot.

250. Greek rt. ἀλθ.

ἀλθ-αίνω, ἀλθήσκω, to heal; ἀλθ-ήεις, healing, wholesome.

251. Greek rt. ἀθ, ἀνθ.

ἄνθ-ος, blossom, flower; ἀνθ-έω, to blossom, bloom; ἀνθ-ηρός, blooming; ἀνθ-ερεών, the chin; ἀνθ-έριξ, the beard of an ear of corn; the ear itself; Ἀθήνη (the blooming one), Athene.

252. St. ἐθ (σϜεθ).

ἔθος, ἦθος, custom, habit, [*ethics, ethical*]; εἴ-ω-θα (pf.), to be accustomed; ἐθ-ίζω, to accustom.

sŭesco, to become or be accustomed, (compd. w. ad, com, de, in); **consŭētūdo,** *custom;* **mansuesco** (*manus, suesco*), (lit. to accustom to the hand), to tame; **mansŭētūdo,** tameness, mildness; **desŭētūdo,** disuse, *desuetude;* **sŏdālis,** a boon-companion.

253. rudh; rudh; ἐρυθ (ε prothetic); **rud, ruf, rub, rob;** red.

ἐρεύθ-ω, to make red; ἐρυθ-ρός, red, ruddy, [*rust*]; ἔρευθος, redness; ἐρυθριάω, to blush; ἐρυσίβη, mildew.

rŭb-er, rub-rus, rŭb-eus, rŏb-eus, rŏb-ius, rŏb-us, red, [*ruby*]; **rŭb-eo,** to be red; **sur-rŭb-eo** (*sub-rubeo*), to be somewhat red; **rŭbĕ-facio** (*rubeo, facio*), to make red; **rŭb-esco** (inch.), to grow red; **rŭb-ēdo, rŭb-or,** redness; **rŭb-ellus** (dim.), reddish; **rŭb-us,** a bramble-bush, blackberry-bush; **rŭbrīca** (fr. *ruberica*), red earth, the title of a law, the *rubric;* **rŏb-ĭgo, rūb-ĭgo,** rust, blight; **rūf-us,** red, red-haired; **Rufus, Rufio,** Roman proper names; **rūf-esco** (inch.), to become reddish; **rŭ-tĭlus** (=*rud-tilus*), red, shining; **rŭ-tĭlo,** to make red, to be red.

254. dha; dha; θα, θη; fe, fi; suckle, suck.

θῆ-σαι, to suckle; θῆ-σθαι, to milk; θή-σατο, he sucked; θη-λή, teat; θη-λώ, θη-λαμών, θη-λάστρια, a nurse; τι-θή-νη, τίτ-θη, a nurse; τιτ-θός, a *teat;* θῆ-λυς, female; γαλα-θη-νός, sucking.

fello, to suck; fē-mina, a *female*, [*feminine*]; fī-lius, a son; fī-lia, a daughter, [*filial*]. *Fēmina, fīlius,* and *fīlia* may be derived from the root *fu.*

255. Greek rt. **θαF.**

(Dor.) θᾱ-έομαι, (Ion.) θη-έομαι, Att. θε-ά-ομαι, to look on, gaze at; θαῦ-μα, a wonder; θε-ωρία, a looking at, contemplation, *theory;* θέ-α, a view, a sight; θέᾱ-τρον, a place for seeing, esp. for dramatic representation, a *theatre.*

256. dha; dha; θε; da, fa, fa-c; place, make, do.

τί-θη-μι, to place, to make, to *do*, [*deed, deem, doom*]; θέ-μα, that which is placed or laid down; θέ-σις, a placing, a *thesis;* θε-σμός, that which is laid down and established, a rule, a law; θέ-μις, that which is laid down and established, law (not as fixed by statute, but) as established by custom; θε-μέλια, θέ-μεθλα (pl.), the foundations, the lowest part; θή-κη, a case to put anything in, a chest; ἀποθήκη, a storehouse, repository, [*apothecary*].

ab-do, to put away, to conceal; con-do, to put together, to form, to put away carefully for preservation, to conceal; in-do, to put into or upon; ob-do, to place at or before; sub-do, to place under; abs-condo, to put out of sight, conceal carefully, [*abscond*]; re-condo, to put back again, to stow away, conceal, [*recondite*]; condĭtor, a maker, builder, founder; crēdo (Sk. çrat, çrad, trust and dha), to put faith in, to trust, [*credit, creditor, credence, credential, credible, credulous, creed*]; făm-ŭlus (masc.), făm-ŭla (fem.), a servant; făm-ilia, a household establishment, a *family;* fă-ber, a maker, a worker (in hard materials), an artificer; fa-brĭca, the workshop or the business of an artisan; fa-brĭcor, to make, prepare, [*fabricate*]; fa-brĭcātor, an artificer, a contriver; făc-io, to make, to do, (compd. [in form -ficio] w. ad, com, de, ex, in, ob, per, prae, pro, re, sub); fi-o (=fa-i-o), to be made, to become; āre-făcio (areo, facio), to make dry, to dry up; assŭe-făcio (assuesco, facio), to accustom; calĕ-făcio (caleo, facio), to make warm or hot; commone-făcio (commoneo, facio), to remind forcibly, to put in mind; con-călĕ-facio (cum, calefacio), to warm thoroughly; lăbĕ-facio (labo, facio), to make to reel, to shake violently; mădĕ-făcio (madeo, facio), to make wet; pătĕ-făcio (pateo, facio), to make or lay open; tĕpĕ-făcio (tepeo, facio), to make moderately warm; af-fic-io, to do something to a person or thing, to treat in any way; con-fic-io, to make thoroughly, to complete; de-fic-io, to make to be away, to make one's self to be away, revolt, fail, [deficient]; ef-fic-io, to make out, work out, bring to pass, effect; in-fic-io, to put in, dip in a liquid, stain, infect; inter-ficio, (to make something to be between the parts of a thing, so as to separate and break it up), to destroy, to kill; of-fic-io, to do over against, to hinder, to oppose; per-fic-io, to make or do completely, to finish; prae-fic-io, to set over, place in authority over; pro-fic-io, to go forward, make progress, [proficient]; re-fic-io, to make again, to rebuild; suf-fic-io, to make or cause to be under, to dip, dye, affect, furnish, [sufficient]; affectio (adf.), disposition toward, affection; affec-to (better adfecto), (freq.), to strive after, imitate, affect, [affectation]; fac-to (freq.), to make, to do; fac-tĭto (freq. fr. facto), to make or do frequently, to be wont to make or do; fac-esso (intens.), to do eagerly or earnestly; pro-fic-iscor, (to make, i.e. put one's self forward), to set out, depart, proceed; făc-ilis, easy to do, easy, facile; dif-fic-ilis, (far from easy to do), difficult; fac-ilĭtas, ease, facility; fac-ultas, capability, power, supply, [faculty]; dif-fic-ultas, difficulty; fac-tum, that which is done, a deed, a fact; fac-tor, a maker, doer, [factor]; fac-tio, a making, a company of persons, a party, faction; fac-tiōsus, seditious, factious; fac-ĭnus, a deed, a crime; ef-fĭc-ax, efficacious; prŏ-fec-to (=pro facto), actually, certainly; běnĕ-fĭcus, generous, *beneficent;* **mălĕ-fĭcus,** evil-doing, wicked; **aedĭ-fĭc-o** (*aedes, facio*), to build, build up, *edify;* **ampli-fĭc-o** (*amplus, facio*), to enlarge, *amplify.*

257. ghan; han; θεν; fend; beat, strike.

θείν-ω, to strike.

‡**fend-o,** the primitive word of the compounds, *defendo, offendo, infensus* and *infestus;* **de-fend-o,** to ward off, repel, *defend, fend,* [*defence, fence* (n. and. v.), *fender*]; **of-fend-o,** to strike, injure, *offend;* **in-fen-sus,** hostile; **in-fes-tus** (for *infenstus*), made unsafe, disturbed, *infested,* that renders unsafe, hostile; **mani-festus** (*manus, fendo,* i.e., that one hits with the hand), clear, evident, *manifest.*

258. Greek rt. θεF.

θέ-ω (θεύ-σομαι), to run; θο-ός, swift; θο-άζω, to move quickly; Βοη-θόος (βοή, θέω), hasting to the battle-shout, warlike, helping.

259. θήρ, Aeol. φήρ, θηρ-ίον, a wild beast; θηρ-άω, to hunt; θήρ-α, the chase.

fĕr-us, wild; **fĕr-us,** m., **fĕr-a,** f., a wild beast; **ef-fĕr-o,** to make wild; **fer-ĭtas,** wildness; **fĕr-ox,** wild, bold, *fierce,* [*ferocious*]; **fĕr-ōcia, fĕr-ōcĭtas,** wild or untamed courage, fierceness, *ferocity.*

260. dhars; dharsh; θαρσ, θρασ; fars; dare.

θρασ-ύς, bold; θάρσ-ος, boldness, courage; θαρσ-έω (θαρρ-έω), to be of good courage, [*dare*]; θαρσ-ύνω, to encourage.

fas-tus (full form *farstus*), scornful contempt, arrogance; **fas-tidium** (for *fasti-ti-dium*), loathing, aversion; **fas-tidiōsus,** (full of disgust or aversion), disdainful, *fastidious.*

261. dhar, dhra; dhar; θρα; fĭr, for; hold, support, bear up.

θρή-σασθαι, to seat one's self, to sit; θρᾶ-νος, a bench; θρῆ-νυς, a footstool; θρό-νος, a seat, chair, *throne.*

fir-mus, *firm*, strong; in-fir-mus, feeble, *infirm;* fir-mitas, fir-mitudo, firmness; fir-mo, to make firm, support, strengthen, (compd. w. ad, com, in, ob), [*affirm, confirm*]; fir-mātor, an establisher; fir-mamentum, a support, [*firmament*]; for-tis, strong, brave, [*fort, fortress, fortify, force, forte*]; for-titūdo, strength, firmness, *fortitude;* frē-tus, leaning or supported on something, relying upon; frē-num, a bridle.

262. Greek rt. θρε.

θρέ-ομαι, to cry aloud; θρό-ος, a noise; θρῆ-νος, a dirge; θρηνῳδία (θρῆνος, ᾠδή), a lament, dirge, *threnode, threnody;* θόρυ-βος, a noise.

263. dhugh-atar; duh-i-tâ; θυγ-ά-τηρ; —; *daughter.*

264. Primary (Indo-Eur.) form, *dhur, dhvar*. Sk. *dvara-m, dvâr*, door.

θύρ-α, θύρ-ετρα, *door;* θύρ-ᾱσι, at the door; θὔρ-ίς, a window; θυρ-εός, a door-stone; θαιρός, hinge, axle.

fŏr-is (more freq. in pl. fŏr-es), a door; fŏr-is (adv., an abl. form from an obs. nom. *fora*), out of doors; fŏr-ās (adv., an acc. form from an obs. nom. *fora*), out through the doors, forth.

265. dhu; dhu; θυ; fu. Of this root the primary meaning is that of a violent movement, and from this spring three modifications: 1. to rush, excite; 2. to smoke, fumigate; 3. to sacrifice.

θύ-ω, to rush, to sacrifice; θύ-ν-ω, to rush along; θῦ-νος, a violent movement onward, an attack; θύ-ελλα, a hurricane, whirlwind; θυ-ι-άς, θυ-άς, a mad or inspired womam, a Bacchante; θυ-μός, the soul, courage, passion, feeling; θῦ-μα, θῦ-σία, a sacrifice; θύ-ος, a sacrifice, incense; θὔ-ήεις, smoking or smelling with incense, fragrant; θὔ-μος, θὔ-μον, *thyme.*

fū-mus, smoke, *fume,* [*dust*]; fū-mĕus, smoky; fū-mĭdus, fū-mōsus, full of smoke, smoky; fū-mo, to smoke, steam, *fume;* fū-mĭgo (*fūmus, ago*), to smoke, *fumigate;* suf-fi-o, sub-fi-o (*fio* = θύω), to fumigate, scent; suf-fi-tio, fumigation; suf-fī-men, suf-fī-mentum, fumigation, incense; fē-teo (less correctly foeteo, faeteo), to have an ill smell, to stink; fē-tĭdus (faetidus, foetidus), that has an ill smell, stinking, *fetid;* foe-dus, foul, filthy; foe-do, to make foul, to defile, disfigure; fū-nus, a funeral procession, burial, *funeral*.

266. sku, kudh; gudh; κυθ; cud; cover, conceal.

κεύθ-ω, to cover, hide; κεῦθ-ος, κευθ-μών, a hiding-place.

cus-tos (= *cud-tos*), a guard; cus-tōdia, a guarding, *custody*, a guard; cus-tōdio, to watch over, to guard.

267. μισθός, pay, [*meed*].

268. vadh; vadh; ὀθ; od; thrust, strike, beat.

ὠθ-έω, to thrust, push; Ἐν-οσί-χθων, Ἐννοσίγαιος, Earth-shaker (epithet of Poseidon).

ŏd-i, to hate; ŏd-ium, hatred, *odium;* ŏd-iosus, hateful, *odious*.

269. οὖθ-αρ, an udder.

ūb-er, a teat, an *udder*, [*exuberant*].

270. bhandh; bandh; πενθ; —; join, bind, [*bond, band*].

πενθ-ερός, a father-in-law, brother-in-law, son-in-law; πενθ-ερά, a mother-in-law; πεῖσ-μα, a rope.

271. bhandh; bandh; πιθ; fid; join, bind, unite, trust.

πείθ-ω, to persuade; πείθ-ομαι, to obey; πέ-ποιθ-α, trust (vb.); πίσ-τις, faith; πειθ-ώ, persuasion, persuasiveness; πεῖ-σα, obedience.

fĭd-es, trust, *faith*, [*affiance, affidavit*]; fĭd-ēlis, faithful; fĭd-ēlĭtas, faithfulness, *fidelity;* Fĭd-ius, a surname of Jupiter; Dius Fidius, the god of truth; medius fidius, by the god of truth, most certainly; per-fĭd-us (*per, fides*), faithless; per-fid-iōsus, full of perfidy, *perfidious;* fĭd-us, faithful; fĭd-o, to trust; con-fĭd-o, to trust confidently, *confide* in, [*confident, confidánt*]; dif-fĭd-o, to distrust; [*diffident, defy*]; foed-us, a league, compact, [*federal*]; foed-ĕro, to establish by treaty; foed-erātus, leagued together, *federate*.

272. —; budh; πυθ; —; awake, inquire, perceive, know.

πυνθ-άνομαι, πεύθ-ομαι, to ask, inquire; πύσ-τις, πεῦ-σις, an asking; πύσ-μα, a question; πευθ-ήν, an inquirer.

273. bhu, bhu-dh; budh; πυθ, πυνδ; fund; grow.

πυθ-μήν, the bottom, the stock of a tree; πύνδ-αξ, the bottom of a vessel.

fund-us, the bottom of anything, the soil, a farm; fund-o, to lay the bottom or foundation of a thing, to *found;* fund-āmentum, foundation, [*fundamental*]; prŏ-fund-us, (having the bottom forward, i.e., at some distance off), deep, *profound*.

Π

p; p, ph; π; p.

274. ἀπό, from, away from; ἄψ, back, back again.

ap, af, ab, (av) au-, ā, ă, aps, abs, as-, from, away from, by, [*off, of*].

275. rap, rup; —; ἁρπ; rap; seize.

Ἁρπ-υιαι, the Snatchers, the storm-winds (personified), (in later mythology) the *Harpies;* ἁρπ-η, a bird of prey; ἅρπ-αξ (adj.), robbing; ἅρπ-αξ (subst.), rapine, a robber; ἁρπ-ἄλέος, grasping, greedy; ἁρπ-άζω, to snatch away, seize, plunder; ἁρπ-άγη, a hook, a rake; ἁρπ-αγή, rapine, robbery, booty.

răp-io, to seize and carry off, (compd. w. ab, ad, com, de, di, e, prae, pro, sub), [*rap, rape, reave* (obs.), *bereave, rob, rapture, ravage, ravish*]; răp-ax, grasping, *rapacious;* răp-ācĭtas, *rapacity;* răp-ĭdus, tearing away, fierce, tearing or hurrying along, swift, *rapid;* răp-īna, robbery, pillage, *rapine,* [*raven, ravin, ravenous, ravine*]; rap-tor, a robber; rap-tus, a carrying off, plundering, abduction; rap-tim (adv.), by snatching or hurrying away, suddenly, hurriedly.

276. ἁρπ-η, a sickle.

sarp-o, to cut off, prune; sar-mentum, the thing lopped or pruned, twigs.

277. var, val; —; Fελπ; vol(u)p; hope, desire.
The root in Greek and Latin is connected with the shorter form in No. 525.

ἐλπ-ω, to make to hope; ἐλπ-ομαι, to hope; ἐλπ-ίς, hope; ἐλπ-ωρή, hope; ἐλπ-ίζω, to hope.

vŏlŭp (shortened for vŏlŭpis), agreeably; vŏlup-tas, pleasure; vŏlup-tuōsus, full of pleasure, [*voluptuous*].

278. ἐμπί-ς, a gnat.

ăpis, ăpes, a *bee*; ăpĭcŭla, a little bee; ăpĭ-ārius, relating to bees; ăpi-ārium, a bee-house, bee-hive, *apiary*.

279. ἐπί, upon, to, toward.

ob (old form obs), toward, at, before, on account of; ăpud, with, near.

280. ἑπτά, seven; ἕβδομος, seventh.

septem, *seven;* septĭmus, septŭmus, seventh; Septem-ber, *September* (the seventh month of the Roman year, reckoning from March); sept-ēni, seven each, seven; sept-ĭes, seven times; septuāginta (for *septuma-ginta, septem-decenta*), seventy, [*Septuagint*].

281. sarp; sarp; ἑρπ; serp, rep (for srep); creep, go with an even motion along the ground.

ἕρπ-ω, to creep, to move slowly; ἑρπ-ύζω, to creep, crawl; ἑρπ-ετόν, a creeping thing, a beast.

serp-o, to creep, crawl; serp-ens, creeping, crawling; serp-ens, a *serpent;* rēp-o (*serp* = *srep* = *rep*), to creep, (compd. w. ad, com, de, in, ob, per, pro, sub); rep-tĭlis, creeping, *reptile;* rep-to (freq.), to creep.

282. Greek rt. λαμπ.

λάμπ-ω, to shine; λαμπ-άς, a torch, [*lamp*]; λαμπ-ρός, bright.

lanterna, laterna, a *lantern*, lamp, torch; limp-ĭdus, clear, bright, *limpid*.

283. rup; lup; λυπ; rup; break, trouble.

λυπ-ρός, wretched, painful; λύπ-η, pain, grief; λῡπ-έω, to pain, distress; λῡπ-ηρός, painful.

rump-o, to break, break asunder, (compd. w. ab, com, di, e, inter, intro, in, ob, per, prae, pro), [*rupture, abrupt, corrupt, eruption, interrupt, irruption*].

284. Greek rt. **νεπ.**

ἀ-νεψ-ιός, a first cousin, any cousin; νέπ-οδες, offspring, descendants.

nĕp-os, a grandson, spendthrift, *nephew*, [*nepotism*]; neptis, a granddaughter.

285. pak, pag; paç; παγ; pag, pac; bind fast.

πήγ-νυμι (ἐ-πάγ-ην), to make fast, to fix; πῆγ-μα, anything fastened or joined together; πηγ-ός, firm, strong; πάγ-ος, a firm-set rock; πάγ-ος, πάχ-νη, παγ-ετός, frost; πάγ-η, anything that fixes or holds fast, a trap; πάσσ-αλος, a peg, a nail.

pa-n-g-o (old form păco, pago), to fix, record, determine (compd. w. com, in, ob, re), [*impinge, impact*]; păc-iscor, păc-isco (old form păco), to make a bargain or agreement; pac-tum, an agreement, compact, *pact;* pax (orig. an agreement, treaty), *peace,* [*appease*]; pāc-o, to make peaceful, to pacify; pāci-fĭco, to make a peace, to *pacify;* pāci-fĭcus, peace-making, *pacific;* păg-us, (prop. a place with fixed boundaries), a district, the country; păg-ănus, of or belonging to the country or to a village, civil, (in eccl. Latin) heathen, pagan; păg-ānus (subst.), a countryman, a civilian, (in eccl. Latin) a heathen, a *pagan;* păg-ĭna, a *page;* com-pāg-es, com-pāg-o, a connection, joint, structure; prŏ-pāg-o, to fasten or fix forward or down, to set slips, *propagate,* prolong; prŏ-pāg-o, a layer, a setting, offspring; pā-lus, pā-lum, a stake; pig-nus, a pledge; pig-nero, to give as a pledge; pĕc-u, (the thing fastened up), a head of the larger cattle, cattle of all kinds, sheep, money; pĕc-us (ŭdis), a head of cattle of any kind; pĕc-us (ŏris), the larger cattle, a herd, cattle of all kinds, animals; pec-ūnia (fr. *pecus;* "omnis pecuniae pecus fundamentum," Var.), property, money; pec-ūniaris, of or belonging to money, *pecuniary.*

286. pu, —, —, —, strike.
παί-ω, to strike.

păv-io, to beat, strike; păv-īmentum, (the thing beaten or rammed down), a hard floor, a *pavement;* păv-imento, to cover with a pavement, to pave; de-pŭv-io, to strike, beat.

287. παλ-άμη, the palm of the hand, the hand.

pal-ma, the *palm* of the hand, the hand, the blade of an oar, the *palm*-tree, [*palmy*]; pal-mus, the palm of the hand; pal-mŭla (dim.), palm of the hand, oar-blade; pal-metum, a palm-grove; pal-mes, a young branch or shoot of a vine.

288. παρά, παραί, πάρ, πά, (w. gen.) from the side of, (w. dat.) at the side of, (w. acc.) to the side of.

per, through, throughout, by means of.

289. pa; pa; πα; pa; nourish, protect.

πα-τήρ, a father; πα-τριά, lineage, a clan; πατρι-άρχης, the father or chief of a clan, a *patriarch;* πατριώτης, a fellow-countryman, [*patriot*].

pă-ter, a *father;* pă-ternus, pă-trītus, pă-trĭcus, pă-trius, of or belonging to one's father, *paternal;* pă-tria, one's fatherland, native country; pă-trīmonium, an estate inherited from a father, a *patrimony;* parrīcīda (for *patricida* from *pater, caedo*), the murder of a father, a *parricide,* a murderer; pa-truus, a father's brother; pa-truēlis, a cousin on the father's side; pă-trōnus, a protector, defender, *patron;* pa-trōcĭnor, to protect; pāpa, a father, *papa,* (in eccl. writers) a spiritual father, a bishop.

290. πάτο-ς, a path; πατέ-ω, to walk, tread.

pons, a bridge.

291. pa; pa; πα, πατ; pa, pen; nourish, protect.

πατ-έομαι, to eat; ἄ-πασ-τος, not having eaten.

pa-sco, to nourish, support by food; pa-scor, to feed upon; pascuus, of or for pasture, grazing; pascuum, pastūra, a *pasture;* pas-tor, a feeder, feeder of cattle, shepherd, *pastor;* pas-torālis, of or belonging to shepherds, *pastoral;* pas-tus, feeding, food; pā-bŭlum, food, fodder; pā-bulor, to seek for food, to forage, to feed; pā-bulātor, a forager, a herdsman; pā-nis, bread; pĕn-us, food, food stored within a place (perhaps through the intermediate idea of storing food within, the root "*pen*" acquired the meaning "*within*"); Penātes, the Penates, (deities of the interior of the house), guardian deities of the household and of the state; pĕn-es, with, in the possession or power of; pĕn-ĕtro, to put into, enter, *penetrate.*

292. pava; —; st. παυ; pau; little.

παύ-ω, to make to end or cease, [*pause*]; παύ-ομαι, to cease from; παῦ-λα, παυ-σωλή, a rest, an end; παῦ-ρος, small, few.

pau-cus, small, little, (pl.) *few;* pau-citas, fewness, *paucity;* pau-cŭlus, very small, (pl.) very few; pau-lus, paullus, little, small; pau-lum, (adv.), a little, somewhat; pau-lō (advbl. abl.), by a little, somewhat; pau-lātim, by little and little, by degrees; pau-lisper, for a little while; pau-per (adj.), poor; pau-per (subst.), a poor person, [*pauper*]; pau-pertas, *poverty;* pau-pĕries (poet. and in post Aug. prose for *paupertas*), poverty; pa-rum (adv.), too little, little.

293. πελλός, πελός, πελιός, πελιδνός, dark-colored, dusky, livid; πολ-ιός, gray.

pal-leo, to be or look pale; pal-lesco (inch.), to grow or turn pale; ex-pal-lesco (inch.), to grow or turn very pale; pal-lĭdus, *pallid, pale,* [*fallow*]; pal-lor, paleness, *pallor;* pul-lus, dark-colored, dusky; pul-lātus, clothed in soiled or black garments; līveo (for *plīveo*), to be of a bluish or lead color; līvĭdus, of a leaden color, blue, *livid;* ob-līv-iscor (*ob, liveo,* to have the mind darkened), to forget; **ob-lĭv-io,** forgetfulness, *oblivion;* **oblĭviōsus,** forgetful, *oblivious.*

294. πέλ-λα, a hide, leather; ἐρυσί-πελας (ἐρυθρός, πέλλα), inflammation of the skin, *erysipelas;* ἐπι-πολή, a surface.

pel-lis, a skin, hide (of a beast) whether on the body or taken off, a *pelt,* a *fell.*

295. Greek rt. πεν, want, toil.

πέν-ομαι, to work, toil, be poor or needy; πέν-ης, πεν-ιχρός, poor, needy; πεν-ία, poverty; πεν-έσται, serfs; πόν-ος, work, esp. hard work, toil; πον-έω, to work hard, toil, distress; πον-ηρός, toilsome, troublesome, bad; πεῖν-α, hunger.

pēn-ūria, paen-ūria, want, *penury.*

296. par; par; περ, πορ; **per, por;** pierce, go through, go over, carry over.

περά-ω, to drive right through, to pass through or over; πόρος, a means of passing, a way; πόρ-θμος, a ferry; πορ-εύω, to make to go, to convey, (pass. to be made to go, to go); πορ-ίζω, to carry, to procure; ἔμ-πορ-ος, a passenger, a merchant; ἐμ-πόρ-ιον, a trading-place, *emporium;* ἐμ-πορ-ικός, commercial; πεῖρ-α, a trial, attempt; πειρ-άω, to attempt, [*pirate*]; ἄ-πειρ-ος (ἀ, πεῖρα), without trial or experience of, ignorant of.

por-ta, a gate; **por-tĭcus,** a colonnade, *porch, portico;* **por-tus,** a harbor, *port;* **ex-pĕr-ior,** to try, prove, attempt; **ex-pĕr-ientia,** a trial, *experience;* **ex-pĕr-ĭmentum,** a proof, *experiment;* **pĕr-ĭtus,** experienced, skilful; **pĕr-ĭcŭlum,** trial, danger.

297. πέρᾱ (adv.), beyond; πέρᾱν (adv.), on the other side, across; περαίν-ω, to bring to an end; περαῖος, on the farther or other side; πέρᾰ-τος (adj.), on the farther or opposite side; περά-τη (sc. χώρα), land on the farther or opposite side; πέρας, πεῖραρ, πεῖρας, an end, a goal; ἄ-πειρος (ἀ, πεῖρας, πέρας), ἀ-πειρ-έσιος, (poet. ἀ-περ-είσιος), boundless, immense.

298. περά-ω (orig. identical with No. 296), to export beyond sea for sale, to sell; πι-πρά-σκω (shortened from πι-περά-σκω, reduplicated from περάω), to sell (often in pass., to be sold, esp. for exportation); πέρ-νημι (poet. mostly Ep. for πιπράσκω), to export for sale, to sell; πρί-αμαι, to buy; πρᾶ-σις, a selling, sale; πρα-τήρ, πρα-τίας, a seller; πόρ-νη, a prostitute.

299. περί (prep.), round, about, all around; περί (adv.), around, above, exceedingly, very; περί (in comp.), around, above, very; πέριξ (strengthened for περί), round about; περισσός, prodigious, extraordinary; -περ (encl. particle), very much, however much.

per- (before adjectives), very; **per-magnus**, very great.

300. These words are probably connected with No. 293.

πηλός, clay, earth, mud; πήλ-ινος, of clay; προ-πηλακ-ίζω, to bespatter with mud, to treat with contumely.

pă-lus, a swamp.

301. These words are probably connected with No. 295.

πῆνος, πήνη, the woof, (pl.) the web; πην-ίον, the quill or spool on which the bobbin is wound for weaving; πην-ίζομαι, to reel, to weave; πηνῖτις (fem.), the weaver.

pannus, a cloth, a garment; **panus**, the thread wound upon the bobbin in a shuttle.

302. pī; pĭ; πι; pĭ; swell, be fat.

πί-ων, πῑ-ἀρός, πῑ-ερός, πῑ-ἀλέος, fat, plump, (of soil) rich; πῖαρ, πιμελή (subst.), fat; πι-αίνω, to fatten.

opīmus (?), rich.

303. πῖλος, wool or hair wrought into *felt*, anything made of felt, esp. a felt cap.

pilleus, pilleum, pileus, a felt cap or hat.

304. par, pal; par; πλα, πλε; plē; fill.

πί-μ-πλη-μι (inf. πιμ-πλά-ναι), to fill; πλήθω, to be full; πλέ-ος, πλεῖ-ος, πλέ-ως, πλή-ρης, full; πλη-θύς, πλῆ-θος, a throng, a crowd; πλοῦ-τος, wealth.

‡ pleo, to fill, fulfil, (compd. w. com, de, ex, in, ob, re, sub), [*complete, deplete*, (adj.) *replete, supply*]; com-plē-mentum, a *complement*, [*compliment*]; ex-plē-tīvus, serving to fill out, *expletive;* im-plē-mentum, a filling up, [*implement*]; sup-plē-mentum, a supply, a *supplement;* plē-nus, full, [*plenary, replenish*]; plebs, plebes, the common people, the *plebeians;* po-pŭlu-s, a *people*, the people; po-pŭl-āris, of or belonging to the people, *popular;* pūb-lĭcus, (contr. from *pŏpŭlĭcus*, from *pŏpŭlus*), *public;* pūblĭce, on the part of the state; pūb-lĭco, to seize and adjudge to the public use, to confiscate; pūb-lĭcānus (subst.), a tax-gatherer, a *publican;* mănĭ-pŭl-us (*manus, pleo*), a handful, a small handle, a company, a *maniple*, [manipulate].

305. plak; —; πλαγ (for πλακ), πληγ; plag, plang; strike, beat.
πλήσσω (ἐ-πλήγ-ην, ἐξε-πλάγ-ην), to strike; πληγ-ή, a blow; πλάζω, to strike, drive off, make to wander.

plang-o, to strike; plang-or, a striking, beating, lamentation; planc-tus, a striking, beating; plāg-a, a blow; plec-to, to strike.

306. plu; plu; πλυ, πλε, πλεϝ; plu. This root denotes movement in water and of water, under four main heads: float, sail, flow, rain.

πλέ-ω, to sail; πλό-ος, a voyage; πλω-τός, floating, fit for sailing; πλω-τήρ, a sailor; πλύν-ω, to wash; πλύ-μα, water in which something has been washed; πλῠ-τός, washed; πλυν-τήρ, πλῠν-ός, a trough, tank.

plŭ-o (usu. impers.), to rain; plŭv-ius, causing or bringing rain; plŭv-ia, rain; plŭv-iālis, plŭv-iātĭcus, of or belonging to rain; lin-ter, (old Latin, lunter = *plunter*), a boat.

307. pnu, plu; —; πνυ, πνε; plu, pul; blow, breathe.
πνέ-ω, to blow, breathe; πνεῦ-μα, wind, air, breath, spirit; πνευ-ματικός, of or belonging to wind or air, *pneumatic;* πνο-ή, a blowing, a blast; πνεύ-μων, πλεύ-μων, the lungs; πνευ-μονία, a disease of the lungs, *pneumonia;* πέ-πνῡ-μαι (old Epic perf. pass. of πνέω, with pres. sense), to have breath or soul, to be wise; πε-πνυ-μένος, πῐνῠ-τός, wise, discreet; πῐνῠ-τή, under-

standing; ποι-πνύ-ω, to be out of breath, to puff, to bustle about.

pul-mo (= *plu-mon*), a lung, (pl.) the lungs; **pul-moneus,** of or belonging to the lungs, *pulmonic*; **pul-monārius,** pertaining to the lungs, *pulmonary*.

308. pa, pu, po; pâ; πο, πι; po, bi; drink.

πί-νω, to drink; πο-τός (adj.), drunk, for drinking; πο-τόν (subst.), drink; πό-τος, a drinking, a drinking-bout; πό-σις, a drinking, drink; πό-μα, πῶ-μα, a drink; πό-της, a drinker; πο-τήριον, a drinking-cup; πῖ-νον, liquor made from barley, beer; πι-πί-σκω, to give to drink; πῖ-σος (prob. used only in the plural), meadows; πί-σα, πί-στρα, a drinking-trough, drink.

pō-tus, pō-tio, a drinking, a drink, a *potion;* pō-tor, a drinker, a drunkard; pō-to, to drink (usually from passion, habit, etc.), to tipple, (compd. w. e, prae, per); pō-tatio, a drinking, a *potation;* pō-cŭlum, a drinking-vessel, cup, bowl; bĭ-bo, to drink (from natural thirst), (compd. w. com, e, in, per, prae), [*imbibe*]; bĭ-bŭ-lus, drinking readily, *bibulous;* im-bŭ-o (a sort of causative to *imbibo*), to cause to drink in, to fill, to *imbue*.

309. ποι-μήν, a shepherd. This word is to be traced to the root *pa*, meaning protect.

310. pu; pu; ποι; pu; cleanse, purify.

ποι-νή, a penalty; ἄ-ποι-να (pl.), a ransom, recompense, penalty.

pŭ-tus, purified, pure; pŭ-to, (lit. to clean, cleanse, trim, prune, [in this lit. sense very rare]), (very freq. in the trop. sense) to make clear, set in order, reckon, compute, consider; am-pŭ-to, to cut around, to cut off, [*amputate*]; com-pŭ-to, to reckon, *compute;* dē-pŭ-to, to prune, consider, (in late Latin) to destine, allot, [*depute, deputy, deputation*]; dis-pŭ-to, to calculate, consider well, discuss, *dispute;* ex-pŭ-to, to prune, consider well, comprehend; inter-pŭ-to, to prune out here and there; re-pŭ-to, to count over, compute, reflect upon, [*repute, reputation, reputable*]; pŭ-tāmen, prunings, waste; pŭ-tātor, a pruner; **pū-rus,** clean, *pure,* [*puritan*]; **im-pū-rus,** unclean, *impure;* **pū-ri-fĭco** (*purus, facio*), to cleanse, *purify;* **pū-rĭtas,** cleanness, *purity;* **purgo** (contr. for *purĭgo,* from *purum, ago*), to cleanse, *purge;* **ex-purgo,** to purge completely, [*expurgate*]; **pur-gātio,** a cleansing, *purgation;* **pur-gātor,** a cleanser; **purgatorius,** cleansing, purgative, *purgatory;* †**poena,** expiation, *penalty,* [*penal*]; **pū-niǫ,** (arch. from **poe-nio**), to punish; **impūnĭtas,** *impunity;* **pae-niteo** (less correctly **poe-niteo**), to cause to repent, to *repent,* [*penitent*]; **pae-nĭtet** (less correctly **poenĭtet**), it repents one, etc., i.e., I, you, etc., repent; **pae-nitentia,** *repentance, penitence.*

311. This group is related to No. 304.

πόλι-ς, a city; πολί-της, a citizen; πολῑτεία, citizenship, administration, civil *polity,* [*policy, police*]; πολιτικός, civil, *political,* [*politic, politics*]; μητρόπολις (μήτηρ, πόλις), the mother-state, the mother-city, a *metropolis;* κοσμοπολίτης (κόσμος [world], πολίτης), a citizen of the world, a *cosmopolitan.*

312. par, pal; par; πλε; ple; fill (connected with No. 304).

πολύ-ς (by stem πολλο), much, [*poly-,* in compds., e.g., *polysyllable*]; πλε-ί-ων, more, [*pleonasm*]; πλήν, besides.

plūs (= *ple*[*i*]*os*), more, [*plus*]; old Latin form **plous** (= *plo*[*i*]*os*), more; **plū-rĭmus** (= old Latin *plo-irŭmus* = *ploisimus*), very much, (pl.) very many; old Latin **pli-sĭmus** (= *ple-isimus*), very much; **plu-rālis,** relating to more than one, *plural;* **plē-rus,** very many, a very great part; **plē-rusque** (a strengthened form from *plerus*), very many, the most, (rare in sing., freq. in pl.).

313. par; —**; πορ; par;** place, make, perform, do.

ἔ-πορ-ον, brought to pass, gave; πέ-πρω-ται, it has been fated; πορ-σύνω, to offer, prepare.

păr-o(?), to prepare (compd. w. ad, com, prae, re, se), [*prepare, repair, separate*]; **im-pĕr-o**(?), [*in, paro*], to command, [*imperative*]; **im-pĕr-ium**(?), a command, authority, dominion, *empire,* [*imperial*]; **pro-pĕrus,** quick, speedy; **pro-pĕro,** to hasten;

păr-io, to bring forth, to produce; a-pĕr-io (*ab, pario*), (lit. to get from), to uncover, to open; o-pĕr-io (*ob, pario*), (lit. to get for, put upon), to cover, conceal; păr-ens, a *parent;* par-tŭrio (desid.), to desire to bring forth, to bring forth; par-tŭritio, *parturition;* vīpera (*vivus, părio*), (lit. that brings forth living young), a *viper;* pars, a *part,* [*parboil,* (prob. from *part* and *boil*), *partake, partial, partner*]; par-tĭcŭla, a small part, a *particle;* par-tĭcŭlaris, of or concerning a part, *particular;* par-tio, to divide, (compd. w. dis, in); particeps (*pars, capio*), sharing; particeps (subst.), a partaker; participium, a sharing, (in gram.) a *participle;* particĭpo, to share, to *participate;* ex-pers (*ex, pars*), having no part in, destitute of; por-tio, a share, *portion;* por-to (probably belongs here, though by some it is connected with *fĕro*), to carry, (compd. w. abs, ad, com, de, ex, in, prae, re, sub, trans), [*comport, deport, deportment, export, import, report, support, transport*]; pār-ĕo (intrans. form of *păro,* to make ready, and of *pario,* to bring forth; hence, to be ready, be at hand), to come forth, *appear,* appear (as a servant), obey, (compd. w. ad, com), [*apparent*].

314. Indo-Eur. rt. pa; guard, protect.

πόσι-ς (for πότι-ς), a husband; πότ-νια (fem.), revered; δεσ-πότ-ης, a master, a *despot;* δέσ-ποινα, mistress; δεσ-πόσυνος, of or belonging to the master or lord; δεσ-πόζ-ω, to be lord or master.

pŏt-is, powerful, able; pŏt-ior, more powerful, preferable; pŏt-ior, to become master of, acquire, possess; com-pos (*com, potis*), partaking of, possessing, sharing in; impos (*in, potis*), not master of, not possessed of; possum (*potis, sum*), to be able, [*possible, power*]; pot-ens, able, powerful, *potent;* pot-entia, might, power, *potency,* [*potential*]; pot-estas, ability, power; ut-pŏte, as namely, inasmuch as.

315. Greek rt. πρα.

πίμ-πρη-μι (inf. πιμ-πρά-ναι), to burn; πρή-θω, to blow up, blow out, blow into a flame, intr. to blow; ἔ-πρη-σεν (Hom.), blew, caused to stream; πρη-δών, an inflammation; πρη-σ-τήρ, a flash of lightning, a hurricane; πρη-μαίνω, to blow hard.

316. pra; pra; προ, πρω, πρι; pra, pro, pri; before.

πρό, before; πρό-τερος (compar.), before (in place, time, or rank); πρῶ-τος (sup. contr. fr. πρότατος), first, foremost; πρό-μος, the foremost man, a chief; πρύ-τανις, a prince, a president; πρίν (= προ-ιν, προ-ιον), before, before that; πρω-ί, early, early in the day; πρώ-ην, lately, day before yesterday; πρό-σσω, πρό-σω, πόρ-σω, πόρρω, forwards, far.

prae (= *pra-i,* loc.), before, [*pre-,* e.g., *predetermine*]; **prae-ter** (*prae,* with the demonstr. suffix *-ter*), past, by, beyond, before; **prae-postĕrus,** the last part foremost, reversed, perverted, *preposterous;* **prae-stō** (adv., a sup. form from *prae*), at hand, ready; **prī-mus,** the first, foremost, [*prime, prim, primer, primitive, primary*]; **princeps** (*primus, capio*), first, chief; **principālis,** first, *principal;* **principātus,** the first place, pre-eminence, dominion; **principium,** a beginning; **prī-or,** former, *prior* (adj.), [*priority, prior* (subst.), *priory*]; **pris-cus** (for *prius-cus,* a comparative form), of or belonging to former times, ancient; **pris-tĭnus** (for *prius-tĭnus,* a comparative form), former, *pristine;* **prī-dem,** a long time ago, long since; **prī-die,** on the day before; **pran-dĭum** (Sk. *pra*), a late breakfast, luncheon, a meal; **pran-deo,** to take breakfast, to eat; **pran-sus,** that has breakfasted or fed; **pran-sor,** one that eats breakfast, a guest; **prō** (perhaps old abl. form, of which *prae* is the loc.) (adv.), according, just as; **prō** (prep.), before, in front of, for; **prŏ-pĕ,** adv. and prep. (*pro* and dem. suffix *-pe*), near, nearly; **prŏ-pior** (adj. compar. from obs. *propis*), nearer; **proxĭmus** (proxŭmus), nearest, next, [*proximate, proximity*]; **prŏpĕ-diem,** at an early day, very soon; **prŏpĕ-modum, prŏpĕ-mŏdo** (*prope, modus*), nearly, almost; **prŏ-pĭtius,** favorable, *propitious;* **prŏ-pĭtio,** to *propitiate;* **prŏ-pinquus,** near, neighboring, related; **prŏ-pinquĭtas,** nearness, *propinquity,* relationship; **propter** (contr. for *propĭter*), (adv.) near, (prep.) near, on account of; **proprius**(?), one's own, *proper;* **prō-nus,** turned forward, bending down, *prone;* **prūīna** (for *provīna*), (the thing belonging to the early morning), hoar-frost; **por-ro,** forward, further on; **rĕciprŏcus**(?) (perhaps from *reque proque*, back and forth), turning back the same way, alternating, *reciprocal*.

317. προ-τί (πο-τί), πρό-ς (πό-ς), (w. gen.) from, (w. dat.) by, (w. acc.) to; προσ-θε(ν), (adv.), before.

po (old Latin prep. **port**), insep. prep., a prefix denoting power or possession, or that renders emphatic the meaning of a verb; **polleo** (*po, valeo*), to be strong; **pollĭceor** (*port, liccor*), (lit. to bid or offer largely), to offer, promise; **pos-sĭdeo** (*port, sĕdeo*), to be master of, *possess;* **possīdo** (causat. of *possideo*), to take possession of; **pō-nŏ** (for *posno, posĭno,* from *port, sĭno*), to put or set down, to place, (compd. w. ante, ad, circum, com, contra, de, dis, ex, in, inter, ob, post, prae, pro, re, se, sub, super, trans), [*positive, position, apposite, apposition, compose, composite, composition, deponent, depose, dispose, expose, impose, interpose, oppose, postpone, prepositive, preposition, propose, proposition, repose, suppose, superpose, superposition, transpose, transposition*].

318. spju, spu; shtiv; πτυ, πυτ; spu; spit.

πτύ-ω, to spit; πτύ-αλον, spittle; πῦτ-ίζω, to spit frequently, spurt; ψύττ-ω, to spue.

spŭ-o, to *spit, spew, spue*, (compd. w. com, de, ex, in, re); spu-tum (subst.), spit, spittle; **spŭ-ma,** foam, *spume;* **spu-mĕus, spu-mĭdus,** foaming; **spŭ-mo,** to foam, to cause to foam; **pĭtu-ĭta** (*pitu = sputu*), slime, phlegm, *pituite*.

319. pu; pu; πυ; pu; rot, stink, be foul.

πύ-θω, to make to rot; πύ-θο-μαι, to rot; πυ-θεδών, putrefaction; πύ-ον, pus.

pūs, *pus;* **pū-rŭlentus,** full of pus, *purulent;* **sup-pū-ro** (*sub, pus*), to form pus, *suppurate;* **pū-tor,** a stench, rottenness; **pū-teo,** to stink, to be rotten; **pū-tĭdus,** stinking, rotten; **pŭ-ter pŭ-tris,** stinking, rotten; **pŭ-trĭdus,** rotten, *putrid;* **pŭ-treo,** to be rotten; **pŭ-tresco** (inch.), to grow rotten, putrefy; **pŭtre-făcio,** to make rotten, (pass.) *putrefy*.

320. pug; —; πυγ; pug; strike, thrust, prick.

πύξ (adv.), with clenched fist; πύκ-της, πυγ-μάχος, a boxer; πυγ-μή, a fist.

pu-n-g-o (pf. *pŭ-pŭg-i*), to prick, puncture, (compd. w. com, ex, inter, re), [*pungent, compunction, expunge*]; punc-tus, a puncture, a *point*, [*punctilious, punctual, punctuate*]; pŭg-io, a dagger; pug-nus, a *fist;* pŭg-il, a boxer, *pugilist;* pug-na, a fight, a battle; pug-no, to fight, (compd. w. de, ex, in, ob, pro, re), [*impugn, repugnant*]; pug-nax, fond of fighting, contentious, *pugnacious.*

321. πῦρ, *fire;* πῠρ-ετός, burning heat, fever; πυρ-ά, a funeral-pile, a *pyre;* πυρ-σός, a firebrand; πυρρό-s, flame-colored.

prū-na, a burning or live coal.

322. pu; pô, pu; —; pu; beget.

πῶλο-s, a *foal*, a *filly*, a young animal; πωλ-ίον (dim.), a pony; ποιέ-ω(?), to make; παῖς(?), a child, son, daughter; παιδ-αγωγός(?) (παῖς, ἄγω), a trainer and teacher of boys, [*pedagogue, pedant*].

pŭ-er, a child, a boy, a girl; pŭ-ĕra, girl; pu-ella (dim. fr. *pŭ-ĕra*), a girl; pŭ-ĕrĭlis, childish, *puerile;* pŭ-eritia, childhood; pū-pus, a boy, a child; pū-pillus (dim.), an orphan boy, a ward, [*pupil*]; pū-pa (puppa), a girl, a doll, a *puppet;* pū-pilla (dim.), an orphan girl, a ward, the *pupil* of the eye; pū-sus, a boy, a little boy; pŭ-sillus (dim.), very little; pŭ-sillanimis (*pusillus, animus*), of small spirit, *pusillanimous;* pū-bes, pū-ber, pū-bis, of ripe age, adult; pū-bertas, the age of maturity, *puberty;* pullus, a young animal, a young fowl, [*pullet*].

323. spar, sphar, spur, spal, sphal, pal; sphar, sphur; σπαρ, σπαλ, παλ; **sper, spur, pal, pul, pol.**

The fundamental meaning of the root is that of a quick movement, especially, 1. with the feet (whence the meaning, to spurn) and 2. with the hands (whence the meanings, to scatter, strew, shake, lift).

σπαίρ-ω, ἀ-σπαίρ-ω, to pant, gasp, struggle convulsively; σπείρ-ω, to sow seed, to scatter like seed, to strew; σπαρ-άσσω, to tear, to rend in pieces; πα-σπάλ-η, παι-πάλ-η, the finest meal; πάλ-η, the finest meal, any fine dust; πάλ-λω, to shake, to quiver, to swing; παλ-άσσω, to besprinkle, (in pf. pass.) of men drawing lots, because these were shaken in an urn; πάλ-ύνω, to strew or sprinkle upon; πᾶλ-ος, the lot (cast from a shaken helmet); παλ-μός, a quivering motion, pulsation.

sper-n-o, to sever, reject, despise, *spurn*, [*spur*]; **a-spern-or** (*ab, spernor*), to reject, despise; **sprē-tio**, contempt; **sprē-tor**, a despiser; **spŭr-ius**, illegitimate, *spurious;* **păl-ĕa**, chaff; **pul-vis**, dust; **pul-vĕro**, to scatter dust, [*pulverize*]; **pul-verŭlentus**, full of dust, dusty; **pollen, pollis**, fine flour, fine dust.

324. svap; svap; ὑπ; sop; sleep.

ὕπ-νος (for σύπ-νος), sleep; ὑπ-νόω, to put to sleep, to sleep; ὑπ-νωτικός, inclined to sleep, putting to sleep, *hypnotic*.

sŏp-or (= *svop-or*), sleep; **sŏp-ōrus**, causing sleep, *soporous, soporiferous, soporific;* **sŏp-io, sŏp-ōro**, to put to sleep; **som-nus** (= *sop-nus*), sleep; **som-nium**, a dream; **som-nio**, to dream; **som-nĭ-fer**, sleep-bringing, *somniferous;* **somni-fĭcus**, causing sleep, *somnific;* **somnŭlentus, somnŏlentus**, full of sleep, *somnolent;* **in-som-nis**, sleepless; **in-som-nia**, sleeplessness; **in-som-nium**, a dream, sleeplessness.

325. ὑπέρ, ὑπείρ, *over;* ὕπερθεν, from above; ὕπερος, ὕπερον, pestle; ὑπέρα, upper rope.

sŭper, above, over; **in-sŭper**, above, moreover; **sŭpernus, sŭperus**, upper, celestial, *supernal;* **sŭpĕrior**, higher, *superior;* **suprēmus**, highest, *supreme;* **summus** (from *sup-ĭmus, sup-mus*), highest, [*summit*]; **sum-ma** (sc. *res*), the summit, the main thing, the *sum;* **sūprā**, above, before; **sŭp-ĕro**, to go over, to overcome, surpass; **sŭperbus**, haughty, magnificent, *superb;* **con-summo**, to sum up, finish, *consummate*.

326. ὑπό, ὑπαί, under, [*up*]; ὕπτιος (= supīnus), laid back.

sub, under; **subter**, below, beneath; **sŭpīnus**, bent back, upturned, *supine;* **sursum** (*sub-vorsum*), from below, upwards, on high.

B

b; b; β; b. The correspondence here shown is found in but few instances.

327. βάρβαρος, *barbarous*, i.e., not Greek, foreign; βαρβαρίζω, to behave or speak like a barbarian or foreigner.

†barbărus, foreign, *barbarous* (opp. to Greek or Roman); balbus, stammering; balbutio, to stammer.

328. βλη-χή, a bleating; βληχ-άς, a bleating sheep; βληχάομαι, to *bleat*.

bālo, to *bleat*; bālātus, a bleating.

329. βολβό-ς, a bulbous root.

bulbus, a *bulb*, an onion; bulbōsus, *bulbous*.

330. bargh, bhrag; barh; βραχ; —; tear, tear off, torn off, short.

βραχ-ύς, short; βράχ-εα, shallows; βραχ-ύτης, shortness; βρᾰχ-ύνω, to abridge, shorten.

Φ

bh; bh; φ; f and (in the middle of a word) b.

331. arbh, rabh, labh; rabh; ἀλφ; lab; lay hold of, work. The root ἀλφ- is probably akin to λαβ-, λαφ-.

ἀλφ-άνω, to bring in, yield, earn; ἀλφ-εσίβοιος, bringing in oxen; ἀλφ-ή, ἄλφ-ημα, produce, gain.

lăb-or, lăb-os, *labor;* lăb-ōro, to *labor*, strive, (compd. w. ad, e, in), [*elaborate*]; lăb-oriōsus, full of labor, *laborious*.

332. ἀλφό-ς, a dull-white leprosy.

albus, white (prop. a dead white, not shining); albātus, clothed in white; albūmen, the white of an egg, *albumen;* albeo, to be white; albesco (inch.), to become white; Alba, Alba Longa, the mother-city of Rome; Albānus, *Alban;* Alpes, the *Alps* (from the whiteness of their snowy summits).

333. ἀμφί, on both sides, about; ἀμφίς, on both sides, apart; δι-αμφί-διος, utterly different.

ambi, amb-, am-, an-, (prep. used only in compos.), around, round about; **am-plus** (prob. from *am* and *plus*, akin to *pleo*, full all round), large, *ample;* **am-plio,** to enlarge; **am-plifico,** to enlarge, *amplify;* **annus** (for *am-nus*, that which goes around), a year; **annuus,** that lasts a year, that returns every year, yearly, *annual;* **biennis, biennālis,** lasting two years, [*biennial*]; **biennium,** a period of two years; **triennium,** the space of three years, [*triennial*]; **annālis,** relating to the year or age; **annāles** (sc. *libri*), a historical work in which the occurrences of the year are chronologically recorded, *annals;* **anniversārius** (*annus, verto*), that returns every year, yearly, *anniversary;* **annōna,** the yearly produce, means of subsistence, grain; **annōsus,** of many years, old; **perennis** (*per, annus*), that lasts the whole year through, everlasting, *perennial;* **sollemnis** (less correctly **solemnis, sollennis, solennis, sollempnis**), (*sollis*, i.e. *totus, annus*), (esp. in religious language, of solemnities), yearly, established, *solemn,* customary; **ānŭlus,** a ring; **anulāris,** relating to a signet-ring, [*annular*]; **omnis(?),** all, [*omnibus, omni-* (in compos.)].

334. ἄμφω, both; ἀμφό-τερος (more freq. plural or dual), both.

ambo, *both.*

335. nabh; nabh; νεφ; neb, nub; veil, cover.

νέφ-ος, νεφ-έλη, a cloud; συν-νεφ-έω, to collect clouds; συν-νεφ-εῖ, συν-νέ-νοφ-ε, it is cloudy; νεφ-όομαι, to be clouded over.

něb-ŭla, a mist, [*nebular*]; **něb-ŭlōsus,** full of mist or vapor, cloudy, *nebulous;* **nūb-es, nūb-is,** a cloud; **nūb-ĭlus,** cloudy; **nūb-ĭlum,** a cloudy sky; **nūb-ĭlo,** to be cloudy; **nūb-o,** to cover, to veil, to marry; **nūb-ĭlis,** marriageable; **nup-ta,** a bride; **nup-tiae,** marriage, *nuptials;* **co-nūb-ium** (less correctly **connū-bium**), marriage; **co-nūb-iālis** (less correctly **con-nūb-iālis**), pertaining to marriage, *connubial.*

336. ὀρφ-ανό-s, *orphaned,* [*orphan*]; ὀρφ-ανίζω, to make orphan; ὀρφανιστής, one who takes care of orphans; ὀρφ-ανεύω, to take care of orphans.

orb-o, to bereave; orb-us, bereaved; orb-ĭtas, orbĭtūdo, bereavement, orphanhood.

337. ῥοφ-έω, ῥυφ-έω, ῥοφ-άνω, to sup greedily up; ῥόμ-μα, ῥόφ-ημα, thick gruel; ῥοπ-τός, to be supped up.

sorb-eo, to sup up, to drink down, (compd. w. ab, ex, ob, per, re), [*absorb*]; sorb-illo (dim.), to sip; sorb-ĭtio, a drinking, a drink.

338. Greek rt. ὐφ.

ὑφ-ή, a weaving, a *web;* ὗφ-ος, a web; ὑφ-αίνω, ὑφ-άω, to *weave.*

339. bha, bha-n, bha-s, bha-v, bha-k, bha-d; bha; φα, φαν, φαF; fa, fa-n, fa-s, fa-v, fa-c, fa-t; bring to light, make known, declare, say.

Rt. φα. φη-μί, φά-σκ-ω, to declare, make known, say, affirm; φά-τις, φή-μη, a voice, saying, report; φω-νή, voice, sound, language, [*phonics, phonetic, phonography, phonology, phonotype, -phone* in compounds (e.g., *telephone,* from τῆλε, far off, and φω-νή)].

Rt. φαν. φαίν-ω, to bring to light, to show, to shine, [*phenomenon*]; φαν-τάζω, to make visible, (pass. to become visible, appear); φάν-τασμα, an appearance, *phantom, phantasm, fantasm;* φαν-ταστικός, able to represent, [*fantastic*]; φαν-τᾰσία, a making visible, an appearance, [*fancy*]; φᾰν-ερός, visible, evident; φᾰν-ή, a torch; φά-σις, information, appearance, a saying; φά-σ-μα, an apparition, a vision.

Rt. φαF. φά-ε (= φάFε, Hm.), appeared; ὑπό-φαυσις, a small light showing through a hole, a narrow opening; φά-ος, φῶς, φέγγ-ος, light, [*photo-* in compds., e.g., *photograph*]; φα-έθω, to shine; Φᾰ-έθων, son of Helios and Clymene, famous in later legends for his unlucky driving of the sun-chariot, [*phäcton*]; φα-είνω, to shine, to bring to light; φαει-νός, shining; φᾱ-νός, light, bright; πι-φαύ-σκω, to show.

Rt. fa. for (inf. fā-ri), to speak, say, (compd. w. ad, ex, inter, prae, pro); af-fā-bĭlis (better adf.), that can be easily spoken to, *affable;* prae-fā-tio, (lit. a speaking beforehand), a *preface;* fā-tum, a prophetic declaration, destiny, *fate;* fā-ma, report, reputation, *fame;* in-fā-mia, *infamy;* in-fā-mis, ill spoken of, *infamous;* in-fā-mo, to defame; dif-fā-mo, to spread abroad, to publish; fā-mōsus, much talked of (well or ill), *famous,* infamous; fā-num, a place dedicated to some deity by forms of consecration, a temple, a *fane;* fā-no, to dedicate; fā-nātĭcus, of or belonging to a temple, inspired by a divinity, enthusiastic, frantic, [*fanatic*]; pro-fā-nus (*pro, fānum,* prop. before the temple, i.e., outside of it; hence opp. to the temple as a sacred object), unholy, not sacred, common, *profane;* fā-bŭla, a story, a *fable;* fā-bŭlōsus, *fabulous;* fā-cundus, eloquent; fā-cundia, eloquence; in-fans, that cannot speak, not yet able to speak, *infant,* [*infantry*]; infandus, unutterable, abominable; ne-fandus, (not to be mentioned), execrable.

Rt. fa-n. fĕn-estra, a window,

Rt. fa-s. fas, that which is right, divine law; ne-fas, that which is contrary to divine law; fas-tus, a day on which judgment could be pronounced; nĕ-fas-tus (*dies*), a day on which judgment could not be pronounced, irreligious, inauspicious; nĕ-fārius, execrable, *nefarious.*

Rt. fa-v. făv-illa, hot cinders or ashes; făv-eo (?), to *favor.*

Rt. fa-c. fax, a torch; făc-ies, form, appearance, *face;* super-fĭc-ies, the upper side, *surface, superficies;* super-fĭc-iālis, of or belonging to the surface, *superficial;* făc-ētus, elegant, polite, *facetious;* făc-ēte, elegantly, pleasantly, *facetiously;* făc-ētiae, witty sayings.

Rt. fa-t. făt-eor, to confess; con-fĭt-eor, to acknowledge fully, to *confess;* pro-fĭt-eor, to declare publicly, to *profess;* in-fĭt-ior, not to confess, to deny; confessio, a *confession;* professio, a public acknowledgment, a *profession;* prŏfessor, a public teacher, *professor,* one who makes instruction in any branch a business.

340. Greek rt. φαγ.

φαγ-εῖν, to eat; φαγ-άς, glutton.

341. bhar; —; φαρ; for; bore, pierce, tear.

φάρ-ος, a plough; φαρ-όω, to plough; ἄ-φαρ-ος, ἀ-φάρ-ωτος, unploughed; φάρ-σος, a piece cut off or severed; φάρ-αγξ, a mountain-cleft or chasm, a ravine; φάρ-υγξ, the throat.

fŏr-o, to *bore*, to pierce, (compd. w. per, trans), [*perforate*]; fŏr-āmen, an opening or aperture produced by boring, a hole.

342. —; bhi; φεβ; —; fear.

φέβ-ομαι, to flee affrighted; φόβ-ος, flight, panic fear; φοβ-έω, to put to flight, to terrify; φοβ-έομαι, to be put to flight, to flee affrighted; φοβ-ερός, fearful (act. or pass.), causing fear, feeling fear.

343. Greek rt. φεν, φα, kill.

Aor. ἔ-πε-φν-ον, killed; φα-τός, slain; φόν-ος, φον-ή, murder; φον-εύς, a murderer; ἀνδρ-ει-φόν-της, man-slaying; φόν-ιος, φοίν-ιος, bloody.

344. bhar; bhar; φερ; fer; bear. The meanings of these words may be grouped under three main classes: 1. to bear a burden; 2. to bear (with reference to the effect, the produce, and so), to bring forth; 3. to bear (considered as a movement).

φέρ-ω, φορ-έω, to *bear*, [*birth, bairn*]; φέρ-μα, that which is borne, a load, a burden, fruit; φέρ-ετρον, a bier, a litter; φαρ-έτρα, a quiver; φώρ, one who carries off, a thief; φόρ-ος, that which is brought in, tribute; φορ-ός, bearing; φορ-ά, a carrying, motion, a load; φορ-μός, a basket, a mat; φόρ-τος, a load; φερ-νή, a dowry.

fĕr-o, to bear, (compd. w. ad, ante, circum, com, de dis, ex, in, intro, ob, per, post, prae, pro, re, sub, super, trans), [*circumference, confer, conference, defer, deference, differ, infer, inference, offer, prefer, preference, proffer, refer, reference, referable, referrible, suffer, sufferance, transfer*]; fer-tus, fĕr-ax, fer-tĭlis, *fertile;* fer-tilĭtas, *fertility;* fer-cŭlum, that on which anything is carried, a frame, a litter; fors, (whatever brings itself, i.e., happens, occurs), chance; **fors-an** (ellipt. for *fors sit an*), **forsĭtan** (contr. from *fors sit an*), **fortasse, fortassis** (*forte an si vis*), perhaps; **for-tūna** (lengthened from *fors*), chance, *fortune;* **for-tŭĭtus,** casual, *fortuitous;* **far,** a sort of grain, spelt; **far-rāgo,** mixed fodder for cattle, mash, a medley, hodge-podge, *farrago;* **făr-ĭna,** meal, flour, *farina;* **fūr,** a thief; **fur-tum,** theft; **fur-tīvus,** stolen, secret, *furtive;* **fur-tim,** by stealth; **fūr-or,** to steal.

345. bhal, bhla, bhlu; —; φλα, φλαδ, φλε, φλι, φλιδ, φλυ, φλυδ, φλυγ; fla, flo, flu, fle; bubble over, overflow, blow, swell, flow.

a. Rt. φλα. ἐκ-φλαίν-ω, to burst or stream forth. Rt. φλαδ. ἔ-φλαδ-ον, rent with a noise; φλασ-μός, empty boasting; πα-φλάξ-ω, to boil, to foam.

Latin rt. **fla. flo,** to blow, (compd. w. ad, circum, com, de, dis, ex, in, per, pro, re, sub), [*blow, inflate*]; **flā-tus,** a blowing, a breeze; **flā-men,** a blowing, a blast; **flā-bra,** blasts; **flos,** a flower, [*bloom*]; **flō-reo,** to *bloom,* to *flower,* to *blow,* to *flourish;* **flō-resco** (inch.), to begin to blossom, (compd. w. de, ex, prae, re), [*efflorescence*]; **Flō-ra,** the goddess of flowers, [*floral*].

b. Rt. φλε. φλέ-ω, to swell, overflow; φλέ-δων, an idle talker; φλήν-ᾰφος, idle talk.

c. Rt. φλι. Φλί-ᾱς, son of Dionysus. Rt. φλιδ. φλιδ-άω, to overflow with moisture.

d. Rt. φλυ. φλύ-ω, φλύ-ζω, to boil over, to overflow with words; φλύ-ος, φλύ-αρος, idle talk; φλυ-ᾱρέω, to talk nonsense, to play the fool; φλύ-αξ, a jester. Rt. φλυδ. ἐκ-φλυδ-άνειν, to break out (of sores); φλυδ-άω, to have an excess of moisture. Rt. φλυγ. οἰνό-φλυξ, given to drinking wine; φλύκ-τις, φλύκ-ταινα, a blister.

Latin rt. **flu. flu-o,** to *flow,* to overflow, (compd. w. ad, circum, com, ex, in, inter, per, prae, praeter, pro, re, subter, super), [*fluent, affluent, affluence, circumfluent, confluent, confluence, effluent, effluvium, efflux, influence, influx, refluent, reflux, superfluous*]; **flŭ-ĭto** (freq.), to flow, float; **flu-ēsco** (inch.), to become fluid; flū-men, a stream, a river; flu-ĭdus, flowing, *fluid;* fluc-tus, a flowing, a wave, a billow; fluc-tuo, to move to and fro, to *fluctuate;* fluv-ius, a river, [*flue*]; flux-us, flowing, loose, careless; flux-us (subst.), a flowing, a *flux;* fle-o (= *flev-o*), to weep, (compd. w. ad, de); flē-tus, a weeping, lamentation.

e. St. φλοι. φλοί-ω, to burst out, to swell; φλοι-ός, φλο-ός, the inner bark of trees. St. φλοιδ. φλοιδ-έω, to have an excess of moisture; φλοῖσ-βος, any confused, roaring noise, as of a large mass of men, or of the sea.

346. bhark, bhrak; —; φρακ; farc, frequ; press hard, shut up fast, cram.

φράσσ-ω, to fence in, to secure; φράγ-μα, a fence, protection; φραγ-μός, a shutting up, a fence; δρύ-φακ-τος (δρύ-φρακ-τος), a partition.

farc-io, to stuff; con-ferc-io, to stuff or cram together; con-fertus, pressed close, crowded; re-ferc-io, to fill up, to cram; rĕ-fef-tus, stuffed, crammed; frequ-ens, repeated, *frequent;* frequ-ento, to visit frequently, to repeat; frequ-entia, a throng.

347. φράτρα, φράτρη, φρήτρη, φρᾱτρία, a brotherhood, a clan, a political division of the people; φράτηρ, φράτωρ, a member of a φράτρα; φρατρ-ίζω, φρατρι-άζω, to belong to the same φράτρα.

frā-ter, a brother; frā-ternus, brotherly, *fraternal;* frā-ternĭtas, brotherhood, *fraternity.*

348. bhu; bhû; φυ; fu, fo, fe; grow, become, be.

φύ-ω, to bring forth, to beget; φύ-ομαι (pass.), to grow, to spring forth, to come into being, [*be, boor*]; φυ-ή, growth; φŭ-σις, nature; φŭ-σικός, natural, *physical,* [*physics, physic, physician, physiognomy, physiology*]; φῦ-μα, a growth; φυ-τός, shaped by nature, fruitful; φŭ-τεύω, to plant, to beget; φῦ-λον, φῦ-λή, a race, a clan; φί-τῡμα (= φύ-τῡμα) (poet. φῖ-τυ), a shoot, a scion; φῑ-τύω (= φυ-τύω), to plant, to beget; φι-τύομαι (mid.), to bear.

fu-ăm, fu-ās, fu-ăt, fu-ant, for *sim, sis, sit, sint;* fu-ī, I have been; fŭ-tū-rŭs, about to be, *future;* fŏ-rĕm, fŏ-rēs, fŏ-rĕt, fŏ-rent, for *essem, esses, esset, essent;* fŏ-rĕ, for *futurus esse;* fē-tus, foe-tus, a bearing, offspring, fruit; fē-to, foe-to, to breed; ef-fē-tus, that has brought forth young, exhausted, worn out by bearing, [*effete*]; fē-cundus, fruitful; fē-cundĭtas, fruitfulness, *fecundity;* fē-cundo, to make fruitful, to *fecundate;* fē-lix, fruitful, favorable, happy; fē-lĭcĭtas, fruitfulness, happiness, *felicity;* fē-lĭcĭter, fruitfully, happily; fae-num (less correctly fē-num), hay; fae-nus (less correctly fē-nus), the proceeds of capital lent out, interest; fae-nĕror (less correctly fēn, foen), to lend on interest; fae-nĕrator (less correctly fēn, foen), a money-lender.

349. φύλλον (= φύλ-ιον), a leaf.

folĭum, a leaf, [*foliage, foil* (a leaf or thin plate of metal)]. These words are identical in their origin, and may be from the root shown in 345, *d*, or from that in 348.

N

n; n; v; n.

350. an; an; αν; an; breathe, blow.

ἄν-εμος, wind.

ăn-ĭma, air, breath, the animal life, the animal principle of life; ăn-ĭmus, the rational soul in man (in opp. to the body, *corpus*, and to the physical life, *anima*), the mind; ăn-ĭmo, to fill with breath or air, to *animate;* ex-ăn-ĭmo, to deprive of life or spirit, to terrify greatly; ăn-ĭmātio, a quickening, [*animation*]; ăn-ĭmatus, *animated;* ăn-ĭmōsus (fr. *anima*), full of air or life; ăn-ĭmōsus (fr. *animus*), full of courage; ăn-ĭmōsĭtas, boldness, vehemence, enmity, *animosity;* ăn-ĭmal, a living being, an *animal*.

351. ἀνα-, ἀν-, ἀ-, a negative prefix, Eng. *un-*, *in-*, *im-*, not; ἄνευ, without.

in-, an inseparable negative prefix, Eng. un-, *in-*, *im-*, not; in-tŏlĕrābĭlis, unbearable, *intolerable*.

352. ἀνά, up, upon, *on;* ἄνω (adv.), up, upward.

an-hēlo (*an, halo*), to draw breath up, to breathe with difficulty, to pant.

353. γένυ-ς, the under jaw, the cheek, the *chin*, an edge; γέν-ειον, the chin; γνά-θος, γναθ-μός, the jaw, an edge.

gĕn-a, a cheek (more freq. in pl. gĕn-ae, the cheeks).

354. nak; naç; ἐνεκ (the initial ε is a vowel prefix); **nac;** reach, obtain, carry away.

ἠνέχ-θην, ἐν-ήνοχ-α, ἤνεγκ-ον, ἤνεγκ-α, carry; δουρ-ηνεκ-ές, a spear's throw or distance off; δι-ηνεκ-ής, continuous; ποδ-ηνεκ-ής, reaching down to the foot; ἠνεκ-ής, bearing onward, far-stretching.

nanc-i-sc-or (pf. pt. nac-tus), to obtain, to find.

355. ἐν (poet. ἐνί, εἰν, εἰνί), in, (in some dialects, also) into; εἰς, ἐς, (= ἐνι-ς, ἐν-ς), into, to; ἐν-τός, ἔν-δον, within; εἴσ-ω, ἔσ-ω (= ἔν-σω), adv., to within, into, within; ἔν-εροι (= Lat. inferi), those below, those beneath the earth (used of the dead or of the gods below); ἔνερ-θε, from beneath, beneath; ὑπ-ένερθε, beneath; ἐνέρ-τερος, deeper; ἔν-τερον (usu. in pl. ἔν-τερα), inward parts, intestines, *entrails*.

in (old form endŏ, indŭ), *in*, into; in-ter, between, among, [*under*]; interim, adv. (*inter* and old acc. of *is*), meanwhile, [*interim*]; intrā (contr. from intĕrā, sc. *parte*), on the inside, within; intrō, adv. (contr. from intĕro, sc. *loco*), inwardly, to the inside; in-tĕrior, inner, *interior;* in-tĭmus, inmost, [*intimate*]; in-tus (*in* and the abl. termination *-tus*), on the inside, to the inside, from within; intestīnus, internal, *intestine*.

356. ἐννέα, nine; ἔνατος, ἔννατος, (poet. εἴνατος), ninth; ἐνάκις, ἐννάκις, nine times; ἐνακόσιοι, ἐννακόσιοι, nine hundred; ἐνενήκοντα (Hom. ἐννήκοντα), ninety.

nŏvem, *nine;* nōnus (for *novenus,* fr. *novem*), the ninth; nōnānus, of or belonging to the ninth legion; nŏvies, noviens, nine times; nōnāginta, ninety; non-genti, nine hundred; Nŏvember, the ninth month of the old Roman year, *November;* Nōnae, the *Nones,* the ninth day before the Ides; nŏvendiālis, that lasts nine days; nundĭnae (sing. nundĭna), the ninth day.

357. ἕνο-ς, ἕνη, belonging to the former of two periods, old.
sĕn-ex, old; sĕn-ior, older, [*senior, sire, sir*]; sĕn-ex (subst.), an aged person; sĕn-ectus (adj.), aged, very old; sĕn-ecta, sĕn-ectus, old age; sĕn-īlis, of or belonging to old people, *senile;* sĕn-ium, the feebleness of age; sĕn-eo, to be old, to be feeble; sĕn-esco (inch.), to grow old, (compd. w. com, in); sĕn-ātor, a *senator;* sĕn-ātus, the council of the elders, the *Senate.*

358. ma, ma-d, ma-dh, ma-n, mna; man; μεν, μαν; man, men. The meanings of this root have taken three main directions: 1. Thought accompanied by effort, striving. 2. Excited thought: hence, (*a*) to be inspired, raving, wrathful; (*b*) to remain (as one engrossed in thought stands still). 3. To keep in mind, remember, (causatively) to remind.

μέν-ω, to remain; μέ-μον-α (pl. μέμαμεν), to wish, to strive; μέν-ος, might, strength, spirit, courage; Μέν-τωρ, *Mentor,* [*mentor*]; Μέν-της; ’Αγα-μέμνων; μαίν-ομαι, to rage, to rave; μαν-ία, madness, *mania,* [*maniac*]; μάν-τις, one who divines, a seer; μῆν-ις, wrath. St. μνα. μέ-μνη-μαι, to remember; μνά-ομαι, to keep in mind, to think much of, to woo to wife; μνησ-τήρ, μνησ-τής, a wooer, a suitor; μνησ-τεύω, to woo; μι-μνή-σκω, to remind (mid. and pass. to call to mind, to remember); μνή-μη, μνη-μοσύνη, memory, [*mnemonic*]. St. μαθ. μανθ-άνω (2 aor. ἔ-μαθ-ον), to learn; μαθ-ηματικός, disposed to learn, of or for the sciences, esp. *mathematical;* ἡ μαθ-ηματική (with or without ἐπιστήμη), *mathematics.* St. μηνυ. μηνύ-ω, to reveal, inform.

măn-eo, to stay, to remain, (compd. w. com, e, per, ob, re), [*permanent, remain*]; man-sĭto (freq.), to remain, to dwell; man-sio, a staying, a place of abode, a *mansion;* mĕ-mĭn-i, to remember, [*mind* (vb.), *mean* (vb.)]; com-mĕmĭni, to recollect a thing in all its particulars; com-min-iscor, to devise something by careful thought; re-min-iscor, to recall to mind, to recollect, [*reminiscence*]; com-men-tum, an invention, a contrivance; com-men-tor, to study thoroughly, to contrive, to *comment* upon; com-men-tārius, com-men-tārium, a note-book, a *commentary;* men-tio, a calling to mind, a mentioning, *mention;* Min-erva, *Minerva;* mens, the *mind,* [*mental*]; a-mens, out of one's senses, frantic; de-mens, out of one's mind, raving, foolish, *demented;* vĕhĕ-mens, vē-mens, (vē, mens), (lit. not having mind, unreasonable), violent, *vehement;* men-tior, (to form in the mind, hence in a bad sense), to lie, (compd. w. com, ex, prae, sub); men-dax, given to lying, *mendacious;* mŏn-ĕo, to remind, to admonish, (compd. w. ad, com, e, prae, sub), [*admonish*]; mon-ĭtor, one who reminds, a *monitor;* ad-mon-itio, a reminding, an *admonition;* mŏn-ĭtus, a reminding, warning; mŏn-ŭmentum (mŏn-ĭmentum), a memorial, a *monument;* mon-strum, a divine omen indicating misfortune, an evil omen, a *monster;* mon-stro, to show, instruct, (compd. w. com, de, prae), [*demonstrate, remonstrate*]; Mŏn-ēta, (the reminding one): 1. The mother of the Muses; 2. A surname of Juno, in whose temple at Rome money was coined; mŏn-ēta, the place for coining money, the *mint, money,* [*monetary*]; mĕd-eor, to heal, to restore; mĕd-ĭcus, of or pertaining to healing, *medical;* mĕd-ĭcus (subst.), a physician; mĕd-ico, to heal; mĕd-ĭcīnus, of or pertaining to a physician; mĕd-ĭcīna, the healing art, *medicine;* rĕ-mĕd-ium, a *remedy,* a relief; mĕd-ĭtor, to think upon, to *meditate,* (compd. w. com, prae), [*premeditate*].

359. ναῦς, a ship; ναύ-της, a sailor; ναυ-τικός, of or for a ship, *nautical;* ναυ-τία, ναυ-σία, sea-sickness, *nausea.*

nāvis, a ship; nāvālis, of or belonging to ships, *naval;* nau-ta (ante-class., poet., and late Lat. nāvĭta), a sailor; nāvĭgo (*nāvis*, *ago*), to sail, to *navigate*. The root of these words is perhaps the same as of No. 370.

360. nam; —; νεμ; nem, num; allot, number, pasture.

νέμ-ω, to distribute, to hold as one's portion, to possess, to hold sway, to pasture; νωμ-άω, to distribute, to govern; νέμ-ησις, a distribution; νομ-ή, a pasture, distribution; νεμ-έτωρ, a dispenser of rights; νομ-εύς, a shepherd, a distributer; νέμ-εσις, righteous indignation, resentment; Νέμ-εσις, Nemesis, the impersonation of divine wrath; νεμ-εσάω, νεμ-εσσάω, to feel righteous indignation; νεμ-εσίζομαι, to be wroth with; νόμ-ος, custom, law; νομ-ίζω, to own as a custom, to acknowledge, consider as; νόμ-ισμα, a custom, the current coin; νέμ-ος, a wooded pasture or glade; Νεμ-έα, a wooded district between Argos and Corinth; νομ-ός, a pasture, a dwelling.

nŭm-ĕrus, a *number;* nŭm-ĕrōsus, *numerous;* nŭm-ĕro, to count, to *number,* (compd. w. ad, com, di, e, per, re, trans), [*numerate, enumerate*]; nŭm-ĕrator, a counter, numberer, the *numerator;* nummus, numus, a piece of money, money; nummārius, numārius, of or belonging to money; nĕm-us, a wood with much pasture-land, a grove.

361. —; nas; νεσ; —; go, return.

νέ-ομαι, to go or come; νίσ-σομαι, to go; νόσ-τος, a return home; νοσ-τέω, to go or come home, to return.

362. The words under this number are probably from the pronominal stem *nu*, No. 368.

νέ-ος (νεϝ-ος), young, *new;* νε-ός, νει-ός, (new land), fallow land; νε-ᾰρός, young, new; νε-ανίας, a youth; νε-οσσός, a young bird, a young animal; νε-οττία, νε-οσσία, a nest; νε-οχμός, new; νε-βρός, a fawn; νέ-ατος, the last, the latest; νε-ωστί, lately; νεί-αιρᾰ, the latter, the lower; Νέ-αιρα, the Younger.

nŏvus, *new;* nŏv-ellus (dim.), new, [*novel*]; nŏv-ĭtas, newness; nŏv-ālis, that is ploughed anew or for the first time; nŏv-o, to make anew, (compd. w. in, re), [*renovate*]; dē-nŭo (contr. from *dē nŏvo,* which never occurs), anew, a second time; nū-per (for *novum-per*), newly, lately; nŏv-erca (for *noverica*, the new one), a step-mother; nŏv-ācŭla, a razor (which gives a new appearance to the face), a knife.

363. νεῦρον, a sinew, cord, nerve, [*neuralgia*]; νευρά, a bow-string.

nervus, a sinew, nerve; nervōsus, sinewy, *nervous*; ē-nervis (*e, nervus*), nerveless, weak; ē-nervo, to *enervate*, to weaken.

364. sna; nah; νε; ne; spin.

νέ-ω, νή-θω, to spin; νῆ-μα, yarn, thread; νῆ-σις, spinning; νῆ-τρον, a spindle.

ne-o, to spin, (compd. w. per, re), [*needle, net*]; nē-tus, a thread, yarn.

365. The words of this group are probably from the pronominal root *na* (Indo-Eur.).

νη-, insep. privative (= negative) prefix, [*nay*].

nĕ (old form nei, nī), (adv.) not, (conj.) that not, lest; -nĕ, interrog. and enclit. particle (weakened from *nē*) throwing emphasis on the word to which it is attached; nĕ-, a negative adverb used in composition, e.g., nĕ-que (= *nec*), nĕ-fas; nec-nĕ, or not; nī-si (= *si, ni*), if not, unless; nī-mīrum, [nī (= *nē*), *mirum*], (not wonderful), doubtless; nōn (probably contracted from *ne, oenum* or *unum*, old form nēnum or noenum), *not, non-* (e.g., *non*-performance), [*no, none*].

366. nig; —; νιγ, νιβ; —; wash.

νίζ-ω, νίπ-τω, to wash (usually said of the washing of a part of the person, while λούομαι is used of bathing); χέρ-νιβα (acc. fr. χείρ, νίζω), water for washing the hands; νίπ-τρον, water for washing.

367. snigh; snih; νιφ; nig, niv (for *nigv*); snow.

νίφ-α (acc.), snow; νιφ-άς, a snow-flake; νιφ-ετός, νίφ-ετος, a snow-storm; νίφ-ει, νείφ-ει, it snows.

nix (gen. *nĭv-is* = *nig-vis*), snow; nĭv-ĕus, nĭv-ālis, snowy; nĭv-ōsus, full of snow; ning-it, ningu-it, it snows.

368. These forms are connected with those of No. 362.

νῦν, now; νῦ-ν-ί (Att. form of νῦν, strengthened by -ῖ demonstrative), now, at this moment; νύν, νυ (postpos. and encl.), a weakened form of νῦν, used to denote sequence or inference, or to strengthen a command or question.

num (an acc. m. of which nam is the acc. f.), an interrog. particle usually implying that a negative answer is expected; nun-c (num and the demonstrative suffix ce, just as tunc from tum and the demonstrative suffix ce), now.

369. nu; —; νυ; nu; nod.

νεύ-ω, to nod, incline; νεῦ-μα, a nod; νεῦ-σις, a nodding, inclination; νευ-στάζω, νυ-στάζω, to nod, to sleep; νυ-στᾰλός, drowsy.

-nŭo (used only in derivatives and in compound words), to nod; ab-nŭo, rĕ-nŭo, to deny, refuse; ad-nuo, annuo, innuo, to nod to, give assent, promise, [innuendo]; nū-tus, a nod, command, will; nū-men, a nod, will, the divine will, a divinity; nū-to (freq.), to nod, to waver; nū-tātio, a nodding, nutation.

370. sna, snu; snu; νυ, σνυ; na, nu; flow, swim.

νέ-ω (for σνέϝω), to swim; νεῦ-σις, a swimming; νευ-στήρ, a swimmer; νά-ω (for σναϝω), to flow; ἀέ-να-ος, ever-flowing.

no, to swim, (compd. w. ad, de, e, in, prae, re, trans); nă-to (freq.), to swim, float, fluctuate, (compd. w. ad, de, e, in, prae, re, super, trans); nū-trio, (lit. to make to flow), to suckle, to nourish; nū-trix, a nurse, [nursery]; nū-trīcius, nūtrītius, that nourishes, [nutritious, nutrition]; nū-trīmentum, nourishment, nutriment.

371. νυός (for σνυσός), a daughter-in-law.

nŭrus (for snusus), a daughter-in-law.

372. na; —; st. νω; —.

νῶ-ϊ, we two.

nōs, we, us.

373. οἴνη, the ace on dice; οἶος, alone, single.

ūnus (old forms *oinus* and *oenos*), one, [*uni-*, e.g., *universal*]; ūnio (subst.), the number one, unity, *union;* ūnio (vb.), to join together, *unite,* [*unit*]; ūnīcus, one and no more, only, only of its kind, *unique*.

374. gan, gna, gno; —; γνο, γνω; gno; perceive, know.

ὄ-νο-μα, (prob. = ὄ-γνο-μα), a name; ὀνοματοποίησις, ὀνοματοποιία, the making of a name or word (esp. to express a natural sound), *onomatopoeia;* ἀν-ώνῠ-μος, ν-ώνῠμος, nameless; ὀνομάζω, ὀνομαίνω, to name.

co-gnō-men, a surname; i-gnō-minia, disgrace, *ignominy;* nō-men (for *gnō-men*), a *name,* [*noun, nomenclature* (*călo,* to call)]; nō-mĭnālis, *nominal;* no-minatīvus, of or belonging to naming, *nominative;* nō-mĭno, to call by name, to name, to *nominate,* (compd. w. co, de, trans), [*denominate, denomination*].

375. ὄνυξ, a claw, a *nail.*

ungu-is, a nail (of a person's finger or toe), a claw, talon; ungu-icŭlus, (dim.), a little nail of the finger; ungŭ-la, a hoof, a claw; ungŭ-latus, having claws or hoofs.

376. ὦνο-ς, price of purchase; ὠνή, a purchasing, purchase; ὠνέ-ομαι, to buy.

vĕn-us, vĕn-um (occurring only in the forms *vĕnui, vĕno,* and *vĕnum*), sale; vĕn-eo [*venum, eo*], (to go to sale), to be sold; vēnālis, of or belonging to selling, purchasable, [*venal*]; ven-do (*venum, do*), to sell, vend, [*vender, vendor, vendee, venduc*].

M

m; m; μ; m.

377. —; —; ἀμ, ὀμ; sim; like.

ἅμ-α, at the same time; ὁμό-ς, one and the same, common; ὁμογενής, of the same race or family, of the same kind, *homogeneous;* ὁμ-οῦ, together; ὁμό-θεν, from the same place;

ὁμό-σε, to one and the same place; ὅμο-ιος, ὅμο-ῖος, like; ὁμοί-ιο-ς, resembling; ὁμοιοπάθεια, likeness of condition or feeling, [*homeopathy, homoeopathy*]; ὁμα-λός, ὁμα-λής, even, level; ὁμα-λίζω, to make even or level.

sĭm-ĭlis, like, *similar;* dis-sĭmĭlis, unlike, *dissimilar;* sĭm-ul (adv.), at the same time, [*simultaneous*]; sim-ultas, dissension, strife; sĭm-ŭlo, sĭm-ĭlo, to imitate, *simulate;* dis-sim-ulo, to *dissemble, dissimulate*, conceal; in-sĭm-ŭlo, to bring a charge against any one; sĭm-ŭlātor, an imitator, a pretender; sĭm-ĭlitūdo, resemblance, *similitude;* sĭm-ŭlācrum, an image, likeness; sim-ĭtu, (old Lat.), at once; sĕm-el, once; sem-per (-*per* = παρά), ever, always; sim-plex (*sim-, plico*), *simple*, uncompounded; sin-gŭli, one to each, *single;* sin-gŭlāris, one by one, single, *singular.*

378. ἀμά-ω, to cut or reap corn; ἄμη-τος, a reaping, a harvest; ἀμη-τός, the crop or harvest gathered in; ἄμαλλα, ἀμάλη, a sheaf.

mĕ-to, to *mow* or reap; mes-sis, a harvest; més-sor, a reaper.

379. mav; mĭv; —; mov; push, push out of place.

ἀ-μείβ-ω (Pind. ἀμεύω), to change; ἀ-μείβ-ομαι, to change one with another, to reply; παρ-αμείβ-ω, to change, pass by, excel; ἀ-μοιβ-ή, compensation, change.

mŏv-eo, to *move*, (compd. w. a, ad, com, de, di, e, ob, per, pro, re, sub, se, trans); mō-bĭlis (for *movibilis*), easy to be moved, *movable, mobile*, [*mob, mobility, mobilize, mutiny*]; mō-mentum (for *mŏvĭmentum*), *movement, momentum*, a *moment* (of time), *moment*, (importance), [*momentous, momentary*]; mō-tio, a moving, *motion*, a removing, [*emotion*]; mō-tus, a moving, motion, disturbance; com-mō-tio, a *commotion;* mū-to (freq. = *mŏvĭto*), to move, to change, (compd. w. com, de, in, per, sub, trans), [*commute, transmute*]; mū-tābĭlis, changeable, *mutable*, [*immutable*]; mū-tŭus, borrowed, lent, in exchange, *mutual.*

380. mu; mu; μυν; mu; bind, enclose, protect.

ἀμύνω, to keep off; ἀμύν-ομαι, to defend one's self; ἀμύν-τωρ, ἀμύν-τηρ, a helper; ἄμυνα, defence; μύν-η, a pretence.

mū-nis, ready to be of service, obliging; **com-mū-nis** (serving together), *common,* [*commune* (subst.)]; **com-mū-nĭco,** (to do or have in common), to *communicate,* impart, share, *commune;* **im-mū-nis** (*in, munis*), exempt from a public service, free from; **im-mū-nĭtas,** exemption from public service, *immunity;* **mū-nia,** (that to which one is bound), duties; **mū-nĭceps** (*munia, capio*), [one undertaking a duty], an inhabitant of a municipium or free town, a citizen; **mū-nĭcĭpĭum,** a free town; **mū-nĭcĭpālis,** of or belonging to a municipium, *municipal;* **mū-nĭfĭcus** (*munus, facio*), liberal, *munificent;* **mū-nus,** a service, duty; **mū-nĕro, mū-nĕror,** to give, bestow; **re-mūnĕror,** to repay, *remunerate;* **mū-nio** (old form **moenio**), to build a wall, to build a wall around, to fortify, (compd. w. circum, com, e, per, prae); **mū-nimentum,** a fortification, [*muniment*]; **mū-nitio,** a fortifying, fortification, [*munition, ammunition*]; **moe-nia,** defensive walls, ramparts; **mū-rus,** a wall; **mū-rālis,** of or belonging to a wall, *mural;* **po-mē-rium, po-moe-rium** (*post, moerus = mūrus*), an open space within and without the walls of a town.

381. vam; vam; ἐμ, Fεμ; vom; vomit.

ἐμ-έω, to vomit; ἔμ-ετος, ἔμ-εσις, a vomiting; ἐμ-ετικός, inducing to vomit, *emetic.*

vŏm-o, to *vomit,* (compd. w. com, e, pro, re); **vŏm-ĭto** (freq.), to vomit often; **vŏm-ĭtus, vŏm-ĭtio,** a vomiting.

382. This number is related to No. 377, since from the idea 'like,' the idea of like parts or halves is naturally developed.

ἡμῐ-, insep. prefix, half-; ἥμῐ-συς, half.

sēmi-, half-, demi-, *semi-;* **sēmi-s,** a half; **sē-lībra** (*semi, libra*), a half-pound; **ses-tertius** (*sēmis, tertius*), a *sesterce,* a small silver coin equal to two and a half asses.

383. mad; mad; μαδ; mad; be wet, flow.

μαδ-αρός, melting away; μαδ-άω, to be moist or wet.

măd-eo, to be moist, wet, or dripping; măd-esco (inch.), to become moist or wet; mădĕ-făcio, to wet, moisten, intoxicate; măd-ĭdus, moist, soaked, intoxicated; mā-no (?) (prob. for *madno*), to flow, run, (compd. w. de, dis, e, per, re).

384. makh; —; μαχ; mac; kill, slaughter.

μάχ-ομαι, to fight; μάχ-η, battle, [*logomachy*, from λόγος, μάχη]; μάχ-ιμος, warlike; πρό-μαχος, fighting before; πρό-μαχος (subst.) a champion; μάχ-αιρα, a knife, a sword.

măc-ellum, meat-market; mac-to, to slaughter (in sacrifice), to slaughter, kill, destroy.

385. ma; ma; με; me; pronom. denoting the first person.
με, ἐμε, me.
me, *me*; me-us, my.

386. ina, mi; mâ; με; ma, me = *mai*, men; measure.

μέ-τρον, a measure, *metre* [-*meter* in compos., e.g., *thermometer* (θερμός, μέτρον)]; με-τρικός, of or for measure or metre, *metrical;* μέ-τριος, within measure, moderate; μῑ-μέ-ομαι, to imitate, *mimic;* μί-μη-σις, imitation, *mimesis;* μῖ-μος, an imitator.

mē-ta (the measuring thing), the goal; mē-to, to measure, mete, survey; mē-tor, to measure, mark off, encamp, traverse; mē-tior, to *measure*, *mete*, mark off, encamp, traverse, (compd. w. de, e, per, re), [*immense*]; men-sūra, a measuring, *measure*, [*mensuration, mensurable, commensurate, commensurable*]; men-sa, a table; nĭ-mis (*ni-*, *ne-*, and root *ma*), beyond measure, too much; mă-nus (as the measurer, feeler, shaper), the hand, [*manual, manufacture, manumit, manuscript*]; mā-nus (old Latin for *bonus*), good; immānis (negative of *mānus*), monstrous, (in size) immense, (in character) frightful, fierce; mā-ne, (in good season), the morning, early in the morning; Mānes, (the good spirits), manes; mos(?) (from this root or from No. 379), (a measuring or guiding rule of life), custom, usage, (in pl. manners, *morals*, character).

387. mag, magh; mah; μεγ; mag; great. From the root *ma* there probably came at an early time three related roots, *mak* (No. 82), *mag*, and *magh*, all three existing together and having the common meaning of extension.

μέγ-ας (by-stem μεγαλο), great, [*mega-* in compos., e.g., *megatherium*, *megalosaurus*]; μεί-ζων (= μεγ-ίων), greater; μεγ-αλύνω, to magnify; μεγ-αίρω, to look at a thing as great or too great, to grudge; μέγ-εθος, greatness.

mag-nus, great; **mag-nitudo,** greatness, *magnitude;* **magnanimus** (*magnus, animus*), great-souled, *magnanimous;* **major** (= *mag-ior*), greater, *major,* [*majority, mayor*]; **maj-estas,** greatness, grandeur, *majesty;* **măg-is,** in a higher degree, more; **măg-ister,** a *master,* [*magisterial*]; **măg-istratus,** *magistracy, magistrate;* **măg-istŏro, măg-istro,** to rule; **mālo** (*măgis, volo*), to wish rather, to choose, prefer.

388. smi; smi; μει; mi; smile, wonder.

μεῖ-δος, μεί-δημα, a smile; μει-δάω, μει-διάω, to *smile*.

mī-ror (to smile upon, i.e., in indication of approval), to *admire*, to wonder at, (compd. w. ad, e); **mī-rābĭlis,** wonderful, *admirable;* **mī-rācŭlum,** (that which causes to wonder), a wonder, a *miracle;* **mī-rus,** wonderful; **nĭ-mī-rum** (*ni, ne, mīrum*), doubtless, certainly.

389. marl; mard (for *marl*); μελλ, μειλ; —; mild.

μείλ-ια, soothing things, propitiations; μείλ-ιχος, gentle, kind; μειλ-ίχιος, gentle, soothing, *mild*, gracious; μειλ-ĭχία, gentleness, kindness; μειλ-ίσσω, to soothe, to treat kindly.

390. μέλι, honey; μελί-φρων (φρήν), sweet to the mind, delicious; μέλισσᾰ, a bee.

mel. (gen. *mell-is* = *melt-is*), honey; **mellifluus** (*mel, fluo*), flowing with honey, *mellifluous*.

391. smar; smar; μερ, μαρ; mor; keep in mind.

μέρ-μηρ-α, μέρ-ιμνα, care, anxious thought; μερ-μαίρω, μερμηρ-ίζω, to be full of cares; μέρ-μερα ἔργα, warlike deeds; μέρμερ-ος, peevish, baneful; μάρ-τυς, μάρ-τυρ, a witness, (later) a *martyr;* μαρ-τύριον, a testimony, proof; μαρ-τύρομαι, to call to witness.

mĕ-mor, mindful of, remembering; **mĕ-mŏr-ia,** *memory;* **mĕ-mŏr-iālis,** *memorial;* **mĕ-mŏr-o,** to remind of, to relate; **com-mĕmŏro,** to recall an object to memory in all its particulars, [*commemorate*]; **mĕ-mŏr-ābĭlis,** *memorable;* **mĕ-mŏr-ĭter,** from memory, accurately; **mŏr-a,** a delay; **mŏr-or,** to delay, (compd. w. com, de, in, re), [*demur, demurrage*].

392. mar; —; μερ; **mer;** measure out, distribute to.

μείρ-ομαι, (ἔμ-μορ-α, εἴ-μαρ-ται), to receive as one's portion; μέρ-ος, μέρ-ις, a part, share; μερ-ίζω, to divide; μόρ-ος, fate, destiny; μοῖρ-α, part, share, destiny, one's due; μόρ-α, a division (of the Spartan army); μόρ-σιμος, appointed by fate.

mĕr-eo, mĕr-eor (to receive as one's share), to deserve, *merit,* earn, obtain, (compd. w. de, e, pro); **mĕr-ĭtum,** that which one deserves, reward, punishment, *merit;* **merx,** (the gainful thing), merchandise; **com-mer-cium,** *commerce;* **mer-c-ēs,** hire, pay, recompense; **mer-c-or,** to trade, (compd. w. com, e, prac); **mer-cans** (pres. part.), trading, [*mercantile*]; **mer-cans** (subst.), a buyer, purchaser, [*merchant, merchandise*]; **mer-c-ātor,** a merchant; **mer-c-ēnārius, mer-c-ennārius** (in old Mss.), doing anything for reward or pay, *mercenary.*

393. mar; mar; μερ, μορ, μαρ, μρο; **mor, mar-c;** waste away, die.

βρο-τός, μορ-τός, mortal; ἄ-μβρο-τος (ἀ-μβρόσ-ιος), immortal; ἀ-μβροσ-ία, *ambrosia,* the food of the gods; μαρ-αίνω, to put out or quench, pass. to waste away, [*amaranth*]; μαρ-ασ-μός, μάρ-ανσις, decay.

mŏr-ior, to die, (compd. w. de, e, in, inter, prae); **mors,** death, [*murder, mortify*]; **mor-tālis,** *mortal;* **mor-bus,** a sickness, disease; **mor-bĭdus,** sickly, diseased, *morbid;* **mar-c-eo,** to wither, to be feeble; **mar-c-esco** (inch.), to wither, to become feeble.

394. mad; madhjas; μεθ; **med, mĭd;** middle.

μέσσος (= μεθ-jος), μέσος (a still further weakened form), middle; μεσσ-ηγύ(ς), μεσ-ηγύ(ς), between.

měd-ius, *middle, mid-*, [*midst*]; měd-ium, the middle, a *medium;* měd-io, to divide in the middle, to be in the middle, [*mediate*]; med-iator, a *mediator;* měd-iocris, middling, ordinary, *mediocre;* dī-mĭd-ius (*dis, midius*), half; dī-mid-io, to divide into halves, to halve; měditerraneus (*medius, terra*), midland, inland, *mediterranean;* meri-dies (for *medi-dies*), midday, noon; měrīdiānus, of or belonging to mid-day, *meridian;* měrīdionālis, southern, *meridional*.

395. ma; mâ; (st.) μηνs; men; measure.

μήν, μής, μείς, a *month;* μή-νη, the moon; μην-ιαῖος, monthly.

mens-is, a month; -mestris, (= *mensitris*); bi-mes-tris, of two months duration; tri-mes-tris, of three months; mens-truus, monthly, *menstrual*.

396. ma; mâ; μα, μη; ma; measure, fashion, make.

μή-τηρ, μά-τηρ, a *mother;* μα-ῖα, good mother.

mā-ter, a mother; mā-ternus, *maternal;* mā-trĭmōnium, marriage, *matrimony;* mā-trōna, a married woman, wife, [*matron*]; mā-trix, a breeding-animal, a public register; mā-tricula (dim.), a public register, [*matriculate*]; mā-teria, mā-teries, *matter*, materials, wood; mā-teriālis, of or belonging to matter, *material*.

397. mĭk; mĭc; μιγ; misc; mix.

μίσγ-ω, μίγ-νυ-μι, to *mix;* μίγ-α, μίγ-δα, μίγ-δην, confusedly; μιγ-άs, mixed pell-mell; μῖξ-ις, a mixing.

misc-eo, to mix, mingle, (compd. w. ad, com, inter, re); misc-ellus, mixed; misc-ellāneus, mixed, *miscellaneous;* mis-tio, mix-tio, mis-tura, mix-tura, a mixing, a *mixture;* prō-misc-uus, mixed, *promiscuous*.

398. ma, mĭ; mĭ; μιν, με; man, min, men; diminish.

μιν-ύθω, to make less, become less, perish; μίν-υνθα, a little, a short time; μῐν-υνθάδιος, short-lived; με-ίων, less; με-ιόω, to diminish.

man-cus, maimed; men-da, men-dum, a fault, a defect; men-dōsus, full of faults, faulty; ē-men-do, to *amend, emend, mend;* men-dīcus, beggarly; men-dīcus, a beggar, a *mendicant;* men-dīco, men-dīcor, to beg; mĭn-uo, to diminish, (compd. w. com, de, di, in), [*diminish, mince*]; mĭn-ūtus, small, *minute;* mĭn-ūtum, the smallest piece of money, pl. very small parts, [*minute*]; mĭn-or, mĭn-us, less, [*minor, minus*]; mĭn-ĭmus, very little, least, [*minimum, minim*]; mĭn-ister, adj., (a double comparative in form, from *minus* and compar. ending *-ter*, Gr. -τερ-ος), serving; mĭn-ister (subst.), a servant, a *minister*, [*minstrel*]; mĭn-istĕrium, service, *ministry;* min-istro, to serve, supply, *minister*, (compd. w. ad, prae, sub).

399. μορ-μύρ-ω, μυρ-μύρ-ω (formed by redupl. from μύρ-ω), (of water) to roar and boil.

mur-mur (formed perhaps by onomatopoeia), a *murmur*, rushing, roaring; mur-mŭr-o, to *mur-mur*, rustle, roar.

400. mu; mu; μυ; mu; bind, close. (Cf. No. 380.)

μύ-ω, to close (eyes, mouth); μύ-σις, a closing (of the lips, eyes, etc.); μυ-ίνδα, blindman's-buff; μύ-ωψ, blinking, short-sighted, [*myops, myope, myopy*]; μυ-χός, the innermost place or part; μυ-έω, to initiate into the mysteries, to instruct; μύσ-της (fem. μύσ-τις), one initiated; μυσ-τήριον, a *mystery* or secret doctrine; μυ-άω, to compress the lips; μύ-ζω, to murmur with closed lips, to moan; μυ-γμός, a moaning; μυ-χθίζω, to moan, to sneer; μυ-κτήρ, the nose; μυν-δός, μύ-δος, dumb; μύ-ζω, to drink with closed lips, to suck in; μυ-ζάω, to suck; μυ-ττός, μύ-της, dumb.

mū-tus, dumb, *mute;* mū-tesco (inch.), to become dumb, (compd. w. in, ob), mū-tio, muttio, to *mutter;* mu-sso, mu-ssĭto (intens.), to speak low, to mutter.

401. mus; mush; μυσ; mus; steal. (Cf. No. 403.)

μυ-ῖα (for μυσ-ῖα), a fly.

mu-sca, a fly, [*midge, mosquito, musquito*].

402. mar, mal; —; μυλ; mol; rub, grind.

μύλ-η, μύλ-ος, a *mill*, a millstone, [*meal*]; μυλ-ωθρός, a miller; μύλ-αι, μυλ-όδοντες, μυλ-ῖται, the molar teeth, the grinders.

mŏl-o, to grind; mŏl-a, a *mill*, millstone, *meal;* mŏl-āris, of a mill, of grinding, *molar;* im-mŏl-o (*in, mola*), to sprinkle a victim with sacrificial meal, to sacrifice, to *immolate*.

403. mus; mush; μυσ; mus; steal. (Cf. No. 401.)
μῦς, a *mouse*, a muscle (shell-fish).

mus, a mouse; mus-cŭlus (dim.), a little mouse, a sea *muscle* (*mussel*), a *muscle* (of the body), [*muscular*]; mus-cĭp-ŭla, mus-cĭp-ŭlum, (*mus, capio*), a mouse-trap.

404. Perhaps these words are from the root mu (No. 400).

μωρός, dull, foolish; μωρία, folly; μωρόομαι, to become dull, be stupefied; μωραίνω, to be silly, to be foolish.

mōrus, foolish; mōrōsus, self-willed, peevish, *morose*.

405. ὄμβρος, rain; ὄμβριος, rainy; ὀμβρέω, to rain.

imber, rain, a rain-storm, a shower of rain; imbrex, a hollow tile, pantile (used in covering roofs, for conducting off the rain).

406. ὠμός, raw, fierce; ὠμότης, rawness, fierceness.
amārus, bitter.

407. ὦμος, the shoulder; ὠμοπλάτη, the shoulder-blade.
ŭmĕrus (incorrectly spelled hŭmĕrus), the upper part of the arm, the shoulder.

P

r; r; ρ; r (sometimes l).

408. ar; ar; ἀρ; ar; fit, join closely. The Indo-European root *ar* has the fundamental meaning of motion in the direction of something. From this arise the meanings of attaining a goal, close union, fitness, closeness, narrowness. The root *ar* is in Sanskrit retained unchanged in form. In Greek it appears under three forms, ἀρ, ἐρ, ὀρ; and to each of these forms a definite meaning is attached, to the one with *a* that of fitting (No. 408) and ploughing (No. 410), to the one with ε that of rowing (No. 411), to the one with ο that of raising or arousing (No. 414). Comparing the Latin words, *artus, rēmus, ŏrior*, we find a similar special meaning attached to each of the corresponding vowels.

ἀρ-αρ-ίσκω, to join, to fit together, to be joined closely together, to fit or suit; ἄρ-μενος, fitting, fitted or suited; ἄρ-θρον, a joint, (pl. limbs); ἀρ-τύω, to prepare; ἀρ-τύς, ἀρ-θμός, a bond, friendship; ἀρ-ιθμός, a number, a numbering; ἀρ-ιθμητικός, of or for numbering; ἡ ἀριθμητική (sc. τέχνη), arithmetic; ν-ήρ-ιτος, ν-ήρ-ιθμος, ἀν-άρ-ιθμος, countless; ἀρ-μός, a joint, the shoulder-joint; ἄρ-τι, just, exactly; ἄρ-τιος, suitable, exactly fitted; ἀρ-τίζω, to prepare; ἀρῐ-, insep. prefix, used to strengthen the meaning of its compound; ἀρ-είων, better; ἄρ-ιστος, best; ἀρ-έσκω, to make good, make amends, please; ἀρ-ετή, goodness, excellence, manhood, valor; ἀρ-ετάω, to be fit or proper; ἐρί-ηρ-ος, fitting exactly; ἄρα (ἄρ, ῥά), then, straightway.

ar-ma, armor, *arms;* ar-mo, to *arm*, [*army, armada*]; ar-matūra, armor, [*armature*]; ar-mus, the shoulder, the *arm;* ar-tus, fitted, close, narrow, severe; ar-tum, a narrow place; ar-te, closely; ar-tus, a joint, (pl. limbs); ar-ticŭlus (dim.), a joint, (of discourse) a part, a division, *article;* ar-ticŭlo, to utter distinctly, to *articulate;* ars, skill in joining something, skill in producing, occupation, *art*, [*artist, artisan, artifice, artificer, artificial, artful, artless, artillery*]; in-ers (*in, ars*), unskilled in any art, inactive, *inert*, [*inertia*]; sollers, solers (*sollus* [old word meaning 'entire'], *ars*), [having all art], skilled, intelligent.

409. ark (expanded fr. rt. ar); —; —; —; spin.

ἀράχ-νης, a spider; ἀράχ-νη, a spider, a spider's web; ἀράχ-νιον, a spider's web.

arā-nea (= *araknea*), a spider, a spider's web; arā-neus, a spider; arā-neum, a spider's web.

410. ar; —; ἀρ; ar; move, plough.

ἀρ-όω, to plough; ἀρ-οτήρ, a ploughman; ἄρ-οτος, a crop or cornfield, ploughing, seed-time; ἄρ-οτρον, a plough; ἄρ-ουρα, tilled land.

ăr-o, to plough, [*arable*]; ăr-ātor, a ploughman; ăr-atio, a ploughing; ăr-ātrum, a plough; ar-vus, ploughed, arable; ar-vum, an arable field; ar-mentum (?), cattle for ploughing, a drove, a herd.

411. ar, ra; ar; ἐρ; ra, re; move, move with oars. (Cf. No. 408.)
ἀμφ-ήρ-ης, fitted on both sides, with oars on both sides; ἁλι-ήρ-ης, sweeping the sea; τρι-ήρ-ης, a galley with three banks of oars, a trireme; πεντηκόντ-ορο-ς, a ship of burden with fifty oars; ἐρ-έ-της, a rower; ὑπ-ηρ-έ-της, an under-rower, under-seaman, servant; εἰρ-εσία, ἐρ-εσία, a rowing, a crew; ἐρ-έσσω, to row; ἐρ-ετμόν, an oar.

ră-tis, a raft, boat, vessel; rē-mus, an *oar*, [*rudder*]; rē-migium, a rowing, the oars, the rowers; tri-rē-mis (adj.), having three banks of oars; tri-rē-mis (subst.), a vessel having three banks of oars, a *trireme*.

412. var; —; ἐρ, Fερ; ver; speak.
εἴρ-ω, to say, (ἐρ-έω, εἴρ-ηκα [for ἔ-Fρη-κα], ἐρρήθην, ῥη-τός [for Fρη-τός]); ῥή-τωρ, a public speaker; ῥη-τορικός, *rhetorical;* ἡ ῥη-τορική (sc. τέχνη), *rhetoric;* ῥή-τρα, a verbal agreement, an unwritten law, a law; ῥῆ-μα, a word; ῥῆ-σις, a speaking, speech; εἰρήνη, peace.

ver-bum, a *word*, a *verb;* ver-bālis, *verbal;* ver-bōsus, full of words, *verbose;* ad-verbium, an *adverb;* prōverbium (*pro, verbum*), a *proverb*.

413. var; —; —; —; cover.
εἶρ-ος, ἔρ-ιο-ν, wool; ἐρ-ίν-εος, ἐρεοῦς, woollen.
vell-us, a fleece, *wool;* vill-us, shaggy hair.

414. ar; ar; ὀρ; or; arouse, rouse one's self, rise. (Cf. No. 408.)
ὄρ-νυμι, ὀρ-ίνω, ὀρ-οθύνω, to stir up, excite, arouse; ὀρ-ούω, to rise and rush violently on or forward; ἀν-ορ-ούω, to start up; οὖρ-ον, a boundary; δίσκ-ουρ-α (pl.), a quoit's cast.

ŏr-ior, to stir one's self, to rise, to have one's origin from, (compd. w. ab, ad, com, ex, in, ob, sub); or-tus, a rising, origin, birth; **abortus, abortio**, a premature birth, *abortion;* **ŏr-iens**, the rising sun, the East, the *Orient;* **ŏr-ientālis**, *oriental;* **ŏr-īgo**, birth, origin, [*aborigines, aboriginal*]; **ŏr-īgĭnālis**, primitive, *original*.

415. var; —; ὅρ, Foρ; **ver;** be watchful, wary.

ὅρ-ομαι, to watch; οὖρ-ος, a watcher, guardian; ἐπί-ουρ-ος, a guardian; φρουρός (προ-ορός), a watcher; φρουρά, a looking out, a watch, guard; τῑμά-ορο-ς, τῑμωρός, upholding honor, helping, avenging, punishing; πυλα-ωρός, πυλωρός, a gate-keeper; θυρ-ωρός, a door-keeper; ὥρα, care, heed; ὁρά-ω, to see; ὅρα-μα, a sight, [*cosmorama* (κόσμος, world), *diorama* (διά, through), *panorama* (πᾶν, all)]; ἀ-όρᾱ-τος, invisible.

vĕreor, to reverence, to fear; **rĕ-vĕr-eor**, to honor, *reverence, revere,* [*reverent, reverend*]; **vĕr-ēcundus**, feeling shame, modést.

416. ὁρ-μή, 1. a violent movement onward, a rush, an attack; 2. the first stir or start in a thing, effort, attempt; 3. a start on a march, etc.; ὁρ-μάω, to set in motion, to urge on, (more commonly intrans.), to hurry on, to start; ἀφ-ορ-μή, ὁρ-μη-τήριον, a starting-place, an incentive.

417. ὠρυγ-ή, ὠρυθμός, a howling, a roaring.

rŭg-io, to roar, to bellow; **rŭg-ītus**, a roaring.

418. var; var; —; —; cover.

οὐρ-ανός (ὠρ-ανός, ὀρ-ανός), the vault or firmament of heaven, a ceiling, the roof of the mouth, palate; οὐρ-άνιος, heavenly; Οὐρανίωνες, the gods.

419. ῥῖγ-ος, frost, cold; ῥίγ-ιον, more frosty or cold, more horrible; ῥιγ-έω, to shudder with the cold, to shudder at anything; ῥιγ-όω, to be cold, to shiver from frost or cold.

frīg-us (subst.), cold; **frīg-eo**, to stiffen with cold, to be cold; **frīg-ĭdus**, cold, *frigid*.

420. ῥίζ-α, a root.

rādix, a *root*, [*wort, radical*].

421. sru; sru; ῥυ, σρυ; ru, rou, ro; flow, break forth, come out with vehemence.

ῥέ-ω (ῥεύ-σω, ἐ-ῤῥύη-ν), to flow, to run; ῥέ-ος, ῥεῦ-μα, ῥο-ή, a stream; ῥύ-σις, ῥεῦ-σις, a flowing; ῥῠ-τός, flowing; ῥευσ-τός, made to flow, fluctuating; ῥεῖθρον, ῥέ-εθρον, a stream, the bed of a stream; ῥύ-αξ, a stream that bursts forth, esp. a stream of lava; ῥύ-μη, the force, swing, rush of a body in motion; ῥυ-θμός, any motion, esp. a regular, recurring, vibratory motion, time (in music), *rhythm*. From the root ῥυ comes the stem ῥω. ῥώ-ομαι, to move with speed or violence, to rush; ῥώ-ννυμι, to strengthen, to put forth strength; ῥώ-μη, strength, force; Ῥώ-μη, Rome; ἐ-ρω-ή, a quick motion, rush; ἐ-ρω-έω, to rush, rush forth.

Ru-mo, an older name of the Tiber; **Ro-ma** (= *Srou-ma*, *Rou-ma*, stream-town), *Rome*; **ru-o** (= *srov-o*), to rush down, fall down, go to ruin, (compd. w. com, de, di, e, in, ob, pro, sub, super); **ru-īna,** a falling or tumbling down, *ruin*.

422. svar, sar; sar; σερ, ἐρ, ἔρ, σειρ, εἰρ, ἀερ; ser, src, sor; swing, hang, bind; (Latin) arrange, put together.

σειρ-ά, a rope; ὅρ-μος, 1. a chain, necklace, 2. a roadstead, anchorage, place where the ships swing or ride at anchor, where ships are bound or fastened, 3. = ἕρ-μα, ear-ring; (ὅρμος, with the second signification, is by some referred to ὁρμάω, No. 416); ὁρ-μαθός, a string or chain (as of beads, etc.); ὁρ-μία, a fishing-line; ἕρ-μα, an ear-ring (prob. of strung pearls); ἕρ-μα, prop, support, ballast, (prob. belongs with this root); εἴρ-ω (simple verb rare; compds. w. ἀν-, δι, εν, ἐξ, σύν), to fasten together in rows, to string; εἰρ-μός, a train, series (as of things bound or fastened together); εἴρ-ερος, bondage; ἀείρ-ω [Ionic], (Att. αἴρ-ω, Aeol. ἀέρρω), to raise, to lift; ἄορ, a hanger, a sword; ἀορ-τήρ, a strap over the shoulder to hang anything to, a sword-belt; αἰώρα, a machine for suspending bodies, a being suspended or hovering in the air, oscillation; ἀρ-τάω, to fasten to or hang one thing upon another; ἀρ-τάνη, that by which something is hung up, a rope, cord.

sĕr-o, to join or bind together, to plait, to entwine, (compd. w. ad, de, dis, ex, in, inter, pro, sub, trans), [*insert*]; **disserto** (freq. fr. *dissĕro*), to discuss, to treat, [*dissertation*]; **in-ser-to** (freq. fr. *insĕro*), to put into, to insert; **ser-mo** (may be referred to No. 422 or to No. 423), a speaking, discourse, [*sermon*]; **ser-tum** (rare in sing., freq. in pl.), a wreath of flowers; **sĕr-ies**, a row, succession, *series;* **rē-te** (= *sre-te*), a net; **rē-ticŭlum** (dim.), a little net, [*reticule*]; **rē-ticulatus**, made like a net, *reticulated;* **circum-rētio**, to enclose with a net, ensnare; **ir-rētio**, to take in a net, catch, ensnare, hinder; **sĕr-a**, a bar for fastening doors; **ob-sĕr-o**, to bolt, bar, fasten; **rĕ-sĕr-o**, to unlock, unclose, open; **ser-vus**, slavish; **ser-vus, ser-va**, a slave, a *servant;* **ser-vitium**, slavery, the class of slaves, [*service*]; **ser-vĭtūdo**, *servitude;* **ser-vīlis**, slavish, *servile;* **ser-vio**, to be a servant or slave, to *serve*, (compd. w. ad, de, in, sub); **sors(?)**, anything used to determine chances, a lot, (*sĕro* : *sors* = *fĕro* : *fors*); **sor-tio(?), sor-tior(?)**, to cast or draw lots; **con-sors(?)**, having an equal share with another or others, partaking of in common; **con-sors(?)** (subst.), a sharer, partner, *consort;* **ex-sors(?)**, without lot, having no share in.

423. svar; svar; συρ; sur; tune, sound.

σῦρ-ιγξ, a musical pipe; συρ-ίζω, to pipe, to make any whistling or hissing sound; σῦρ-ιγμός, a shrill piping sound, a hissing.

ab-sur-dus, 1. out of tune, giving a disagreeable sound, harsh, 2. incongruous, silly, *absurd;* **su-sur-rus**, a humming, whispering; **su-sur-ro**, to hum, buzz, whisper.

424. ὥρα, any limited time or period (as fixed by natural laws and revolutions), whether of the year, month, or day, a season, spring-time, part of a day, hour, the right or fitting time; ὥρος, time, a year; ὥρᾱσι, in season; ὡραῖος, timely, seasonable; ἄωρος, untimely.

hōra, (lit. a definite space of time fixed by natural laws), an *hour*, a season.

425. ru; ru; ὠρυ (ω is here a prefixed vowel); ru, rau; sound.
ὠρύ-ομαι, howl, roar; ὠρυ-θμός, a howling, roaring; ὀρυ-μαγδός, a loud noise, din.
rū-mor, common talk, *rumor*; rū-mĭfĭco (*rumor, facio*), to report; rau-cus, rāv-us, hoarse; rāv-is, hoarseness.

Λ

l; l; λ; l. L is sometimes represented by r.

426. al; —; ἀλ; al, ol, ul; grow, make to grow, nourish.
ἀν-αλ-τος, insatiable; ἀλ-σος, a grove; Ἀλ-τις, the sacred grove of Zeus at Olympia.
ăl-o, to nourish, support; ăl-esco (inch.), to grow up; co-ălesco (inch.), to grow together, become united, *coalesce;* ăl-imentum, nourishment, *aliment;* ăl-imonium, sustenance, support, *alimony;* al-tor, (fem. *al-trix*), a nourisher; ăl-umnus (adj.), that is nourished; ăl-umnus (subst.), a foster-son, pupil, *alumnus;* ăl-umna, a foster-daughter, a pupil; ăl-umno, to nourish, educate; al-mus, nourishing, cherishing, kind; al-tus (lit. grown or become great), high, [*old*]; al-tĭtūdo, height, *altitude;* ex-al-to, to elevate, *exalt;* ĕl-ĕmentum, a first principle, *element;* ăd-ŏl-eo, to cause to grow up, to magnify; ad-ul-tus, grown up, *adult;* ăd-ŏl-esco (inch.), to grow up; ad-ŭl-escens, ăd-ŏl-escens, growing up; ăd-ŭl-escens (subst.), a youth; sub-ŏl-es, a sprout, offspring; ind-ŏl-es, inborn or native quality; prō-les (= *pro-ol-es*), offspring; obs-ŏl-esco (inch.), to wear out, fall into disuse, become obsolete; obs-ŏl-ētus, worn out, *obsolete*.

427. ἄλλος, another; ἄλλως, otherwise; ἀλλ-ήλους, one another; ἀλλά, (in another way), but; ἀλλ-οῖος, of another kind; ἀλλ-άσσω, to make other than it is, to change, exchange; ἀλλ-ότριος, of or belonging to another, foreign, strange.

ăli-us, another (of many), other, *else;* ăllo, to another place, elsewhere; ălia (sc. *via*), in another way; alĭ-as, at another time; ălĭter, otherwise; alĭ-bi (contr. fr. *aliubi*), elsewhere; ali-ēnus, that belongs to another person, place, object, etc., *alien;* ali-ēno, to transfer, *alienate;* alĭ-quantus (*alius, quantus*), somewhat, some; alĭ-quando, at some time, sometimes; alĭ-quis (*alius, quis*), some one, something; alĭ-quot (*alius, quot*), some, several, [*aliquot*]; al-ter (a comparative form of *alius*), the other of two, one of two, [*alter, alterative*]; al-ternus (adj.), *alternate, alternative;* al-terno, to *alternate;* al-tercor, to dispute, quarrel, *altercate;* al-tercatio, a dispute, *altercation;* altĕr-ŭter, one of two, either; ad-ul-ter (*ad, alter*), an *adulterer.*

428. γλῠκύ-ς, sweet; γλῠκύ-της, sweetness; γλευκ-ος, must; ἀ-γλευκ-ής, not sweet, sour.

dul-cis (perhaps from *gulcis*, by dissimilation), sweet, [*dulcet*]; dul-cēdo, sweetness.

429. var; val; Fελ, Fαλ; vol; wind, roll, grind.

ἑλύ-ω, to wind, to twist together; εἰλύ-ω, to roll, enfold; εἴλυ-μα, a wrapper; ἔλυ-τρον, a cover; ἴλιγξ, a whirling; ἰλλά-ς, a rope; ὀλοί-τροχος, ὀλοί-τροχος, a rolling stone; ὄλ-μος, a round stone, a mortar; οὐλαί, coarsely-ground barley; ἀλέω, to grind; ἄλευρον, ἀλείατα, wheaten flour; ἀλέτης, a grinder; ἀλε-τός, a grinding, meal; ἀλε-τρίβ-ανος, a pestle; ἀλο-άω, to thresh; ἀλω-ή, ἅλως, a threshing-floor.

volv-o, to roll, (compd. w. ad, circum, com, de, e, in, ob, per, pro, re, sub, super), [*walk, well* (vb.), *convolve, convolution, devolve, evolve, evolution, involve, involution, revolve, revolution, revolt, revolver*]; vŏl-ūto (freq.), to roll; vŏl-ūbĭlis, rolling, whirling, (of speech) rapid, *voluble;* vŏl-ūmen, a roll, *volume.*

430. ἔλαιον, olive-oil; ἐλαί-α (Att. ἐλά-α), the olive-tree, the fruit of the olive-tree, an olive.

ŏlĕu-m, *oil*, olive-oil, [*oleaginous*]; ŏlīva, an *olive*, olive-tree.

431. ἕλος (Ϝελος), low ground.
valles, vallis, a *valley*.

432. ἧλος, a nail; ἐφ-ηλο-ς, nailed on or to; ἐφ-ηλό-ω, to nail on.
vallu-s, a stake, a palisade; **vallum,** a rampart set with palisades, a fortification; **vallo,** to surround with a rampart and palisades, (compd. w. circum, com, e), [*circumvallation*]; **inter-vallum,** the space between two palisades, an *interval*.

433. las; lash; λα, λασ; las; wish, long for.
λά-ω, to wish; λῆ-μα, λῆ-σις, will; λι-λα-ίομαι, to desire earnestly; λε-λίη-μαι (pf.), to strive eagerly; λία-ν, very, exceedingly.
las-c-īvus, playful, wanton, *lascivious*, [*lust*].

434. λαιός, left, i.e., on the left side.
laevu-s, left, i.e., on the left side.

435. λάξ, λάγδην, with the foot; λακ-τίζω, to kick with the heel or foot; λακ-πάτητος, trampled on.
calx, the *heel;* **calc-o,** to tread under foot; **circum-calco, circum-culco,** to trample around; **con-culco,** to crush or bruise by treading; **de-culco,** to tread down; **pro-culco,** to tread down, to despise; **ex-culco,** to tread out or down; **in-culco,** to tread into or upon, to impress on, to *inculcate;* **oc-culco,** to trample upon or down; **re-calco,** to tread again, retrace; **calcar,** a spur; **calc-eus,** a shoe; **calc-ĭtro,** to kick, to be stubborn, [*recalcitrate, recalcitrant*].

436. λᾱ-ός, the people; λά-ϊτον, λή-ϊτον, the town-hall or council-room; λειτουργός, (λέϊτος or λεῖτος, ἔργον), a public servant; λειτ-ουργία, a burdensome public office or duty, any public service, the public service of the gods, [*liturgy*]; λειτ-ουργέω, to perform public duties; βασιλεύς (prob. from rt. βα and Ionic λευ = λαο), a king (as leader of the people).

437. lu, lav; —; λαF; lu, la; gain, get booty.

λά-ω, ἀπο-λαύ-ω, to enjoy; λεία, Ion. ληίη, Dor. λαία, ληίς, λαίς, booty; ληίζομαι, to seize as booty; ληῖτις, she who gives booty, epithet of Athena; λά-τρις, a hired servant; λα-τρεύω, to work for hire, to serve; λω-ίων (for λω-Fίων), better.

lŭ-crum, gain, [*lucre*]; lŭ-cror, to gain; lŭ-cratīvus, *lucrative;* lă-tro, a hired servant, a hired soldier, a freebooter, a robber; lă-trŏcĭnor, to practise robbery on the highway; lă-trocinium, freebooting, robbery, piracy.

438. lap; —; λαπ; lab; lick.

λάπ-τω, to *lap* with the tongue, to drink; λαφ-ύσσω, to swallow greedily.

lăb-rum, lăb-ia, lăb-ea, lăb-ium, a *lip*, [*labial, labiate*]; lamb-o, to lick, *lap*, (compd. w. circum, de, prae, praeter).

439. λάχ-νη, soft, woolly hair; λάχ-νος, wool; λαχ-νήεις, woolly, shaggy; λαχ-νέομαι, to grow hairy; λῆ-νος, wool.

lā-na, wool; lā-nū-go, down; lā-neus, woollen; lā-nicius, woolly, fleecy.

440. rag, lag; —; λεγ; leg; collect, gather.

λέγ-ω, to pick, collect, count, tell, speak (the meaning 'speak' is the latest, and is developed through the intermediate notion of 'counting one's words'); λεκ-τός, chosen, spoken; λογ-άς, gathered, chosen; δια-λέγ-ομαι, to converse with, [*dialect, dialectic*]; διάλογος, a conversation, *dialogue;* κατα-λέγ-ω, to lay down, to pick out, to recount; συλ-λογ-ή, a collecting, levying; ἐκ-λογ-ή, a picking out, election, selection; λόγ-ος, a word, speech, reason, [*logarithm* (λόγος, ἀριθμός), *logic, logomachy* (λόγος, μάχη), *-logy* in compds., e.g., *geology* (γῆ, λόγος)]; λέξ-ις, a speaking, speech; λογ-ίζομαι, to reckon, to consider, [*syllogize, syllogism*].

lĕg-o, to collect, gather, hear, see, read, (compd. w. ad, com, de, e, inter, per, prae, se, sub), [*lecture, collect, elect, select*]; dĭ-lĭg-o (*dis, lĕgo*), (to distinguish one by selecting him from others), to esteem highly, to love; intellĕgo, less correctly intellĭgo, [*inter, lĕgo*], (to choose between), to perceive, understand, distinguish, [*intelligent, intellect*]; **neg-lĕg-o**, less correctly **neg-lĭg-o, nec-lĕg-o,** [*nec, lĕgo*], (not to gather), to *neglect*, to slight; **rĕ-lĕg-o,** to collect again, go over again, read again; **lec-tio,** a gathering, a reading, *lection;* **lec-tor,** a reader; **leg-ĭbĭlis,** *legible;* **lĕg-io,** (prop. a levying), a body of soldiers, a *legion;* **lĕg-ionarius,** *legionary;* **dĭ-lĭg-ens** (prop. esteeming, loving), attentive, *diligent;* **neg-lĕg-ens, neg-lĭg-ens,** heedless, *negligent;* **ē-lĕg-ans** (another form of *eligens*), luxurious, *elegant;* **rĕ-lig-io,** in poetry also **rel-lig-io** (by some authorities derived from *rĕligare*), reverence for God (the gods), *religion;* **col-lĕg-a,** one who is chosen at the same time with another, a *colleague;* **col-lĕg-ium,** persons united by the same office or calling, a *college,* a corporation; **leg-ūmen,** (that which is gathered), pulse, any *leguminous* plant; **lec-tus,** a reading; **sŭpel-lex** (*super, lĕgo*), household utensils, furniture; **lig-num,** (that which is gathered), wood, firewood, (*lignum* is by some derived from Sk. rt. *dah,* burn).

441. ll; —; λει; lev; smooth, polish.

λεῖ-ος, λευ-ρός, smooth, even, level; λει-ότης, smoothness; λε-αίνω, λει-αίνω, to smooth, to polish.

lēv-is, smooth; **lēv-ĭtas,** smoothness; **lēv-o,** to smooth, to polish; **lēv-ĭgo,** 1. to make smooth, 2. to make small, pulverize, *levigate.*

442. lak; —; —; —; bend.

λέχ-ριος, slanting, crosswise; λέχ-ρις (adv.), slanting, crosswise; λοξ-ός, slanting, crosswise, indirect.

lic-ĭnus, bent or turned upward; **oblīquus,** slanting, *oblique;* **oblīquo,** to turn aside or in an oblique direction; **lī-mus,** sidelong, aslant; **lī-men,** (prop. a cross-piece), a threshold; **ē-lī-mĭno,** to turn out of doors, [*eliminate*]; **sub-lī-mis** (etym. dub., perhaps *sub, limen,* up to the lintel; or *sub, lĕvo*), uplifted, high, *sublime;* **lī-mes,** a cross-path, boundary, *limit;* **lī-mĭto,** to enclose within boundaries or limits, to *limit;* **lux-us** (adj.), dislocated; **lux-um, lux-us,** a dislocation; **lux-o,** to dislocate, to *luxate,* [*luxation*].

443. rĭ, lĭ, lĭb; —; λιβ; rĭ, lĭ, lĭb. From the fundamental idea 'melt' have been developed two meanings, viz.: 1. flow, drop, melt away, pass away; 2. melt on to, adhere to.

λείβ-ω, to pour, to let flow; λοιβ-ή, a drink-offering; λίψ, λῐβ-άς, λίβ-ος, anything that drops or trickles, a drop, a stream; λιβ-ρός, wet; λείβ-ηθρον, a wet country or place; λιβ-άδιον, a small stream, a wet place; λίμ-νη, a pool; λι-μήν, a harbor; λει-μών, a moist, grassy place, a meadow.

rī-vus, a small stream of water, a brook, [*river*]; **rī-vŭlus** (dim.), a small brook, a *rivulet;* **rī-vālis** (adj.), of or belonging to a brook; **rī-vāles** (subst.), those who have or use the same brook; **rī-vālis,** a competitor in love, a *rival;* **rī-vo,** to lead or draw off; **de-rī-vo,** to draw off, divert, *derive,* [*derivation*]; **cor-rī-vo,** to conduct streams of water together; **lĭ-no, lĭ-nio,** to daub, spread over, (compd. w. ad, circum, com, de, ob, per, prae, sub, super); **lĭ-tus, lĭ-tura,** a smearing, anointing; **lĭ-nĭmentum,** smearing-stuff, *liniment;* **lĭ-tus,** the sea-shore; **littĕra** (less correctly **lītera),** a *letter,* a word, (pl. an epistle); **litterālis, literālis,** of or belonging to letters or writing, *literal;* **litteratura, literatura,** philology, *literature;* **oblittero, oblitero,** to blot out, *obliterate;* **de-le-o,** to destroy; **lĭb-o,** to take a little of, to taste of, to pour out in honor of a deity, to make a libation, (compd. w. de, prae, pro); **lĭb-atio,** a *libation;* **lĭb-um, lĭb-us,** a consecrated cake, a cake; **de-lĭb-uo,** to besmear, anoint; **Lĭb-er,** an old Italian deity who presided over planting and fructification, afterwards identified with the Greek Bacchus.

444. λίνο-ν, anything made of flax, linen; λίνεος (adj.), of flax, linen.

lĭn-um, flax, *linen;* **lĭn-eus** (adj.), of flax, of linen; **lĭn-ea,** a linen thread, a *line;* **lĭn-eāris,** of or belonging to lines, *linear;* **lĭn-eālis,** consisting of lines, *lineal;* **lĭn-eāmentum,** a line (made with a pen, pencil, brush, etc.), a feature, *lineament;* dē-līn-eo, (lit. to make a line down), to sketch out, to *delineate;* lin-teus, of or belonging to linen or flax.

445. λίς, λέων, *lion;* λέ-αινα, lioness.
leo, lion.

446. λί-ς (st. λιτ), smooth; λῖτ-ός, smooth, plain; λισσό-ς, λίσ-πος, λίσ-φος, smooth; λίσ-τρον, a tool for levelling or smoothing, a spade; γλοι-ός, sticky oil; γλί-α, γλοι-ά, glue.
‡glu-o, to draw together; glus (for the usual *gluten*), *glue;* glū-ten, glū-tĭnum, glue; glū-tĭno, to glue, (compd. w. ad, com, de, re).

447. lubh; lubh; λιφ; lĭb, lŭb; desire, long for.
λίπ-τω, λίπ-τομαι, to be eager, to long for; λίψ, a longing.
lĭb-et, lŭb-et, (impers.), it pleases, it is pleasing; lĭb-eo, lŭb-eo, to please; prō-lŭb-ium, desire, pleasure; lĭb-ĭdo, lŭb-ĭdo, desire, passion; lĭb-er, doing as one desires, free; lĭb-ĕro, to *liberate;* lĭb-ĕratio, *liberation;* lĭb-erātor, a *liberator;* lĭb-ertas, *liberty;* lĭb-ertus, a freedman (in reference to the manumitter); lĭb-ertīnus (adj.), of or belonging to the condition of a freedman; lĭb-ertīnus (subst.), a freedman (in reference to his condition or class), [*libertine*]; lĭb-erālis, of or belonging to freedom, noble, *liberal;* lĭb-eralĭtas, a disposition befitting a freeman, a noble spirit, *liberality.*

448. lu; lu; λυ; lu; loose, release, ransom.
λύ-ω, to *loose,* [*lose, -less*]; λύ-η, λύ-α, dissolution, separation; λύ-σις, a loosing, release, [*analysis*]; λυ-τήρ, a deliverer; λύ-τρον, a ransom.
lŭ-o, to loose, release; rĕ-lŭo, to redeem; solvo (= *se-lu-o*), to loose, (compd. w. ab, dis, per, re), [*solve, solution, absolve, absolute, absolution, dissolve, dissolute, dissolution, resolve, resolute, resolution*].

REGULAR SUBSTITUTION OF SOUNDS. 159

449. lu; —; λυ, λο, λου; lu, luv, lav; wash.

λῦ-μα, filth or dirt removed by washing, defilement; λύ-θρον, defilement; λύ-μη, 1. outrage, ruin, 2. defilement; λυ-μαίνομαι, to outrage, to ruin; λού-ω (orig. form λό-ω), to wash; λου-τρόν (= λοϝετρόν), a bath; λου-τήρ, a bathing-tub; λού-τριον, water that has been used in washing.

lŭ-o, to wash, cleanse, expiate, (compd. w. ab, ad, circum, dis, e, per, praeter, pro, sub), [*ablution, dilute, dilution*]; pol-luo, to defile, to pollute; lŭ-tum, lŭ-tus, mud, clay, [*lute*]; lŭ-to, to daub with mud or clay; lu-s-trum (that which is washed, covered with water or flooded), a muddy place, a haunt or den of wild beasts; lu-s-trum, (that which washes out or expiates), an expiatory offering, a period of five years, a *lustrum*, [*lustral*]; dē-lū-brum, a temple or shrine (as a place of expiation); al-lŭv-ies, a pool of water occasioned by the overflowing of the sea or a river; al-lŭv-ius, *alluvial;* dī-lŭv-ium, dī-lŭv-ies, dī-lŭv-io, an inundation, *deluge*, [*diluvial*]; lăv-o, to wash, bathe, *lave;* lau-tus (part.), washed; lau-tus (adj.), elegant, noble; lō-tio, a washing, a *lotion*.

450. λώβ-η, maltreatment, outrage; λω-βάομαι, to maltreat, outrage; λωβ-εύω, to mock; λω-βητήρ, a slanderer, a destroyer.

lăb-es, a spot, a stain.

451. mal; mal; μελ; mal; be dirty.

μέλ-ας, black; μελ-αίνω, to blacken; μολ-ύνω, to stain.

măl-us, bad; măl-e, badly, ill, (in Eng. *male-, mal-*, e.g., *malevolent, maltreat*); măl-itia, badness, *malice;* măl-ignus (for *maligenus*, from *malus* and *gen*, root of *gigno*), of an evil nature or disposition, *malignant, malign;* măle-făcio, to do or act wickedly; mălĕ-factor, an evil-doer, *malefactor;* măle-dīco, to speak ill of, revile, curse; măle-dictio, evil-speaking, *malediction*.

452. For this group of words, there is assumed a stem-form *mluva*. *Ml* was softened in Greek by means of the auxiliary vowel *o*, while *m* in Latin, being in immediate contact with *l*, was changed into *p*.

μόλυβος, μόλιβος, μόλυβδος, lead; μολ-ύβδαινα, a ball of lead; μολιβοῦς, μολυβοῦς, leaden.
plumbum, lead, [*plumb, plumber, plumbago*]; plumb-eus, of or belonging to lead, leaden.

453. ul; ul; ὐλ; ul; howl.
ὀλολύζω, to cry aloud; ὀλολυγή, ὀλολυγμός, any loud cry.
ŭlŭla, a screech-owl, [*owl*]; ŭlŭlo, to howl, to shriek; ŭlŭlatus, a howling, wailing, shrieking.

454. οὖλε, hail (a salutation); ὄλβος, happiness; ὄλβιος, happy, blessed.
salv-us, safe, [*save, salve, salver, salvage, salvation, savior*]; salv-eo, to be well; săl-us, health, safety; săl-ūbris, healthful, *salubrious*.

455. σάλ-ος, unsteady, tossing motion, the open sea; σαλεύω, to toss; σόλ-ος, a quoit.
săl-um, the open sea.

456. σίαλον, spittle; σίαλος, fat, grease.
salīva, spittle, *saliva*.

457. spal; sphal; σφαλ; fal; deceive, disappoint.
σφάλλ-ω, to make to fall, to mislead; σφάλμα, a false step, a fall; ἀ-σφαλ-ής, firm, sure; σφαλ-ερός, likely to make one fall, ready to fall.
fall-o, to deceive, [*fall*]; fal-sus, *false;* fall-ax, deceitful, *fallacious;* fall-acia, deceit, trick, [*fallacy*].

458. ὕλη, a wood, forest; ὑλήεις, woody; ὕλημα, under-wood.
silva, a wood, forest; silvestris, of or belonging to a wood or forest; silvōsus, full of woods, [*sylvan*].

Σ

s; s; σ; s (or usually, when between two vowels, **r**).

459. as; as; ἐσ; es. The three principal meanings of this root are probably developed in the following order: *breathe, live, be.* The distinction of this root from the root *bhu* (No. 348) is that the root *as* denotes, like respiration, a uniform, continuous existence, while the root *bhu* implies a becoming. By short and natural steps, we have the successive meanings, *living, real, true, good.*

εἰ-μί (Aeol. ἐμ-μί = ἐσ-μί), *am*, ἐσ-τί, *is*; εὐ-εσ-τώ (εὖ, εἰμί), well-being; ἐσ-θλός, good, excellent; ἐΰς, good, brave, noble; ἐτεός, true, real; ἔτ-υμος, true; τὸ ἔτ-υμον (as subst.), the true, literal sense of a word according to its origin, its etymology or derivation, the *etymon* or root; ἐτυμο-λογία, the analysis of a word so as to find its origin, its *etymology*; ἕτ-οιμος, ready, certain, real.

ōs, mouth; ōro, to speak, plead, entreat, (compd. w. ex, per), [*oral*]; **ōrātio**, a speech, *oration*; **ōrātor**, a speaker, *orator*; **orac̄ulum**, a divine announcement, an *oracle*; **os-c̄ulum** (dim.), a little mouth, a pretty mouth, a kiss; **os-c̄ulor**, to kiss, (compd. w. de, ex, per); **os-culatio**, a kissing, *osculation*; **orificium** (*os, facio*), an opening, *orifice*; **orārium**, a napkin, handkerchief; **cōram** (prob. from *co = cum, os*), in the presence of; **os-cĭto, os-cĭtor** (*os, cieo*), to open the mouth wide, to gape; **sum** (= *esum*), am, (compd. w. ab, ad, de, in, inter, ob, post, potis, prae, pro, sub, super). Whenever *s* of the stem *es* comes between two vowels, *e* is dropped, as in *sum, sunt*, or *s* is changed to *r*, as in *eram, ero*. **essentia,** the being or *essence* of a thing; **absens,** *absent*; **praesens,** *present*; **praesento,** to place before, to present; **repraesento,** to bring before one, to bring back, to *represent*; **sons,** (prop. he who was it, the real person, the guilty one) [adj.], guilty, criminal; **insons,** guiltless, innocent; **sontĭcus,** dangerous, serious.

460. vas; vas; ἐσ, Fεσ; ves; cover around, clothe.

ἔν-νυμι, to clothe; εἶ-μα, a dress, a garment, clothing; ἱ-μάτιον, a piece of dress, a cloak; ἐσ-θής, dress, clothing; ἐ-ᾰνός, a fine robe; ἐ-ᾱνός, good for wear.

ves-tis, clothing, [vest, vestment, vesture]; ves-tio, to clothe, to vest, (compd. w. circum, com, de, in); vas (gen. vasis), a vessel, utensil, [vase]; vas-culum (dim.), a little vessel, [vascular].

461. Under this number the root is perhaps the same as of No. 460.

ἕσπερος, evening (subst. and adj.); ἑσπέρα, evening; ἑσπέριος, ἑσπερινός (adj.), toward evening, western.

vesper, the evening, evening-star, the west, [vesper, vespers]; vespĕra, the evening; vespertīnus, belonging to evening.

462. sa; —; σαο, σω; sa; save, safe, whole and sound.

σάο-ς, σόο-ς, σῶ-ος, σῶ-ς, safe and sound; σῶ-κος, strong; σώ-ζω (lengthened from σά-ω, σαό-ω, σώ-ω), to save; σω-τήρ, a savior, preserver; ἄ-σω-τος, without salvation, abandoned.

sā-nus, sound, whole, sane; sā-no, to make sound, heal, restore; sā-nĭtas, soundness of body, soundness of mind, sanity; in-sā-nus, unsound in mind, insane; sos-pes (prob. from σῶς and the root pa, nourish, or from σῶς and peto), saving, delivering; sos-pes (subst.), a savior, deliverer; sā-cer, 1. dedicated to a divinity, sacred, 2. devoted to a divinity for destruction, forfeited, accursed; sacrum, a holy or sacred thing, a sanctuary; sa-cellum (dim.), a little sanctuary, a chapel; sa-cro, to declare or set apart as sacred, to consecrate; con-sĕ-cro, to devote, to consecrate; ex-sĕ-cror, to curse, to execrate; ob-sĕ-cro, (lit., to ask on religious grounds), to beseech, implore; rĕ-sĕ-cro, to beseech again, to free from a curse; sā-crāmentum, 1. the thing set apart as sacred, the sum deposited by the two parties to a suit, 2. the thing setting apart as sacred, the military oath of allegiance, a solemn obligation or engagement, 3. (in eccl. and late Lat.) something to be kept sacred, a mystery, revelation, sacrament; sā-cerdos, a priest, a priestess, [sacerdotal]; sancio, to render sacred or inviolable, to confirm, to sanction; **sanctio,** an establishing, a decree, ordinance, *sanction;* **sanctifico** (*sanctus, facio*), to make holy or treat as holy, to *sanctify*. (The words *sacer* and *sancio* with their derivatives are by some considered to come from the root *sak*, shown in No. 497.)

463. sa, si; —; σα, ση; sa, sa-p, se, si; sow.
σά-ω, σή-θω, to sift; σῆ-στρον, a sieve.

sĕ-ro (= *se-s-o*) (*sē-vi, să-tus*), to sow, plant, beget, bring forth, (compd. w. circum, com, in, inter, ob, pro, re, sub); **să-tio,** a sowing, planting; **să-tor,** a sower, planter, father; **in-sĭ-tio,** an ingrafting; **sē-men,** seed; **sē-mĭno,** to sow, (compd. w. dis, in, prae, pro, re), [*disseminate*]; **sē-mĭnārium,** a nursery, nursery-garden, seed-plot, *seminary;* **saeculum, seculum** (perhaps to be referred to *secus, sĕquor*), a race, a generation, an age; **saeculāris, seculāris,** of or belonging to a saeculum, temporal, *secular;* Sa-turnus, (the Sower), *Saturn;* **pro-sāpia,** a stock, race.

464. στλεγγ-ίς, στελγ-ίς, στεργ-ίς, iron for rubbing or scraping. **strig-ĭlis,** a scraper. The root is the same as that of No. 465.

465. strag, strang; —; στραγγ (st.); **strag, strang, strĭg, string.**
This root has two principal meanings: 1. to draw or force through, to press; 2. to strip.

στράγξ, a drop; στραγγ-εύω, to force through, to twist, (in middle voice) to turn one's self backward and forward, hesitate; στραγγ-άλη, a halter; στραγγαλ-ιά, a knot hard to unloose; στραγγ-αλίζω, to *strangle.*

string-o, to draw tight, press together, touch, strip off, (compd. w. ad, com, de, dis, in, ob, per, prae, re), [*strong, strain, string, stringent, astringent, strict, stricture, restrict, restriction, constrict, constriction*]; **strang-ŭlo,** to choke, *strangle.*

466. si, siu, siv; siv; συ; su. The root *si* means 'bind,' *su* means 'sew.'
κασ-σύ-ω (prob. contr. from κατα-σύ-ω), καττύω, to stitch or sew together like a shoemaker; κάσ-σῡ-μα, κάτ-τυ-μα, anything stitched of leather; κασ-σύ-ς, κατ-τύ-ς, a piece of leather.

sŭ-o, to *sew*, (compd. w. ad, in, ob, prae, sub, trans); sū-tor, a shoemaker, cobbler; sū-tūra, a seam, *suture;* sū-tēla, (prop. a sewing together), a cunning device; sū-bŭla, an awl.

467. σύς, ῦς, a swine, a pig.

su-s (the prolific animal), a *swine*, boar, *sow*, pig.

468. σφήξ, a wasp.

vespa, a *wasp*.

Ξ

ks; ksh; ξ; hs, chs.

469. ἀλέξ-ω, to ward or keep off, to help; ἀλεξητήρ, a helper. These words are formed on an expansion of the root ἀλκ (No. 3).

470. ἄξ-ων, an axle; ἅμ-αξ-α, ἅμ-αξ-α (ἁμ is for ἅμα, No. 377), a wagon.

ax-is, an axle-tree, *axle, axis*, of the earth, the pole, the heavens. We may consider ἀξ as an expanded ἀγ (No. 104), and the Latin *ax* as an expanded *ag* (No. 104).

471. vaks; vaksh; αὔξ; —; increase.

αὔξ-ω, αὐξ-άνω, to increase; αὔξ-η, αὔξ-ησις, αὔξ-ημα, growth, increase. Cf. No. 138. By adding *s*, the root *vag* becomes *vaks* (Sk. *vaksh*), Greek Ϝεξ, with prothetic *a* ἀϜεξ, with a 'thinning' from Ϝε to *v,* αὐξ.

472. ἐξ, ἐκ (Locr. ἐ), from out of, out of, forth from.

ex, ec, e, out of, from; ex-ter, ex-tĕrus, outward; ex-terior, outer, *exterior;* ex-tremus, outermost, *extreme;* ex-tra (contr. from *extera*), (adv.), on the outside, (prep.) outside of, without, beyond, [*extra*]; ex-trāneus, external, *extraneous;* ex-ternus, outward, *external;* ex-trinsĕcus (adv.), from without, [*extrinsic*].

473. ἕξ (from Ϝεξ), six; ἑκ-τός, the sixth.

sex (from a primitive Graeco-Italic form *svex*), *six;* sextus, the sixth.

F

v; v; F; v.

474. αἰές, αἰέν (ἀεί), always, even, for ever; ἀί-διος, everlasting; αἰών, lifetime, an age, a long space of time.

aevu-m, lifetime, age, an age or generation, long time, eternity, [*aye, ever*]; **aetas** (contr. from *aevitas*), lifetime, age, an age or generation; **aeternus** (contr. from *aeviternus*), eternal; **aeternālis,** everlasting, *eternal.*

475. av; av; ᾱF; av, au; hear, attend to, help, treat affectionately or tenderly.

ἀίω, to hear, to perceive; ἐπ-α-ί-ω, to hear, to understand; ἀ-ΐ-τας (Dor.), a beloved youth.

au-di-o, to hear, understand, listen to, (compd. w. ex, in, ob, sub), [*audible, audience, audit*]; **ob-oe-dio, ob-ē-dio** (*ob, audio*), to hearken to, to obey; **ob-oe-diens, ob-ē-diens,** *obedient;* **ăv-us,** a grandfather; **ăv-ia,** a grandmother; **ăv-uncŭlus** (dim.), *uncle;* **ăv-ĕo,** to desire earnestly, to be or fare well; **ăv-ĭdus,** longing eagerly for something; **ăv-ĭdĭtas,** eagerness, *avidity;* **ăv-ārus,** covetous, avaricious; **ăv-aritia, ăv-arities,** *avarice;* **au-deo** (for *avideo,* from *avidus,* prop. to be eager about something), to dare, to be bold; **audax,** daring, courageous, *audacious.*

476. av, va; vû; aF, Fa; va, ve, a; breathe, blow.

ἄ-ω, ἄ-ημι, to blow, breathe hard; ἀή-της, a blast, gale, wind; ἄ-ελλα, a stormy wind, a whirlwind; αὔ-ρα, air in motion, a breeze; οὖ-ρος, a fair wind; ἀ-ήρ, the lower air or atmosphere, air, [*aerolite* (λίθος), *aeronaut* (ναύτης)]; ἀίσθω, to breathe out; ἄσθ-μα, short-drawn breath, panting, *asthma;* αὔω, to shout, to call aloud; ἀϋ-τή, a cry, shout, war-cry; ἀϋ-τέω, to cry, to shout; ἰ-ω-ή, a shout or cry; αὐ-δή, the human voice, speech.

ven-tus, *wind;* ven-tŭlus (dim.), a slight wind, a breeze; ven-tĭlo, to blow gently, to *ventilate;* van-nus, a *fan,* a *van;* āēr, the *air,* (prop.) the lower atmosphere; āĕrius, āĕreus, *aerial,* airy, high, [*aerate, aeriform*].

477. ἀϋτ-μήν, ἀϋτ-μή, breath; ἀτ-μός, smoke, vapor, [*atmosphere*]. These words are derived from No. 476, the root being expanded by ατ.

478. ἔαρ, ἦρ (= Fέσ-αρ = Fέαρ), spring; ἐαρ-ινός, of spring.

ver (= *ves-er* or *ver-er*), the spring; ver-nus, of spring; vernālis, of spring, *vernal.*

479. ἰο-ν (= Fίον), the violet; ἰώδης (ἴον, εἶδος), violet-like, dark-colored, [*iodine*].

vĭŏla, the *violet.*

480. ἰ-ός, an arrow, rust, poison.

vīrus, a slimy liquid, a poisonous liquid, poison, *virus;* vīrŭlentus, poisonous, *virulent.*

481. ἴ-ς (pl. ἴν-ες), sinew, strength; ἰν-ίον, nape of the neck; ἴφι, strongly, mightily; ἴφιος, strong; ἴφθῑμος, strong, mighty, goodly.

vīs (pl. vīres for *vīses*), strength; vī-ŏlo, to treat with violence, to *violate;* vĭŏlentus, forcible, *violent.* For these words there is assumed a Graeco-Italic stem *vi,* which, coming from the √*vi,* plait, (No. 482), meant *band* or *cord,* then (like *nervus,* No. 363) *sinew,* and finally *strength.* The stem is expanded in Greek in some forms by ν, in Latin by *s* (afterwards becoming *r*).

482. va, vi; vja, va; ι; vi; plait, entwine.

ἴ-τυς, shield-rim, felloe of a wheel; ἰ-τέα, a willow, [*withe*].

vĭ-ĕ-o, to plait, weave; vī-men, a pliant twig, a withe; vitta, a band, a fillet; vī-tis, a vine; vĭ-tĭum, (prop. a twist), a fault, defect, *vice;* vĭ-tŭpĕro (*vitium, paro*), to censure, *vituperate.*

483. οἶ-νος (orig. Foῖνος), *wine;* οἴ-νη, vine; οἰ-νάς, οἴν-αρον, a vine-leaf, a tendril; οἰν-άνθη, vine-shoot, vine-blossom.

vī-num, *wine.* The Indo-European root is probably *vi* as in No. 482.

484. ŏ-ïs (orig. ŏϜις), οἶς, a sheep. (Sk. *av-is*, a sheep.)
ŏvi-s, a sheep; ŏvīle, a sheep-fold.

The Sanskrit *avis*, as an adjective, means *devoted, attached*, and is probably derived from the root *av* (No. 475). The sheep may have been called pet, favorite, from its gentleness.

485. οἰ-ωνό-ς, a large bird. (Sk. *vis*, a bird.)
ăvis, a bird; ăvĭarium, a place where birds are kept, an *aviary*; au-ceps, (contr. for *aviceps*, from *avis, capio*), a bird-catcher; augur (*avis* and Sk. *gar*, to call, show, make known), an *augur*, soothsayer; augŭro, augŭror, to act as augur in any matter; ex-augŭro, to desecrate; in-augŭro, to practise augury, to consecrate, *inaugurate*; auspex (a contraction of *avispex*, from *avis-spicio*), (lit. a bird-seer), an augur, soothsayer; auspicium, augury from birds, *auspices*, [*auspicious*]; augŭrium, *augury*, prophecy. The root is probably *va, av*, blow, as in No. 476. We may assume the Indo-European stem *avi*, from which came Greek ὄϜι = ὄï. In Sk. the initial vowel was lost.

486. ᾠ-όν (ὤιον), an egg.
ōvu-m, an egg, [*oval, ovate, ovary*]. .

The older Graeco-Italic form was *ōvjo-m*, of which the Roman suppressed the *j*, and the Greek suppressed the *Ϝ*.

Spiritus Asper.

A Greek spiritus asper is in the following words the representative of an Indo-European initial *s* followed by a vowel, which *s* is retained in the Sanskrit and the Latin.

487. Prefix ἁ-, ἀ-, ὁ-, with. (Sk. *sa, sam*, with). The aspirated form is found in only two words, ἁ-θρό-ος and ἅ-πας; but the so-called ἀ copulative, expressing union, participation or likeness, is very common with the spiritus lenis; e.g., from ἀ copulative and κοίτη, bed, we have ἀκοίτης, husband, ἄκοιτις, wife. This prefix is not related to σύν, ξύν, or to Latin *com-*, but it is probably akin to ἅ-μα (No. 377) and perhaps to No. 488.

488. ἁ in ἅπαξ (formed from ἁ and the root παγ, No. 285), once; ἁ-πλό-ος, single.

sim-plex (*sim* = Sk. *sam, plico*), *simple;* **singuli,** one to each, separate. These words are derived from a stem *sam, sa*, with the meaning *one*, and are probably akin to No. 487 and 377.

489. Pronominal stem, ἑ, Ϝε (for σϜε), σφε, (οὗ, οἷ, ἕ), himself, herself, themselves; ἑ-ός, ὅς, σφός, own, his own, her own, their own; ἴ-διο-ς, one's own, private, personal; ἰ-διώ-της, a private person, one who has no professional knowledge, [*idiot*]; ἰ-δίω-μα, a peculiarity, *idiom.*

se, himself, herself, itself, themselves; **suus,** of or belonging to himself, herself, itself, themselves, [*suicide*].

The Spiritus Asper appears in the following words as the representative of an original *j* or *y*, which in Sk. and Latin may be retained or replaced by *i* or *e*.

490. ya; ja; (st. ό, fem. ά, ή); **i;** pronominal forms.
ὅ-ς, who; ὥς, as.

ϊ-s, he; **e-a,** she; **i-d,** it; **iste** (compounded of two pronominal stems, *i* and *to*), this, that, this of yours, that of yours; **ipse** (*is* and *pse* for *pte;* the suffix *pte* being from the same root as *potis*, No. 314), he himself; **i-bī** (from the pronominal root *i*, with dative ending *bi* [as in *tibi, sibi*], in locative sense [as in *ubi*]), there; **ϊ-ta,** thus; **ϊ-tem** (from the pronominal root *i* and *-tam*), just so, in like manner, also, [*item*]; **i-dem** (from the pronom. rt. *i* and the demonstrative suffix *-dem*, meaning *just, exactly*), the same, [*identical, identity, identify*]; **ϊ-tĕrum,** (acc. sing. neut. of a comparative form from the pronom. rt. *i*), further, again; **ϊ-tĕro,** to do a thing a second time, to repeat, [*iterate, reiterate*].

In the following words (Nos. 491–495), in Greek a simple vowel is the representative of the Indo-European vowel corresponding to it: ă, ε, ο, representing original ă; ā, η, ω, representing original ā; ι and υ representing original *i* and *u;* and the original vowels are retained in Sk. and Latin, sometimes in a fuller form.

491. vas, us; ush, us; —; us; burn.
εὕω, εὔω, to singe; αὔω, to kindle.

ūr-o (= us-o) (us-si, us-tus), to burn, (compd. w. ad, amb, com, de, ex, in, per, prae); us-tor, a burner of dead bodies; combūro (com, būro = ūro), to burn entirely, to consume; com-bus-tio, a burning, *combustion;* bus-tum, the place where the bodies of the dead were burned and buried, a tomb.

492. ἠώς, Aeol. αὔως, Att. ἕως, the dawn; Ἐωσ-φόρος, Bringer of morn, (Lat. Lucifer), the Morning-star; αὔριο-ν, to-morrow; ἦ-ρι (adv.), early; ἠρι-γένεια, child of morn; ἠέριος (adj.), early; ἄριστον, morning-meal, breakfast.

aurōra (for *aus-os-a*), the dawn, morning. Of these words the Indo-Eur. rt. is *us*, burn, shine.

493. i; i; ι; ἰ; go.
"As the root *i* has been expanded in Sk. to *ja*, so Greek ι has been expanded to ἰε, which occurs in ἰέναι. From the same *ja* in a causative sense comes ῖ-η-μι, i.e., *ji-jā-mi*, and, with the addition of a *c*, Lat. *jacio*." Curtius.

εἶ-μι (pl. ἴ-μεν), to go; ἴ-της, ἰ-τα-μός, headlong, eager; οἶ-μος, a way, path; οἴ-μη, the course of a song; οἶ-τος, fate, doom; ἵημι (causal of εἶμι), to put in motion, to send.

e-o (pl. i-mus), to go, (compd. w. amb, ab, ad, ante, circum, com, ex, in, inter, intro, ob, per, prae, praeter, pro, re, retro, sub, trans), [*exit, transient, transit, transition, transitive, transitory*]; Itus, Itio, a going; ambĭtio, a going round, a soliciting for votes, *ambition;* cŏmes (com, eo), a companion; I-ter (for i-*tiner*), a going, a journey, [*itinerant*]; in-It-ium, a going in, a beginning, [*initial*]; in-It-io, to begin, to *initiate;* ex-It-ium, a going out, destruction; sĕd-It-io (sed, i.e., sine, itio), a going apart, dissension, *sedition;* subĭtus, that has come on stealthily or unexpectedly, sudden, unexpected; cŏĭtus, coetus, a coming together, an assemblage; praetor (for *praeitor*), a leader, a praetor (*pretor*); jă-c-io, (to make go, cause to go, hence), to throw, (compd. w. ab, ad, circum, com, de, dis, e, in, inter, ob, prae, pro, re, sub, super, trans), [*adjective, conjecture, dejected, eject, inject, interject, interjection, object, projéct, próject, reject, subjéct, súbject*]; **amĭcĭo** (*am = ambi, jăcio*), to throw around, to wrap about; **amictus**, an outer garment, clothing; **jac-to** (freq.), to throw, to hurl; **jac-tūra**, that which is thrown overboard, loss; **jac-ŭlus** (adj.), that which is thrown, cast, or hurled; **jac-ŭlum**, a net, a dart; **jac-ŭlor**, to hurl a javelin, to throw, [*ejaculate*]; **ŏbex** (*ob, jacio*), a bolt or bar, a barrier; **jăc-eo** (intrans. of *jăcio*), (lit. to be thrown or cast, hence), to lie, (compd. w. ad, circum, inter, ob, prae, sub), [*adjacent, circumjacent*]; **Jānus**, an old Italian deity (the month of January, as the beginning of the year, was sacred to him, as were also the beginnings of things in general; and the doors of houses were under his special protection); **Jānuarius** (adj.), of or belonging to Janus; **Jānuarius** (sc. *mensis*), *January*; **jă-nua**, a door; **jānĭtor**, a door-keeper, a *janitor*.

494. ĭs; ĭsh; ἰσ; —; wish, long for.

ἰό-της, will, desire; ἵ-μερος, a longing or yearning after.

495. οὖς, the ear.

aur-is (= *aus-is*), the ear, [*aurist, auricular*]; **aus-culto** (freq.), to listen to, give ear to, [*auscultation*]. The Indo-Eur. rt. of these words is probably *av* (shown in No. 475). By adding *s* we have the stem *aus* shown in the Latin *auris* (= *ausis*).

PART III.

Irregular Substitution of Sounds.

——∞°○°∞——

k; k, p; π; qu.

496. vak; vak'; Fεπ; vŏc, vec; sound, speak, call.

ἔ-(F)ειπον, εἶπον, I spoke, I said; ἔπ-ος, a word, (pl.) epic poetry; ἐπ-ικός, *epic;* ὄψ, a voice; ἐν-οπ-ή, a cry, voice, sound.

vox (st. *vŏc*), a *voice,* sound; **vŏc-o,** to call, (compd. w. a, ad, com, de, e, in, pro, re, se), [*convoke, evoke, invoke, provoke, revoke*]; **vŏc-ābulum,** an appellation, name, [*vocabulary*]; **vŏc-ālis,** that utters a voice, *vocal;* **vŏc-ātio, vŏc-ātus,** a calling, summoning, [*vocation, avocation, convocation, invocation, provocation, revocation*]; **vŏc-ĭfĕror** (*vox, fero*), to cry out, *vociferate;* **con-vīc-ium** (= *con-vec-ium*), a violent or loud noise, loud or violent reproaching; **invīto** (= *in-vic-ito* = *in-vec-ito*), to *invite,* ask.

497. sak; sak'; ἑπ (for σεπ); **sequ, sec, soc;** follow.

ἕπ-ω, to be about or with; ἕπ-ομαι, to follow; ἑ-σπ-όμην (2 aor.), I followed; ἑπ-έτης, a follower, attendant; ὅπ-λον, an implement, (pl.) arms.

sĕqu-or, to follow, (compd. w. ad, com, ex, in, ob, per, pro, re, sub), [*sue, suit, ensue, pursue, sequence, consequent, consequence, subsequent, consecutive, persecute, prosecute*]; **sec-tor** (freq.), to follow continually or eagerly, (compd. w. ad, com, in); **as-sec-la (ad-sec-la),** a follower; **sĕqu-ester,** a depositary, a trustee; **sĕqu-estro,** to give up for safe-keeping, surrender, [*sequester, sequestrate*]; **sĕc-undus,** following, the following in time or order, the next, the *second,* [*secondary*]; sĕc-undo, to favor, to *second;* sĕc-us, adv. (prop. following later in rank or order), otherwise; sŏc-ius (adj.), sharing, associated; sŏc-ius (subst.), a sharer, partner, companion; sŏc-ialis, of or belonging to companionship, *sociable, social;* sŏc-io, to associate, to share a thing with another, (compd. w. ad, com, dis), [*associate, association, consociate, consociation, dissociate, dissociation*]; sŏc-ietas, *society.*

498. ik; —; ἰπ; ic; hit.

ἵπτομαι, to press hard, to hurt; ἴψ (st. ἰπ), a noxious worm; ἴπ-ος, (in a mouse-trap) the piece of wood that falls and catches the mouse, a fuller's press.

Ic-o, to strike, to hit; ic-tus, a blow, a stroke, (in prosody or music) a beating time, a beat.

499. ἵππος (ἴκκος), a horse; ἱππό-τα, a driver or rider of horses, a horseman, knight; ἵππιος, of or pertaining to horses; ἱππεύς, a horseman; ἱππό-δρομος, a chariot-road, race-course, *hippodrome;* ἱππο-πόταμος, the river-horse, *hippopotamus.*

ĕquu-s, a horse; ĕqu-īnus, of or belonging to horses, *equine;* ĕqu-es, a horseman; Equ-ĭtes, the order of knights; ĕqu-ester, of horsemen, of cavalry, *equestrian;* ĕq-uĭto, to ride, (compd. w. ad, in, inter, ob, per, praeter). The Indo-Eur. root of these words is probably *ak* (No. 2).

500. rik; rik'; λιπ; liqu, lic; leave, leave free.

λείπ-ω, λιμπ-άνω, to leave; λεῖμ-μα, λείψ-ανον, a remnant; λοιπ-ός, remaining, the rest; ἔλ-λευψ-ις, a leaving out, *ellipsis, ellipse.*

linqu-o (līqu-i, lic-tum), to *leave;* de-linquo, to fail, to be wanting in one's duty, [*delinquent*]; rĕ-linquo, to leave behind, *relinquish,* [*relic, relict*]; dē-rĕlinquo, to forsake entirely, [*derelict*]; rĕ-līqu-us, that is left behind, remaining; reliquiae, relliquiae, the remains, *relics;* līc-et (it is left to one, open to one), is is lawful, permitted, (*licet,* being the intrans. to *linquĕre,* as *pendet* to *pendĕre*, *jăcet* to *jăcĕre*), [*licit, illicit*]; lĭc-entia, freedom, *license;* lĭc-eo, to be for sale; lĭc-eor, to bid at an auction; pol-lĭc-eor, [to bid or offer largely, cf. No. 317), to offer, to promise; lĭqu-eo, to be fluid or liquid, to be clear or evident; liqu-esco (inch.), to become fluid or liquid, to become clear; lĭqu-ĭdus, flowing, fluid, *liquid*, clear; lĭqu-or, to be fluid or liquid, to flow; lĭqu-or, fluidity, a fluid or liquid, *liquor*.

501. mark; març; μαρπ, μαπ; mulc; touch, seize.

μάρπ-τω (2 aor. ἔ-μαπ-ον), to catch, seize; μάρπ-τις, a seizer, ravisher.

mulc-o, ‡mulc-to, to maltreat, injure; mulc-eo, to stroke, to touch lightly, (compd. w. com, de, per, re).

502. ak; aç, ak-sh; ὀπ; oc; see.

√ὀπ (ὄπ-ωπ-α, ὄψ-ομαι), see; ὄμ-μα, the eye, a sight; ὤψ, the eye, countenance; ὄψις, the look or appearance of a person or thing, countenance, sight; ὀπ-τήρ, a spy, a scout; ὀπ-ιπεύω, ὀπ-ιπτεύω, to look around after; ὀπ-ή, an opening, a hole; ὀπ-εας, an awl; ὀπ-τικός, of or for sight, *optic, optical*, [*optics, optician*]; ὀφ-θαλμός, the eye; ὀφ-θαλμία, a disease of the eyes, *ophthalmia, ophthalmy*.

ŏc-ŭlus, an eye, [*ocular, oculist, daisy*]; ŏc-ŭlo, to make to see, to make visible, [*ogle*]; in-ŏcŭlo, to *inoculate*, i.e., to ingraft an eye or bud of one tree into another; ex-ŏcŭlo, to deprive of eyes.

503. ὀπ-ός, juice, (properly) the milky juice which flows naturally from a plant or is drawn off by incision; σαφ-ής, clear, sure (prop. of a keen, decided taste); σοφ-ός, skilful, intelligent, wise, [*sophist, philosopher*]; σοφ-ία, skill, intelligence, wisdom; σοφ-ίζω, to make wise, to become wise.

sūg-o, to suck; ex-sūgo, to suck out; sūc-us (succus), juice; sūc-ulentus, full of juice or sap, *succulent;* sū-men (= sug-imen, sug-men), breast; săp-a, must or new wine boiled thick, [*sap*]; †sāpo, soap, [*saponaceous*]; săp-io, to taste, to have taste, to have good taste, to be wise; **săp-iens**, wise, *sapient;* **săp-or**, taste; **săp-ĭdus**, well-tasted, relishing, savory, wise; **in-sĭp-ĭdus**, tasteless, *insipid*.

504. πέντε, five; πέμπ-τος, the fifth.
quinque, five; quintus (= *quinc-tus*), the fifth.

505. pak, kak; pak'; πεπ; **coqu, coc**; cook, ripen.
πέπ-ων, cooked by the sun, ripe, soft, tender.; πεπ-τός, cooked; πέψ-ις, a ripening, cooking, digestion; δυσ-πεψ-ία, indigestion, *dyspepsia, dyspepsy;* πέπ-τω, to soften or ripen, to cook; πέμ-μα, any kind of dressed food, (but mostly in plur.) pastry; πόπ-ανον, a sacrificial cake.
cŏqu-o, to *cook*, (compd. w. com, de, dis, ex, in, per, prae, re), [*decoction*]; cŏqu-us (cŏquos, cŏcus), a *cook;* coqu-īna, a *kitchen;* cŭ-lĭ-na, (= *coc-lina*), a kitchen, [*culinary*].

506. ka; ka; πο, κο; quo; pronominal roots.
πό-θῐ, ποῦ, where; πό-θεν (Ion. κό-θεν), whence? πῶς (Ion. κῶς), *how?* πότε (Ion. κότε), when? πό-τερος (Ion. κό-τερος), which of two? πό-στος (πόσος), which in a series? πο-ῖος (Ion. κοῖος), of what nature, of what sort? πό-σος (Ion. κόσος), of what quantity?
quo-d, that, because; quo (prop. dat. or abl. of *qui*), where, whither; ŭ-bĭ (for *quo-bi*), *where;* qua-m (adverbial acc. of *qui*), how; quan-do, *when;* ŭter (for *cu-ter,* or *quo-tero-s,* in form a comparative of *quis*), which of the two, [*whether*]; ŭterque (*uter, que*), each (of the two), one and the other, one as well as the other; quo-t, how many, as many; quŏtiens, quŏties, how often, how many times, as often as, [*quotient*]; quŏ-tus, which or what in number, order, etc., [*quota*]; quantus (*quam*), how great, [*quantity*]; quā-lis, of what sort or kind, [*quality*].

507. √σεπ, say.
ἔ-σπ-ετε, say; ἔν-ι-σπ-εν, said.

IRREGULAR SUBSTITUTION OF SOUNDS. 175

508. tark; —; τρεπ, τραπ; **torqu, torc;** turn, wind.

τρέπ-ω (Ion. τράπω), to turn; τροπ-ή, a turning round; τρόπ-ος, a turn, manner, *trope;* τροπ-ικός, belonging to a turn or turning, [*tropic, tropical*]; τροπ-αῖος, of a turning, of or belonging to a defeat or rout; τρόπ-αιον, a *trophy*, a monument of the enemy's defeat (τροπή); τρόπ-ις, a ship's keel; τροπ-ήιον, τροπ-εῖον, a press; τραπ-έω, to tread grapes; εὐ-τράπ-ελος, easily turning, versatile.

torqu-eo, to turn, to twist, (compd. w. com, de, dis, ex, in, ob, per, prae, re), [*torsion, tort, tortoise, contòrt, contortion, distort, distortion, extort, extortion, retort, retortion*]; **tor-to** (freq.), to torture; **tor-tor,** an executioner, torturer; **tor-tura,** a twisting, *torture;* **tor-tus,** a twisting, winding; **tor-tuōsus,** full of crooks or turns, *tortuous;* **tor-mentum,** an engine for hurling missiles, an instrument of torture, torture, *torment;* **torqu-is, torqu-es,** a necklace; **torc-ŭlum, torc-ŭlar,** a press.

g; g; β; b, v, g.

509. ga, gva, (g)va-n, ba; ga, gam; βα; bi, bi-t, bu, (ven), go.

2 aor. ἔ-βη-ν, I went; Hom. pres. part., βι-βά-s, going; (iterative) βά-σκε, go; (verbal adj.) βα-τός, passable; pres. βαίν-ω, I go; βῆ-μα, a step, a raised place to speak from; βω-μός, an altar (with a base or steps); βη-λός, the threshold; βέ-βη-λος, allowable to be trodden, profane; βά-σις, a stepping, step, *base, basis;* ἀνά-βα-σις, a going up; βά-θρον, that on which anything steps or stands, a pedestal, step, the ground; βά-δ-ος, a walk; βα-δ-ίζω, to walk or go slowly, to march; βέ-βα-ιος, firm, steady; βι-βά-ζω (causal of βαίνω), to make to mount, to lift up.

vĕn-io, to come, (compd. w. ad, ante, com, de, dis, e, inter, in, ob, per, prae, pro, re, sub, super), [*advent, adventure, convene, cònvent, event, intervene, invent, inventory, prevent, supervene*]; **ven-tĭto** (freq.), to come often; **ad-vĕn-a,** one who comes to a place, a foreigner, a stranger; **ven-tio,** a coming, [*intervention, invention, prevention, supervention*]; **con-ven-tio,** a meeting, *convention,* agreement; **con-tio** (less correctly **concio**) (= *con-ventio*), a meeting, a discourse; **contiōnor, conciōnor,** to be convened in an assembly, to deliver an oration; **bă-cŭlum, bă-cŭlus,** a staff; **bē-to, bae-to, bī-t-o,** to go, (compd. w. ad, e, in, inter, per, praeter, re); **ar-bĭ-t-er** (*ar* = *ad, bito*), one that goes to something in order to see or hear it, a spectator, one who approaches a cause in order to inquire into it, an *arbiter;* **ar-bĭ-tror,** to hear, judge, believe, *arbitrate;* **ar-bĭ-trium,** judgment, decision; **ar-bi-trarius,** of arbitration, uncertain, depending on the will, *arbitrary;* **am-bŭ-lo** (= *ambi-bŭ-lo*), to go about, to walk, (compd. w. circum, de, in, ob, per, re), [*ambulant, ambulance, ambulatory, amble, perambulate*].

510. —; **gal;** βαλ, βελ, βολ; —; fall, glide, slip away, let slip, let fly, throw.

βάλ-λω, to throw, (intr.) to fall; δια-βάλ-λω, to throw over or across, to slander; διά-βολ-ος, a slanderer, the Slanderer, the *Devil;* δια-βολ-ικός, slanderous, devilish, *diabolical;* βλή-μενος, βλη-τός, hit; βλῆ-μα, a throw, a missile, a wound; βέλ-ος, a missile; βέλ-εμνον, a dart; βελ-όνη, a point, a needle; βολ-ή, a throw, a stroke; βόλ-ος, a throw with a casting-net, a net; βολ-ίς, a missile, the sounding-lead.

511. βăρύ-ς, heavy; βăρύ-τονος (βăρύς, τόνος), deep-sounding, [*barytone, baritone*]; βăρ-ος, βαρύ-της, weight, [*barometer*]; βαρέ-ω, to weigh down; ἐπι-βαρέ-ω, to weigh down, press heavily upon.

grăv-is (= *gar-uis*), heavy, *grave,* [*grief*]; **grăv-ĭtas,** weight, *gravity;* **grăv-o,** to load, to weigh down, (compd. w. ad, de, in, prae), [*grieve, aggrieve, aggravate*]; **grăv-esco** (inch.), to become burdened or heavy; **grăv-ĭdus,** pregnant, laden; **brū-tus** (kindred with βαρύς, perhaps contracted from *bărūtus*), heavy, dull, irrational, *brute,* [*brutal*].

512. gĭ, gvĭ-v, gvĭ-g; g'ĭv; βι; vĭ, vĭ-v, vĭ-g; live.

βί-ος, βί-οτος, βι-οτή, life, course of life, livelihood, [*biography, autobiography, biology*]; βι-όω, to live.

vīt-a, life; **vīt-ālis,** *vital;* **vīv-us,** living, *quick;* **vīv-ĭdus,** living, animated, *vivid;* **vīv-ax,** tenacious of life, vigorous, *vivacious;* **vīv-ācĭtas,** natural vigor, liveliness, *vivacity;* **vīv-o,** to live, (compd. w. com, pro, re, super), [*revive, revival, survive*]; **vic-tus,** that upon which one lives, provisions, *victuals.*

513. gu; gu; βο; bo; cry aloud, roar, bellow.

βο-ή, a loud cry, a shout; βο-άω, to cry aloud, to shout.

bŏ-o, bŏv-o, to cry aloud, to roar; **re-bŏ-o,** to bellow back, resound, re-echo; **bŏv-īnor,** to bellow at, to revile.

514. gar, gal; gar; βορ, βρο; vor (for gvor), **gur, gul, glu;** swallow, devour.

βι-βρώ-σκω, to eat; βορ-ά, meat; βορ-ός, gluttonous; βρῶ-μα, food; βρω-τήρ, eating.

vŏr-o (= *gvoro*), to devour; **dē-vŏro,** to swallow down, to *devour;* **vŏr-ax,** swallowing greedily, *voracious;* **vŏr-ācĭtas,** greediness, *voracity;* **vŏr-āgo,** (that which swallows up), an abyss, whirlpool; **gur-ges,** a raging abyss, a whirlpool, [*gorge*]; in-**gur-gĭto,** to pour in like a flood or whirlpool; **gur-gŭl-io,** the gullet, windpipe; **gŭl-a,** the *gullet,* throat, [*gully*]; **glū-tio, gluttio,** to swallow or gulp down, [*glut, deglutition*]; **in-glŭvies,** the crop, maw.

515. gu; gu; βο; bo; bellow.

βοῦς, an ox, a cow; βου-κόλος, a herdsman; βου-κολικός, pastoral, *bucolic.*

bōs, an ox, a cow, [*bos, bossy, bovine*].

k; k'; τ; qu.

516. τε, and.

que, and. This particle is probably derived from the interrogative stem (No. 506).

517. τέσσαρες, four; τέταρτος, τέτρατος, the fourth; τετράκις, four times.

quattuor, quatuor, *four;* quartus, the fourth, [*quarter, quart, quartan, quartette, quarto*]; quăter, four times; quădro, to make square, [*quadrate*]; quadrans, a fourth part, [*quadrant*]; quadrīgae (contr. from *quadrijugae, quatuor, jugum*), a set or team of four; quadrŭpēs (*quattuor, pes*), a four-footed animal, a *quadruped.*

518. √τι, pay.

τί-ω, to pay honor to a person, to honor, to value; τί-νω, to pay a price, (mid.) to have a price paid one, to exact a penalty; τι-μή, honor, value; τι-μάω, to honor, to value; τί-μημα, valuation, census; τι-μη-τής, one who estimates, the censor; τί-σις, payment by way of return or recompense, vengeance.

519. ki; —; τι; qui; interrog. pronom. roots.

τί-s, τί (interrog. pronoun), *who? what?* τις, τι (indef. pronoun enclitic), any one, anything.

qui-s, qui-d, (interrog. pronoun), *who? which? what?* qui-s, qui-d, (indef. pronoun), any one, anything. These forms are to be referred to *ki*, the weaker form of the interrogative stem; the stronger form is shown under No. 506.

In the following example the corresponding letters are **gh; gh; θ; f.**

520. ghar; ghar; θερ; for, fur; hot, warm.

θέρ-ομαι, to become hot or warm; θέρ-ος, summer; θερ-μός, hot, *warm,* [*thermometer*]; θέρ-μη, heat; θέρ-μαι (pl.), hot springs; θέρ-μετε (vb.), heat; θερ-μαίνω, to warm, to heat.

for-mus, for-mĭdus, warm; fur-nus, for-nus, an oven; for-nax, a *furnace,* an oven; for-ceps (*formus, capio*), (lit. that which takes hold of what is hot), a pair of tongs, pincers, *forceps.*

In Nos. 521 and 522 we find a change of an original **b** or **bh** to Greek **F.**

521. Sk. **bhañg' (bhanag'-mi),** break, burst; **bhang-as,** breach.

Greek √**Fαγ.** ἄγ-νυμι, to break; ἀγ-ή, breakage, a fragment, the place where the waves break, the beach; ἀ-αγ-ής, unbroken, not to be broken.

522. bargh, bhrag; —; Fραγ, Fρηγ; frag; break.

ῥήγ-νυμι, to break, break or burst through; ῥῆγ-μα, a fracture, a rent; ῥηγ-μίς, ῥηγ-μίν, breakers; διαρρώξ, rent asunder; ῥωγαλέο-ς, broken, cleft, torn.

frang-o, to break, (compd. w. com, de, dis, e, in, inter, ob, per, prae, re, sub), [*frangible, fraction, infringe, infraction, refract, refraction, refractory*]; **frag-men, frag-mentum,** a piece broken off, a *fragment;* **frăg-or,** a breaking, a crashing; **frăg-ĭlis,** easily broken, *fragile, frail;* **frac-tūra,** a *fracture.*

In the following words we find in Greek an interchange of λ and ρ.

523. sar; sar; ἁλ; sal; leap.

ἅλλ-ομαι, to spring, leap; ἅλ-μα, a spring, leap; ἁλ-τικός, good at leaping, active.

săl-io, to leap, (compd. w. ad, dis, ex, in, prae, pro, re, sub, trans), [*salient, assail*]; **sal-tus,** a leaping, a bound; **sal-to** (freq.), to dance, (compd. w. ad, de, dis, ex, in, per, prae, sub, trans), [*assault, desultory, exult, insult*]; **săl-ax,** fond of leaping, *salacious;* **săl-ebra,** a jolting-place, roughness in a road; **prae-sul,** one who leaps or dances before others.

524. ἅλ-ς (m.), salt; ἅλ-ες (pl.), intellectual 'salt,' wit; ἅλ-ς (f.), the sea; ἅλ-ιος, marine; ἁλ-ιεύς, one who has to do with the sea, a fisher, a sailor; ἅλ-μη, sea-water, brine; ἁλ-μυρός, salt, briny; ἁλ-ίζω, to salt.

sal, *salt,* the sea, intellectual acuteness, wit; **săl-io, sălo, sallo,** to salt down, to salt; **sal-sus,** salted, salt.

525. var, val; var; βολ, βουλ; vol; will, choose.

βούλ-ομαι (Hom. βόλ-εται, ἐ-βόλ-οντο), to will, to wish; βουλ-ή, will, plan; βούλ-ησις, a willing, a purpose; βούλ-ημα, a purpose; βουλ-εύω, to take counsel, to plan.

vŏl-o, to *will,* to wish, [*volition*]; **nō-lo** (= *ne, volo*), to wish or will ... not, to be unwilling; **vŏl-untas,** will, choice; **vŏluntarius,** willing, *voluntary, volunteer;* **vel** (old imperative of *vŏlo,* take your choice) (conj.), or; **vel ... vel,** either ... or.

526. —; **var; Fελ;** —; press, restrain, shut in, protect.

εἰλ-ω, εἰλ-έω, to pack close, to collect; εἰλ-αρ, a close covering, a defence; οὐλ-ἄμός, a throng of warriors; εἰλ-η, ἰλ-η, a crowd, a troop; ὅμῑλος (ὁμός, ἴλη), a crowd, a throng; ὁμῑλέω (ὅμῑλος), to be together with, be associated with.

527. ὅλο-ς (Ion. οὖλος), whole, [*catholic*].

sollu-s (old Latin form, retained in the compounds, *sollennis, sollers, sollicitus, sollifereus*), whole, entire; **sŏl-ĭdus,** firm, *solid*.

528. svar; (svar, heaven); σερ (for σϝερ), σειρ, σελ (for σϝελ); **ser, sor, sol;** shine, burn.

σείρ-ιος = σειρ-ός, hot, scorching; Σείρ-ιος, Sirius, the dog-star; σειρ-ιάω, to be hot and scorching; σέλ-ας, light; σελ-ήνη, the moon, [*selenography*].

sĕr-ēnus, clear, bright, *serene;* **sĕr-ēno,** to make clear or fair; **sōl,** the sun; **sōl-āris,** *solar.*

PART IV.

Application of the Principles of the New School.

CHAPTER I.

ABLAUT I.

THE three root-forms which are treated under the names of ablaut I., II., and III., each occur regularly in Greek, as in the other languages of the family, only in certain kinds of formations, or, conversely, a certain Greek word has but one historically correct root-form or ablaut. But as in language everywhere, so especially in a language of the rich, independent life of the Greek, disturbing forces have operated against the laws which originally shaped the several word formations, and have in certain cases succeeded in almost obliterating the effects of these laws. The unfriendly forces at work are best defined as: 1. *Assimilation* by what is generally termed 'false analogy' or form association. 2. *New formation* upon some already existing form, or upon the material abstracted from such a form. A single example to illustrate each will not be amiss.

(1) The noun bases in ες, generally serving as abstracts (θέρ-ος, κλέF-ος, etc.), are made with ablaut I. According to this rule are made βένθ-ος and πένθ-ος, both occurring in Homer, but going out of common use about the time of Herodotus. In the later language there appear in addition to these βάθ-ος and πάθ-ος, illegitimately made with ablaut III. These are evidently formed after the analogy of βαθ-ύς, ἔ-παθ-ον, etc., forms which regularly have ablaut III., and with which the abstracts were associated in the minds of the

language-users until they crowded out the historically correct βένθ-ος and πενθ-ος, because there were no forms by mental association with which they could be kept alive.

(2) The present ῥάπ-τω is made with ablaut III. Ordinarily the theme of the present stands in no formal relation with the themes of the other tenses, e.g., the present πάσχω is made with ablaut III., but future πείσομαι (πένθ-σομαι) with ablaut I., as the future regularly is. But the future and sigmatic aorist corresponding to ῥάπτω are made according to its root-vowel: ῥάψω, ἔρραψα, where we should expect ῥέμψω, ἔρρεμψα; cf. ῥομ-φεύς.

Verbal Formations.

1. The singular of non-thematic (root) presents originally was accented on the root, which appears in its first strong form. The material in Greek is very meagre: εἶ-μι, εἶ and Hom. εἶ-σθα, εἶ-σι : ἴ-μεν. — εἶ-μί (ἐσ-μί), Dor. ἐσ-σί, ἐσ-τί : Dor. (σ)-εντί; further the Hom. infinitive ἔδ-μεναι; cf. Lat. es-t = Sk. at-ti. An Indo-European irregularity is contained in κεῖ-ται = Sk. çé-te, because ablaut I. appears in the middle. From Class BB there is another example: φη-μί, φή-s, φη-σί : φᾰ-μέν. Sanskrit has this class largely represented: é-mi, i-más; ás-mi, s-más; hán-mi; ghn-ánti; vác-mi; uc-más, etc. The only Latin instance which preserves the difference between strong and weak forms is contained in es-t : s-unt.

2. The entire system, active and middle, of thematic presents, when corresponding to the Hindu I. class, is made with ablaut I. They are to be found in Curt. Verb. I^2, 210 and 223. Examples: ἔχ-ω, δέχ-ομαι, τεί-ω, κε(y)-ομαι, κλέ(F)-ω, ἀλεύ-ομαι, δέρ-ω, πέλ-ομαι, μέν-ω, φείδ-ομαι, φεύγ-ω, τέρσ-ομαι, σπέν-δω, μέμφ-ομαι, etc. Of Class BB: λήθ-ω, τήκ-ω, ἤδ-ομαι, etc. Lat. leg-o, reg-o, trem-o, dīc-o (= deic-o), fīd-o (=feid-o), dūc-o (= deuc-o), ūr-o (= eus-o), clep-o, serp-o, etc.

3. A considerable number of presents of the iota-class are made (irregularly) with ablaut I.: πέσσω, σείω (σεF-yω), πλείω

(πλεϝ-γω), κλείω (κλεϝ-γω), τείρω, φθείρω, σπείρω, ἀγείρω, ἐγείρω, δείρω, κείρω, μείρομαι, πείρω, εἴρω (σερ-γω), τελλω, δελλω and ζέλλω, ὀφείλω, ὀφέλλω, στέλλω, κέλλω, ὀκέλλω, μελλω, σκέλλω, τείνω, γείνομαι, θείνω, κτείνω, λεύσσω, ἔρδω (= ϝεργ-γω).

4. The future systems, active and middle, are made with ablaut I.: ἐδ-οῦμαι, κεί-σομαι, πλευ-σοῦμαι, δερ-ῶ, στελ-ῶ, τεν-ῶ, νεμ-ῶ, λείψω, φευξοῦμαι, τέρψω, βλέψω, πέμψω, etc.

5. The sigmatic (first) aorist system, active and middle, is made with ablaut I.: ἔλεξα, ἔ-δδει-σα, ἐ-ρρευ-σα, ἔ-φθειρα, ἔ-στειλα, ἔ-μεινα, ἔ-λειψα, ἔ-θρεψα, etc. To these correspond the simple s-aorists in Sk. (Whitney, §§ 878, 879): a-çro-ṣ-i, a-ne-ṣ-i, etc.

6. The first aorist passive, a special Greek formation, is made with this ablaut with very few exceptions. It differs in this important respect from the second aorist passive, which is made with ablaut III. The following are the instances from roots of Class AA: ἠνέχ-θην, ἐ-πέφ-θην, ἐ-πέχ-θην, ἐ-στέφ-θην, ἐ-λέχ-θην, ἐ-πνεύσ-θην, ἐ-πλεύσ-θην, ἠγέρ-θην (ἀγείρω), ἠγέρ-θην (ἐγείρω), ἐ-κέρ-θην, ἐ-πείσ-θην, ἠλείφ-θην, ἠρείχ-θην, ἐ-λείφ-θην, ἠμείφ-θην, ἐλείχ-θην, ἐ-δείχ-θην, ἐ-ψεύσ-θην, ἐ-τεύχ-θην, ἐ-ζεύχ-θην, ἐ-γεύσ-θην, εὑ-θείς, ἐ-κλέφ-θην, ἐ-θέλχ-θην, ἐ-πλέχ-θην, ἐ-βλέφ-θην, ἐ-φλέχ-θην, ἐ-δέρχ-θην, ἐ-στρέφ-θην, ἐ-τρέφ-θην, ἐ-θρέφ-θην, ἐ-σπέρχ-θην, ἐ-τέρφ-θην, ἐ-βρέχ-θην, ἐ-στέρχ-θην, ἐ-σπείσ-θην, (= ἐ-σπένδ-θην), ἐ-μέμφ-θην, ἐ-πέμφ-θην; of Class BB cf. ἐ-λήφ-θην and ἐ-δήχ-θην.

Seeming exceptions are the Doric ἐ-στράφ-θην, ἐ-τράφ-θην, etc. Their vowels are on the same level with, and are to be explained like τράφ-ω, στράφ-ω, τράχ-ω, etc., as a special dialectic peculiarity.

Interesting are the cases in which first and second aorist passive occur from the same root: ἐ-κέρ-θην : ἐ-κάρ-ην; ἠλείφ-θην : ἐξ-ηλίφ-ην, ἠρείφ-θην : ἠρίπ-ην; ἐ-ζεύχ-θην : ἐ-ζύγ-ην; ἐ-κλέφ-θην : ἐ-κλάπ-ην; ἐ-πλέχ-θην : ἐ-πλάκ-ην; ἐ-δέρχ-θην : ἐ-δράκ-ην; ἐ-στρέφ-θην : ἐ-στράφ-ην; ἐ-τέρφ-θην : ἐ-τάρπ-ην; ἐ-τρέφ-θην : ἐ-τράπ-ην; ἐ-θρέφ-θην : ἐ-τράφ-ην; ἐ-βρέχ-θην : ἐ-βράχ-ην; cf. from Class AA ἐ-τήχ-θην : ἐ-τᾰκ-ην.

Nominal Formations.

7. Nominal and adjectival bases in ες are made with ablaut I.: (F)έπος, νέφ-ος, ἔχεσ-φιν; ἔτ-ος, πέκ-ος, λέπ-ος, πέ(σ)-ος, κτέ-ος, στέγ-ος, τέγ-ος, ἔρεβ-ος, λέχ-ος, ἕδ-ος, ῥέγ-ος, ῥέθ-ος, στέφ-ος; δέ(y)-ος; ῥέ(F)-ος, κλε(F)-ος, σκεῦ-ος; δέρ-ος, μέρ-ος, θέρ-ος, εἶρ-ος, ἔρ-ος; ἕλ-ος, βέλ-ος, τέλ-ος, σκέλ-ος, μέλ-ος; μέν-ος, γέν-ος, σθέν-ος, νέμ-ος, γέμ-ος; εἶδ-ος, μεῖδ-ος, τεῖχ-ος; γλεῦκ-ος, κεῦθ-ος, ζεῦγ-ος, ἔρευθ-ος, τεῦχ-ος, ψεῦδ-ος; κέρδ-ος, ἔρκ-ος, θέρσ-ος, στρέφ-ος; βλέπ-ος, φλέγ-ος, ἕλκ-ος, κλέπ-ος, βένθ-ος, πένθ-ος, ῥέγκ-ος, (ῥέγχ-ος), ἔγχ-ος, ἔλεγχ-ος, φέγγ-ος, λέμβ-ος, λέμφ-ος.

Adjectives: ποδ-ηνεκής, εὐ-μενής, ἰο-δνεφής, εὐ-σεβ-ής, Ἐτεο-κλῆς (theme: -κλεF-ες), Εὐ-πτερής, νημερτής, περι-σκελής, ζα-φλεγής, ἀ-τενής, ἀμφι-ρρεπής, ἀ-σπερχές, ἀ-μερφές.

As first members of compounds: φερέσ-βιος, ἐγερσί-μαχος, θελξί-νοος, etc.

Cf. also nouns in ας: σέβ-ας, δέμ-ας, σέλ-ας, γέρ-ας, σκέπ-ας, κρέ-ας, λέπ-ας.

Formed by association with βαθ-ύς, θρασ-ύς, κρατ-ύς, etc., are made πάθ-ος, βάθ-ος, θάρσ-ος and θράσ-ος, κράτ-ος and κάρτ-ος, etc.; some historically correct forms, πένθ-ος, etc., are also preserved. Otherwise irregular are λάχ-ος, ὄχ-ος; εὐ-τυχής and δυσ-πονής are denominative formations.

Lat., *gen-us, nem-us, vct-us*, etc. In comp., *de-gener*.

8. Bases in τωρ, τηρ, της are formed with ablaut I.: Ἔκ-τωρ, Νέσ-τωρ, Μέν-τωρ, Στέν-τωρ, νεμ-έ-τωρ, ἔρκ-τωρ, κέν(τ)-τωρ, θέλκ-τωρ, τεῦκ-τωρ;— θελκ-τήρ, θρεπ-τήρ, στρεπ-τήρ, ζευκ-τήρ, πευσ-τήρ, τευκ-τήρ, ἀλειπ-τήρ, πεισ-τηρ (: πείθω), γεν-ε-τήρ;— ἐπ-έ-της, νεφελ-ηγερέ-της, ἐρ-έ-της, Μέν-της, αὐθ-έν-της, ἀλείπ-της, ψεύσ-της, πεύσ-της, κλέπ-της, Θερσί-της.

The secondary suffix τρο- follows the same norm: λέκ-τρον κέν(τ)-τρον, δέρ-τρον, φέρ-τρον, τὰ θρέπ-τρα; φέρετρον and τέρ-ε-τρον.

Lat., *sec-tor, emp-tor, vec-tor, lec-tor, tex-tor, gen-i-tor*, etc.

9. Noun-bases in *man* (neuters in μα-τ; masculines in μων) are made with ablaut I.: εἶ-μα; Aeol. ἔμ-μα (root Fεσ), πέμ-μα, λέμ-μα, ζέσ-μα, στέμ-μα, βδέσ-μα, ὄρεγ-μα, ῥέγ-μα; δεῖ-μα, χεῖ-μα, πνεῦ-μα, ῥεῦ-μα, χεῦ-μα, νεῦ-μα, δεῦ-μα; τέρ-μα, φέρ-μα, σπέρ-μα, ἔρ-μα, δέρ-μα, κέρ-μα; πέλ-μα, τέλ-μα, σέλ-μα; ἄλειμ-μα, ἔρειγ-μα, ἔρεισ-μα, λεῖμ-μα, δεῖγ-μα, ψεῦσ-μα, τεῦγ-μα, κεῦθ-μα, ζεῦγ-μα, γεῦ-μα; βλέμ-μα, κλέμ-μα, θέλγ-μα, πλέγ-μα, φλέγ-μα, ἔργ-μα, δέργ-μα, στρέμ-μα, θρέμ-μα, πεῖσ-μα (= πενθ-μα). As an example of an exception χύ-μα is late; χεῦ-μα Homeric.

Sk., kár-man, bhár-man, tok-man, várt-man, etc.

Lat., ger-men, seg-men, ter-men, lū-men (= leuc-men).

Nouns in μων: χει-μών, λει-μών, πλεύ-μων, πνεύ-μων, τέρ-μων; τερ-ά-μων and τελ-α-μών; derivatives: φλεγ-μον-ή, βέλ-ε-μν-ον, στελ-μον-ίαι; in comp. ἀν-εί-μων, 'unclad': εἶ-μα.

Lat., ter-mo, ser-mo.

10. The comparatives and superlatives in ιων and ισ-τος are formations accented on the root-syllable, and are regularly made with ablaut I.: κερδ-ίων, κέρδ-ιστος; μείζων, μέγ-ιστος, μεί-(γ)ων; κρείσσων (κρέτ-γων), Doric-Ionic κρέσσων; the superlatives κράτ-ιστος and κάρτ-ιστος (abl. III.) have been attracted to the vocalic condition of the positive κρατ-ύς.

11. Formations in ανο, ανη, ονη (υνη) seem to be pretty equally divided between ablauts I. and II. With ablaut I.: ἐδ-ανός, σφεδ-ανός, σκεπ-ανός, στεγ-ανός; σκέπ-ανον, δρέπ-ανον, λείψ-ανον; ἐρκ-άνη, σφενδ-όνη, περ-όνη, βελ-όνη, ἀμπ-εχ-όνη; cf. τέμ-ενος.

With ablaut II.: ζό(F)-ανον, ὄργ-ανον, πόπ-ανον, ὄχ-ανον, χό(F)-ανος; χόδ-ανος, ὀρφ-ανός, ῥοδ-ανός, οὐρ-ανός (= Fορ-ανός), ὀρκ-άνη (ὀρχ-άνη), τορ-ύνη.

CHAPTER II.

ABLAUT II.

Verbal Formations.

THE Greek, as well as the Indo-European, perfect is a non-thematic or root-formation. Like the non-thematic present, it originally exhibited the difference of accent and root-form between the singular active on the one hand and the dual-plural active and entire middle on the other. The singular active, having the accent on the root, contained and still regularly contains strong forms; in case of Class AA, ablaut II.: ἔ-οικ-α, μέ-μον-α : ἔ-ϊκ-τον, μέ-μα-τον ; of Class BB : λέ-ληθ-α, πέ-φην-α : λέ-λᾶσ-ται, πέ-φᾰν-ται. The perfects with o are given in Curt. Verb. II., 185 and 188. Examples: τέ-τοκ-α, δέ-δοι-κα, ἔ-φθορ-α, ἔ-Ϝολ-α, κέ-κον-α, δέ-δρομ-α, πέ-ποιθ-α, ἐλ-ήλουθ-α ; δέ-δορκ-α, κέ-κλοφ-α, πέ-πονθα, λέ-λογχ-α, πέ-πομφ-α.

Lat., o in the old perfects: *mo-mord-i, spe-pond-i,* and *tc-tond-i.*

[NOTE. Many are the intrusions which have been made upon this rule of root-vowels for the singular active. So the vowel-group ευ, as is well known, has, with the exception of the single ἐλ-ήλουθ-α, supplanted the group ου : τέ-τευχ-α, πέ-φευγ-α, κέ-κευθ-α, πέ-πνευ-κα. Not infrequently the weak forms of the perfect have intruded upon the singular, as vice versa the strong forms have generally usurped the territory of the weak in the active dual and plural : δέ-δι-α with δέ-δοι-κα ; ἔ-φθαρ-κα with ἔ-φθορ-α ; ἔ-σπαρ-κα, κέ-καρ-κα, ἔ-σταλ-κα, τέ-τα-κα, ἀλ-ήλιφ-α, ἐρ-ήριπ-α ; the frequency of κ-perfects among these attests the fact that these are later formations, made after the accentual law, the cause of the difference between strong and weak forms, had become extinct. A few perfects are made upon the theme of the present: κέ-χανδ-α : χανδάνω ; (ἔ-πτᾱρ-α : πταίρ-ω) ; εἴ-ληχ-α by the side of λέ-λογχ-α is made like εἴ-ληφ-α, λέ-ληθ-α, etc.; λα-γ-χ-άνω, ἔ-λαχ-ον (root-syllable λῠχ), apparently equal to λα-μ-β-άνω, ἔ-λαβ-ον (root-syllable λᾰβ) show the reason.]

2. Derived verbs in *aya*, Gr. ε(y)ω, take ablaut II.: ὀχ-έω, ἐκ-ποτ-έομαι, φοβ-έω, φορ-έω, ῥοφ-έω, πον-έω, στοιχ-έω, πορθ-έω, στροφ-έω, τροπ-έω, τροφ-έω, στοργ-έω, τρομ-έω, στροβ-έω, ῥομβ-έω, ὀρχ-έομαι; the same formations are contained in μεμόρ-ηται, βε-βόλ-ημαι, ἀπ-ε-κτόν-ηκα, σπορ-ητός, δομ-ήτωρ, etc.; an exception is στιβ-έω, made directly upon στίβ-ος.

Lat., *mon-eo, noc-eo, tond-eo, tong-eo, spond-eo*, etc.

Nominal Formations.

3. A special Greek formation made in close junction with the preceding are the themes in ευς : τοκ-εύς, χο(F)εύς, τορ-εύς, φορ-εύς, φθορ-εύς, σπορ-εύς, γον-εύς, φον-εύς, δρομ-εύς, τομ-εύς, νομ-εύς, πορθ-εύς, στροφ-εύς, τροφ-εύς, ἀμοργ-εύς, ἀμολγ-εύς, πλοκ-εύς, κλοπ-εύς, ῥομφ-εύς, πομπ-εύς, etc.; στιβ-εύς occurs like στιβ-έω.

4. Themes in *a* (Greek *o*, masculine and neuter, *η* feminine) are formed with ablaut II. The accent in historical times is generally found on the suffix in the case of *feminines;* on the suffix also in the case of *masculines* when they have the function of *adjectives* or *nomina agentis;* but on the root in the case of *masculines* when they are *abstracts* or *names of objects.* Accordingly there are: —

(α) Feminines: ἐν-(F)οπ-ή, σκοπ-ή, ῥο(F)-ή, πνο(F)-ή, βολ-ή, στολ-ή, φον-ή, τομ-ή, στοιβ-ή, σπουδ-ή, κλοπ-ή, πομπ-ή, etc.

(β) Adjectives and Nomina Agentis : δοχ-ός, σκοπ-ός, λοιπ-ός, σμοι-ός, θο(F)ός, βορ-ός, τομ-ός, ἀοιδ-ός, ἀμοιβ-ός, τροφ-ός, κλοπ-ός, ὁλκ-ός, πομπ-ός, φορ-ός (cf. φόρ-ος), τροχ-ός (cf. τρόχ-ος), etc.

(γ) Abstracts and Names of Objects : τόκ-ος, φόβ-ος, λόγ-ος, χο(F)-ός, σό(F)-ος, νόμ-ος, φόν-ος, δρόμ-ος, βόλ-ος, στόλ-ος, πτόρ-ος, φόρ-ος, στοῖχ-ος, τρόχ-ος, δνόφ-ος, μόμφ-ος, ῥόγχ-ος, etc.

Exceptionally forms with ablaut I.: φειδ-ός, λευκ-ός, Δελφ-οί, ἔργ-ον; with ablaut III.: φυγ-ή, ζυγ-όν, στίχ-ος, etc.

Lat., dol-u-s, mod-u-s, tog-a.

5. Themes in ι are made with ablaut II.: τρόχ-ις, τρόφ-ις, τρόπ-ις, χρόμ-ις, μόμψ-ις, δρόπ-ις. Those in ιδ are pretty evenly divided between ablauts I. and II., and generally have the tone on the suffix: ἐλπ-ίς, σκελ-ίς and σχελ-ίς, σελ-ίς, λεπ-ίς, κερκ-ίς; ζο(F)-ίς, βολ-ίς, λοπ-ίς, φλογ-ίς, βροχ-ίς.

6. A special Greek formation (probably secondary) with ablaut II. are the nouns in άδ: λογ-άς, σπορ-άς, στολ-άς, λοιπ-άς, ὁλκ-άς, πλοκ-άς, λοπ-άς, δρομ-άς, ὀργ-άς, δορκ-άς, φορβ-άς, νομ-άς, ὀρχ-άς, τροχ-άς, φοιτ-άς, Στοιχ-άδες, Στροφ-άδες; exceptions with ablaut III.: φυγ-άς, νιφ-άς, μιγ-άς.

7. Themes in ma (μος, μη, μον; ιμος, αμος) are regularly formed with ablaut II.; the accent wavers between root and suffix, except in the case of those in ιμος: γόν-ιμος, λόπ-ιμος, μόρσ-ιμος, τρόφ-ιμος, πλόκ-ιμος, σπόρ-ιμος, φθόρ-ιμος. Those without intervening vowel are, (a) With the accent on the root: πότ-μος, οἶ-μος, τόρ-μος, ὄρ-μος, ὄλ-μος, ὄρκ-μος; λόχ-μη, οἴ-μη, τόλ-μη. (b) With the accent on the suffix: ῥογ-μός, ἀλοι-μός, λοι-μός, συν-εοχ-μός, κορ-μός, φορ-μός, στολ-μός, βροχ-μός, ῥωχ-μός, πλοχ-μός, φλογ-μός; δοχ-μή, ὀρ-μή; also a base κοι-μα- in κοι-μά-ω. In αμος: πλόκ-αμος, ὄρχ-αμος; οὐλ-αμός (= Fολ-), ποτ-αμός.

Lat., for-ma (Sk. root dhar); for-mus (Sk. root ghar).

8. Themes in ta (το, τη) which are not verbal adjectives are regularly accented on the root-syllable and take ablaut II.: οἶ-τος, κοῖ-τος, κόν(τ)-τος, νόσ-τος, φόρ-τος, χόρ-τος.

Lat., hor-tus = κόρ-τος.

CHAPTER III.

ABLAUT III.

This root-form is the one which appears when the accent of a word rests on some formative element, not on the root itself. The special Greek law of accentuation has, however, engrafted itself upon the old Indo-European accentual system, leaving but a few fossilized remnants, which have resisted the new law (infinitives of second aorist, verbal adjectives in τός, etc.).

Verbal Formations.

1. The dual and plural active and the middle of non-thematic presents were originally accented on the personal suffixes, leaving the root-syllable without accent, which therefore appears in its weakest form, ablaut III.: ἴ-τον, ἴ-μεν : εἰμι ; Doric (σ)-ἐντί : ἐσ-τί ; the vowel is inorganically restored in ἐσ-μέν, ἐσ-τόν, etc., as is shown by Sk. *s-mas*, Lat. *s-umus*, etc. Of Class BB : φα-μέν, φα-τόν : φη-μί ; ἔ-φα-μεν, ἔ-φα-τον : ἔ-φη-σθα. Sk. *s-mas* : *ás-mi;* *i-más* : *é-mi;* *ha-thás* : *hán-mi.* Lat., *s-unt* : *es-t.* With the same ablaut are formed the optative and participle of non-thematic presents : ἰ-οίην, ἰ-όντος : εἰ-μι ; (σ)-όντος and (σ)-ἐτεός = Sk. *sat-yá-s;* cf. φα-ίην, φά-μενος : φη-μί.

2. Reduplicated thematic presents are formed with ablaut III. : γί-γν-ο-μαι, μί-μν-ω, ἴ-σχ-ω, πί-πτ-ω and τίκτω for τί-τκ-ω. Lat. *gi-gn-o.*

3. Presents whose formative element is the inchoative suffix σκ added immediately to the root are formed with ablaut III.: βά-σκω (βν-σκω) = Sk. *gá-chāmi;* πάσχω (= πνθ-σκω) : πένθ-ος ; μίσγω (μίγ-σκω) : Μειξίας ; ἴσκω (Ϝικ-σκω) : ἔ-Ϝοικ-α. Cf. of Class BB : φά-σκω: φη-μί ; λάσκω (λάκ-σκω) : λέ-λᾱκ-α ; χάσκω (χάν-σκω) : κέ-χην-α.

4. Only a small number of presents of the *iota*-class (IV. class) are formed with ablaut III., though this is the historically correct formation: πταίρω (πτρ-yω) : Ἐυ-πτέρ-ης ; σπαίρω and ἀσπαίρω ; βάλλω (βλ-yω) : βέλ-ος ; δαίρω : δέρ-μα ; μαίνομαι (μν-yομαι) : μέν-ος ; καίνω : κέ-κον-α. Roots of Class BB : φαίνω (φᾰν-yω) : πέ-φην-α ; πάλλω (πᾰλ-yω) : ἔ-πηλ-α. With reduplication : τι-ταίνω (τι-τν-yω).

5. A number of nasal formations are made with ablaut III.

(*a*) Those in ανω : ἱκ-άνω : ἵκ-ω (= εἰκ-ω), ἁμαρτ-άνω : νημερτ-ής ; α-ὐξ-άνω : ἀ-Ϝέξ-ω ; δαρθ-άνω.

(*b*) Those with double nasals are uniformly made with ablaut III. : θι-γ-γ-άνω ; λι-μ-π-άνω ; τυ-γ-χ-άνω ; ἐρυ-γ-γ-άνω ; πυ-ν-θ-άνομαι ; φυ-γ-γ-άνω ; λα-γ-χ-άνω (= λν-γ-χ-άνω) : λέ-λογχ-α ; χα-ν-δ-άνω (χν-ν-δ-άνω) : χείσομαι (= χενδ-σομαι) ; πα-ν-θ-άνω (πν-ν-θ-άνω) : πενθ-ος ; of roots of Class BB : ἁ-ν-δ-άνω : ἔ-ᾱδ-α ; λᾰ-μ-β-άνω : λήψομαι ; λᾰ-ν-θ-άνω : λήθ-ω ; μᾰ-ν-θ-άνω.

(*c*) Presents with nasals and υ : ἐρυθ-αίνω : ἔρευθ-ος ; ἀλιτ-αίνω : ἀλεί(τ)-της ; α-ὐ(σ)-αίνω and α-ὐ(σ)αίνω : Lat. *ūr-o* (= *eus-o*) and Sk. *oṣ-ati*; παθ-αίνω : πένθ-ος, μαρ-αίνω : Sk. *már-ate*. So also πεπ-αίνω ; but ablaut III. of roots of the type A does in most cases not differ graphically from ablaut I. With reduplication : τε-τρ-αίνω.

6. The non-thematic second aorist (μι-form) is historically an imperfect belonging to a non-thematic present, and accordingly shares with it the peculiarity of differentiating the root-form of the singular active (ablaut I.) from that of the remaining persons of the indicative, active and middle, the entire optative, and the participles (ablaut III.).

In roots from Class BB the Greek has ἔ-πτη-ν : ἐ-πτά-μην, πτᾰ-ί-ην ; ἔ-βη-ν : βᾰ-ί-ην ; ἔ-τλη-ν : ἔ-τλᾰ-ν, τλᾰ-ί-ην ; ἔ-φθη-ν : φθᾰ-ν, etc.

In roots of Class AA this original vocalic difference appears also upon close search. There occur in the first place the following forms with ablaut III. : ἐ-χύ-μην, ἐ-σσύ-μην, κλῦ-θι, and κλύ-μενος ; ἀπο-υρά-ς and ἀπο-υρά-μενος : ἀπό-(Ϝ)ερ-σε ; ἔ-κτα-το : κτόν-ος ; ἀπ-έ-φα-το.

For traces of formations containing ablaut I. and supplementing these, we must look to a set of peculiar aorists: ἔ-χευ-α and ἔ-χε(F)-α, ἔ-σσευ-α, ἠλευ-άμην, and ἠλε(F)-άμην. These are not sigmatic aorists which have dropped their σ, but they are strong forms of root-aorists, whose corresponding weak forms live in ἐ-χύ-μην and ἐ-σσύ-μην. An old conjugation was ἔ-χευ-α (for ἔ-χευ-μ), ἔ-χευ-ς, ἔ-χευ-τ : ἔ-χυ-μεν, etc., precisely as the imperfect of a μι-verb : ἐ-τί-θη-ν, etc. : ἐ-τι-θε-μεν, etc. But the strong forms attracted the weak forms of the active to their vowel condition in accordance with that same tendency towards uniformity which has disturbed the original difference between the singular and the dual-plural of the perfect active. Ἔ-χευ-α, ἔ-σσευ-α, etc., are therefore conjugated independently through the active like sibilant aorists, and even middle forms (ἠλευ-άμην) occur; but ἐ-χύ-μην and ἐ-σσύ-μην have preserved the historically correct root-forms belonging to all the persons, except the singular active.

7. The common second aorist is a formation which corresponds to an imperfect of a thematic present which has the accent on the thematic vowel, therefore ablaut III. The true accentuation, which is the cause of the weak root-form, appears in the infinitives and participles: πιθ-εῖν ; πιθ-έσθαι, πιθ-ών, πιθ-όμενος. From roots of type A : ἔ-σχ-ον, ἐ-πτ-ό-μην, ἔ-σπ-ον : ἕπ-ω, ἔ-σπ-ον : Lat. in-sec-e; ἤ-νεγκ-ον. Irregularly with ablaut I. : ἔ-τεκ-ον. From roots of type B : ἄμ-πνυ-ε, ἔ-κλυ-ον, ἔ-πταρ-ον, ἠγρ-όμην : ἐ-γείρω ; ἀγρ-όμενος : ἀγείρω, ὦφλ-ον, ἔ-καν-ον, ἔ-κταν-ον, ἔ-ταμ-ον, ἔ-δραμ-ον. Irregularly with ablaut I. : ἀγερ-έσθαι : ἀγρ-όμενος (both Homeric) ; ὤφελ-ον : ὦφλ-ον ; ἔ-τεμ-ον (late) : ἔ-ταμ-ον. From roots of type C : ἔ-πιθ-ον, ἤρικ-ον, ἤριπ-ον, ἔ-φλιδ-ον (Hesych.), εἶδ-ον, ἱκ-όμην, ἔ-λιπ-ον, ἤλιτ-ον, ἔ-στιχ-ον, ἔ-θιγ-ον, ἔ-δικ-ον, ἔ-ψυθ-εν, ἔ-τυχ-ον, ἔ-φυγ-ον, ἤλυθ-ον, ἔ-κυθ-ον, ἐ-πυθ-όμην, ἤρυγ-ον, ἔ-πραθ-ον, ἔ-δρακ-ον, ἔ-τραπ-ον, ταρπ-ώμεθα and τραπ-είομεν, ἔ-βραχ-ον, ἤμαρτ-ον and ἤμβροτ-ον, ἔ-δαρθ-ον and ἔ-δραθ-ον, ἔ-δραπ-ον, ἔ-παθ-ον, ἔ-δακ-ον, ἔ-χαδ-ον, ἔρ-ραφ-ον, ἔ-λαχ-ον. From roots of Class BB : ἔ-λαθ-ον, ἔ-λαβ-ον, δι-έ-τμαγ-ον, ἔ-λακ-ον, etc.

8. The reduplicated thematic aorist is formed with ablaut III.: ἔειπον (= ἐ-Ϝε-Ϝπ-ον); ἐ-σπ-ό-μην; ἐ-κε-κλ-ό-μην, ἔ-πε-φν-ον, ἔ-τε-τμ-ον, πε-πιθ-ό-μην, πε-φιδ-ό-μην, τε-τυκ-ό-μην, πε-πυθ-ό-μην, τε-ταρπ-ό-μην; from Class BB: λε-λαθ-ό-μην : λήθ-ω.

9. The second aorist passive system is formed with ablaut III., differing remarkably in this respect from the first passive system, which is formed with ablaut I.: ἐ-ῤῥύ-ην, ἐ-σσύ-ην, ἐ-πτάρ-ην, ἐφθ-άρ-ην, ἐ-σπάρ-ην, ἐ-δάρ-ην, ἐ-κάρ-ην, ἐ-πάρ-ην, ἐ-(Ϝ)άλ-ην, ἐ-στάλ-ην, ἐ-κάν-ην, ἐξ-ηλίφ-ην, ἠρίπ-ην, ἐ-μίγ-ην, ἐ-λίπ-ην, ἐ-ζύγ-ην, ἐ-κλάπ-ην, ἐ-πλάκ-ην, ἐ-λάπ-ην, ἐ-δράκ-ην, ἐ-στράφ-ην, ἐ-τράπ-ην, ἐ-τράφ-ην, ἐ-τάρπ-ην, ἐ-βράχ-ην, ἐ-ῤῥάφ-ην. Exceptions with ablaut I.: ἐ-φλέγ-ην, ἐ-πλέκ-ην, variant for ἐ-πλάκ-ην; ἐ-τέρσ-ην. From roots of Class BB: ἐ-τᾰκ-ην : τέ-τηκ-α; ἐ-σᾰπ-ην : σέ-σηπ-α; ἐ-σφᾰλ-ην : ἔ-σφηλ-α; ἐ-φάν-ην : πέ-φην-α, etc.

10. The domain of ablaut III. in the perfect, it has been seen, regularly is: The dual and plural active and the entire middle of the indicative; the optative, active and middle, and the participles.

In Greek this relation has been disturbed by the inroads of the strong forms of the singular active (ablaut II.), so that, as a rule, the perfect system follows their norm through all forms of the active, showing ablaut II. However, the traces of the old regime of ablaut III. in the active are not wanting, especially in the older language. Of the indicative and participle active from roots of Class AA there are to be found: ἔ-ϊκ-τον, ἐ-ϊκ-την : ἔ-οικ-α; cf. middle: ἔ-ϊκ-το and ἤ-ϊκ-το; ἐ-πέ-πιθ-μεν : πέ-ποιθ-α; ἴσ-τον, ἴδ-μεν, ἰδ-υῖα : οἶδ-α; δεί-δι-μεν and δέ-δι-μεν, ἐ-δε-δί-την, δε-δι-ώς : δεί-δοι-κα and δέ-δοι-κα; ἐλ-ηλύθ-αμεν : εἰλ-ήλουθ-α; ἐκ-γέ-γα-τον, γέ-γα-μεν, γε-γα-ώς : γέ-γον-α; μέ-μα-τον, μέ-μα-μεν, με-μα-ώς : μέ-μον-α; πέ-πασ-θε, πε-παθ-υῖα : πέ-πον-θα. From roots of Class BB: τέ-τλᾰ-μεν, τε-τλᾰ-ί-ην : τέ-τλη-κα; κέ-κρᾱχ-θι : κέ-κρᾱγ-α; ἔ-στᾰ-τον, ἔ-στα-μεν : ἔ-στη-κα; δε-δᾰ-υῖα : δέ-δη-ε; με-μᾰκ-υῖα : με-μηκ-ώς; τε-θᾰλ-υῖα : τέ-θηλ-α; λε-λᾰκ-υῖα : λέ-ληκ-α; σε-σᾱρ-υῖα :

σε-σηρ-ώς; ἀρ-ἄρ-υῖα : ἀρ-ηρ-ώς. Apparently of all forms of the active the feminine participle has resisted longest the attacks of assimilation.

In the perfect middle system ablaut III. has generally survived : εἶμαι (Fε-Fσ-μαι) : ἔσ-σα; κέ-κλι-μαι, ἔ-σσυ-μαι; κέ-χυ-μαι, ἔ-φθαρ-μαι; ἔ-σπαρ-μαι, δέ-δαρ-μαι, κέ-καρ-μαι, πέ-παρ-μαι, τέ-ταλ-μαι, ἔ-σταλ-μαι, τέ-τα-μαι, πέ-φα-ται, ἀλ-ήλιμ-μαι, ἐρ-ήριγ-μαι, ἐρ-ήριμ-μαι, μέ-μιγ-μαι, τέ-τυγ-μαι, πέ-φυγ-μαι, πέ-πυσ-μαι, ἔ-στραμ-μαι, τέ-τραμ-μαι, τέ-θραμ-μαι. In roots of type A, ablaut III., as usual, necessarily coincides with ablaut I. : ἔ-ζεσ-μαι, ἔ-στεμ-μαι, ἐν-ήνεγ-μαι, εἴ-λεγ-μαι, λέ-λεγ-μαι; such forms as these have given rise to others made with the same vowel, where ablaut III. would be historically correct and possible : πέ-πλεγ-μαι (cf. ἐ-πλάκ-ην), κέ-κλεμ-μαι (cf. ἐ-κλάπ-ην), βέ-βρεγ-μαι, πέ-φλεγ-μαι, ἔ-στεγ-μαι, for κέ-κλαμ-μαι, etc.; then also forms ἔ-ζευγ-μαι, δέ-δειγ-μαι, λέ-λειμ-μαι, etc. From roots of Class BB: λέ-λᾱσ-μαι : λέ-ληθ-α; πέ-πο-ται : πέ-πω-κα; πέ-φαν-ται : πέ-φην-α.

Nominal Formations.

11. Verbal adjectives in τός and τέος = Sk. pass. participles in -tas accent the suffix and accordingly appear with ablaut III. In Greek this condition appears in the following cases: ἄ-τι-τος, ῥυ-τός, πλυ-τός, κλυ-τός, μορ-τός and βρο-τός, φθαρ-τός, σπαρ-τός, δρα-τός and δαρ-τός, καρ-τός, σταλ-τός, βα-τός, τα-τός, αὐτό-μα-τος, φα-τός, ἐρα-τός, πισ-τός, ἐρικ-τός, ἄ-ϊσ-τος, στιπ-τός, ἄ-θικ-τος, τυκ-τός, φυκ-τός, ἀνά-πυσ-τος, ῥαπ-τός. Roots of type A as usual cannot differentiate ablaut III. from I. : ἐκ-τός, λεπ-τός, πεκ-τός, πεπ-τός, ζεσ-τός, λεκ-τός, etc.; they perhaps were the starting point of illegitimate formations containing ablaut I. where III. was possible, e.g., ἐγερ-τέον, φερ-τός, ἄ-δερκ-τος, ἄ-φλεκ-τος, στρεπ-τός, μεμπ-τός, and even ἐρεικ-τός, δεικ-τέον, πευσ-τός, ζευκ-τός, etc. These false formations, in the course of the development of the language away from its original laws and materials, have become on the whole the

more common method for verbals. From roots of Class BB: θε-τός, δο-τός, ἄ-λασ-τος, πακ-τός, etc.

The abstract nouns in ti (σι) originally had the tone on the suffix, therefore ablaut III.: τί-σις, ῥύ-σις, χύ-σις, δάρ-σις, κάρ-σις, στάλ-σις, τά-σις, (κτά-σις in) ἀνδρο-κτα-σί-α, πίσ-τις, τύξις, φύξις, πύσ-τις, ῥάψις, ἀγαρρίς. From roots of type Λ necessarily: πέψις, ξε-σις, λέξις, ὄρεξις. Thence the ε has spread over by far the largest part of these nouns: δέρ-ρις (with δάρ-σις), ῥεῦ-σις (with ῥύ-σις), φεῦξις (with φύξις), πεῦσις (with πύσ-τις), πλέξις, θρέψις, μέμψις, etc. From roots of Class BB: φἄ-τις, στᾰ-σις, δό-σις, θέ-σις, etc. Cf. Latin stă-tio-(n), rā-ti-o(n), af-fă-tim.

13. A number of adjectives in ra (ρο-) have the accent on the suffix and ablaut III.: ἐρυθ-ρός = Sk. rudh-irás = Lat. ruber; ψυδ-ρός, λιβ-ρός, λυγ-ρός, στιφ-ρός, ἐλαφ-ρός, γλυκ-ερός, στυγ-ερός; from roots of Class BB: μᾰκ-ρός : μήκ-ιστος ; σᾰπ-ρός ; τᾰκ-ερός, πᾰγ-ερός, etc.

CHAPTER IV.

ARRANGEMENT OF THE ROOTS.

In the present chapter, the roots assigned are to be taken in accordance with the principles laid down in Part I., Ch. VI., and Part IV., Ch. I.–III. It is impossible to arrange the entire etymological material of a language under designated roots, because the roots are not all known. According to the most recent views, the roots of a certain group of words are one and the same element, which appears in different forms when modified by certain surroundings and laws. For instance, φερ, φορ, φρ are one root: φερ and φορ change with each other in certain formations, the law of the variation being not as yet ascertained; it is clear, however, that there is *some* law: on the other hand, φρ varies with both φερ and φορ according to the well-known original accentual difference. Here we know the law.

In *all* roots we look for processes and explanations as reasonable as this, but as yet only the variations described under ablaut I.–III. are understood with anything like satisfactory clearness. Other material, in cases involving variation of the root-vowel, is more or less obscure. Nevertheless, even in such cases, we may often assign roots that are fairly warranted by the evidence of comparison and that will be of practical benefit in associating related words.

In the following sets, the numbers (1–528) are the same as in the body of the work; the definitions of the roots are also the same. It is not necessary to restate the Sanskrit roots; and the omission of them secures a form which exhibits regularly side by side for each set: 1. the Indo-European root; 2. the Greek root; 3. the Latin root.

1. ak, ank; ἀγκ; anc, unc.
2. ak; ἄκ, ἄκ; āc, ăc.
3. ark; ἀρκ, ἀλκ; arc.
5. —; δακ; —.
9. derk, dork, dr̥k; δερκ, δορκ, δρκ (δρακ); —.
10. deik, dik; δεικ, δικ; dīc, dĭc.
11. —; δοκ; dĕc, dĭc.
12. douk, douk, duk; δυκ; dūc, dŭc.
14. vik; Fικ, ἰκ; vīc.
16. —; Fεκ, ἐκ; vīc.
18. —; Fελκ, Fολκ; lăc.
21. —; ἰκ; —.
22. —; ἐλκ, ἰκ; —.
25. Pron. stems: ka, ki; κα, κο; —.
26. —; κακ; —.
28. kal; καλ; kăl, căl, clā.
29. kal; καλ; cāl, căl, cĕl.
32. kan; καν; căn.
33. kap; καπ; căp.
35. kvap; καπ; văp (for cvap).

40. —; καρπ, κραπ; —.
41. skarp; —; carp.
42. kar; —; —.
43. —; κᾱF, καυ; —.
44. kei, ki; κει; qui, ci.
45. sēk; σκε, σκα; sĕc, sci.
48. kel, kl̥; κελ, κλ; cĕl.
51. sker, skor, skr̥; κερ, κορ, κρ (καρ); —.
53. skap; σκαπ; —.
54. kei, ki; κει, κι; cī, cĭ.
55. klep, klop, kl̥p; κλεπ, κλοπ, κλπ; clĕp.
56. sklav; κλᾱF; clav, clau.
57. kli; κλι; cli.
58. kleu, klū; κλευ, κλῠ; clu.
59. klu; κλυ; —.
60. skav; κοF; cav, cau.
62. ku; —; —.
64. —; κοπ; —.
66. kard; κραδ; card.

67. —; κρα, κραν; cer, cre.	123. verg; Ϝεργ, Ϝρεγ; —.
69. ker, kri; κρι; cer, cri.	124. verg; Ϝεργ; urg.
70. kru; κρυ; cru.	125. jeug, jŭg; ζευγ, ζῠγ; jŭg.
71. —; κτεν (κεν), κτον, κτᾰ; —.	126. dheigh, dhigh; θειγ, θιγ; fīg.
72. —; κτει, κτῑ; —.	127. lag; λαγ; lag.
73. —; κοϜ, κυ, κοι; cav, cau.	129. rug, lug; λυγ; lŭg.
74. kur; κυρ, κυλ; —.	130. lig; λυγ; lĭg.
76. kŏ; κω; cō, cŭ.	131. —; μελγ, μολγ; mulg.
77. —; λᾱκ, λᾰκ; lōqu, lŏc.	132. —; μεργ, μοργ; merg.
78. lak; λακ; lāc.	133. —; ὀργ; virg.
80. reuk, rouk, rk; λυκ; lūc, lŭc.	134. rēg; ὀργ, ὀρεγ; reg.
82. mak; μακ; mac.	135. steg; στεγ; steg, tĕg, tĕg, tŏg.
83. —; νεκ; nĕc, nŏc	138. veg, aug; ὑγ; vĕg, vĭg, aug.
85. vik; Ϝικ; vīc.	140. —; φλεγ; flag, fulg.
87. —; πεκ, ποκ; pec.	141. —; φρυγ; frīg.
89. —; πευκ, πυκ; —.	142. bheugh, bhŭgh; φευγ, φῠγ; fūg, fŭg.
90. pik, pig; πικ; pic, pig.	143. —; ἀρχ; —.
91. plak; πλακ; plac.	144. agh, angh; ἀχ, ἀγχ; ang.
92. —; πλεκ, πλοκ; plăg, plĕc, plĭc.	145. —; βρεχ, βροχ; rīg.
95. —; —; scalp.	146. —; λαχ; lĕv (for legv).
96. scad, scand; σκαδ; scad.	147. —; Ϝεχ, ἐχ; vĕh.
97. skap; σκαπ, σκιπ; scap.	148. —; σεχ, σχ, ἐχ; —.
98. —; σκαπ; —.	149. —; ἀχ, ἀγχ; —.
99. —; σκεπ, σκοπ; spĕc.	150. —; λεχ; lĕc.
101. sku; σκυ; scu.	151. reigh, roigh, righ, ligh; λιχ; lĭg.
102. —; σκυλ; —.	152. steigh, stĭgh; στειχ, στῐχ; stig(?).
104. ag; ἀγ, ἀγ; āg, ēg, ăg.	153. —; τρεχ, τροχ; —.
105. —; ἀγ; —.	154. gha, ghi; χα, χαν; hi.
107. arg; ἀργ; arg.	155. —; χενδ, χᾰδ; hend.
108. gau; γαυ, γᾱϜ, γα; gau.	156. ghrad; χλαδ; grad.
111. —; γεμ, γομ; gĕm.	158. ghar, ghra; χαρ; grā.
112. gen, gon, gn; γεν, γον, γν(γα); gĕn, gn, gnā.	159. —; χερ; hir, her.
115. geus, gous, gus; γευ; gus.	160. ghjes; —; —.
117. gar; γαρ; gar.	161. ghi; χι; hi.
118. grabh; γλαφ; —.	163. —; χρεμ, χρομ; —.
119. glubh; γλυφ; —.	164. —; χρι; fri.
120. gan, gnā, gnō; γνω, γνο; gnā, gnō.	165. gheu, ghou, ghŭ; χευ, χου, χῠ; fū, fŭd.
122. —; γραφ; scrib, scrob, scrof.	

167. ster, str; ἀστρ; ster, astr.
173. pet, pt; πετ, ποτ, πτ, πτᾰ; pĕt.
175. stā̆, stă; στᾰ, στη, στᾰ; stā̆, stă.
176. stel, stol, stḷ; στελ, στολ, στλ (σταλ); stol.
177. —; στεμφ, στεμβ, στομφ, στοβ; —.
178. —; στεν, στον; —.
179. —; στερ; —.
181. —; στεφ; stĭp, stĭp.
183. stig; στιγ; stĭg, stĭg.
185. ster, stor; στρω, στορ; strā, ster, stor.
186. —; στευ, στυ; —.
188. ten, ton, tṇ; τεν, τον, τν (τα, ταν); tĕn, tŏn.
189. stag; ταγ; tāg, tăg.
190. ta; τᾰκ, τᾰ́κ; ta.
192. tva; τε (for τϝε); tŏ, tu.
194. tek, tok, tḳ,—teuk, tŭk; τεκ, τοκ, τκ,—τευκ, τῠκ,—τευχ, τῠχ; tec.
195. tel, tol, tḷ; τλᾰ, τλη, τλᾰ,—τελ, τολ, τᾰλ; tol, tul, tlā.
196. tem, tom, tṃ; τεμ, τομ, τμ, τμᾱγ; tem, tom.
197. —; τερ; ter, tra.
198. —; τερ; ter, tor, tri.
199. —; τερπ, ταρπ,—τρεφ, τροφ, τραφ; —.
200. —; τερσ, ταρσ; tors.
202. tres; τρεσ; tors.
203. —; τρεμ, τρομ; trŏm.
204. Stems: tri; τρι; tri.
205. tu; τυ; tu.
206. stud; τυδ; tŭd.
207. —; τυπ; —.
208. tvar; —; —.
209. svad; σϝαδ, ἀδ; suad.
210. da, da-k; δᾰ, δακ; dŏc.

211. —; δα; —.
212. —; δᾰυ, δᾰϝ; —.
213. —; δαμ; dŏm.
214. —; δαπ, δεπ; dăp.
215. —; δαρθ; dorm.
218. —; δη, δε; —.
219. dem, dom; δεμ, δομ; dŏm.
220. dek; δεξ; dex.
221. der, dor, dṛ; δερ, δορ, δρ (δαρ); —.
223. dei, doi, di; δει, δοι, δι; di.
224. di, div; δι, διϝ; di, div.
225. dō, dŏ; δω, δο, δωκ; dō, dă.
227. —; δρᾱ; —.
228. —; δρα; —.
229. —; δρεμ, δρομ, δραμ; —.
233. ēd, ĕd; ηδ, ἐδ, ὠδ; ēd, ĕd.
234. sed; ἐδ; sēd, sĕd.
235. sed; ἐδ; sēd, sĕd.
236. veid, void, vĭd; ϝειδ, ϝοιδ, ϝιδ (ἰδ); vīd, vĭd.
237. svid; σϝιδ, ἰδ; sud (for svid).
238. —; μεδ; mŏd.
239. —; μελδ; —.
240. od; ὠδ, ὀδ; ŏd, ŏl.
242. —; πεδ, ποδ; pĕd.
243. —; σκεδ, σχεδ, κεδ; scand.
244. skid; σκιδ, σχιδ; scid, cid, caed.
245. spad, spand; σφαδ; fund.
247. vad, ud, und; ὐδ; und.
248. —; ϝεθ; văd.
249. aidh, idh; αἰθ; aed.
250. —; ἀλθ; —.
251. —; ἀθ, ἀνθ; —.
252. svēdh; σϝηθ; sōd, sŏd, sued.
253. reudh; ἐρυθ; rud, ruf, rub.
254. —; θα, θη; fē, fī.
255. —; θαϝ; —.
256. —; θη, θε; dă, fă, fă-c.
257. ghen; θεν; fend.

258. —; θευ (θεϝ), θὔ, θο; —.
260. dhars; θαρσ, θρασ; fars.
261. dhar, dhra; θρα; fir, for.
262. drĕ; θρη, θρε; —.
265. dhu; θυ; fu.
266. keudh, kŭdh; κενθ, κὔθ; cud.
268. —; ὀθ; ŏd, ŏd.
270. —; πενθ; —.
271. bheidh, bhoidh, bhidh; πειθ, ποιθ, πιθ; fīd (= feid), foed (= foid), fĭd.
272. —; πευθ, πὔθ; —.
273. bhudh; πυθ, πυνθ; fund.
275. rap; ἁρπ; răp.
276. sarp; ἁρπ; sarp.
277. —; ϝελπ, ἐολπ; vol(u)p.
281. serp; ἑρπ; serp, rĕp (for srep).
282. —; λαμπ; —.
283. reup, roup, rup, lup; λυπ; rup.
284. —; νεπ; —.
285. pak, pag; πᾱγ, πηγ; pāg, păg, pāc, păc.
286. pav; παϝ; păv.
291. pa; πα; pā, pĕn.
292. pau; παυ; pau.
295. —; πεν, πον; —.
296. per, por, pṛ; περ, πορ, παρ; pĕr, pŏr.
302. pi; πι; pī.
304. pel, pol, pḷ; πελ, πολ, πλ, πλη; ple.
305. plak; πλᾱγ, πληγ, πλᾰγ; plāg.
306. pleu, plŭ; πλευ (πλεϝ), πλὔ, — πλω, πλο; plu.
307. —; πνευ (πνεϝ), πνὔ; —.
308. pō; πω, πο, πι; pō, bī.
310. pu; ποι; pū, pū.
312. —; πλε; ple.
313. —; πρω, πορ; pàr.
314. pa; —; —.

315. —; περ, πρ, πρα; —.
316. pra; πρω, προ, πρι; pra, pro, pri.
318. spju, spu; πτυ, πυτ; spu.
319. pu; πυ; pū, pū.
320. pug; πυγ; pŭg.
322. pu; —; pū, pū.
323. spher, sphor, sphṛ, — sphel, sphol, sphḷ; σπερ, σπορ, σπρ (σπαρ), — πελ, πολ, πλ (παλ); spĕr, sprē, spŭr, pŏl, păl, pŭl.
324. —; ὑπ; sŏp, sŏp.
330. bargh; βραχ; —.
331. arbh, rabh, labh; ἀλφ; lăb.
335. —; νεφ; nĕb, nŭb.
339. bhā, bha-n, bha-s, bha-v, bha-k, bha-d; φᾱ (φη), φᾰ, — φα-ν, φᾱυ (φαϝ); fā, fă, — fa-n, fa-s, fa-v, fa-c, fa-t.
340. —; φαγ; —.
341. bhar; φαρ; fŏr.
342. —; φεβ, φοβ; —.
343. —; φεν, φον, φν (φα); —.
344. bhcr, bhor, bhṛ; φερ, φορ, φρ; fĕr, for.
345. —; φλα, φλαδ, φλε, φλι, φλιδ, φλυ, φλυδ, φλυγ; flā, flō, flŭ, fle.
346. —; φρακ; farc, frĕqu.
348. bhu; φῦ, φὔ; fū, fŏ, fĕ.
350. an; ἀν; ăn.
354. —; ἐνεκ, ἐνοκ; nac.
358. men, mon, mṇ, — madh; μεν, μον, μν (μα, μαν), — μενθ, μαθ; mĕn, mŏn, măn.
360. —; νεμ, νομ; nĕm, nŭm.
361. —; νεσ, νοσ; —.
364. —; νε; ne.
366. nig; νιγ, νιβ; —.
367. snigh; νιφ; nig, nīv (for nigv).

369. nu; νυ; nu.
370. snā, snŭ; νευ (νεϝ), νŭ; nā, nă, nŭ.
372. —; νω; nō.
374. gan, gna, gno; γνω, γνο; gnō.
377. —; ἀμ, ὀμ; sīm.
379. —; —; mŏv, mŏv.
380. mu; μυ-ν; mū.
381. —; ϝεμ, ἐμ; vŏm.
383. mad; μαδ; măd.
384. makh; μαχ; măc.
385. ma, me; με; me.
386. ma, mi; με; ma, mĕ = mai, men.
387. mag, meg; μεγ; măg.
388. smi; μει; mī.
389. —; μελλ, μειλ; —.
391. —; μερ, μαρ; mŏr.
392. mer, mor, mar; μερ, μορ, μαρ; mĕr.
393. mer, mor, mar; μερ, μορ, μαρ, μρο, βρο; mŏr, mar-c.
394. —; μεθ; mĕd, mīd.
395. —; —; men.
396. ma; μα, μη; mā.
397. mik; μιγ; misc.
398. —; μιν, με; man, min, men.
400. mu; μυ; mū.
401. mus; μυσ; mus.
402. —; μυλ; mŏl.
403. mus; μυσ; mus.
408. ār; ἀρ, ἀρ; ar.
409. ark; —; —.
410. ar; ἀρ; ar.
411. ar, ra, er; ἐρ; ră, rē.
412. ver; ϝερ, ἐρ; vĕr.
413. ver; —; —.
414. or; ϝορ, ὀρ; ŏr.
415. —; ϝορ, ὀρ; vĕr.
417. raug; —; —.
421. sreu, srou, srū; ρευ (ρεϝ), ρου (ροϝ), ρŭ, ρŭ; ru, rou, rō.
422. sver, ser; σϝερ, σερ; sĕr, srĕ.
423. —; συρ; sur.
425. rau; —; rŭ, rau.
426. āl; ἀλ; ăl, ŏl, ŭl.
428. —; γλευκ, γλŭκ; —.
429. —; ϝελ, ϝαλ; vŏl.
433. las; λασ, λα; las.
437. lau, lav; λαϝ; lav, lu, la.
438. lap; λαπ; lăb.
440. leg, log; λεγ, λογ; lĕg, lĕg.
441. —; λει; lĕv.
443. leib, loib, lib; λειβ, λοιβ, λιβ; rī, lī, lī, līb.
447. —; λιφ; līb, līb, lūb.
448. lu; λυ; lu.
449. —; λου, λυ, λο; lăv, lŭ, lŭv.
451. —; μελ; măl.
453. ul; ὑλ; ŭl.
455. sal; σαλ; săl.
457. sphal; σφαλ; făl.
459. es, s; ἐσ, σ; ĕs, s.
460. ves; ϝεσ, ἐσ; ves.
462. —; σαο, σω; sā, sā.
463. —; σα, ση; sā, sē, sĕ, sī.
466. siu, siv; συ; sŭ
471. —; αὐξ; —.
475. av; ἀϝ; av, au.
476. av, va; ϝη, ϝε, ἀϝ, ϝα; —.
482. —; ι; vī, vī.
490. Pron. stems: ja; ὁ (fem. ἀ, ἡ); i.
491. us; —; ūs, ŭs.
492. aus; αὐσ; aus.
493. ei, i; εἰ, ι, — ἡ, ἑ (ἵημι); ī, ĭ.
494. is; ἰσ; —.
496. vek, vok, vk; ϝεπ; vŏc, vŏc, vĕc.
497. sek, sk; σεπ, σπ; sĕqu, sĕc, sŏc.
498. ik; ἰπ; īc.

500. reik, roik, rik; λειπ, λοιπ, λιπ; līqu, lĭqu, lĭc.
501. mark; μαρπ, μαπ; mulc.
502. —; ὠκ, ὠτ, ὀπ; ὀc.
503. sap; σαπ, σαφ; săp, săp.
505. —; πεπ; cŏqu, cŏc.
506. —; πω, πο, κο; quo.
507. —; σεπ, σπ; —.
508. terk, tork, tṛk; τρεπ, τροπ, τραπ; torqu, torc.
509. gem, gom, gm; βᾱ, βη, βᾰ; bī, bĭ, bi-t, bu, vēn, vĕn.
510. —; βελ, βολ, βλ (βαλ), βλη; —.

512. gi, gvi-v, vi-g; βι; vī, vī-v, vī-g.
513. —; βο; bŏ.
514. —; βρω, βορ; vŏr, gŭr, gŭl, glŭ, glŭ.
515. gou; βο; bo.
518. —; τει, τί; —.
519. ki; τι; qui.
520. —; θερ; for, fur.
521. —; ϝαγ; —.
522. vrĕg, bhrĕg; ϝρηγ, ϝρωγ, ϝραγ; frăg.
523. sar, sal; ἁλ; săl.
525. —; βουλ, βολ; vŏl.
526. —; ϝελ; —.

SUPPLEMENTARY LIST OF GREEK ROOTS.

The following list comprises some roots not included in the foregoing sets. These roots, with words to which they apply, are stated in accordance with the principles of the new school.

529. βενθ, βαθ. βένθος, βαθύς, βάθος.
530. βλω (for μλω), μολ, μλο, βλο. βλώσκω, ἔμολον.
531. βρεμ, βρομ. βρέμω, βρόμος.
532. βω, βο. βόσκω.
533. γρα. γράω, γρώνη.
534. (ἐ)γερ, (ἐ)γρ. ἐγείρω, ἠγρόμην.
535. ἐλευθ, ἐλουθ, ἐλῡθ. ἐλεύσομαι, ἐλήλουθα, ἦλθον (ἤλυθον).
536. ϝαχ. ἰάχω.
537. ϝcιϝ, ϝοιϝ, ϝιϝ. εἴκω (= ϝείκω), ἔοικα (= ϝέ-ϝοιϝ-α), ἔϊκτον (= ϝέ-ϝιϝ-τον).
538. ϝελ. ἴλλω, ἐελμένος.
539. ϝερ. ἀπούρας.

540. ζη. ζητέω.
541. ζωσ, ζοσ. ζώννῡμι.
542. ἡσ. ἧμαι.
543. θᾰγ. θήγω.
544. θαϝ. θαῦμα.
545. θᾰλ. θάλλω.
546. θνᾰ, θνη, θᾰν. θνᾴσκω, ἔθᾰνον.
547. θρω, θορ. θρῴσκω, ἔθορον.
548. κᾰδ, κηδ, κᾰδ. κήδω, κεκᾰδήσομαι.
549. κᾰφ, κᾰπ. κάπτω.
550. κλᾱγ. κέκληγα.
551. κλᾱϝ, κλᾱυ. κλαίω, κλαύσω.
552. λᾱβ, λᾱφ, λᾰβ. λαμβάνω, ἔλᾰβον.
553. λᾱθ, λᾰθ. λανθάνω, ἔλᾰθον.

554. λεγχ, λογχ, λᾰχ. λαγχάνω, λέλογχα, ἔλᾰχον.
555. μακ. μεμᾰκυῖα.
556. νᾱϝ. ναίω.
557. ξᾱν. ξαίνω.
558. πελ, πλ. πέλομαι, ἔπλετο.
559. πτερ. πτάρνυμαι.
560. πεμπ, πομπ. πέμπω, πέπομφα, πομπή.
561. πενθ, πονθ, (πνθ) παθ. πάσχω, πείσομαι, πέπονθα, ἔπᾰθον.
562. περθ, πορθ, πραθ. πέρθω, πορθέω, ἔπραθον.
563. πτᾱκ. πτήσσω.
564. σᾱπ. σήπω.
565. σᾱρ. σαίρω, σεσαρυῖα.
566. σευ, σῠ. σεύω, ἔσσῠτο.
567. σκᾱλ. σκάλλω.
568. σκλη. ἀποσκλῆναι.
569. στειβ, στοιβ, στῐβ. στείβω, στοιβή, στῐβάς.
570. στεργ, στοργ. στέργω, ἔστοργα.
571. στρεφ, στροφ, στρᾰφ. στρέφω, ἔστροφα, στρᾰφήσομαι.
572. τελ, ταλ. τέλλω, ἐτέταλτο.
573. τᾰφ, τᾰφ. ταφεῖν.
574. τρω. τιτρώσκω.
575. φᾱγ, φᾰγ. ἔφᾰγον.
576. φειδ, φῐδ. φείδομαι, πεφῐδέσθαι.
577. φθᾱ, φθᾰ. φθανω, ἔφθᾰκα.
578. φθει, φθῐ. φθίω, φθίνω, ἔφθῐτο.
579. φθερ, φθορ, φθρ, φθαρ. φθείρω, ἔφθαρμαι, φθορά.
580. χη, χε. κίχημι, κιχείην.

GREEK INDEX.

[The figures refer to the numbers of the sets.]

A.

ἀ-	351	√ἀδ	209	αἰθός	249	ἀλέω	429
ἀ-	487	ἀδάμαστος	213	αἶθοψ	249	√ἀλθ	250
ἀ-	487	ἀδάματος	213	αἴθρα	249	ἀλθαίνω	250
ἀ (st.)	490	ἄδμης	213	αἴθρη	249	ἀλθήεις	250
ἀαγής	521	ἄδμητος	213	αἴθω	249	ἀλθήσκω	250
√ἀγ	104	ἄδραστος	227	αἴθων	249	ἁλιεύς	524
√ἀγ	105	ᾄδης	236	αἴρω	422	ἁλίζω	524
Ἀγαμέμνων	358	Ἀΐδης	236	ἀϊσθω	476	ἀλιήρης	411
ἄγαν	104	ἀέθλιον	248	ἄϊτας	475	ἅλιος	524
ἀγή	521	ἄεθλον	248	ἀΐω	475	√ἀλκ	3
ἀγήνωρ	104	ἀεί	474	αἰών	474	ἀλκή	3
ἁγίζω	105	ἀείρω	422	αἰώρα	422	ἀλλά	427
ἀγινέω	104	ἄελλα	476	√ἀκ	2	ἀλλάσσω	427
ἅγιος	105	ἀέναος	370	ἄκαινα	2	ἀλλήλους	427
√ἀγκ	1	√ἀερ	422	ἄκανος	2	ἀλλοῖος	427
ἄγκος	1	ἀέρρω	422	ἀκέφαλος	52	ἄλλομαι	523
ἄγκυλος	1	√ἀϝ	475	ἀκοή	60	ἄλλος	427
ἄγκυρα	1	√ἀϝ	476	ἀκοίτης	487	ἀλλότριος	427
ἀγκών	1	ἄζομαι	105	ἄκοιτις	487	ἄλλως	427
ἀγλευκής	428	ἄημι	476	ἀκολουθέω	47	ἄλμα	523
ἀγνός	105	ἀήρ	476	ἀκόλουθος	47	ἄλμη	524
ἄγνυμι	521	ἀήτης	476	ἀκουή	60	ἀλμυρός	524
ἀγός	104	√ἀθ	251	ἀκούω	60	ἀλοάω	429
ἄγος	105	Ἀθήνη	251	ἄκρις	2	ἄλοχος	151
ἄγρα	104	ἀθλεύω	248	ἄκρος	2	ἅλς	524
ἀγρεύω	104	ἀθλέω	248	ἄκτωρ	104	ἄλσος	426
ἀγρέω	104	ἀθλητήρ	248	ἄκων	2	ἀλτικός	523
ἄγριος	106	ἀθλητής	248	√ἀλ	523	Ἄλτις	426
ἀγριόω	106	ἆθλον	248	√ἀλ	426	√ἀλφ	331
ἀγρός	106	ἆθλος	248	ἀλαλκεῖν	3	ἀλφάνω	331
ἀγυιά	104	ἁθρόος	487	ἀλείατα	429	ἀλφεσίβοιος	331
√ἀγχ	144, 149	ἀΐδιος	474	ἀλεξητήρ	469	ἀλφή	331
ἄγχι	144	αἰέν	474	ἀλέξω	469	ἄλφημα	331
ἀγχόνη	144	αἰές	474	ἄλες	524	ἀλφός	332
ἀγχοῦ	144	√αἰθ	249	ἀλέτης	429	ἀλωή	429
ἄγχω	144	αἰθήρ	249	ἀλετός	429	ἅλως	429
ἄγω	104	Αἰθίοψ	249	ἀλετρίβανος	429	√ἁμ	377
ἀγών	104	αἶθος	249	ἄλευρον	429	ἅμα	377

ἀμάλη	378	ἀνορούω	414	ἀρετάω	408	ἀστήρ	167
ἄμαλλα	378	ἄντα	166	ἀρετή	408	√ἀστρ	167
ἄμαξα	470	ἀντάω	166	ἀρθμός	408	ἄστρον	167
ἅμαξα	470	ἄντην	166	ἄρθρον	408	ἀσφαλής	457
ἀμάω	378	ἀντί	166	ἀρι-	408	ἄσωτος	462
ἀμβροσία	393	ἀντιάω	166	ἀριθμητική	408	ἀτάλαντος	195
ἀμβρόσιος	393	ἀντικρύ	166	ἀριθμητικός	408	ἀτενής	188
ἄμβροτος	393	ἀντίος	166	ἀριθμός	408	ἀτμός	477
ἀμείβω	379	ἄντομαι	166	ἀριστοκρατία	67	ἀτρέμας	203
ἀμείβομαι	379	ἄνυδρος	247	ἄριστον	492	ἀτροφία	199
ἄμελξις	131	ἄνω	352	ἄριστος	408	αὐδή	476
ἀμέλγω	131	ἀνώνυμος	374	√ἀρκ	3	αὐξάνω	471
ἀμέργω	132	ἄξιος	104	ἀρκέω	3	αὔξη	471
ἀμεύω	379	ἀξιόω	104	ἄρκιος	3	αὔξημα	471
ἄμητος	378	ἄξων	470	ἄρκτος	4	αὔξησις	471
ἀμητός	378	ἄορ	422	ἄρμενος	408	αὔξων	471
ἀμοιβή	379	ἀόρατος	415	ἀρμός	408	√αὐξ	471
ἀμολγαῖος	131	ἀορτήρ	422	√ἀρ	410	αὔριον	492
ἀμολγεύς	131	ἅπαξ	488	ἀροτήρ	410	αὔρα	476
ἀμοργός	132	ἅπας	487	ἄροτρον	410	√αὐσ	492
ἄμυνα	380	ἄπαστος	291	ἄροτος	410	αὐτέω	476
ἀμύνομαι	380	ἀπειρέσιος	297	ἄρουρα	410	αὐτή	476
ἀμύντωρ	380	ἄπειρος	297	ἀρόω	410	αὐτμή	477
ἀμυντήρ	380	ἄπειρος	296	√ἀρπ	275	αὐτμήν	477
ἀμύνω	380	ἀπερείσιος	297	√ἀρπ	276	αὐτοκρατής	67
ἀμφήρης	411	ἁπλόος	488	ἁρπαγή	275	αὔω	476
ἀμφί	333	ἀπό	274	ἁρπάγη	275	αὔω	491
ἀμφιδέξιος	220	ἀποδρᾶναι	227	ἁρπάζω	275	αὔως	492
ἀμφικτίονες	72	ἀποθήκη	256	ἅρπαξ	275	ἀφαρός	341
ἀμφιλύκη	80	ἄποινα	310	ἁρπαλέος	275	ἀφάρωτος	341
ἀμφίς	333	ἀπολαύω	437	ἅρπη	275	ἀφορμή	416
ἀμφότερος	334	ἀποσκλῆναι	568	ἅρπη	276	√ἀχ	144, 149
ἄμφω	334	ἀπόστολος	176	Ἅρπυιαι	275	ἀχεύω	144
√ἀν	350	ἀπούρας	539	ἀρτάνη	422	ἀχέω	144
ἄν	351	√ἀρ	408	ἀρτάω	422	ἄχθομαι	144
ἀνά	352	ἄρ	408	ἄρτι	408	ἄχθος	144
ἀνα-	351	ἄρα	408	ἀρτίζω	408	ἄχνυμι	144
ἀνάβασις	509	ἀραρίσκω	408	ἄρτιος	408	ἄχομαι	144
ἄναλτος	426	ἀράχνη	409	ἀρτύς	408	ἄχος	144
ἀνάριθμος	408	ἀράχνης	409	ἀρτύω	408	ἄψ	274
ἀναρχία	143	ἀράχνιον	409	√ἀρχ	143	ἄω	476
ἀνδάνω	209	√ἀργ	107	ἀρχή	143	ἄωρος	424
ἀνδρειφόντης	343	ἀργεννός	107	ἀρχός	143		
ἄνεμος	350	ἀργής	107	ἄρχω	143	**B.**	
ἀνεψιός	284	ἄργιλλος	107	ἄρχων	143		
√ἀνθ	251	ἀργινόεις	107	ἄσθμα	476	√βα	509
ἀνθέω	251	ἄργιλος	107	ἄσμενος	209	βαδίζω	509
ἀνθερέων	251	ἀργός	107	ἀσπαίρω	323	βάδος	509
ἀνθέριξ	251	ἄργυρος	107	ἀσπάλαξ	95	√βαθ	529
ἀνθηρός	251	ἀρείων	408	ἀστερόεις	167	βάθος	529
ἄνθος	251	ἀρέσκω	408	ἀστεμφής	177	βάθρον	509

βαθύς	529	√βολ	525	γάνος	108	γλύπτης	119
βαίνω	509	βολβός	329	γάνυμαι	108	√γλυφ	119
√βαλ	510	βόλεται	525	γαστήρ	110	γλύφανος	119
βάλλω	510	βόλη	510	√γαυ	108	γλύφω	119
βάρβαρος	327	βολίς	510	γαῦρος	108	√γν	112
βαρβαρίζω	327	βόλος	510	√γαυ	108	γναθμός	353
βαρέω	511	√βορ	514	γέα	116	γνάθος	353
βάρος	511	βορά	514	γείνομαι	112	γνήσιος	112
βαρύς	511	βορός	514	γείτων	116	√γνο	374
βαρύτης	511	βόσκω	532	√γεμ	111	√γνο	120
βαρύτονος	511	βουκολικός	515	γεμίζω	111	γνύξ	121
βασιλεύς	436	βουκόλος 48,	515	γέμω	111	√γνω	374
βάσις	509	√βουλ	525	√γεν	112	√γνω	120
βάσκε	509	βουλεύω	525	γενεά	112	γνώμη	120
βατός	509	βουλή	525	γένειον	353	γνωρίζω	120
βέβαιος	509	βούλημα	525	γένεσις	112	γνῶσις	120
βέβηλος	509	βούλησις	525	γενέτειρα	112	γνωστός	120
√βελ	510	βούλομαι	525	γενέτηρ	112	γνωτός	120
βελόνη	510	βοῦς	515	γενέτης	112	√γομ	111
βέλεμνον	510	√βραχ	330	γένος	112	γόμος	111
√βενθ	529	βράχεα	330	γένυς	353	γομόω	111
βένθος	529	βραχύνω	330	γέρανος	113	√γον	112
βέλος	510	βραχύς	330	γέρων	114	γόνυ	121
βηλός	509	βραχύτης	330	√γευ	115	γουνάζομαι	121
βῆμα	509	√βρεμ	531	γεῦμα	115	γουνόομαι	121
√βι	512	βρέμω	531	γεύομαι	115	γράμμα	122
βιβάζω	509	√βρεχ	145	γεῦσις	115	γραμμή	122
βιβάς	509	βρέχω	145	γεύω	115	γραῦς	114
βιβρώσκω	514	√βρο	393	γῆ	116	√γρα	533
βίος	512	√βρο	514	γηθέω	108	√γραφ	122
βιοτή	512	√βρομ	531	γῆθος	108	γραφή	122
βίοτος	512	βρόμος	531	γηθοσύνη	108	γραφικός	122
βιόω	512	βροτός	393	γηθόσυνος	108	γραφίς	122
√βλ	510	√βροχ	145	γῆρας	114	γράφω	122
√βλη	510	βροχετός	145	γηρυ (st.)	117	γράω	533
βλῆμα	510	√βρω	514	γῆρυς	117	γυνή	112
βλήμενος	510	βρῶμα	514	γηρύω	117	γρώνη	533
βλητός	510	βρωτήρ	514	γίγνομαι	112		
βληχάομαι	328	√βω	532	γιγνώσκω	120		
βληχάς	328	βωμός	509	√γλαφ	118	**Δ.**	
βληχή	328			γλάφυ	118		
√βλο	530	**Γ.**		γλαφυρός	118	√δα	210
√βλω	530			γλάφω	118	√δα	211
βλώσκω	530	√γα	108	√γλευκ	428	δαδύσσεσθαι	12
√βο	515	√γα	112	γλεῦκος	428	√δαϜ	212
√βο	513	γαϜ	108	γλία	446	δαίζω	211
√βο	532	γαῖα	116	γλοιά	446	δαίνυμαι	211
βοάω	513	γαίω	108	γλοιός	446	δαίνυμι	211
βοή	513	γάλα	109	√γλυκ	428	δαίρω	221
βοηθόος	258	γαλαθηνός	254	γλυκύς	428	δαΐς	212
√βολ	510	γαλακτ (st.)	109	γλυκύτης	428	δαίς	211
						δαίτη	211

206 GREEK INDEX.

δαιτρός	211	δεινός	223	διάβολος	510	√δρ	221
δαιτυμών	211	δεῖξις	10	διαδέω	218	√δρα	228
δαιτύς	211	δεῖπνον	214	διάδημα	218	√δρα	227
δαίω	211	δειράς	222	διαλέγομαι	440	√δρακ	9
δαίω	212	δειρή	222	διάλογος	440	δράκων	9
√δακ	5	δείρω	221	διαμφίδιος	333	√δραμ	229
√δακ	210	√δεκ	7	διαρρώξ	522	δρᾶμα	228
δάκνω	5	δέκα	8	διδάσκω	210	δρᾶνος	228
δάκος	5	δέκομαι	7	δίδημι	218	δρασμός	227
δάκρυ	6	δέλεαρ	226	διδράσκω	227	δραστοσύνη	228
δάκρυον	6	√δεμ	219	δίδωμι	225	δράω	228
δακρύω	6	δέμας	219	δίεμαι	223	√δρεμ	229
δάκτυλος	7	δέμω	219	√διϜ	224	δρηστήρ	228
δαλός	212	δένδρεον	230	διηνεκής	354	δρηστοσύνη	228
√δαμ	213	δένδρον	230	√δικ	10	√δρκ	9
δαμάζω	213	√δεξ	220	δίκη	10	√δρομ	229
δαμάλης	213	δεξιός	220	δινεύω	223	δρομεύς	229
δάμαρ	213	δεξιτερός	220	δινέω	223	δρόμος	229
δαμάω	213	δέος	223	δῖνος	223	δρυμός	230
δαμνάω	213	√δεπ	214	δίνω	223	δρυοτόμος	230
δάμνημι	213	√δερ	221	δίομαι	223	δρῦς	230
-δαμος	213	δέργμα	9	δῖος	224	δρυτόμος	230
√δαπ	214	δέρη	222	δίς	231	δρύφακτος	346
δαπάνη	214	√δερκ	9	δίσκουρα	414	√δυκ	12
δαπανηρός	214	δέρκομαι	9	δισσός	231	δύο	231
δάπανος	214	δέρμα	221	δίχα	231	δυσ-	232
δάπτω	214	δέρος	221	διχθά	231	δυσεντερία	232
√δαρ	221	δέρρις	221	δίω	223	δυσμενής	232
√δαρθ	215	δέρω	221	Διώνη	224	δυσπεψία	
δαρθάνω	215	δέσις	218	δμώς	213		505, 232
δασμός	211	δεσμός	218	√δο	225	δυσχερής	159
δάσος	216	δεσπόζω	314	δοάσσατο	224	δυσώδης	234
δασύνω	216	δεσπόσυνος	314	√δοι	223	δύω	231
δασύς	216	δεσπότης	314	δοιή	231	δυώδεκα	231
δατέομαι	211	δέσποινα	314	δοιοί	231	δῶ	219
√δαυ	212	δετή	218	√δοκ	11	√δω	225
δαυλός	216	Δευτερονόμιον		δοκέω	11	δώδεκα	231
δαψιλής	214		231	δόλος	226	√δωκ	225
-δε	217	δεύτερος	231	√δομ	219	δῶμα	219
√δε	218	√δεχ	7	δόξα	11	δῶρον	225
δέατο	224	δέχομαι	7	δόμος	219	δώς	225
δεδάασθαι	210	δέω	218	√δορ	221	δωτήρ	225
δέδαε	210	√δη	218	δορά	221	δωτίνη	225
δεδαώς	210	δῆγμα	5	√δορκ	9	δῶτις	225
√δει	223	δῆλος	224	δορκάς	9	δωτύς	225
δεῖγμα	10	δημοκρατία	67	δόρυ	230		
δείδω	223	√δι	223	δόσις	225	**E.**	
√δεικ	10	√δι	224	δοτήρ	225		
δείκνυμι	10	διά	231	δουράτεος	230	ἑ	472
δειλός	223	διαβάλλω	510	δούρειος	230	ἑ (st.)	489
δειμός	223	διαβολικός	510	δουρηνεκές	354	ἕ	489

GREEK INDEX.

√ἑ	493	εἴλυμα	429	ἕλκος	19	√ἐνοκ	354
ἕαδον	209	εἰλύω	429	ἕλκω	18	ἐνοπή	496
ἐᾱνός	460	εἴλω	526	ἑλλειψις	500	ἔνος	357
ἐᾱνός	460	εἶμα	460	ἕλος	430	Ἐνοσίχθων	268
ἔαρ	478	εἵμαρται	392	√ἐλουθ	535	ἔντερον	355
ἐαρινός	478	εἶμι	493	ἐλπίζω	277	ἐντός	355
ἕβδομος	280	εἰμί	459	ἐλπίς	277	ἐξ	472
ἔβην	509	εἰν	355	ἔλπομαι	277	ἔξ	473
ἐβόλοντο	525	εἴνατος	356	ἔλπω	277	ἐξείης	148
ἐγείρω	534	εἰνί	355	ἐλπωρή	277	ἐξεπλάγην	305
√(ἐ)γερ	534	εἶπον	496	√ἐλυθ	535	ἑξῆς	148
√(ἐ)γρ	534	√εἰρ	422	ἔλυτρον	429	ἔοικα	537
ἔγχελυς	149	εἰργμός	124	ἐλύω	429	√ἐολπ	277
√ἐδ	233	εἴργω	124	√ἐμ	381	ἐός	489
√ἐδ	234	εἴργω	124	ἔμαπον	501	√ἐπ	497
√ἐδ	235	εἴρερος	422	ἔμαθον	358	ἔπαθον	561
ἐδάην	210	εἰρεσία	411	ἔμε	385	ἐπαίω	475
ἐδανός	209	εἴρηκα	412	ἔμεσις	381	ἐπέτης	497
ἔδαφος	235	εἰρήνη	412	ἐμετικός	381	ἔπετον	173
ἔδεσμα	233	εἰρκτή	124	ἔμετος	381	ἔπεφνον	343
ἐδητύς	233	εἰρμός	422	ἐμέω	381	ἐπί	279
ἐδίδαξα	210	εἶρος	413	ἔμμορα	392	ἐπιβαρέω	511
ἕδος	234	εἴρω	422	ἔμολον	530	ἐπικός	496
ἕδρα	234	εἴρω	412	ἐμπίς	278	ἐπίουρος	415
ἔδραμον	229	εἰς	355	ἐμπορικός	296	ἐπιπολή	294
ἕδω	233	εἶσα	234	ἐμπόριον	296	ἐπισκύνιον	101
ἐδωδή	233	εἴσω	355	ἔμπορος	296	ἔπλετο	558
ἐελμένος	538	εἴωθα	252	ἐν	355	ἐπλήγην	305
ἔϝιδον	236	√ἐκ	16	ἐναγίζω	105	ἕπομαι	497
ἕζομαι	234	ἐκ	472	ἐνάκις	356	ἔπορον	313
ἐθ (st.)	252	ἑκατόν	15	ἐνακόσιοι	356	ἔϝος	496
ἐθάνον	546	ἔκηλος	16	ἐναντίος	166	ἐπράθον	562
ἔθιγον	126	ἔκητι	16	ἔνατος	356	ἔπρησεν	315
ἐθίζω	252	ἐκλογή	440	ἔνδιος	224	ἑπτά	280
ἔθορον	547	ἐκτός	473	ἔνδον	355	ἕπω	497
ἔθος	252	ἔκυρα	17	√ἐνεκ	354	√ἐρ	411
ἔ(ϝ)ειπον	496	ἐκυρός	17	ἐνενήκοντα	356	√ἐρ	412
√εἰ	493	ἐκφλαίνω	345	ἔνερθε	355	√ἐρ	422
εἶδαρ	233	ἐκφλυνδάνειν	345	ἔνεροι	355	√ἐρ	422
εἴδομαι	236	ἑκών	16	ἐνέρτερος	355	ἐργάζομαι	123
εἶδον	236	ἔλδα	430	ἔνη	357	ἔργω	124
εἶδος	236	ἔλαβον	522	ἐνήνοχα	354	ἔρδω	123
εἴδωλον	236	ἔλαθον	553	ἐνί	355	ἐρεοῦς	413
√εἰκ	22	ἐλαία	430	ἔνισπεν	507	ἐρεσία	411
εἴκοσι	13	ἔλαιον	430	ἐννάκις	356	ἐρέσσω	411
εἴκτον	537	ἔλακον	77	ἐννακόσιοι	356	ἐρέτης	411
εἴκω	14	ἔλαχον	554	ἔννατος	356	ἐρετμόν	411
εἴκω	537	ἐλαχύς	146	ἐννέα	356	ἔρευθος	253
εἴλαρ	526	√ἐλευθ	535	ἐννήκοντα	356	ἐρεύθω	253
εἰλέω	526	ἐλεύσομαι	535	Ἐννοσίγαιος	268	ἐρέω	412
εἴλη	526	ἐλήλουθα	535	ἔννυμι	460	ἐρίηρος	408

GREEK INDEX.

ἐρίνεος	413	εὐτράπελος	508	√Fεχ	147	ἠέριος	492
ἔριον	413	ἐΰς	459	Fη	476	ἦθος	252
ἕρμα	422	εὐχερής	159	√Fιδ	236	Ἠλέκτρα	20
√ἐρπ	281	εὕω	491	Fίδον	236	ἤλεκτρον	20
ἐρπετόν	281	εὕω	491	√Fικ	14	ἠλέκτωρ	20
ἐρπύζω	281	ἔφαγον	575	√Fικ	22	ἦλθον	535
ἕρπω	281	ἔφηλος	432	√Fικ	85	ἧλος	432
ἐρρήθην	412	ἐφηλόω	432	√Fικ	537	ἧμαι	542
ἐρρύης	421	ἔφθᾰκα	577	Fίκατι	13	ἡμι-	382
√ἐρυθ	253	ἔφθαρμαι	579	√Fλακ	78	ἥμισυς	382
ἐρυθρός	253	ἔφθιτο	578	√Fοιδ	236	ἤνεγκα	354
ἐρυσίβη	253	ἔφλαδον	345	√Fοικ	537	ἤνεγκον	354
ἐρυσίπελας	294	√ἐχ	147	Fοῖκος	85	ἠνεκής	354
ἐρωέω	421	√ἐχ	148	Fοῖνος	483	ἠνέχθην	354
ἐρωή	421	√ἐχ	148	√Fολκ	18	ἦρ	478
√ἐσ	460	ἐχεπευκές	89	√Fορ	415	ἦρι	492
√ἐσ	459	ἐχθές	160	√Fορ	414	ἠριγένεια	492
ἐς	355	ἔχιδνα	149	√Fραγ	522	√ἠσ	542
ἐσθής	460	ἔχις	149	√Fρακ	78	ἠώς	492
ἐσθίω	233	ἔχομαι	148	√Fρεγ	123		
ἐσθλός	459	ἐχυρός	148	√Fρηγ	522	**Θ.**	
ἔσθω	233	ἔχω	148	√Fρωγ	522		
ἑσπέρα	461	ἑώς	492			√θα	254
ἑσπερινός	461	Ἑωσφόρος	492			√θᾰγ	543
ἑσπέριος	461			**Z.**		θαέομαι	255
ἕσπερος	461	**F.**				√θαF	255
ἔσπετε	507			√ζευγ	125	√θαF	544
ἑσπόμην	497	√Fα	476	ζεῦγμα	125	θαιρός	264
ἔσσυτο	566	√Fαγ	521	ζεύγνυμι	125	√θᾰλ	545
ἔστην	175	√Fαλ	429	ζεῦγος	125	θάλλω	545
ἐστί	459	√Fαχ	536	Ζεύς	224	√θᾰν	546
ἔστοργα	570	Fε (st.)	489	√ζη	540	θαρρέω	260
ἔστροφα	571	√Fε	476	ζητέω	540	√θαρσ	260
ἔσω	355	√Fεθ	248	√ζοσ	541	θαρσέω	260
ἐτάκην	190	√Fειδ	236	√ζυγ	125	θάρσος	260
ἔταμον	196	√Fεικ	537	ζυγόν	125	θαρσύνω	260
ἔτεκον	194	√Fειργ	124	ζυγός	125	θαῦμα	255
ἐτεός	459	√Fεκ	16	ζώννυμι	541	θαῦμα	544
ἐτέταλτο	572	√Fελ	429	√ζωσ	541	√θε	256
ἐτησίαι	169	√Fελ	526			θέα	255
ἐτήσιος	167	√Fελ	538	**H.**		θεάομαι	255
ἔτι	168	√Fελκ	18	ἡ (st.)	490	θέατρον	255
ἕτοιμος	459	Fέλος	430	√ἠ	493	√θεF	258
ἔτος	169	√Fελπ	277	ἡγέομαι	104	√θειγ	126
ἐτυμολογία	459	√Fεμ	381	ἡγρόμην	534	θείνω	257
ἔτυμον	459	√Fεπ	496	√ἡδ	233	θέμα	256
ἔτυμος	459	√Fερ	412	ἥδομαι	209	θέμεθλα	256
ἔτυχον	194	√Fερ	539	ἡδονή	209	θεμέλια	256
εὐδία	224	√Fεργ	123	ἦδος	209	θέμις	256
εὐεστώ	459	√Fεργ	124	ἥδυμος	209	√θεν	257
ἐϋκτίμενος	72	√Fεσ	460	ἡδύς	209	√θερ	520

GREEK INDEX.

θερμαίνω	520	θρῆνυς	261	ἵημι	493	ἴτυς	482
θέρμαι	520	θρηνῳδία	262	√ἰκ	21	ἴφθιμος	481
θέρμετε	520	θρήσασθαι	261	√ἰκ	14	ἶφι	481
θέρμη	520	θρόνος	261	√ἰκ	22	ἴφιος	481
θερμός	520	θρόος	262	ἱκανός	22	ἴψ	498
θέρομαι	520	√θρω	547	ἱκάνω	22	ἰώδης	479
θέρος	520	θρώσκω	547	ἱκέτης	22	ἰωή	476
θέσις	256	√θυ	265	ἴκκος	499		
θεσμός	256	√θῠ	258	ἱκμαίνω	21	**K.**	
√θευ	258	θυάς	265	ἴκμας	21		
θεύσομαι	258	θυγάτηρ	263	ἴκμενος	22	√κα	25
θέω	258	θύελλα	265	ἱκνέομαι	22	√κᾱδ	548
θεωρία	255	θυήεις	265	ἱκτήρ	22	√κᾰδ	548
√θη	254	θυιάς	265	ἵκω	22	κάδος	23
√θη	256	θῦμα	265	ἴλη	526	√καF	43
θήγω	543	θύμον	265	ἴλιγξ	429	καθαίρω	24
θηέομαι	255	θύμος	265	ἰλλάς	429	καθαρός	24
θήκη	256	θυμός	265	ἴλλω	538	κάθαρσις	24
θηλαμών	254	θῦνος	265	ἱμάτιον	460	καί	25
θηλάστρια	254	θύνω	265	ἴμεν	493	καίνω	71
θηλή	254	θύος	265	ἵμερος	494	καίω	43
θῆλυς	254	θυοσκόος	60	ἰνδάλλομαι	236	√κακ	26
θηλώ	254	θύρα	264	ἰνίον	481	κάκη	26
θήρ	259	θύρᾱσι	264	ἴον	479	κακός	26
θήρα	259	θυρεός	264	ἰός	480	κακόω	26
θηρίον	259	θυρέτρα	264	ἰότης	494	κακύνω	26
θηράω	259	θυρίς	264	√ἰπ	498	√καλ	28
θῆσαι	254	θυρωρός	415	ἶπος	498	√καλ	29
θήσατο	254	θυσία	265	ἱππεύς	499	καλαμεύς	27
θῆσθαι	254	θύω	265	ἵππιος	499	καλάμη	27
√θιγ	126			ἱππόδομος	499	κάλαμος	27
θιγγάνω	126	**I.**		ἱππόδρομος	229	καλέω	28
√θνᾱ	546			ἵππος	499	καλιά	29
√θνη	546	√ἰ	493	ἱπποπόταμος	499	καλιάς	29
θνήσκω	546	√ἰ	482	ἱππότα	499	κάλιος	29
θίγημα	126	ἰάχω	536	ἵπτομαι	498	καλλίων	30
√θο	258	√ἰδ	236	√ἰσ	494	καλλονή	30
θοάζω	258	√ἰδ	237	ἴς	481	κάλλος	30
θοός	258	ἴδιος	489	ἵστημι	175	καλλύνω	30
√θορ	547	ἰδίω	237	ἱστορέω	236	καλός	30
θόρυβος	262	ἰδίωμα	489	ἱστορία	236	κάλπη	40
√θρα	261	ἰδιώτης	489	ἱστός	75	καλυβ (st.)	29
θρᾶνος	261	ἴδον	236	ἴστωρ	236	καλύβη	29
√θρασ	260	ἴδος	237	ἴστωρ	236	καλύπτω	29
θρασύς	260	ἴδρις	236	ἰσχανάω	148	καμάρα	31
√θραφ	199	ἰδρόω	237	ἰσχάνω	148	√καν	32
√θρε	262	ἰδρύω	234	ἴσχω	148	κανάζω	32
θρέομαι	262	ἰδρώς	237	Ἰταλός	170	κανάσσω	32
√θρεφ	199	ἰέναι	493	ἰταμός	493	καναχή	32
√θρη	262	ἱεράρχης	143	ἰτέα	482	√καπ	33
θρῆνος	262	ἵζω	234	ἴτης	493	√καπ	35

GREEK INDEX.

√κᾰπ	549	κελανεφής	46	√κλευ	58	κοπιάω	64
κάπετος	98	κελαινός	46	κλέω	58	κόπις	64
καπηλεύω	34	κέλευθος	47	κληῒς	56	κοπίς	64
καπηλεία	34	κελεύω	48	κλῆσις	28	κόπος	64
κάπηλος	34	κέλης	48	κλητεύω	28	κόπτω	64
καπνός	35	κέλλω	48	κλητήρ	28	√κορ	51
κάπρος	36	κέλομαι	48	κλήτωρ	28	κόραξ	65
κάπτω	549	√κεν	71	√κλι	57	κόρη	51
καπύω	35	√κερ	51	κλίμα	57	κορμός	51
√καρ	51	κεραΐζω	51	κλῖμαξ	57	κόρος	51
κάρα	37	κεραός	49	κλίνη	57	κορυφή	37
κάρανος	37	κέρας	49	κλίνω	57	κορώνη	65
καρανόω	37	κερασός	50	κλισία	57	κορώνη	74
καρδία	38	κέρμα	51	κλιτύς	57	κορωνίς	74
καρκίνος	39	√κευθ	266	√κλοπ	55	κορωνός	74
√καρπ	40	κεῦθος	266	κλοπεύς	55	κοσμοπολίτης	
καρπάλιμος	40	κευθμών	266	κλοπή	55		311
κάρπιμος	41	κεύθω	266	√κλπ	55	κόσος	506
καρπός	41	κεφάλαιος	52	√κλυ	58	κότε	506
καρπόω	41	κεφαλή	52	√κλυ	59	κότερος	506
κάρτερος	67	√κηδ	548	κλύδων	59	κουρά	51
κάρτος	67	κήδω	548	κλύζω	59	κουρεύς	51
καρύα	42	κῆπος	53	κλυτός	58	κούρη	51
κάρυον	42	κῆρ	38	κλύω	58	κουρίδιος	51
κάσσυμα	466	κήρ	51	κλώψ	55	κοῦρος	51
κασσύς	466	κηραίνω	51	√κο	25	√κρ	51
κασσύω	466	√κι	54	κο (st.)	506	√κρα	67
καταλέγω	440	κινέω	54	κόγχη	61	√κραδ	66
κάττυμα	466	κίνυμαι	54	κόγχος	61	κραδαίνω	66
καττύς	466	κίρκος	74	κοέω	60	κραδάω	66
καττύω	466	κιχείην	580	√κοϝ	60	κράδη	66
√καυ	43	κίχημι	580	√κοϝ	73	κραδίη	38
καυλός	73	κίω	54	κόθεν	506	κράζω	65
καῦμα	43	√κλ	48	√κοι	73	κραίνω	67
καυστικός	43	√κλαγ	550	κοιλία	73	κραιπάλη	40
καυστός	43	√κλᾱϝ	551	κοῖλος	73	κραιπνός	40
√κᾱφ	549	√κλαίω	551	κοιμάω	44	√κραν	67
κεδζω	45	√κλαῦ	551	κοῖος	506	κράνεια	50
κέαρ	38	κλαύσω	551	κοίτη	44	κρανίον	37
κέαρνον	45	√κλει	56	κόκκυ	62	κράνον	50
√κεδ	243	√κλειδ	56	κόκκυξ	62	κράντωρ	67
√κει	44	κλεινός	58	κοκκύζω	62	√κραπ	40
κει (st.)	44	κλείς	56	κολοφών	63	κραταιός	67
√κει	54	κλειτός	58	κολώνη	63	κρατέω	67
κεῖμαι	44	κλείω	58	κολωνός	63	κράτος	67
κείρω	51	κλείω	56	κόμμα	64	κρατύνω	67
κείω	45	κλέος	58	κόναβος	32	κρατύς	67
κεκαδήσομαι	548	√κλεπ	55	√κοπ	64	κρέας	68
κεκαφηώς	35	√κλεπ	29	κοπάζω	64	κρεῖον	68
κέκληγα	550	κλέπτης	55	κοπεύς	64	κρείων	67
√κελ	48	κλέπτω	55	κοπή	64	κρέων	67

GREEK INDEX. 211

κρήδεμνον	218	κώπη	33	λαχνόομαι	439	λιβάδιον	443
κρήνη	37	κῶς	506	λάχνος	439	λιβάς	443
√κρι	69	κωφός	64	λάω	433	λίβος	443
κρίμνον	69			λάω	437	λιβρός	443
κρίνω	69	Δ.		λέαινα	445	λιλαίομαι	433
κριός	49			λεαίνω	441	λίμνη	443
κρίσις	69	√λα	433	√λεγ	440	λιμήν	443
κριτήριον	69	√λᾰβ	552	√λεγχ	554	λιμπάνω	500
κριτής	69	√λᾱβ	552	λέγω	440	λίνεος	444
κριτικός	69	√λαγ	127	√λει	441	λίνον	444
Κρόνος	67	λαγαρός	127	λεία	437	√λιπ	500
√κρυ	70	λαγγάζω	128	λειαίνω	441	λίπτομαι	447
κρυμός	70	λάγνος	127	√λειβ	443	λίπτω	447
κρυόεις	70	λαγχάνω	554	λείβω	443	λίς	445
κρυόομαι	70	√λαϝ	437	λείβηθρον	443	λίς	446
κρύος	70	√λᾰθ	553	λείμμα	500	λίσπος	446
κρυσταίνομαι	70	√λᾱθ	553	λειμών	443	λισσός	446
κρύσταλλος	70	λαία	437	λεῖος	441	λίστρον	446
κρώζω	65	λαιός	434	λειότης	441	λίσφος	446
κρώπιον	41	λαῖς	437	√λειπ	500	λιτός	446
√κτα	71	λάϊτρον	436	λείπω	500	√λιφ	447
√κταν	71	√λακ	78	λειτουργέω	436	√λιχ	151
√κτει	72	√λακ	77	λειτουργία	436	λιχανός	151
κτείνω	71	λακερός	77	λειτουργός	436	λιχμάω	151
√κτεν	71	λακερός	78	λείχω	151	λιχμάζω	151
√κτι	72	λακίς	78	λείψανον	500	λίχνος	151
κτίζω	72	λάκκος	78	λεκτός	440	λίψ	447
κτίσις	72	λάκος	78	λέκτρον	150	λίψ	443
κτόνος	71	λακπάτητος	435	λέλακα	77	√λο	449
√κυ	73	λακτίζω	435	λελίημαι	433	√λογ	440
κύαρ	73	λαμβάνω	522	λέλογχα	554	λογάς	440
κυέω	73	√λαμπ	282	λέξις	440	λογγάζω	128
κύημα	73	λαμπάς	282	λευγαλέος	129	λογίζομαι	440
√κυθ	266	λαμπρός	282	λευκός	80	λόγος	440
κύκλος	74	λάμπω	282	λευρός	441	√λογχ	554
κύκνος	32	λανθάνω	553	λεύσσω	79	√λοιβ	443
κυλίνδω	74	λάξ	435	√λεχ	150	λοιβή	443
κυλίω	74	λαός	436	λέχος	150	λοίγιος	129
κυλλός	74	√λαπ	438	λέχριος	442	λοιγός	129
κῦμα	73	λάπτω	438	λέχρις	442	√λοιπ	500
κύος	73	√λασ	433	λέων	445	λοιπός	500
√κυρ	74	λάσκω	77	λητίζομαι	437	λοξός	442
κυρτός	74	λατρεύω	437	λήϊη	437	√λου	449
κύτος	73	λάτρις	437	λήϊς	437	λουτήρ	449
κύτος	101	√λαφ	552	λήϊτις	437	λούτριον	449
κύων	75	√λᾱφ	552	λήϊτον	436	λουτρόν	449
κώμη	44	λαφύσσω	438	λῆμα	433	λούω	449
κῶμος	44	√λαχ	146	λῆνος	439	λοχεία	150
κωμῳδός	44	√λαχ	554	λῆσις	433	λοχεύω	150
κωμῳδία	44	λάχνη	439	λίαν	433	λόχμη	150
κῶνος	76	λαχνήεις	439	√λιβ	443	λόχος	150

GREEK INDEX.

√λυ	448	μάντις	358	μείων	398	μῆνις	358
√λυ	449	√μαπ	501	√μελ	451	μηνσ (st.)	395
λύα	448	√μαρ	393	μελαγχολία	162	μηνύω	358
√λυγ	129	√μαρ	391	μελαίνω	451	μής	395
λυγ (st.)	130	√μαρ	392	μέλας	451	μήστωρ	238
λυγισμός	130	μαραίνω	393	√μελγ	131	μήτηρ	396
λύγος	130	μάρανσις	393	√μελδ	239	μητρόπολις	311
λυγόω	130	μαρασμός	393	μέλδομαι	239	√μιγ	397
λυγρός	129	√μαρπ	501	μέλδω	239	μίγα	397
λύη	448	μάρπτις	501	μέλι	390	μιγάς	397
λύθρον	449	μάρπτω	501	μέλισσα	390	μίγδα	397
√λυκ	80	μάρτυρ	391	μελίφρων	390	μίγδην	397
λύκος	81	μαρτύριον	391	√μελλ	389	μίγνυμι	397
λῦμα	449	μαρτύρομαι	391	μεμᾰκυῖα	555	μιμέομαι	386
λυμαίνομαι	449	μάρτυς	391	μέμνημαι	358	μίμησις	386
λύμη	449	μάτηρ	396	μέμονα	358	μιμνήσκω	358
√λυπ	283	√μαχ	384	√μεν	358	μῖμος	386
λυπέω	283	μάχαιρα	384	√μενθ	358	√μιν	398
λύπη	283	μάχη	384	μένος	358	μινύθω	398
λυπηρός	283	μάχιμος	384	Μέντης	358	μινυνθάδιος	398
λυπρός	283	μάχομαι	384	Μέντωρ	358	μίξις	397
λύσις	448	√με	398	μένω	358	μίσγω	397
λυτήρ	448	√με	386	√μερ	391	μισθός	267
λύτρον	448	με (st.)	385	√μερ	392	√μλο	530
λύχνος	80	με	385	√μερ	393	√μν	358
λύω	448	√μεγ	387	√μεργ	132	μνήμη	358
λωβάομαι	450	μεγαίρω	387	μέριμνα	391	μνημοσύνη	358
λωβεύω	450	μεγαλύνω	387	μερίζω	392	μνάομαι	358
λώβη	450	μέγας	387	μέρις	392	μνηστήρ	358
λωβητήρ	450	μέγεθος	387	μερμαίρω	391	μνηστής	358
λωΐων	437	√μεδ	238	μέρμερα	391	μνηστεύω	358
		μέδιμνος	238	μέρμερος	391	μοῖρα	392
		μέδομαι	238	μέρμηρα	391	√μολ	530
M.		μέδοντες	238	μερμηρίζω	391	√μολγ	131
		μέδω	238	μέρος	392	μόλιβος	452
√μα	358	√μεθ	394	μεσηγύ(s)	394	μολιβοῦς	452
√μα	396	√μει	388	μεσσηγύ(s)	394	μολύβδαινα	452
√μαδ	383	μειδάω	388	μέσος	394	μόλυβδος	452
μαδαρός	383	μείδημα	388	μέσσος	394	μολυβοῦς	452
μαδάω	383	μειδιάω	388	μετά	171	μόλυβος	452
√μαθ	358	μεῖδος	388	μέταζε	171	μολύνω	451
μαθηματικός	358	μείζων	387	μεταξύ	171	√μον	358
μαῖα	396	√μειλ	389	μετρικός	386	μονάρχης	143
μαίνομαι	358	μείλια	389	μέτριος	386	μόναρχος	143
√μακ	82	μειλίσσω	389	μέτρον	386	√μορ	392
√μακ	555	μειλιχία	389	μήδομαι	238	√μορ	393
μάκαρ	82	μελίχιος	389	μῆδος	238	μόρα	392
μακρός	82	μείλιχος	389	μῆκος	82	√μοργ	132
√μαν	358	μειδόω	398	μήν	395	μορμύρω	399
μανθάνω	358	μείρομαι	392	μήνη	395	μόρος	392
μανία	358	μείς	395	μηνιαῖος	395	μόρσιμος	392

GREEK INDEX. 213

μορτός	393	ναυτία	359	νη-	365	**Ξ.**		
√μρο	393	ναυτικός	359	νήθω	364			
√μυ	400	√νε	364	νῆμα	364	ξαίνω	557	
μυάω	400	Νέαιρα	362	νήριθμος	408	√ξᾶν	557	
μυγμός	400	νεανίας	362	νήριτος	408			
μύδος	400	νεαρός	362	νῆσις	364	**O.**		
μυέω	400	νέατος	362	νῆτρον	364			
μυζάω	400	νεβρός	362	√νιβ	366	ὁ (st.)	490	
μύζω	400	νεϝός	362	√νιγ	366	ὁ-	487	
μυῖα	401	νείαιρα	362	νίζω	366	ὕγδοος	86	
μυῖνδα	400	νειός	362	νίσσομαι	361	ὄγκος	1	
μυκτήρ	400	νείφει	367	νίπτρον	366	ὑγμος	104	
√μυλ	402	√νεκ	83	νίπτω	366	√ὀδ	240	
μύλαι	402	νεκρός	83	√νιφ	367	ὀδεύω	235	
μύλη	402	νέκυς	83	νίφα	367	ὀδίτης	235	
μυλῖται	402	√νεμ	360	νιφάς	367	ὀδμή	240	
μυλόδοντες	402	Νεμέα	360	νίφει	367	ὀδός	235	
μύλος	402	νεμεσάω	360	νιφετός	367	ὀδός	235	
μυλωθρός	402	νεμεσίζομαι	360	νίφετος	367	ὀδούς	241	
√μυν	380	νέμεσις	360	νοέω	120	ὕδωδα	240	
μυνδός	400	Νέμεσις	360	√νομ	360	ὄζω	240	
μύνη	380	νεμεσσάω	360	νομεύς	360	√ὀθ	268	
μυρμύρω	399	νεμέτωρ	360	νομή	360	οἴ	489	
√μυσ	401	νέμησις	360	νομίζω	360	οἶδα	236	
√μυσ	403	νέμος	360	νόμισμα	360	οἰκέτης	85	
μῦς	403	νέμω	360	νόμος	360	οἰκέω	85	
μύσις	400	νέομαι	361	νομός	360	οἰκία	85	
μυστήριον	400	νεός	362	νόος	120	οἰκόνδε	217	
μύστις	400	νέος	362	√νοσ	361	οἶκος	85	
μύστης	400	νεοσσία	362	νοστέω	361	οἴμη	493	
μύτης	400	νεοσσός	362	νόστος	361	οἶμος	493	
μυττός	400	νεοττία	362	νύ	368	οἰνάνθη	483	
μυχθίζω	400	νεοχμός	362	√νυ	369	οἴναρον	483	
μυχός	400	√νεπ	284	√νυ	370	οἰνάς	483	
μύω	400	νέποδες	284	νυκτ (st.)	84	οἴνη	373	
μύωψ	400	√νεσ	361	νυκτερινός	84	οἴνη	483˙	
μωραίνω	404	νεῦμα	369	νυκτερίς	84	οἶνος	483	
μωρία	404	νευρά	363	νύκτερος	84	οἰνόφλυξ	345	
μωρόομαι	404	νεῦρον	363	νύκτωρ	84	οἶος	373	
μωρός	404	νεῦσις	369	νῦν	368	οἷς	484	
		νεῦσις	370	νύν	368	ὄις	484	
		νευστάζω	369	νυνί	368	οἶτος	493	
N.		νευστήρ	370	νύξ	84	οἰωνός	485	
		νεύω	369	νυός	371	ὄκρις	2	
√να	370	√νεφ	335	νυστάζω	369	ὀκτώ	86	
√νᾶϝ	556	νεφέλη	335	νυσταλός	369	ὄλβιος	454	
ναίω	556	νέφος	335	νω (st.)	372	ὄλβος	454	
νάω	370	νεφόομαι	335	νῶϊ	372	ὀλκή	18	
ναῦς	359	νέω	364	νωμάω	360	ὀλκός	18	
ναυσία	359	νεωστί	362	νώνυμνος	374	ὄλμος	429	
ναύτης	359	νέωτα	169	νώνυμος	374	ὀλοίτροχος	429	

ὀλοίτροχος	429	ὄργανον	123	οὖς	495	πατριά	289
ὀλολυγή	453	ὀργάς	133	ὀφθαλμία	502	πατριάρχης	289
ὀλολύζω	453	ὀργάω	133	ὀφθαλμός	502	πατριώτης	289
ὀλολυγμός	453	ὀργή	133	ὀχέομαι	147	√παυ	292
ὅλος	527	ὕργια	123	ὀχετός	147	παυ (st.)	292
√ὀμ	377	ὄργνια	134	ὄχημα	147	παῦλα	292
ὁμαλής	377	ὀργυιά	134	ὀχλέω	147	παύομαι	292
ὁμαλίζω	377	√ὀρεγ	134	ὄχλος	147	παῦρος	292
ὁμαλός	377	ὄρεγμα	134	ὄχος	147	παυσωλή	292
ὀμβρέω	405	ὀρέγνυμι	134	ὀχυρός	148	παύω	292
ὄμβριος	405	ὀρέγω	134	ὄψ	496	παφλάζω	345
ὄμβρος	405	ὄρεξις	134	ὄψις	502	πάχνη	285
ὁμιλέω	526	ὀρεχθέω	134	ὄψομαι	502	√πεδ	242
ὁμιλός	526	ὀριγνάομαι	134			πέδη	242
ὄμμα	502	ὀρίνω	414	Π.		πέδιλον	242
ὁμογενής	377	ὀρμαθός	422			πεδίον	242
ὁμόζυγος	125	ὀρμάω	416	πά	288	πέδον	242
ὁμόθεν	377	ὁρμή	416	√πα	289	πέζα	242
ὁμοῖος	377	ὁρμητήριον	416	√πα	291	πεζός	242
ὁμοιοπάθεια	377	ὁρμιά	422	√παγ	285	√πειθ	271
ὅμοιος	377	ὅρμος	422	παγετός	285	πείθομαι	271
ὁμοῖος	377	ὅρνυμι	414	πάγη	285	πείθω	271
ὄμοργμα	132	ὀροθύνω	414	πάγος	285	πειθώ	271
ὀμόργνυμι	132	ὅρομαι	415	√παϝ	286	πείκω	87
ὁμός	377	ὀρούω	414	√παθ	561	πεῖνα	295
ὁμόσε	377	ὀρυμαγδός	425	παιδαγωγός	322	πεῖρα	296
ὁμοῦ	377	ὀρφανεύω	336	παιπάλη	323	πεῖραρ	297
ὄνομα	374	ὀρφανίζω	336	παῖς	322	πεῖρας	297
ὀνομάζω	374	ὀρφανιστής	336	παίω	286	πειράω	296
ὀνομαίνω	374	ὀρφανός	336	√παλ	323	πεῖσα	271
ὀνοματοποιία	374	ὄρχαμος	143	παλάμη	287	πεῖσμα	270
ὀνοματοποίησις		ὅς	490	παλάσσω	328	πείσομαι	561
	374	ὅς	489	πάλη	323	πέκος	87
ὄνυξ	375	ὀσμή	240	πάλλω	323	πέκω	87
ὀξύς	2	ὀστέϊνος	172	παλμός	323	πεκτέω	87
√ὀπ	502	ὀστέον	172	πάλος	323	√πελ	304
ὄπεας	502	ὄστινος	172	παλύνω	323	√πελ	323
ὀπή	502	οὗ	489	πάρ	288	√πελ	558
ὀπιπεύω	502	οὖδας	235	√παρ	296	πελιός	293
ὀπιπτεύω	502	οὐδός	235	παρά	288	πελιδνός	293
ὅπλον	497	οὖθαρ	269	παραί	288	πέλλα	294
ὀπός	503	οὐλαί	429	παραμείβω	379	πελλός	293
ὀπτήρ	502	οὐλαμός	526	πασπάλη	323	πέλομαι	558
ὀπτικός	502	οὖλε	454	πάσσαλος	285	πελός	293
ὄπωπα	502	οὖλος	527	πάσχω	561	πέμμα	505
√ὀρ	414	οὐράνιος	418	√πατ	291	√πεμπ	560
√ὀρ	415	Οὐρανίωνες	418	πατάνη	174	πεμπτός	504
ὄραμα	415	οὐρανός	418	πατέομαι	291	πέμπω	560
ὀρανός	418	οὖρον	414	πατέω	290	√πενθ	561
ὁράω	415	οὖρος	415	πατήρ	289	√πεν	295
√ὀργ	133	οὖρος	476	πάτος	290	πενέσται	295

GREEK INDEX. 215

πένης	295	πεύθομαι	272	√πλ	304	πνεῦμα	307
√πενθ	270	√πευκ	89	√πλ	323	πνευματικός	307
πενθερά	270	πευκεδανός	89	√πλ	558	πνευμονία	307
πενθερός	270	πεύκη	88	√πλα	304	πνεύμων	307
πενία	295	πεύκινος	88	√πλαγ	305	πνέω	307
πενιχρός	295	πευκών	88	πλάζω	305	√πνθ	561
πένομαι	295	πεῦσις	272	πλακ (st.)	91	πνοή	307
πέντε	504	πεφιδέσθαι	576	πλάκινος	91	√πνυ	307
πεντηκόντοροs		πέψις	505	πλακοῦς	91	πο (st.)	506
	411	√πηγ	285	πλάξ	91	√πο	308
√πεπ	505	πῆγμα	285	√πλε	304	√ποδ	242
πεπνυμένος	307	πήγνυμι	285	√πλε	306	ποδηνεκής	354
πέπνυμαι	307	πηγός	285	√πλε	312	πόθεν	506
πέποιθα	271	πήλινος	300	πλέγμα	92	πόθι	506
πέπονθα	561	πηλός	300	√πλεϝ	306	√ποι	310
πέπομφα	560	πήνη	301	πλεῖος	304	ποιέω	322
πεπτός	505	πηνίζομαι	301	πλείων	312	√ποιθ	271
πέπων	505	πηνίον	301	√πλεκ	92	ποικίλος	90
πέπρωται	313	πηνίτις	301	πλέκω	92	ποιμήν	309
πέπτω	505	πῆνος	301	πλέος	304	ποῖος	506
√περ	296	√πι	302	√πλευ	306	√ποκ	87
√περ	315	√πι	308	πλεύμων	307	πόκος	87
-περ	299	πιαίνω	302	πλέω	306	ποινή	310
πέρα	297	πιαλέος	302	πλέως	304	ποινύω	307
περαίνω	297	πῖαρ	302	√πλη	304	√πολ	304
περαῖος	297	πιαρός	302	πληγή	305	√πολ	323
πέραν	297	πιερός	302	πλῆθος	304	πολιός	293
πέρας	297	√πιθ	271	πληθύς	304	πόλις	311
περάτη	297	√πικ	89	πλήθω	304	πολιτεία	311
πέρατος	297	√πικ	90	√πληγ	305	πολίτης	311
περάω	296	πικρός	89	πλήν	312	πολιτικός	311
περάω	298	πῖλος	303	πλήρης	304	πολύς	312
√περθ	562	πιμελή	302	πλήσσω	305	πόμα	308
πέρθω	562	πιμπλάναι	304	√πλο	306	√πομπ	560
περί	299	πίμπλημι	304	√πλοκ	92	πομπή	560
περιδέξιος	220	πιμπράναι	315	πλόκαμος	92	√πον	295
περικτίονες	72	πίμπρημι	315	πλοκή	92	πονέω	295
πέριξ	299	πῖνον	308	πλόος	306	πονηρός	295
περίοδος	235	πινυτή	307	πλοῦτος	304	√πονθ	561
περισσός	299	πινυτός	307	√πλυ	306	πόνος	295
πέρνημι	298	πίνω	308	πλύμα	306	πόρθμος	296
√πετ	173	πιπίσκω	308	πλυνός	306	πόπανον	505
πετα (st.)	174	πιπράσκω	298	πλυντήρ	306	√πορ	313
πέταλον	174	πίπτω	173	πλύνω	306	√πορ	296
πέταλος	174	πίσα	308	πλυτός	306	πορεύω	296
πετάννυμι	174	πῖσος	308	√πλω	306	√πορθ	562
πέτασμα	174	πίστις	271	πλωτήρ	306	πορθέω	562
πέτασος	174	πίστρα	308	πλωτός	306	πορίζω	296
πέτομαι	173	πίτνημι	174	√πνε	307	πόρκος	93
√πευθ	272	πιφαύσκω	339	√πνεϝ	307	πόρνη	298
πευθήν	272	πίων	302	√πνευ	307	πόρος	296

GREEK INDEX.

πόρρω	316	πρῶτος	316	ῥέζω	123	√σαλ	455
πορσύνω	313	√πτ	173	ῥεῖθρον	421	σάλος	455
πόρσω	316	√πτᾱ	173	ῥέος	421	σαλεύω	455
πός	317	√πτᾱκ	563	√ρευ	421	√σαο	462
πόσις	308	πτάρνυμαι	559	ῥεῦμα	421	σάος	462
πόσις	314	√πτερ	559	ῥεῦσις	421	σαόω	462
πόσος	506	πτέρον	173	ῥευστός	421	√σαπ	503
πόστος	506	πτήσσω	563	ῥεύσω	421	√σᾰπ	564
√ποτ	173	√πτυ	318	ῥέω	421	√σᾰρ	565
ποτάομαι	173	πτύαλον	318	ῥῆγμα	522	√σαφ	503
πότε	506	πτύω	318	ῥηγμίν	522	σαφής	503
πότερος	506	πτῶσις	173	ῥηγμίς	522	σάω	462
ποτήριον	308	√πυ	319	ῥήγνυμι	522	σάω	463
πότης	308	√πυγ	320	ῥῆμα	412	√σελ	528
ποτί	317	πυγμάχος	320	ῥῆσις	412	σέλας	528
πότμος	173	πυγμή	320	ῥητορική	412	σελήνη	528
πότνια	314	√πυθ	272	ῥητορικός	412	√σειρ	422
ποτόν	308	√πυθ	273	ῥητός	412	√σειρ	528
ποτός	308	πυθεδών	319	ῥήτρα	412	σειρά	422
πότος	308	πυθμήν	273	ῥήτωρ	412	σειριάω	528
ποῦ	506	πύθομαι	319	ῥιγέω	419	σείριος	528
πούς	242	πύθω	319	ῥίγιον	419	√σεπ	497
√πρ	315	√πυκ	89	ῥῖγος	419	√σεπ	507
√πρα	315	πύκτης	320	ῥιγόω	419	√σερ	422
√πραθ	562	πυλαωρός	415	ῥίζα	420	√σερ	528
πρᾶσις	298	πυλωρός	415	ῥινόκερως	49	σεσαρυῖα	565
πρατήρ	298	√πυνδ	273	√ροϜ	421	√σευ	566
πρατίας	298	πύνδαξ	273	ῥοή	421	σεύω	566
πρηδών	315	πυνθάνομαι	272	ῥόμμα	337	√σεχ	148
πρημαίνω	315	πύξ	320	ῥοπτός	337	√σϜαδ	209
πρηστήρ	315	πύον	319	√ρου	421	σϜεθ (st.)	252
√πρι	316	πῦρ	321	ῥοφάνω	337	√σϜερ	422
πρίαμαι	298	πυρά	321	ῥοφέω	337	√σϜηθ	252
πρίν	316	πυρετός	321	ῥόφημα	337	√σϜιδ	237
√προ	316	πυρρός	321	√ρυ	421	√ση	463
προ	316	πυρσός	321	√ῥυ	421	σήθω	463
πρόμος	316	πυτάζω	318	ῥύαξ	421	σήπω	564
πρόμαχος	384	πύσμα	272	ῥυθμός	421	σήστρον	463
προπηλακίζω	300	πύστις	272	ῥύμη	421	σῆτες	169
πρός	317	√πυτ	318	ῥύσις	421	σίαλον	456
προσέτι	168	√πω	308	ῥυτός	421	σίαλος	456
πρόσθε	317	·√πω	506	ῥυφέω	337	√σκα	45
πρόσσω	316	πωλίον	322	ῥωγαλέος	522	√σκαδ	96
πρόσω	316	πῶλος	322	ῥώμη	421	σκαιότης	94
πρότερος	316	πῶμα	308	Ῥώμη	421	σκαιός	94
προτί	317	πῶς	506	ῥώννυμι	421	√σκᾰλ	567
πρόχνυ	121			ῥώομαι	421	σκάλοψ	95
πρύτανις	316	**Ρ.**				σκάλλω	567
√πρω	313	ῥά	408	**Σ.**		σκαλπ (st.)	95
√πρω	316	ῥάκος	78	√σ	459	σκανδάληθρον	96
πρωΐ	316	ῥέεθρον	421	√σα	463	σκανδαλίζω	96
πρώην	316	√ρεϜ	421	σαίρω	565	σκάνδαλον	96

GREEK INDEX. 217

√σκαπ	53	√σπ	507	στερέω	179	στραγγεύω	465
√σκαπ	97	σπαίρω	323	στερίσκω	179	στραγγαλία	465
√σκαπ	98	√σπαλ	323	στερίφη	180	στράγξ	465
σκαπάνη	98	σπάλαξ	95	στέριφος	180	στρατός	185
σκάπετος	98	√σπαρ	323	στέρομαι	179	√στραφ	571
σκᾶπος	97	σπαράσσω	323	στερρός	180	στραφήσομαι	571
σκάπτω	98	σπείρω	323	√στευ	186	√στρεφ	571
√σκε	45	√σπερ	323	√στεφ	181	στρέφω	571
√σκεδ	243	√σπορ	323	στεφάνη	181	√στροφ	571
σκεδάννυμι	243	√σπρ	323	στέφανος	181	√στρω	185
σκέδασις	243	√σρυ	421	στέφος	181	στρῶμα	185
√σκεπ	99	√στα	175	στέφω	181	στρωμνή	185
σκεπτικός	99	√σταλ	176	√στη	175	στρώννυμι	185
σκέπτομαι	99	στάλιξ	176	στήλη	176	√στυ	186
σκευάζω	101	σταμίν	175	στήμων	175	στῦλος	186
σκευή	101	στάμνος	175	στήριγξ	180	στύπη	187
σκεῦος	101	στάσις	175	στηρίζω	180	στύπος	187
σκευή	101	στατήρ	175	στία	182	στύω	186
σκηνή	100	√στεγ	135	√στιβ	569	Στωϊκός	186
σκῆπτρον	97	στεγανός	135	στιβάς	569	στωμύλος	184
σκήπτω	97	στέγη	135	√στιγ	183	σύ	192
σκήπων	97	στεγνός	135	στίγμα	183	√σὔ	566
σκιά	100	στέγος	135	στιγμή	183	√συ	466
σκιαρός	100	στέγω	135	στίζω	183	συλλογή	440
σκιάω	100	√στειβ	569	στικτός	183	συννένοφε	335
√σκιδ	244	στείβω	569	√στιχ	152	συννεφεῖ	335
σκίδναμαι	243	στείνομαι	178	στιχάομαι	152	√συρ	423
σκιερός	100	πτεινός	178	στίχος	152	σύριγξ	423
√σκιμπ	97	στεῖνος	178	√στλ	176	συριγμός	423
√σκιπ	97	ςτείνω	178	στλεγγίς	464	συρίζω	423
√σκλη	568	στεῖρα (n.)	180	στοά	186	σύς	467
√σκοπ	99	στεῖρα (adj.)	180	√στοβ	177	√σφαδ	245
σκόπελος	99	√στειχ	152	στοβάζω	177	σφαδάζω	245
σκοπέω	99	στείχω	152	στοβέω	177	σφαδασμός	245
σκοπή	99	√στελ	176	√στοιβ	569	√σφαλ	457
σκοπιά	99	στελγίς	464	στοιβή	569	σφαλερός	457
σκοπός	99	στέλλω	176	στοῖχος	159	σφάλλω	457
σκότος	100	√στεμβ	177	√στολ	176	σφάλμα	457
√σκυ	101	στέμβω	177	στόλος	176	σφε (st.)	489
√σκυλ	102	στέμμα	181	στόμα	184	σφεδανός	245
σκῦλα	101	√στεμφ	177	στόμαχος	184	σφενδονάω	245
σκύλλω	102	στέμφυλον	177	√στομφ	177	σφενδόνη	245
σκῦλον	101	√στεν	178	√στον	178	σφήξ	468
σκῦτος	101	στενάχω	178	στόνος	178	σφίγγω	136
√συν	370	στενός	178	√στορ	185	σφίγξις	136
σόλος	455	στένω	178	√στοργ	570	σφιγκτός	136
σόος	462	√στερ	179	στορέννυμι	185	σφιγμός	136
σοφία	503	√στεργ	570	στόρνυμι	185	σφόδρα	245
σοφίζω	503	στεργίς	464	√στραγγ	465	σφοδρός	245
σοφός	503	στέργω	570	στραγγάλη	465	σφός	489
√σπ	497	στερεός	180	στραγγαλίζω	465	√σχ	148

218   GREEK INDEX.

√σχεδ	243	τε	25	τετράκις	517	τομεύς	196
σχέδη	243	√τε	192	τέτρατος	517	τομή	196
σχεδία	243	τε	516	τετραμαίνω	203	√τον	188
σχεδόν	148	τέγγω	193	τέττα	201	τόνος	188
σχέσις	148	τέγη	135	√τευκ	194	τοξικόν	194
σχῆμα	148	τέγξις	193	√τευχ	194	τοξικός	194
√σχιδ	244	τέγος	135	τεύχω	194	τόξον	194
σχίζα	244	√τει	518	τέχνη	194	τορεύω	198
σχίζω	244	τείνω	188	τεχνικός	194	τορέω	198
σχίσμα	244	τείρω	198	τήγανον	190	τόρνος	198
σχολή	148	√τεκ	194	τηκεδών	190	τόρος	198
√σω	462	τέκμαρ	194	τήκω	190	τορός	198
σώζω	462	τεκμήριον	194	τῆτες	169	τορύνη	198
σῶκος	462	τέκνον	194	√τι	518	√τραπ	199
σῶος	462	τέκος	194	τίθημι	256	√τραπ	508
σῶς	462	τέκτων	194	τιθήνη	254	τραπέομεν	199
σωτήρ	462	√τελ	195	τίκτω	194	τραπέω	508
σώω	462	√τελ	512	τιμάωρος	415	τράπω	508
		τελαμών	195	τιμάω	518	τρασιά	200
		τέλλω	512	τιμή	518	√τραφ	199
T.		√τεμ	196	τίμημα	518	τρεῖς	204
		τέμαχος	196	τιμητής	518	√τρεμ	203
√τα	188	τέμενος	196	τιμωρός	415	τρέμω	203
√ταγ	189	τέμνω	196	τίνω	518	√τρεπ	508
τάγηνον	190	√τεν	188	τίς	519	τρέπω	508
ταινία	188	τένων	188	τις	519	√τρεσ	202
√τακ	190	τεός	192	τίσις	518	τρέσσα	202
τακερός	190	√τερ	197	τιταίνω	188	√τρεφ	199
√ταλ	195	√τερ	198	τίτθη	254	τρέφω	199
√ταλ	572	τέρετρον	198	τιτθός	254	√τρεχ	153
ταλαός	195	τερέω	198	τιτραίνω	198	τρέχω	153
τάλαντον	195	τερηδών	198	τιτράω	198	τρέω	202
τάλαρος	195	τέρην	198	τιτρώσκω	574	τρήρων	202
τάλας	195	τέρθρον	197	τίω	518	√τρι	204
√ταμ	196	τέρμα	197	√τκ	194	τριήρης	411
ταμία	196	τερμιόεις	197	√τλα	195	τρία	204
ταμίας	196	τέρμιος	197	√τλη	195	τρίβω	198
√ταν	188	τέρμων	197	τλήμων	195	τρίπους	242
ταναός	188	√τερπ	199	τλῆναι	195	τρίτος	204
τανυ-	188	τερπνός	199	√τμ	196	τρίς	204
τάνυμαι	188	τέρπω	199	√τμᾶγ	196	τρισσός	204
τανύομαι	188	τερπωλή	199	τμήγω	196	√τρομ	203
τανύω	188	√τερσ	200	τμῆμα	196	τρομερός	203
√ταρπ	199	τερσαίνω	200	√τν	188	τρομέω	203
√ταρσ	200	τέρσομαι	200	√τοκ	194	τρόμος	203
ταρσός	200	τέρψις	199	τοκεύς	194	√τροπ	508
ταρσιά	200	τέσσαρες	517	τόκος	194	τρόπαιον	508
τάσις	188	τεταγών	189	√τολ	195	τροπαῖος	508
ταῦρος	191	τέτανος	188	τόλμα	195	τροπεῖον	508
√τᾶφ	573	τέταρτος	517	τολμάω	195	τροπή	508
√τᾶφ	573	τετραίνω	198	√τομ	196	τροπήιον	508
ταφεῖν	573						

GREEK INDEX. 219

τροπικός	508	ὑδαρός	247	φαγεῖν	340	√φθαρ	579
τρόπις	508	ὕδερος	247	φαίνω	339	√φθει	578
τρόπος	508	ὕδρα	246	φάλκης	103	φθείρω	579
√τροφ	199	ὑδραίνω	247	√φαν	339	√φθερ	579
τροφή	199	ὑδρεύω	247	φανερός	339	√φθι	578
τρόχις	153	ὑδρία	247	φανή	339	φθίνω	578
τρόχος	153	ὕδρος	246	φανός	339	φθίω	578
τροχός	153	ὕδρωψ	247	φαντάζω	339	√φθορ	579
τρῦμα	198	ὕδωρ	247	φαντασία	339	φθορά	579
τρύχω	198	√ὑλ	453	φάντασμα	339	√φθρ	579
τρύω	198	ὕλη	458	φανταστικός	339	√φιδ	576
√τρω	574	ὑλήεις	458	φάος	339	φιμός	136
√τυ	205	ὕλημα	458	√φαρ	341	φίτυμα	348
τυγχάνω	194	√ὑπ	324	φάραγξ	341	φιτύομαι	348
√τυδ	206	ὑπαί	326	φαρέτρα	344	φιτύω	348
Τύδας	206	ὑπείρ	325	φάρος	341	√φλα	345
Τυδεύς	206	ὑπένερθε	355	φαρόω	341	√φλαδ	345
√τυκ	194	ὑπέρ	325	φάρσος	341	φλασμός	345
τύκος	194	ὑπέρα	325	φάρυγξ	341	√φλε	345
τύλος	205	ὕπερθεν	325	φάσις	339	√φλεγ	140
τυλόω	205	ὕπερον	325	φάσκω	339	φλεγέθω	140
τύμμα	207	ὕπερος	325	φάσμα	339	φλεγμα	140
τύμπανον	207	ὑπηρέτης	411	φάτις	339	φλεγυρός	140
Τυνδάρεος	206	ὕπνος	324	φατός	343	φλέγω	140
Τυνδάρης	206	ὑπνόω	324	√φαυ	339	φλέδων	345
√τυπ	207	ὑπνωτικός	324	√φεβ	342	φλέω	345
τυπάς	207	ὑπό	326	φέβομαι	342	φλήναφος	345
τυπή	207	ὑπόφαυσις	329	φέγγος	339	√φλι	345
τύπος	207	ὕπτιος	326	√φειδ	576	Φλίας	345
τύπτω	207	ὗς	467	φείδομαι	576	√φλιδ	345
τύρβα	208	√ὑφ	338	√φεν	343	φλιδάω	345
τυρβάζω	208	ὑφαίνω	338	√φερ	344	φλοιδέω	345
τυρβασία	208	ὑφάω	338	φέρετρον	344	φλοιός	345
τύρβη	208	ὑφή	338	φέρμα	344	φλοῖσβος	345
√τυχ	194	ὕφος	338	φερνή	344	φλοίω	345
τύχη	194			φέρω	344	φλόξ	140
				√φευγ	142	φλοός	345
Υ.		**Φ.**		φεύγω	142	√φλυ	345
		√φα	339	φεύξιμος	142	φλύαξ	345
√ὑγ	138	√φα	343	φεῦξις	142	φλυαρέω	345
ὑγιάζω	138	√φᾶγ	575	√φη	339	φλύαρος	345
ὑγιαίνω	138	√φᾶγ	575	φηγινέος	139	√φλυγ	345
ὑγίεια	138	φδε	339	φήγινος	139	√φλυδ	345
ὑγιεινός	138	φαέθω	339	φηγός	139	φλυδάω	345
ὑγιηρός	138	Φαέθων	339	φηγών	139	φλύζω	345
ὑγιής	138	φαεινός	339	φήμη	339	φλύκταινα	345
ὑγραίνω	137	φαείνω	339	φημί	339	φλύκτις	345
ὑγρός	137	√φαϝ	339	φήρ	259	φλύος	345
ὑγρότης	137	φάϝε	339	√φθᾱ	577	φλύω	345
√ὑδ	247	√φαγ	340	√φθᾰ	577	√φν	343
ὑδαρής	247	φαγάς	340	φθάνω	577	√φοβ	342

GREEK INDEX.

φοβέομαι	342	φυλή	348	χείρων	159	χρίω	164
φοβερός	342	φύλλον	349	√χενδ	155	√χρομ	163
φοβέω	342	φῦλον	348	√χερ	159	χρόμαδος	163
φόβος	342	φῦμα	348	χέρης	159	χρόμη	163
φοίνιος	343	φύξιμος	142	√χεϝ	165	χρόμος	163
√φον	343	φύξις	142	χέ(ϝ)ω	165	√χυ	165
φονεύς	343	φύομαι	348	χειά	154	χυλός	165
φονή	343	φυσικός	348	χεῖμα	161	χύμα	165
φόνιος	343	φύσις	348	χειμάζω	161	χυμός	165
φόνος	343	φυτεύω	348	χειμαίνω	161	χύσις	165
√φορ	344	φυτός	348	χειμέρινος	161		
φορά	344	φύω	348	χειμών	161	**Ψ.**	
φορέω	344	φωνή	339	χέρνιβα	366	ψίττω	318
φορός	344	φώρ	344	√χευ	165		
φόρος	344	φῶς	339	χεῦμα	165	**Ω.**	
φορμός	344			√χη	580	√ὠδ	233
φόρτος	344	**X.**		χήμη	154	√ὠδ	240
√φρ	344			χθαμηλός	157	ὠθέω	268
φράγμα	346	√χα	154	χθές	160	√ὠκ	502
φραγμός	346	√χαδ	155	χθεσινός	160	ὠκυπέτης	173
√φρακ	346	χαίνω	154	χθιζινός	160	ὠκύς	2
φράσσω	346	χαίρω	158	χθιζός	160	ὠμοπλάτη	407
φράτηρ	347	χάλαζα	156	√χι	161	ὦμος	407
φράτρα	347	χαλαζάω	156	χίμετλον	161	ὠμός	406
φράτρη	347	χαμᾶδις	157	χιών	161	ὠμότης	406
φρατρία	347	χαμᾶζε	157	√χλαδ	156	ὠνέομαι	376
φρατριάζω	347	χαμᾶθεν	157	χοή	165	ὠνή	376
φρατρίζω	347	χαμαί	157	χολάω	162	ὦνος	376
φράτωρ	347	χαμηλός	157	χολή	162	ᾠόν	480
φρήτρη	347	√χαν	154	χολικός	162	√ὠπ	502
φρουρά	415	χανδάνω	155	χόλος	162	ὥρα	424
φρουρός	415	χάος	154	χολόω	162	ὥρα	415
√φρυγ	141	√χαρ	158	χόρτος	159	ὡραῖος	424
φρύγανον	141	χαρά	158	√χου	165	ὠρανός	418
φρύγετρον	141	χαρίεις	158	χοῦς	165	ὥρασι	424
φρύγω	141	χαρίζομαι	158	√χρεμ	163	ὦρος	424
φρυκτός	141	χάρις	158	χρεμετίζω	163	√ὠρυ	425
√φυ	348	χάρμα	158	χρεμίζω	163	ὠρυγή	417
√φυγ	142	χάσκω	154	√χρι	164	ὠρυθμός	417
φυγάς	142	χάσμα	154	χρῖμα	164	ὠρυθμός	425
φυγή	142	χαῦνος	154	χρῖσις	164	ὠρύομαι	425
φύζα	142	√χε	580	χριστός	164	ὡς	490
φυή	348	χείρ	159	Χριστός	164	ὤψ	502

LATIN INDEX.

[The figures refer to the numbers of the sets.]

A.

√a	476	adoleo	426	agmen	104	alternus	427
a, ab, abs	274	adolescens	426	agnosco	120	alteruter	427
abdico	10	adolesco	426	ago	104	altitudo	426
abdo	256	adscisco	45	agrarius	106	altor	426
abnuo	369	adulescens	426	agricultura	106	altus	426
abscondo	256	adulter	427	√al	426	alumna	426
absens	459	adultus	426	Alba	332	alumno	426
absurdus	423	aduncus	1	Alba Longa	332	alumnus	426
√āc	2	advena	509	Albanus	332	am-	333
√āc	2	adverbium	412	albatus	332	amarus	406
√ăc	2	√aed	249	albeo	332	amb-	333
ac	168	aedes	249	albesco	332	ambi-	333
accelero	48	aedificium	249	albumen	332	ambiguus	104
accentus	32	aedifico	249, 256	albus	332	ambitio	493
accio	54	aedilicius	249	alesco	426	ambo	334
accipiter	173	aedilis	249	alia	427	ambulo	509
acclino	57	aedituus	249	alias	427	amens	358
accuso	60	aër	476	alibi	427	amicio	493
aceo	2	aëreus	476	alieno	427	amictus	493
acer	2	aërius	476	alienus	427	amplector	92
acerbitas	2	aestas	249	alimentum	426	amplifico	256
acerbus	2	aestivus	249	alimonium	426	amplio	333
acervus	2	aestivo	249	alio	427	amplus	333
acesco	2	aestuo	249	aliquando	427	amputo	310
acetum	2	aestuosus	249	aliquantus	427	√an	350
acidus	2	aestus	249	aliquis	427	an-	333
acies	2	aetas	474	aliquot	427	√anc	1
acrimonia	2	aeternalis	474	aliter	427	anceps	52
actio	104	aeternus	474	alius	427	ancile	1
actor	104	aevum	474	alluvies	449	ancilla	1
actus	104	affabilis	339	alluvius	449	ancillaris	1
acuo	2	affectio	256	almus	426	ancora	1
acus	2	affecto	256	alo	426	ancula	1
acutus	2	afficio	256	Alpes	332	anculus	1
√ad	233	√ăg	104	alter	427	√ang	144
addo	225	ager	106	altercatio	427	angina	144
adnuo	369	agilis	104	altercor	427	ango	144
admonitio	358	agito	104	alterno	427	angor	144

LATIN INDEX.

anguis	149	arbitror	509	augmentum	138	biennis	333
angulus	1	√arc	3	augur	485	biga	125
angustus	144	arca	3	augurium	485	bigae	125
anhelo	352	arcanum	3	auguro	485	bimestris	395
anima	350	arcanus	3	auguror	485	binarius	231
animal	350	arceo	3	Augustus	138	bini	231
animatio	350	Arctos	4	augustus	138	bis	231
animatus	350	ardeo	158	auris	495	√bi-t	509
animo	350	arefacio	256	aurora	492	bito	509
animositas	350	√arg	107	√aus	492	bivira	231
animosus	350	argentum	107	ausculto	495	√bo	513, 515
animus	350	argilla	107	auspex	485	boo	513
annales	333	argumentum	107	auspicium	485	bovinor	513
annalis	333	arguo	107	auxiliaris	138	bovo	513
anniversarius	333	argutus	107	auxilium	138	brutus	511
annona	333	arma	408	√av	475	√bu	509
annosus	333	armatura	408	avaritia	475	bulbosus	329
annuo	369	armentum	410	avarus	475	bulbus	329
annus	333	armo	408	aveo	475	bustum	491
annuus	333	armus	408	avia	475		
ante	166	aro	410	aviarium	485	**C.**	
antea	166	ars	408	aviditas	475		
antecello	63	arte	408	avidus	475	cadus	23
anted	166	articulo	408	avis	485	caecus	100
anterior	166	articulus	408	avunculus	475	√caed	244
ante	166	artum	408	avus	475	caedo	244
anticipo	33	artus	408	axis	470	caelestis	73
antidea	166	arvum	410			caelum	244
antiquitas	166	arvus	410	**B.**		caelum	73
antiquo	166	arx	3			caementum	244
antiquus	166	ascisco	45	baculum	509	caerimonia	67
anularis	333	aspernor	323	baculus	509	√cal	28
anulus	333	assecla	497	baeto	509	√cal	29
anxius	144	assuefacio	256	balatio	328	calamus	27
aperio	313	ast	168	balbus	327	calcar	435
apes	278	√astr	167	balbutio	327	calceus	435
apiarium	278	astrum	167	balo	328	calcitro	435
apiarius	278	at	168	barbarus	327	calco	435
apicula	278	atavus	168	bello	231	calculo	42
apis	278	atque	168	Bellona	231	calculus	42
apud	279	atqui	168	bellum	231	calefacio	256
√ar	408	attingo	189	beneficus	256	Calendae	28
√ar	410	√au	475	beto	509	Calendarium	28
aranea	409	auceps	485	√bi	308	Calendarius	28
araneum	409	auctio	138	√bi	509	caligo	29
araneus	409	auctor	138	√bi	509	calix	29
aratio	410	auctoritas	138	bibo	308	callis	47
arator	410	audax	475	bibulus	308	calo	28
aratrum	410	audeo	475	biceps	352	calx	42
arbiter	509	audio	475	bidens	241	calx	435
arbitrarius	509	√aug	138	biennalis	333	calyx	29
arbitrium	509	augeo	138	biennium	333	camara	31

LATIN INDEX.

camera	31	catus	76	circumretio	422	collegium	440
campus	53	caulae	73	circus	74	collis	63
camur	31	caulis	73	cito	54	color	29
camurus	31	caupo	34	citus	54	coloro	29
√can	32	caupona	34	civicus	44	columen	63
cancer	39	causa	60	civilis	44	columna	63
caninus	75	cautes	76	civis	44	combino	231
canis	75	cautio	60	civitas	44	comburo	491
cano	32	cautus	60	√cla	28	combustio	491
canorus	32	√cav	60	clam	29	comes	493
canticulum	32	√cav	73	clamito	28	commemini	358
canticum	32	caveo	60	clamo	28	commemoro	391
cantillo	32	caverna	73	clamor	28	commentarium	
canto	32	cavus	73	clandestinus	29		358
cantor	32	√cel	29	clarifico	58	commentarius	
cantrix	32	√cel	48	claro	58		358
cantus	32	celer	48	clarus	58	commentor	358
√cap	33	celeritas	48	classicus	28	commentum	358
capacitas	33	celero	48	classis	28	commercium	392
capax	33	cella	29	√clau	56	comminiscor	358
caper	36	cellarium	29	claudo	56	commodum	238
capesso	33	cello	48	claudus	56	commodus	238
capillaris	52	cellula	29	claustra	56	commonefacio	
capillus	52	celo	29	√clav	56		256
capistrum	33	celox	48	clavicula	56	commotio	379
capio	33	celsus	63	clavis	56	communico	380
capitalis	52	centesimus	15	clavus	56	communis	380
Capitolium	52	centum	15	√clep	55	compages	285
capitulum	52	centuria	15	clepo	55	compedio	242
capra	36	centurio	15	√cli	57	compes	242
Capricornus	36	√cer	67	cliens	58	complector	92
captivus	33	√cer	69	clinatus	57	complementum	
capto	33	Cerealis	67	clino	57		304
captor	33	cerebrum	37	clipeum	29	compos	314
capulum	33	Ceres	67	clipeus	29	computo	310
capulus	33	cerimonia	67	clivus	57	concalefacio	256
caput	52	cerno	69	cloaca	59	concelo	29
√cri	69	certe	69	√clu	56	concentus	32
√card	66	certo (vb.)	69	√clu	58	concerto	69
cardinalis	66	certo (adv.)	69	cluens	58	concha	61
cardo	66	certus	69	cluo	59	concilium	28
carina	42	√ci	44	clypeus	29	concio	509
caro	68	√ci	54	√cō	76	concionor	509
carnalis	68	√ci	54	coalesco	426	conculco	435
√carp	41	√cid	244	√coc	505	condemno	225
carpo	41	cieo	54	coelum	73	conditor	256
carptim	41	circa	74	coerceo	8	condo	256
casa	100	circulor	74	coetus	493	condono	225
cassis	100	circulus	74	cognomen	374	confercio	346
castigo	24	circumcalco	435	cognosco	120	confertus	346
castrum	100	circumculco	435	cohors	159	confessio	339
castus	24	circumdo	225	coitus	493	conficio	256

LATIN INDEX.

confido	271	√cre	67	decens	11	devius	147
confiteor	339	creber	67	decerto	69	devoro	514
confuto	165	credo	256	decet	11	√dex	220
congratulor	158	creo	67	decimus	8	dexter	220
conjugalis	125	cresco	67	declaro	58	√di	223
conjugo	125	cribrum	69	declino	57	√di	224
conjunx	125	crimen	69	decoloro	29	Diana	224
conjux	125	criminalis	69	decor	11	√dic	10
connubialis	335	crimino	69	decoro	11	√dic	10
connubium	335	√cru	70	decorum	11	√dic	11
conscientia	45	crudelis	70	decorus	11	dico	10
conscisco	45	crudus	70	deculco	435	dico	10
conscius	45	cruentus	68	decumus	8	dictator	10
consecro	462	cruor	68	decus	11	dictio	10
consors	422	crusta	70	dedico	10	dictito	10
consternatio	185	crusto	70	dedignor	11	dicto	10
consterno	185	√cŭ	76	dediticius	225	dido	225
consuetudo	252	cucullus	29	deditio	225	dies	224
consummo	325	cuculus	62	dedo	225	diffamo	339
contactus	189	√cud	266	defendo	257	diffido	271
contagio	189	culina	505	deficio	256	difficilis	256
contagium	189	culmen	63	delecto	18	difficultas	256
contamino	189	culmus	27	deleo	443	digitus	7
contemplor	196	cunctus	125	delibuo	443	dignitas	11
contextus	194	cuneus	76	delicatus	18	dignor	11
contingo	189	cura	60	deliciosus	18	dignus	11
continuus	188	curiositas	60	delineo	444	diligens	440
contio	509	curiosus	60	delinquo	500	diligo	440
contionor	509	curo	60	delubrum	449	diluvies	449
contusio	206	curtus	51	demens	358	diluvio	449
conubialis	335	curvus	74	dens	241	diluvium	449
conubium	335	custodia	266	denseo	216	dimidio	394
conventio	509	custodio	266	denso	216	dimidius	394
convicium	496	custos	266	densus	216	Diovis	224
√coqu	505	cutis	101	dentatus	241	dirus	223
coquina	505			dentifricium	164	dis-	231
coquo	505	**D.**		dentio	241	disciplina	210
coquus	505			dentitio	241	discipulus	210
cor	38	√da	225	denuo	362	disco	210
coram	459	√da	256	depraedatio	155	discrimen	69
cordatus	38	damno	225	deputo	310	discrimino	69
cornix	65	damnum	225	depuvio	286	disperdo	225
cornu	49	√dap	214	derelinquo	500	disputo	310
cornus	50	dapino	214	derivo	443	disserto	422
corona	74	daps	214	descisco	45	dissimilis	377
corporo	67	dativus	225	deses	234	dissimulo	377
corpus	67	dator	225	desidia	234	distinguo	183
corrivo	443	dea	224	destino	175	diu	224
corvus	65	debello	231	desuetudo	253	diurnalis	224
cos	76	√dec	11	determino	197	diurnus	224
cotidie	224	decem	8	deus	224	dius	224
cottidie	224	December	8	devio	147	Dius Fidius	271

√div	224	dumosus	216	ex	472	fabrica	256
diva	224	dumus	216	exalto	426	fabricator	256
divinus	224	duo	231	exanimo	350	fabricor	256
divus	224	duplex	231	exauguro	485	fabula	339
Djovis	224	duplico	231	excello	63	fabulosus	339
√dō	225	duplus	231	excio	54	√fac	256
-do	217	dux	12	excito	54	√fa-c	339
do	225			exculco	435	facesso	256
√doc	210	**E.**		excuso	60	facete	339
doceo	210	e	472	exerceo	3	facetiae	339
docilis	210	ea	490	exercitus	3	facetus	339
doctor	210	ec	472	exilium	235	facies	339
doctrina	210	√ed	233	exitium	493	facilis	256
documentum	210	edax	233	exoculo	502	facilitas	256
dolus	226	ēdo	225	expallesco	293	facinus	256
√dom	213	ĕdo	233	expecto	99	facio	256
√dom	219	educo	12	expedio	242	factio	256
domesticus	219	effero	257	experientia	296	factiosus	256
domicilium	219	effetus	348	experimentum		factito	256
domina	213	efficax	256		296	facto	256
dominium	213	efficio	256	experior	296	factor	256
dominor	213	effigies	126	expers	313	factum	256
dominus	213	effutio	165	expletivus	304	facultas	256
domitor	213	elegans	440	expurgo	310	facundia	339
domo	213	elementum	426	exputo	310	facundus	339
domus	219	eligens	440	exsecror	462	faenerator	348
donatio	225	elimino	442	exsilium	235	faeneror	348
dono	225	emancipo	33	exsolo	235	faenum	348
donum	225	emendo	398	exsors	422	faenus	348
√dorm	215	enervis	363	exspecto	99	faetidus	265
dormio	215	enervo	363	exstinguo	183	faetio	265
dormīto	215	enormis	120	exsugo	503	faginus	139
dormitorium	215	enormitas	120	exsul	235	fagus	139
dorsualis	222	eo	493	exsulo	235	√fal	457
dorsum	222	eques	499	exter	472	fallacia	457
dorsus	222	equester	499	exterior	472	fallax	457
dos	225	equinus	499	extermino	197	fallo	457
dotalis	225	Equites	499	externus	472	falsus	457
doto	225	equito	499	exterus	472	falx	103
√du	225	equus	499	extra	472	fama	339
dualis	231	era	159	extraneus	472	familia	256
dubito	231	erga	134	extremus	472	famosus	339
dubius	231	ergo	134	extrinsecus	472	famulus	256
√dūc	12	erus	159	exul	235	√fa-n	339
√dŭc	12	√es	459	exulo	235	fanaticus	339
duco	12	esca	233			fano	339
ductilis	12	essentia	459	**F.**		fanum	339
ducto	12	esurio	233			far	344
dudum	224	et	168	√fa	256	√farc	346
duim	225	etiam	168	√fā	339	farcio	346
dulcedo	428	evaporo	35	√fă	339	farina	344
dulcis	428	evidens	236	faber	256	farrago	344

LATIN INDEX.

√fars	260	fidelis	271	fluito	345	fragor	522
√fa-s	339	fidelitas	271	flumen	345	frango	522
fas	339	fides	271	fluo	345	frater	347
fastidiosus	260	Fidius	271	fluvius	345	fraternitas	347
fastidium	260	fido	271	fluxus	345	fraternus	347
fastus	339	fidus	271	√fo	348	frenum	261
fastus	260	√fig	126	foederatus	271	√frequ	346
√fa-t	339	figmen	126	foedero	271	frequens	346
fateor	339	figmentum	126	foedo	265	frequentia	346
fatum	339	figo	136	foedus	271	frequento	346
√fa-v	339	figulus	126	foedus	265	fretus	261
faveo	339	figura	126	foenerator	348	√fri	164
favilla	339	figuro	126	foeneror	348	friabilis	164
fax	339	filia	254	foetidus	265	√fric	164
√fe	254	filius	254	foetio	265	frico	164
√fe	348	√fing	126	foeto	348	frictio	164
fecunditas	348	fingo	126	foetus	348	√frig	141
fecundo	348	fio	256	folium	349	frigeo	419
fecundus	348	√fir	261	fons	165	frigidus	419
fel	162	firmamentum	261	√for	261	frigo	141
felicitas	348	firmator	261	√for	520	frigus	419
feliciter	348	firmitas	261	√for	341	frio	164
felix	348	firmitudo	261	√for	344	√fu	348
fello	254	firmo	261	for	339	√fu	165
femina	254	firmus	261	foramen	341	√fu	265
√fend	257	√fla	345	foras	264	fuam	348
fendo	257	flabra	345	forceps	520	fuant	348
fenerator	348	√flag	140	fore	348	fuas	348
feneror	348	flagitiosus	140	forem	348	fuat	348
fenestra	339	flagitium	140	forent	348	√fud	165
fenum	348	flagito	140	fores	348	√fūg	142
fenus	348	flagro	140	foret	348	√fŭg	142
√fer	344	flamen	140	foris	264	fuga	142
fera	259	flamen	345	formidus	520	fugax	142
ferax	344	flamma	140	formus	520	fugio	142
ferculum	344	flammo	140	fornax	520	fugitivus	142
feritas	259	flatus	345	fornus	520	fugito	142
fero	344	√fle	345	foro	341	fugo	142
ferocia	259	flecto	103	fors	344	fui	348
ferox	259	fleo	345	forsan	344	√fulg	140
fertilis	344	fletus	345	forsitan	344	fulgeo	140
fertilitas	344	√flo	345	fortasse	344	fulgor	140
fertus	344	flo	345	fortassis	344	fulgur	140
ferus	259	Flora	345	fortis	261	fulmen	140
feteo	265	floreo	345	fortitudo	261	fulmino	140
fetidus	265	floresco	345	fortuitus	344	fulvus	140
feto	348	flos	345	fortuna	344	fumeus	265
fetus	348	√flu	345	fractura	522	fumidus	265
√fi	254	fluctuo	345	√frag	522	fumigo	265
fibula	136	fluctus	345	fragilis	522	fumo	265
fictio	126	fluesco	345	fragmen	522	fumosus	265
√fid	271	fluidus	345	fragmentum	522	fumus	265

LATIN INDEX.

√fund	273	genius	112	**H.**		ignosco	120
funda	245	gens	112			illativus	195
fundamentum		gentilis	112	√hend	155	illecebra	18
	273	genu	121	√her	159	illumino	80
fundo	165	genuinus	112	hera	159	illustris	80
fundo	273	genus	112	here	160	illustro	80
fundus	273	gigno	112	hereditas	159	imbellis	231
funus	265	glaber	118	heres	159	imber	405
√fur	520	gloria	58	heri	160	imbrex	405
fur	344	glorior	58	herus	159	imbuo	308
furnus	520	gloriosus	58	hesternus	160	immanis	386
furor	344	√glŭ	514	√hi	154	immolo	402
furtim	344	√glū	514	√hi	161	immunis	380
furtivus	344	glubo	119	hiatus	154	immunitas	380
furtum	344	gluma	119	hiberna	161	impedio	242
fusio	165	gluo	446	hiberno	161	imperium	313
fusus	245	glus	446	hibernus	161	impero	313
futilis	165	gluten	446	hiemo	161	impetus	173
futis	165	glutino	446	hiems	161	implementum	
futtilis	165	glutinum	446	hio	154		304
futurus	348	glutio	514	√hir	159	impos	314
		gluttio	514	hir	159	impunitas	310
		√gna	112	hisco	154	impurus	310
G.		√gnā	120	homo	157	in	355
galea	29	gnaruris	120	hora	424	in-	351
galera	29	gnarus	120	hortus	159	inauguro	485
galerum	29	√gno	374	humanitas	157	incentivum	32
galerus	29	√gnō	120	humanus	157	incentivus	32
gallina	117	√gra	158	humecto	137	incentor	32
gallinaceus	117	√grad	156	humeo	137	incestum	24
gallus	117	√grand	156	humerus	407	incestus	24
√gar	117	grandinat	156	humi	157	inciens	73
garrio	117	grando	156	humidus	137	incito	54
garrulus	117	gratia	158	humilis	157	inclino	57
√gau	108	gratiis	158	humilitas	157	inclitus	58
gaudeo	108	gratuitus	158	humo	157	inclutus	58
gaudium	108	gratulor	158	humus	157	incrusto	70
√gem	111	gratus	158			inculco	435
gemini	112	gravesco	511			incuso	60
geminus	112	gravidus	511	**I.**		indemnis	225
gemitus	111	gravis	511	√i	490	indemnitas	225
gemo	111	gravitas	511	√i	493	indico	10
√gen	112	gravo	511	ibi	490	indigena	112
gena	353	grus	113	√ic	498	indignor	11
gener	112	√gul	514	ico	498	indo	256
genero·	112	gula	514	ictus	498	indoles	426
generosus	112	√gur	514	id	490	inedia	233
genetivus	112	gurges	514	idem	490	iners	408
genetrix	112	gurgulio	514	ignarus	120	infamia	339
genitalis	112	√gus	115	ignavus	120	infamis	339
genitor	112	gusto	115	ignominia	374	infamo	339
genitrix	112	gustus	115	ignoro	120	infandus	339

228 LATIN INDEX.

infans	339	internecinus	83	jugum	125	laevus	434
infensus	257	interstitium	175	jumentum	125	√lag	127
infestus	257	intervallum	432	jungo	125	lambo	438
inficio	256	intestinus	355	Jupiter	224	lana	439
infirmus	261	intimus	355	Juppiter	224	lancus	439
infitior	339	intra	355	jurgo	125	langueo	127
inflammatio	140	intrare	197	juro	125	languesco	127
inflammo	140	intro	355	jus	125	languidus	127
ingemisco	111	intus	355	justitia	125	languor	127
ingemo	111	invidia	236	justus	125	lanicius	439
ingeniosus	112	invidiosus	236	juvenca	224	lanterna	282
ingenium	112	invidus	236	juvencus	224	lanugo	439
ingens	112	invito	496	juvenilis	224	laqueus	18
ingenuus	112	invitus	16	juvenis	224	√las	433
ingluvies	514	ipse	490	juvo	224	lascivus	433
ingurgito	514	ir	159	juxta	125	latro	437
inhumo	157	irretio	422			latrocinium	437
initio	493	irrigo	145	**K.**		latrocinor	437
initium	493	irriguus	145			latus	195
injuria	125	is	490	Kalendae	28	latus	185
innuo	369	iste	490	Kalendarium	28	laudabilis	58
innoculo	502	ita	490	Kalendarius	28	laudo	58
inserto	422	item	490	kalo	28	laus	58
insidiae	234	iter	493	√klu	58	lautus	449
insidiosus	234	itero	490			√lav	437
insimulo	377	iterum	490	**L.**		√lav	449
insipidus	503	itio	493			lavo	449
insitio	463	itus	493	√la	437	laxo	127
insomnia	324			√lab	438	laxus	127
insomnis	324	**J.**		labea	438	√lec	150
insomnium	324			labefacio	256	lectica	150
insons	459	jaceo	493	labes	450	lectio	440
instigo	183	jacio	493	labea	438	lector	440
instinctus	183	jacto	493	labium	438	lectus	150
instinguo	183	jactura	493	labor	331	lectus	440
instrumentum		jaculor	493	laboriosus	331	√leg	440
	185	jaculum	493	laboro	331	legibilis	440
insuper	325	jaculus	493	labos	331	legio	440
integer	189	janitor	493	labrum	438	legionarius	440
integritas	189	janua	493	√lac	18	lego	440
intellego	440	Januarius	493	√lac	78	legumen	440
intelligo	440	Janus	493	lacer	78	leo	445
inter	200	jubeo	125	lacero	78	√lev	146
inter	355	judex	125	lacinia	78	√lev	441
intercalaris	28	judicialis	125	lacio	18	levamentum	146
interdiu	224	judicium	125	lacrima	6	levigo	441
interficio	256	judico	125	lacrimo	6	lĕvis	146
interim	355	√jug	125	lacruma	6	lēvis	441
interior	355	jugerum	125	lacrumo	6	lĕvitas	146
interputo	310	jugo	125	lact (st.)	109	lēvitas	441
internecio	83	jugulo	125	lacuna	78	lĕvo	146
		jugulum	125	lacus	78	lēvo	441

LATIN INDEX. 229

lex	130	linteus	444	luto	449	mancus	398
√li	443	√liqu	500	lutum	449	mane	386
√lib	443	liqueo	500	lutus	449	maneo	358
√lib	447	liquesco	500	√luv	449	Manes	386
libatio	443	liquidus	500	lux	80	manifestus	257
libeo	447	liquor	500	luxo	442	manipulus	304
liber	447	litera	443	luxum	442	mano	383
Liber	443	literalis	443	luxus	442	mansio	358
liberalis	447	literatura	443			mansito	358
liberalitas	447	littera	443	**M.**		mansuesco	252
liberatio	447	litteralis	443			mansuetudo	252
liberator	447	litteratura	443	√ma	386	mănus	386
libero	447	litura	443	√ma	396	mănus	386
libertas	447	litus	443	√mac	82	√mar-c	393
libertinus	447	litus	443	√mac	384	marceo	393
libertus	447	liveo	293	macellum	384	marcesso	393
libet	447	lividus	293	macto	82	mater	396
libido	447	√loc	77	macto	384	materia	396
libo	443	√loqu	77	mactus	82	materialis	396
libum	443	longinquus	128	√mad	383	materies	396
libus	443	longitudo	128	madefacio		maternus	396
√lic	500	longus	128		256, 383	matricula	396
licentia	500	loquax	77	madeo	383	matrimonium	396
liceo	500	loquela	77	madesco	383	matrix	396
liceor	500	loquor	77	madidus	383	matrona	396
licet	500	lotio	449	√mag	387	√me	385
licinus	442	√lu	437	magis	387	√me	386
lictor	130	√lu	448	magister	387	me	385
√lig	130	√lu	449	magistero	387	√med	394
√lig	151	√lub	447	magistratus	387	medeor	358
ligamen	130	lubeo	447	magistro	387	mediator	394
ligamentum	130	lubet	447	magnanimus	387	medicina	358
lignum	440	lubido	447	magnitudo	387	medicinus	358
ligo	130	√luc	80	magnus	387	medico	358
ligurio	151	luceo	80	majestas	387	medicus	358
limen	442	lucerna	80	major	387	medio	394
limes	442	lucesco	80	√mal	451	mediocris	394
limito	442	lucidus	80	male	451	mediterraneus	
limpidus	282	lucror	437	maledictio	451		394
limus	442	lucrum	437	maledico	451	meditor	358
linea	444	luctus	129	malefacio	451	medium	394
linealis	444	√lug	129	malefactor	451	medius	394
lineamentum	444	lugeo	129	maleficus	256	mediusfidius	271
linearis	444	lugubris	129	malignus	451	mel	390
lineus	444	lumen	80	malitia	451	mellifluus	390
√ling	151	lumino	80	malo	387	memini	358
lingo	151	luminosus	80	malus	451	memor	391
linimentum	443	luna	80	√man	358	memoria	391
linio	443	luo	448	√man	398	memorialis	391
lino	443	luo	449	manceps	33	memoriter	391
linguo	500	lupus	81	mancipo	33	memoro	391
linter	306	lustrum	449	mancupo	33	√men	358

LATIN INDEX.

√men	386, 395	miror	388	√mov	379	nanciscor	354
√men	398	mirus	388	moveo	379	narro	120
menda	398	√misc	397	√mu	380	narus	120
mendax	358	miscellaneus	397	√mu	400	nascor	112
mendico	398	miscellus	397	√mulc	501	natio	112
mendicor	398	misceo	397	mulceo	501	nato	370
mendicus	398	mistio	397	mulco	501	natura	112
mendosus	398	mistura	397	mulcto	501	nauta	359
mendum	398	mixtio	397	mulctra	131	navalis	359
mens	358	mixtura	397	mulctrum	131	navigo	359
mensa	386	√mod	238	mulctus	131	navis	359
mensis	395	modernus	238	√mulg	131	navita	359
menstruus	395	moderor	238	mulgeo	131	navus	120
mensura	386	modestus	238	munero	380	√ne	364
mentio	358	modicus	238	munia	380	ne-	365
mentior	358	modifico	238	municeps	380	-ne	365
√mer	392	modium	238	municipalis		nē	365
mercans	392	modius	238		33, 380	√neb	335
mercator	392	modo	238	municipium		nebula	335
mercenarius	392	modulor	238		33, 380	nebulosus	335
merces	392	modulus	238	munificus	380	√nec	83
mercor	392	modus	238	munimentum	380	neco	83
mereo	392	moenio	380	munio	380	necne	365
mereor	392	√mol	402	munis	380	nefandus	339
√merg	132	mola	402	munitio	380	nefarius	339
mergae	132	molaris	402	munus	380	nefas	365
merges	132	molo	402	muralis	380	nefas	339
meridies	394	momentum	379	murmur	399	nefastus	339
meridianus	394	√mŏn	358	murmuro	399	neglegens	440
meridionalis	394	moneo	358	murus	380	neglego	440
meritum	392	moneta	358	√mus	403	negligens	440
merx	392	Moneta	358	mus	403	negligo	440
meta	386	monimentum	358	musca	401	√nem	360
metior	386	monitor	358	muscipula	403	nemo	157
meto	386	monitus	358	muscipulum	403	nemus	360
metor	386	monstro	358	musculus	403	neo	364
meus	385	monstrum	358	mussito	400	nepos	284
√mi	388	monumentum	358	musso	400	neptis	284
√mid	394	√mor	391	mutabilis	379	neque	365
√min	398	√mor	393	mutesco	400	nervosus	363
Minerva	358	mora	391	mutio	400	nervus	363
minimus	398	morbidus	393	muto	379	netus	364
minister	398	morbus	393	muttio	400	nex	83
ministerium	398	morior	393	mutus	400	√nig	367
ministro	398	moror	391	mutuus	379	nimirum	365, 388
minor	398	morosus	404			nimis	386
minuo	398	mors	393	**N.**		ningit	367
minus	398	mortalis	393			ninguit	367
minutum	398	morus	404	√nā	370	nisi	365
minutus	398	mos	386	√nă	370	√niv	367
mirabilis	388	motio	379	√nac	354	nivalis	367
miraculum	388	motus	379	nactus	354	niveus	367

LATIN INDEX. 231

nivosus	367	nubilum	335	obsidio	234	orbitas	336
nix	367	nubilus	335	obsidium	234	orbitudo	336
no	370	nubis	335	obsolesco	426	orbo	336
nobilis	120	nubo	335	obsoletus	426	orbus	336
√noc	83, 84	nudius	224	obstinatus	175	oriens	414
noceo	83	nudius tertius	224	obstino	175	orientalis	414
nocte	84	√num	360	obtusus	206	orificium	459
nocti (st.)	84	num	368	obviam	147	originalis	414
noctu	84	numarius	360	obvio	147	origo	414
noctua	84	numen	369	obvius	147	orior	414
nocturnus	84	numerator	360	√oc	502	oro	459
nolo	525	numero	360	occulco	435	ortus	414
nomen	374	numerosus	360	occulo	29	os (bone)	172
nomenclator	28	numerus	360	occupo	33	os (mouth)	459
nomenclatura	28	nummarius	360	ocior	2	oscito	459
nominalis	374	nummus	360	ociter	2	oscitor	459
nominativus	374	numus	360	octavus	86	osculatio	459
nomino	374	nunc	368	octo	86	osculor	459
non	365	nundinae	356	oculo	502	osculum	459
Nonae	356	nuo	369	oculus	502	osseus	172
nonaginta	356	nuper	362	√od	240	ovile	484
nonanus	356	nupta	335	√od	268	ovis	484
nongenti	356	nuptiae	335	odi	268	ovum	486
nonus	356	nurus	371	odiosus	268		
norma	120	nutatio	369	odium	268	**P.**	
normalis	120	nuto	369	odor	240		
nos	372	nutricius	370	odorarius	240	√pa	289
nosco	120	nutrimentum	370	odoratus	240	√pa	291
nota	120	nutrio	370	odoro	240	pabulator	291
notio	120	nutritius	370	odoror	240	pabulor	291
noto	120	nutrix	370	odorus	240	pabulum	291
novacula	362	nutus	369	offendo	257	pāc	285
novalis	362			officio	256	√păc	285
novellus	362	**O.**		oinos	373	pacifico	285
novem	356			oinus	373	pacificus	285
November	356	ob	279	√ol	240	pacisco	285
novendialis	356	obdo	256	√ol	426	paciscor	285
noverca	362	obediens	475	olefacio	240	păco	285
noviens	356	obedio	475	oleo	240	păco	285
novies	356	obex	493	oleum	430	pactum	285
novitas	362	obliquo	442	olfacio	240	paenitentia	310
novo	362	obliquus	442	olidus	240	paeniteo	310
novus	362	oblitero	443	oliva	430	paenitet	310
nox	84	oblittero	443	olor	240	√pag	285
noxa	83	oblivio	293	omnis	333	paganus	285
noxius	83	obliviosus	293	operio	313	pagina	285
√nu	369	obliviscor	293	opimus	302	pago	285
√nū	370	oboediens	475	√or	414	pagus	285
√nub	335	oboedio	475	oraculum	459	√pal	323
nubes	335	obscurus	101	orarium	459	palea	323
nubilis	335	obsecro	462	oratio	459	palleo	293
nubilo	335	obsero	422	orator	459	pallesco	293

LATIN INDEX.

pallidus	293	patrius	289	perennis	333	√plang	305
pallor	293	patrocinor	289	perficio	256	plango	305
palma	287	patronus	289	perfidiosus	271	plangor	305
palmes	287	patruelis	289	perfidus	271	planus	91
palmetum	287	patruus	289	perfuga	142	√ple	304
palmula	287	patulus	174	pergo	134	√ple	312
palmus	287	√pau	292	periculum	296	plebs	304
palum	285	paucitas	292	peritus	296	plebes	304
palus	285	pauculus	292	perjero	125	√plec	92
palus	300	paucus	292	perjurium	125	plecto	92
pango	285	paulatim	292	perjuro	125	plecto	305
panis	291	paulisper	292	permagnus	299	plerique	312
pannus	301	paullus	292	perneco	83	plenus	304
panus	301	paulo	292	pernicies	83	pleo	304
papa	289	paulum	292	perniciosus	83	plerus	312
√par	313	paulus	292	perpes	173	plerusque	312
parens	313	pauper	292	perpetuus	173	√plic	92
pareo	313	pauperies	292	pertinax	188	plico	92
pario	313	paupertas	292	pes	242	plisimus	312
paro	313	pavimento	286	pessum	242	√plu	306
parricida	289	pavimentum	286	pessumdare	242	√plu	307
pars	313	pavio	286	pessum dare	242	plumbeus	452
participium	313	pax	285	pessumdo	225	plumbum	452
participo	313	√pec	87	pessum ire	242	pluo	306
particula	313	pecten	87	pessundare	242	pluralis	312
particularis	313	pecto	87	√pet	173	plurimus	312
particeps	313	pecu	285	peto	173	plus	312
partio	313	pecunia	285	√pī	302	pluvia	306
parturio	313	pecuniaris	285	√pic	90	pluvialis	306
parturitio	313	pecus	285	√pig	90	pluvius	306
parum	292	√ped	242	√pi-n-g	90	√pō	308
pasco	291	pedalis	242	pictor	90	po	317
pascor	291	pedes	242	pictura	90	poculum	308
pascuum	291	pedester	242	pigmentum	90	poena	310
pascuus	291	pedica	242	pignero	285	poeniteo	310
pastor	291	pedum	242	pignus	285	poenitet	310
pastoralis	291	pejero	125	pileus	303	√pol	323
pastura	291	pellis	294	pilleum	303	pollen	323
pastus	291	√pen	291	pilleus	303	polleo	317
patefacio		Penates	291	pingo	90	polliceor,	
	256, 174	penes	291	pinna	173		500, 317
patella	174	penetro	291	pinnaculum	173	pollis	323
pateo	174	penna	173	pinnatus	173	pomerium	380
pater	289	penus	291	pituita	318	pomoerium	380
patera	174	per	288	√plac	91	pono	317
paternus	289	√per	296	√plag	305	pons	290
patesco	174	per-	299	√plag	92	popularis	304
patina	174	peragro	106	plaga	92	populus	304
patria	289	percello	48	plaga	305	√por	296
patricus	289	perdo	225	plagium	92	porcus	93
patrimonium	289	perduellio	231	planca	91	porrigo	134
patritus	289	peregrinor	106	planctus	305	porro	316

porta	296	praeter	316	propemodum		pulvero	323
porticus	296	praetextus	194		316	pulverulentus	
portio	313	praetor	493	propero	313		323
portus	296	prandeo	316	properus	313	pulvis	323
porto	313	prandium	316	propinquitas	316	punctus	320
possideo	317	pransor	316	propinquus	316	pungo	320
possido	317	pransus	316	propior	316	purifico	310
possum	314	prehendo	155	propitio	316	punio	310
postmoerium	380	prendo	155	propitius	316	pupa	322
postridie	224	√pri	316	proprius	316	pupilla	322
potatio	308	pridie 316,	224	propter	316	pupillus	322
potens	314	pridem	316	prosapia	463	pupugi	320
potentia	314	princeps 33,	316	protinus	188	pupus	322
potestas	314	principalis		proverbium	412	purgatio	310
potio	308		33, 316	providens	236	purgator	310
potior	314	principatus	316	providentia	236	purgatorius	310
potis	314	principium	316	providus	236	purgo	310
poto	308	primus	316	proximus	316	puritas	310
potor	308	priscus	316	prudens	236	purulentus	319
potus	308	pristinus	316	pruina	316	purus	310
√pra	316	√pro	316	pruna	321	pus	319
prae	316	pro	316	√pu	310	pusilanimis	322
praecello	63	procella	48	√pu	319	pusillus	322
praecentor	32	procello	48	√pu	322	pusus	322
praeceps	52	procerus	67	puber	322	putamen	310
praeceptor	33	procreo	67	pubertas	322	putator	310
praecipito	52	procul	48	pubes	322	puteo	319
praeda	155	proculco	435	pubis	322	puter	319
praedatorius	155	proditor	225	publicanus	304	puto	310
praedico	10	prodo	225	publice	304	putor	319
praedium	155	profanus	339	publico	304	putrefacio	319
praedo	155	profecto	256	publicus	304	putreo	319
praedor	155	professio	339	puella	322	putresco	319
praefatio	339	professor	339	puer	322	putridus	319
praeficio	256	proficio	256	puera	322	putris	319
praegnans	112	proficiscor	256	puerilis	322	putus	310
praehendo	155	profiteor	339	pueritia	322		
praejudicium	125	profundus	273	√pug	320	**Q.**	
praeoccupo	33	profusus	165	pugil	320		
praepedio	242	progenies	112	pugio	320	quadrans	517
praepes	173	progenitor	112	pugna	320	quadrigae	517
praeposterus	316	prolato	195	pugnax	320	quadro	517
praes	248	proles	426	pugno	320	quadrupes	517
praescisco	45	prolixus	127	pugnus	320	qualis	506
praesens	459	prolubium	447	√pul	307	quam	506
praeses	234	promiscuus	397	√pul	323	quando	506
prae sento	459	pronus	316	pullatus	293	quantus	506
praesidium	234	propago	285	pullus	293	quartus	517
praesidens	234	prope	316	pullus	322	quater	517
praesto	316	propediem		pulmo	307	quattuor	517
praestolor	176		224, 316	pulmonarius	307	quatuor	517
praesul	523	propemodo	316	pulmoneus	307	que 25,	516

234 LATIN INDEX.

√qui	44	√reg	134	√rou	421	salebra	523
√qui	519	regalis	134	√ru	421	salio	523
quid	519	regio	134	√ru	425	salio	524
quies	44	regnum	134	√rub	253	saliva	456
quiesco	44	rego	134	rubedo	253	sallo	524
quintus	504	regula	134	rubefacio	253	salo	524
quinque	504	relaxo	127	rubellus	253	salsus	524
quis	519	relego	440	rubeo	253	salto	523
√quo	506	religio	440	ruber	253	saltus	523
quo	506	relinquo	500	rubesco	253	salubris	454
quod	506	reliquiae	500	rubeus	253	salum	455
quot	506	reliquus	500	rubigo	253	salus	454
quotiens	506	relligio	440	rubor	253	salveo	454
quoties	506	relliquiae	500	rubrica	253	salvus	454
quotus	506	reluo	448	rubrus	253	sancio	462
		remedium	358	rubus	253	sanctifico	462
R.		remigium	411	√rud	253	sanctio	462
		reminiscor	358	√ruf	253	sanitas	462
√ra	411	remuneror	380	rufesco	253	sano	462
radix	420	remus	411	Rufio	253	sanus	462
√rap	275	renuo	369	rufus	253	√sa-p	463
rapax	275	√rep	281	Rufus	253	√sap	503
rapidus	275	repo	281	rugio	417	√sap	503
rapina	275	repraesento	459	rugitus	417	sapa	503
rapio	275	reptilis	281	ruina	421	sapidus	503
raptim	275	repto	281	rumifico	425	sapiens	503
raptor	275	reputo	310	Rumo	421	sapio	503
raptus	275	requies	44	rumor	425	sapo	503
ratis	411	rescisco	45	rumpo	283	sapor	503
√rau	425	resecro	462	ruo	421	sarmentum	276
raucus	425	resero	422	√rup	283	√sarp	276
ravis	425	resurrectio	134	rutilo	253	sarpo	276
ravus	425	rete	422	rutilus	253	satio	463
√re	411	reticulatus	422			sator	463
rebello	231	reticulum	422			Saturnus	463
reboo	513	revereor	415	**S.**		saxum	45
recalco	435	rex	134	√s	459	√scad	96
receptaculum	33	√ri	443	√sa	462	scaena	100
reciprocus	316	√rig	145	√sa	463	scaevitas	94
reclino	57	rigo	145	√sac	45	scaevus	94
recognosco	120	rivales	443	sacellum	462	scala	96
recreo	67	rivalis	443	sacer	462	√scalp	95
rectus	134	rivo	443	sacerdos	462	scalpellum	95
recuso	60	rivulus	443	sacramentum	462	scalpo	95
redono	225	rivus	443	sacro	462	scalprum	95
reddo	225	√ro	421	sacrum	462	scamnum	97
recondo	256	√rob	253	saecularis	463	√scand	243
refercio	346	robeus	253	saeculum	463	scando	96
refertus	346	robigo	253	√sal	455	scandula	243
reficio	256	robius	253	√sal	523	√scap	97
refugium	142	robus	253	sal	524	scapus	97
refuto	165	Roma	421	salax	523	scena	100

LATIN INDEX.

schola	148	semper	377	sido	234	somnificus	324
√sci	45	senator	357	silva	458	somnio	324
√scid	244	senatus	357	silvestris	458	somnium	324
scientia	45	senecta	357	silvosus	458	somnolentus	324
scindo	244	senectus	357	√sim	377	somnulentus	324
scio	45	seneo	357	similis	377	somnus	324
scipio	97	senesco	357	similitudo	377	sons	459
scisco	45	senex	357	similo	377	sonticus	459
scitum	45	senilis	357	simitu	377	√sop	324
scitus	45	senior	357	simplex 377,	488	sopio	324
scopae	97	senium	357	simul	377	sopor	324
scopio	97	septem	280	simulacrum	377	soporo	324
√scrib	122	September	280	simulator	377	soporus	324
scriba	122	septemtriones	198	simulo	377	√sor	422
scribo	122	septentriones	198	simultas	377	√sor	528
√scrob	122	septeni	280	singularis	377	sorbeo	337
scrobis	122	septies	280	singuli 488,	377	sorbillo	337
√scrof	122	septimus	280	sisto	175	sorbitio	337
scrofa	122	septuaginta	280	√soc	497	sors	422
√scu	101	septumus	280	socer	17	sortio	422
scutum	101	√seq	497	socialis	497	sortior	422
√se	463	√sequ	497	societas	497	sospes	462
se	489	sequester	497	socio	497	√spec	99
√sĕc	45	sequestro	497	socius	497	species	99
√sec	497	sequor	497	socrus	17	specimen	99
seco	45	√ser	528	√sŏd	252	specio	99
sectio	45	√ser	422	√sŏd	252	specto	99
sector	497	sera	422	sodalis	252	spectrum	99
secularis	463	sereno	528	√sol	235	specula	99
seculum	463	serenus	528	√sol	528	speculor	99
secundo	497	series	422	√sol	234	speculum	99
secundus	497	sermo	422	sol	528	√sper	323
securis	45	sero	422	solaris	528	sperno	323
securus	60	sero	463	solea	235	spolium	101
secus	497	√serp	281	solemnis	333	√sprē	323
√sed	234	serpens	281	solennis	333	spretio	323
√sed	235	serpo	281	solicito	54	spretor	323
sedatio	234	serra	45	solidus	527	√spu	318
sedatus	234	serratus	45	solium	234	spuma	318
sedeo	234	sertum	422	sollemnis	333	spumeus	318
sedes	234	servilis	422	sollennis	527	spumidus	318
seditio	493	servio	422	sollempnis	333	spumo	318
sedo	234	servitium	422	sollennis	333	spuo	318
sedulus	235	servitudo	422	sollers 527,	408	√spur	323
segmentum	45	servus	422	sollicito	54	spurius	323
selibra	382	sessio	234	sollicitus 54,	527	sputum	318
sella	234	sestertius	382	solliferreus	527	squaleo	46
semel	377	sex	473	sollus	527	squalidus	46
seme	463	sextus	473	solstitium	175	squalor	46
semi-	382	sexus	45	solum	235	√sre	422
seminarium	463	√si	463	solvo	448	√stă	175
semino	463	sica	45	somnifer	324	√stă	175

236 LATIN INDEX.

stabilis	175	stupeo	187	superstitio	175	tempestas	196
stabulum	175	stupidus	187	superus	325	templum	196
statim	175	stuppa	187	supinus	326	tempto	188
statio	175	√su	466	supplementum		tempus	196
stator	175	√suad	209		304	√ten	188
Stator	175	suadela	209	supplicatio	92	tenax	188
statuo	175	suadeo	209	supplico	92	tendo	188
status	175	suasio	209	suppuro	319	teneo	188
√steg	135	suasor	209	supra	325	tener	188
stega	135	suavis	209	supremus	325	tenor	188
stella	167	suavitas	209	√sur	423	tento	188
√ster	167	suavium	209	surgo	134	tenuis	188
√ster	185	sub	326	surrigo	134	tenuo	188
sterilis	180	subdo	256	surrubeo	253	tenus	188
sterno	185	subitus	493	sursum	326	tepefacio	256
√stig	152	subjugo	125	sus	467	√ter	197
√stig	183	sublimis	442	susurro	423	√ter	198
stilus	183	suboles	426	susurrus	423	ter (st.)	204
stimulo	183	subsidium	234	sutela	466	ter	204
stimulus	183	subtemen	194	sutor	466	terebra	198
√sting	183	subter	326	sutura	466	terebro	198
stinguo	183	subterfugium	142	suus	489	teredo	198
√stip	181	subtilis	194			teres	198
stipa	187	subtilitas	194	**T.**		termen	197
stipator	181	subula	466	√ta	190	termino	197
stipendium	181	suculentus	503	tabeo	190	terminus	197
stipes	181	sucus	503	tabes	190	termo	197
stipis	181	√sud	237	tabesco	190	terni	204
stipo	181	sudo	237	tabum	190	tero	198
stipula	181	sudor	237	tactio	189	terra	200
stipulor	181	√sued	252	tactus	189	terreo	202
stipulus	181	suesco	252	√tag	189	terribilis	202
sto	175	sufficio	256	tagax	189	terrifico	202
√stol	176	suffimen	265	talpa	95	terror	202
stolidus	176	suffimentum	265	tango	189	√ters	202
√stor	185	suffio	265	tata	201	tertius	204
√strā	185	suffitio	265	taurus	191	testa	200
√strag	465	suggrunda	156	taxo	189	testaceus	200
strages	185	sugo	503	√te	192	testu	200
stramen	185	sum	459	√tec	194	testudo	200
√strang	465	sumen	503	tectum	135	testum	200
strata	185	summa	325	√tĕg	135	tetuli	195
stratum	185	summus	325	√tĕg	135	texo	194
stratus	185	suo	466	tegimen	135	textilis	194
√strig	465	supellex	440	tegmen	135	textor	194
strigilis	464	super	325	tego	135	textus	194
√string	465	superbus	325	tegulae	135	tignum	194
stringo	465	superficialis	339	tegumen	135	tigurium	135
strues	185	superficies	339	tegurium	135	tinctura	193
struo	185	superior	325	tela	194	tingo	193
stultus	176	supernus	325	telum	194	tlā	195
stupa	187	supero	325	√tem	196	toga	135

LATIN INDEX. 237

√tol	195	tribunal	204	ulcero	19	vappa	35
tolerabilis	195	tribunus	204	ulcus	19	vas (bail)	248
tolero	195	tribuo	204	uligo	137	vas (vessel)	460
tondeo	196	tribus	204	ulula	453	vasculum	460
tonitrus	188	tributum	204	ululatus	453	√ve	476
tono	188	triennium	333	ululo	453	√vec	496
tonsor	196	triens	204	umecto	137	vecors	38
tonus	188	trimestris	395	umeo	137	vectigal	147
√tor	198	trio	198	umerus	407	vecto	147
√torc	508	triplex	204	umidus	137	vector	147
torcular	508	tripus	242	umor	137	vectura	147
torculum	508	triremis	411	√unc	1	√veg	138
tormentum	508	triticum	198	uncus	1	vegeo	138
torno	198	tritor	198	√und	247	vegeto	138
tornus	198	tritura	198	unda	247	√veh	147
√torqu	508	trituro	198	undo	247	vehemens	358
torqueo	508	trivialis	204	unguiculus	375	vehes	147
torques	508	trivium	204	unguis	375	vehiculum	147
torquis	508	√tru	198	ungula	375	veho	147
torreo	200	trua	198	ungulatus	375	vel	525
torrens	200	tu	192	ungulus	1	vellus	413
torris	200	√tu	205	unicus	373	velo	147
√tors	200	tuber	205	unio	373	velum	147
torto	508	√tud	206	unus	373	√vēn	509
tortor	508	tudes	206	√urg	124	√vĕn	509
tortuosus	508	tugurium	135	uro	491	venalis	376
tortura	508	√tul	195	ursa	4	vendo	376
tortus	508	tuli	195	ursus	4	vendo	225
√tra	197	tulo	195	√us	491	veneo	376
traditio	225	tumefacio	205	ustor	491	venio	509
trado	225	tumeo	205	uter	506	veno	376
trans	197	tumesco	205	uterque	506	venter	110
transfiguro	126	tumidus	205	utpote	314	ventilo	476
transfuga	142	tumor	205	uvesco	137	ventio	509
transtrum	197	tumulus	205	uvidus	137	ventito	509
tre (st.)	204	tundo	206	uvor	137	ventulus	476
√trem	203	turba	208			ventus	476
tremefacio	203	turbidus	208	**V.**		venui	376
tremendus	203	turbo	208			venum	376
tremesco	203	turbulentus	208	√va	476	venus	376
tremisco	203	turma	208	√vad	248	√ver	412
tremo	203	tutudi	206	vadimonium	248	√ver	415
tremor	203	tuus	192	vador	248	ver	478
tremulus	203	tympanum	207	valles	430	verbalis	412
tres	204			vallis	430	verbosus	412
√tri	198	**U.**		vallo	432	verbum	412
tri (st.)	204			vallum	432	verecundus	415
tria	204	uber	269	vallus	432	vereor	415
triarii	204	ubi	506	vannus	476	vernalis	478
tribula	198	√ul	426	√vap	35	vernus	478
tribulo	198	√ul	453	vapidus	35	√ves	460
tribulum	198	ulceratio	19	vapor	35	vescor	233
				vaporo	35		

vescus	233	victus	512	virgo	133	vocatus	496
vespa	468	vicus	85	virulentus	480	vociferor	496
vesper	461	√vid	236	virus	480	voco	496
vespera	461	√vid	236	vis	481	√vol(u)p	277
vespertinus	461	videlicet	236	visitatio	236	√vol	429
vestigium	152	video	236	visito	236	√vol	525
vestigo	152	vieo	482	viso	236	volo	525
vestio	460	√vig	138	vita	512	volubilis	429
vestis	460	√vi-g	512	vitalis	512	volumen	429
veteranus	169	vigeo	138	vitis	482	voluntarius	525
veterasco	169	vigesco	138	vitium	482	voluntas	525
vetulus	169	vigesimus	13	vito	14	volup	277
vetus	169	vigil	138	vitreus	236	voluptas	277
vetustus	169	vigilo	138	vitrum	236	voluptuosus	277
vexillum	147	viginti	13	vitta	482	voluto	429
vexo	147	vigor	138	vitulus	170	volvo	429
√vi	482	villa	85	vitupero	482	√vom	381
√vi	512	villus	413	√vi-v	512	vomitio	381
via	147	vimen	482	vivacitas	512	vomito	381
√vic	14	vinum	483	vivax	512	vomitus	381
√vic	16	vio	147	vividus	512	vomo	381
√vic	85	viola	479	vivo	512	√vor	514
vicensimus	13	violentus	481	vivus	512	voracitas	514
vicesimus	13	violo	481	√voc	496	vorago	514
vicinus	85	vipera	313	vocabulum	496	vorax	514
vicis	14	√virg	133	vocalis	496	voro	514
vicissim	14	virga	133	vocatio	496	vox	496

ENGLISH INDEX OF COGNATE WORDS.

[The figures refer to the numbers of the sets.]

A.

word	#	word	#	word	#	word	#
abdicate	10	acute	2	agility	104	amplify	333, 256
abduce	12	add	225	agitate	104	amputate	310
abduction	12	adduce	12	agrarian	106	anacoluthon	47
abjure	125	adduction	12	agree	158	analysis	448
ablution	449	adjacent	493	agreeable	158	anarchy	143
aboriginal	414	adjective	493	agriculture	106	anchor	1
aborigines	414	adjoin	125	Alban	332	ancient	166
abortion	414	adjudge	125	albumen	332	ancillary	1
abound	247	adjudicate	125	alien	427	anger	144
abrupt	283	adjunct	125	alienate	427	angle	1
abundant	247	admirable	388	aliment	426	anguish	144
abscond	256	admire	388	alimony	426	animal	350
absent	459	admonish	358	aliquot	427	animate	350
absolute	448	admonition	358	alleviate	146	animated	350
absolution	448	adult	426	alligation	130	animation	350
absolve	448	adulterer	427	allocution	77	animosity	350
absorb	337	advent	509	alluvial	449	annals	333
abstain	188	adventure	509	Alps	332	anniversary	333
absurd	423	adverb	412	alter	427	annotation	120
accelerate	48	aedile	249	alterative	427	annual	333
accent	32	aerate	476	altercate	427	annular	333
acclaim	23	aeriform	476	altercation	427	answer	166
acclamation	28	aerolite	476	alternate	427	ante	166
accretion	67	aeronaut	476	alternative	427	antedate	166
accuse	60	affable	339	altitude	426	anterior	166
acephalous	52	affect	256	alumnus	426	anti-	166
acerbity	2	affection	256	am	459	anticipate	33
acetic	2	affectation	256	amaranth	393	antique	166
acid	2	affiance	271	ambiguous	104	antiquity	166
acoustic	60	affidavit	271	ambition	493	anxious	144
acquiesce	44	affirm	261	amble	509	apiary	278
acre	106	affix	136	ambrosia	393	apocope	64
acrid	2	affluence	345	ambulance	509	apostle	176
acrimony	2	affluent	345	ambulant	509	apothecary	256
act	104	agent	104	ambulatory	509	apparent	313
action	104	aggravate	511	amend	398	appear	313
actor	104	aggrieve	511	ammunition	380	appease	285
acumen	2	agile	104	ample	333	appetence	173

appetite	173	astral	167	base	509	cap	52
applicant	92	astringent	465	basis	509	capacious	33
application	92	athlete	248	be	348	capacity	33
apposite	317	athletic	248	bear	344	cape	52
apposition	317	atmosphere	477	because	60	caper	36
apprehend	155	atrophy	199	bedstead	175	capillary	52
apprehension	155	attain	188	bee	278	capital	52
arable	410	attempt	188	belligerent	231	capitol	52
arbiter	509	attend	188	beneficent	256	capitulate	52
arbitrary	509	attribute	204	bereave	275	capricious	36
arbitrate	509	attrition	198	bibulous	308	Capricorn	36
ardent	158	attenuate	188	biennial	333	caprice	36
argent	107	auction	138	binary	231	captain	52
argil	107	audacious	475	bind	270	captive	33
argillaceous	107	audible	475	biography	512	captor	33
argue	107	audience	475	biology	512	cardinal	66
argument	107	audit	475	biped	242	care	60
aristocracy	67	augment	138	birth	344	carnal	68
arithmetic	408	augmentation		bleat	328	carp	41
ark	3		138	blink	140	castigate	24
arm	408	augur	485	bloom	345	cathartic	24
arm (vb.)	408	augury	485	blow	345	catholic	527
armada	408	August	138	bond	279	causal	60
armature	408	august	138	boor	348	cause	60
armor	408	Augustus	138	bore	340	caustic	42
arms	408	auricular	495	bos	515	caution	60
army	408	aurist	495	bossy	515	cautious	60
arson	158	auscultation	495	both	334	cave	73
art	408	auspices	485	bovine	515	cavern	73
artful	408	auspicious	485	bow	142	cavity	73
article	408	author	138	bright	140	celerity	48
articulate	408	authority	138	brother	347	celestial	73
artifice	408	autobiography		brutal	511	cell	29
artificer	408		512	brute	511	cellar	29
artificial	408	autocrat	67	bucolic	48	cellular	29
artillery	408	auxiliary	138	bulb	329	cellule	29
artisan	408	avarice	475	bulbous	329	cellulose	29
artist	408	aviary	485			cement	244
artless	408	avidity	475	**C.**		cent	15
ascend	96	avocation	496			centiped	242
ascribe	122	axis	470	calculate	42	centurion	15
askew	94	axle	470	calculus	42	century	15
aspect	99	aye	474	calendar	28	cereal	67
assail	523			call	117	cerebral	37
assault	523	**B.**		calyx	29	ceremony	67
assess	234			camp	53	Ceres	67
assiduous	234	bairn	344	can	120	certain	69
assist	175	band	270	cancer	39	chamber	31
assize	234	barbarous	327	canine	75	chant	32
associate	497	baritone	511	cant	32	chanticleer	32
association	497	barometer	511	canticle	32	chaos	154
asthma	476	barytone	511	cantillate	32	chapter	52

chasm	154	combustion	491	concrete	67	constriction	465
chaste	24	comedy	44	concretion	67	construct	185
chasten	24	comma	64	condemn	225	construe	185
chastise	24	commemorate	391	condense	216	consummate	325
chin	353			condone	225	contact	189
chirography	159	commensurable	386	conduce	12	contagious	189
Christ	164			cónduct	12	contain	188
circle	74	comment	358	condúct	12	contaminate	189
circulate	74	commentary	358	conduction	12	contemplate	196
circulation	74	commerce	392	cone	76	contemporary	196
circumduct	12	commode	238	confer	344		
circumduction	12	commodious	238	conference	344	contend	188
circumference	344	commodity	238	confess	339	content	188
		common	380	confession	339	context	194
circumfluent	345	commotion	379	confidant	271	contingent	189
circumjacent	493	commune(n.)	380	confide	271	continuous	188
circumspect	99	commune (vb.)	380	confident	271	contort	508
circumstance	175			confirm	261	contortion	508
circumvallation	432	communicate	380	confluence	345	contradict	10
		commute	379	confluent	345	contribute	204
cite	54	compete	173	confuse	165	contrite	198
city	44	competence	173	confute	165	contrition	198
civic	44	competent	173	congratulate	158	contusion	206
civil	44	complement	304	conic	76	convene	509
claim	28	compliment	304	conical	76	convent	509
clamor	28	complete	304	conjecture	493	convention	509
clandestine	29	complex	92	conjoin	125	convocation	496
clarify	58	complexion	92	conjugal	125	convoke	496
class	28	complicate	92	conjugate	125	convolution	429
classical	28	complication	92	conjunction	125	convolve	429
clavicle	56	comport	313	conjunctive	125	cook	505
clear	58	compose	317	conjure	125	cordial	88
client	58	composite	317	connoisseur	120	corn	49
climate	57	composition	317	connubial	335	corner	49
climax	57	comprehend	155	conscience	45	cornet	49
clime	57	comprehension	155	conscious	45	cornucopia	49
close	56			conscript	122	corona	74
coalesce	426	compunction	320	consecrate	462	coronal	74
coerce	3	compute	310	consecutive	497	coronation	74
cognate	112	con	120	consequent	497	coronel	74
cognition	120	conceal	29	consequence	497	coroner	74
cognizant	120	conceit	33	consist	175	coronet	74
cohort	159	conceive	33	consociate	497	corporal	67
colleague	440	concent	32	consociation	497	corporate	67
collect	440	conception	33	consort	422	corporation	67
college	440	concern	69	conspicuous	99	corporeal	67
colloquial	77	concért	69	constant	175	corps	67
colloquy	77	cóncert	69	constellation	167	corpse	67
colonel	74	conch	61	consternation	185	corpulent	67
color	29	conchology	61	constipate	181	correct	134
column	63	concise	244	constitute	175	corrupt	283
combine	231	conclude	56	constrict	465	cosmopolitan	311

ENGLISH INDEX OF COGNATE WORDS.

cosmorama	415	cyclopedia	74	deign	11	desultory	523
council	28	cynic	75	deity	224	detain	188
court	159	cynosure	75	dejected	493	determination	
crabbed	2			delectable	18		197
cranial	37	**D.**		delicate	18	determine	197
cranium	37			delicious	18	detonate	188
create	67	dactyl	7	delight	18	detriment	196
creator	67	daisy	502	delineate	444	deuce	231
creature	67	damage	225	delinquent	500	Deuteronomy	
credence	256	dame	213	deluge	449		231
credential	256	damn	225	demented	358	deviate	147
credible	256	dare	260	democracy	67	Devil	510
credit	256	date	225	demonstrate	358	devious	147
creditor	256	dative	225	demur	391	devolve	429
credulous	256	daughter	263	demurrage	391	devour	514
creed	256	daunt	213	dendriform	230	dexterous	220
crescent	67	day	224	dendrology	230	dextrous	220
crime	69	deceit	33	dendrometer	230	diabolical	510
criminal	69	deceive	33	denominate	374	diadem	218
criminate	69	December	8	denomination		dial	224
crisis	69	decent	11		374	dialect	440
criterion	69	deception	33	denote	120	dialectic	440
critic	69	decimal	8	dense	216	dialogue	440
critical	69	decide	244	dentated	241	dictate	10
criticise	69	deck	135	dentifrice	164	dictator	10
croak	65	declaim	28	dentist	241	diction	10
crook	74	declamation	28	dentition	241	dictionary	10
crow	65	declare	58	depict	90	diduction	12
crown	74	declension	57	deplete	304	differ	344
crude	70	declination	57	deponent	317	difficulty	256
cruel	70	decline	57	deport	313	diffident	271
crust	70	decoction	505	deportment	313	diffuse	165
crystal	70	decorate	11	deplore	317	digit	7
cuckoo	62	decorous	11	depredation	155	dignity	11
culinary	505	decorum	11	deputation	310	diligent	440
culm	27	decrease	67	depute	310	dilute	449
culminate	63	decree	69	deputy	310	dilution	449
cuneiform	76	decrement	67	derelict	500	diluvial	449
cuniform	76	dedicate	10	derivation	443	diminish	398
curate	60	deduce	12	derive	443	diorama	415
curator	60	deduction	12	derm	221	dire	223
cure	60	deed	256	dermatology	221	direct	134
curiosity	60	deem	256	descend	96	direful	223
curious	60	defence	257	describe	122	discern	69
curt	51	defend	257	desist	175	disciple	210
curtail	51	defer	344	despot	314	discipline	210
curved	74	deference	344	destination	175	disclose	56
custody	266	deficient	256	destine	175	discreet	69
custom	252	deflect	103	destitute	175	discriminate	69
cycle	74	defy	271	destroy	185	disdain	11
cycloid	74	degenerate	112	destruction	185	disgust	115
cyclone	74	deglutition	514	desuetude	252	disjoin	125

disjunctive	125	dowry	225	elect	440	exclaim	23
dismal	224	dragon	9	electricity	20	exclude	56
dispose	317	drama	228	elegant	440	excuse	60
dispute	310	drill	198	element	426	execrate	462
dissect	45	dropsy	247	elicit	18	exercise	3
dissemble	377	Druid	230	eliminate	442	exhume	157
dissertation	422	dual	231	ellipse	500	exile	235
disseminate	463	dubious	231	ellipsis	500	exit	493
dissimilar	377	ductile	12	eloquent	77	expect	99
dissimulate	377	duel	231	else	427	expedient	242
dissociate	497	dulcet	428	emancipate	33	expedite	242
dissociation	497	duplicate	231	emend	398	expedition	242
dissolute	448	duplicity	231	emetic	381	experience	296
dissolution	448	dust	265	emotion	379	experiment	296
dissolve	448	dys-	232	empire	313	expletive	304
dissuade	209	dysentery	232	emporium	296	explicate	92
distant	175	dyspepsia		encamp	53	explication	92
distend	188		232, 505	enchant	32	explicit	92
distinguish	183	dyspepsy		enclitic	57	export	313
distort	508		232, 505	enervate	363	expose	317
distortion	508			enormity	120	expunge	320
distribute	204	**E.**		enormous	120	expurgate	310
disturb	208			ensue	497	exscind	244
diurnal	224	eager	2	entrails	355	extant	175
divine	224	ear	495	enumerate	360	extemporaneous	
do	256	eat	233	envious	236		196
docile	210	edacious	233	envy	236	extempore	196
doctor	210	edge (vb.)	2	epic	496	extemporize	196
doctrine	210	edge (n.)	2	equestrian	499	extend	188
document	210	edible	233	equine	499	extenuate	188
domain	213	edict	10	erect	134	exterior	472
dome	219	edifice	249	eruption	283	exterminate	197
domestic	219	edify	256	erysipelas	294	external	472
domicile	219	edit	225	essence	459	extinguish	183
dominant	213	educate	12	eternal	474	extort	508
dominate	213	educe	12	ether	249	extortion	508
domineer	213	eduction	12	ethical	252	extra	472
dominie	213	effect	256	ethics	252	extraneous	472
dominion	213	effete	348	etymology	459	extreme	472
donate	225	efficacious	256	etymon	459	extrinsic	472
donation	225	effigy	126	evaporate	35	exuberant	269
donor	225	efflorescence	345	event	509	exude	237
doom	256	effluent	345	ever	474	exult	523
door	264	effluvium	345	evident	236	eye	502
dormant	215	efflux	345	evoke	496		
dormer	215	effulgent	140	evolution	429	**F.**	
dormitory	215	effuse	165	evolve	429		
dormouse	215	egg (vb.)	2	exalt	426	fable	339
dorsal	222	eight	86	excel	63	fabricate	256
double	231	ejaculate	493	except	33	fabulous	339
doubt	231	eject	493	excite	54	face	339
dower	225	elaborate	331	exclamation	28	facetious	339

244 ENGLISH INDEX OF COGNATE WORDS.

facetiously	339	fiction	126	friable	164	glue	446
facile	256	fidelity	271	fricative	164	glut	514
facility	256	fierce	257	friction	164	glyphic	119
fact	256	figment	126	frigid	419	gorge	514
faction	256	figure	126	fugacious	142	grace	158
factious	256	filial	254	fugitive	142	grammar	122
factor	256	filly	322	fugue	142	-graph	122
faculty	256	fire	321	fulminate	140	graphic	122
faith	271	firm	261	fume	265	grateful	158
falcon	103	firmament	261	fumigate	265	gratis	158
fall	457	fist	320	fund	245	gratuitous	158
fallacious	457	fix	136	fundamental	273	grave	122
fallacy	457	flagitious	140	funeral	265	grave	511
fallow	293	flagrant	140	furnace	520	gravity	511
false	457	flame	140	furtive	344	grief	511
fame	339	flexible	103	fuse	165	grieve	511
family	256	flourish	345	fusion	165	grim	163
famous	339	flow	345	futile	165	grum	163
fan	476	flower	345	future	348	gullet	514
fanatic	339	fluctuate	345			gully	514
fancy	339	flue	345	**G.**		gush	165
fane	339	fluent	345			gust	115
fantasm	339	fluid	345	gage	248	gustatory	115
fantastic	339	flux	345	gall	162	gutter	165
farrago	344	foal	322	gallinaceous	117		
farina	344	foil	349	garden	159	**H.**	
fastidious	260	foliage	349	garrulous	117		
fate	339	font	165	gastric	110	hale	30
father	289	foot	242	genealogy	112	Harpies	275
fathom	174	force	261	generate	112	harvest	41
feather	173	forceps	520	generic	112	heal	30
fecundate	348	fort	261	generous	112	health	30
fecundity	348	forte	261	genesis	112	heart	38
federal	271	fortitude	261	genital	112	heel	485
federate	271	fortify	261	genitive	112	heir	159
feign	126	fortnight	84	genius	112	hell	29
feint	126	fortress	261	genteel	112	hereditary	159
felicity	348	fortuitous	344	gentile	112	hiatus	154
fell	294	fortune	344	gentle	112	hibernate	161
felt	303	found	273	gentleness	112	hide	101
female	254	fount	165	gentry	112	hierarch	143
feminine	254	fountain	165	genuflection	121	hieroglyphic	119
fence	257	four	517	genuine	112	hippodrome	
fend	257	fraction	522	genus	112		229, 499
fender	257	fracture	522	geode	116	history	236
ferocious	259	fragile	522	geodesy	116	homeopathy	377
ferocity	259	fragment	522	geography	116	home	44
fertile	344	frail	522	geology	440, 116	homestead	175
fertility	344	frangible	522	geometry	116	homicide	157
fetid	265	fraternal	347	get	155	homoeopathy	377
fetter	242	fraternity	347	glorious	58	homogeneous	
few	292	frequent	346	glory	58		377

ENGLISH INDEX OF COGNATE WORDS. 245

hone	76	implicate	92	inflate	345	interrupt	283
horn	49	implication	92	inflect	103	intersect	45
hound	75	implicit	92	influence	345	interstice	175
hour	424	import	313	influx	345	interval	432
how	506	impose	317	infraction	522	intervene	509
human	157	impugn	320	infringe	522	intervention	509
humane	157	impunity	310	infuse	165	intestine	355
humanity	157	impure	310	ingenious	112	intimate	355
humble	157	in	355	ingenuous	112	intolerable	351
humid	137	in-	351	inheritance	159	intonate	188
humility	157	inaugurate	485	inhumate	157	intone	188
humor	137	incantation	32	inhume	157	introduce	12
hydra	246	incentive	32	initial	493	introduction	12
hydrant	247	inceptive	33	initiate	493	introspect	99
hydrate	247	inception	33	inject	493	inundate	247
hydraulic	247	incest	24	injury	125	invent	509
hydrogen	247	incipient	33	innate	112	invention	509
hydrometer	247	incise	244	innuendo	369	inventory	509
hydrophobia	247	incision	244	inoculate	502	invidious	236
hygiene	138	incisive	244	insane	462	invisible	236
hygrometer	137	incite	54	inscribe	122	invite	496
hypnotic	324	inclination	57	insert	422	invocation	496
		incline	57	insidious	234	invoke	496
		inclose	56	insipid	503	involution	429
I.		include	56	insist	175	involve	429
identical	490	incorporate	67	inspect	99	iodine	479
identify	490	incorporation	67	instant	175	irrigate	145
identity	490	increase	67	instigate	183	irruption	283
idiom	489	increment	67	instinct	183	is	459
idiot	489	incrust	70	institute	175	item	490
idol	236	inculcate	435	instruct	185	iterate	490
ignominy	374	indemnity	225	instrument	185	itinerant	493
ignorant	120	indicate	10	insult	523		
ignore	120	indigenous	112	integer	189	**J.**	
illative	195	indignant	11	integrity	189	janitor	493
illicit	500	induce	12	intellect	440	January	493
illuminate	80	induct	12	intelligent	440	join	125
illustrate	80	induction	12	intend	188	journal	224
illustrious	80	inert	408	intercalar	28	journey	224
imbibe	308	inertia	408	intercalary	28	judge	125
imbue	308	infamous	339	intercalate	28	judicial	125
immense	386	infamy	339	intercept	33	jugular	125
immolate	402	infant	339	interception	33	jurist	125
immunity	380	infantry	339	interclude	56	just	125
immutable	379	infect	256	interdict	10	justice	125
impact	285	infer	344	interfused	165	juvenile	224
impede	242	inference	344	interim	355	juxtaposition	125
imperative	313	infested	257	interject	493		
imperial	313	infirm	261	interjection	493	**K.**	
impetuous	173	infix	136	interlocution	77		
impinge	285	inflame	140	internecine	83	ken	120
implement	304	inflammation	140	interpose	317	kitchen	505

kleptomania 55	liberator 447	**M.**	mediterranean 394
klopemania 55	libertine 447		
knee 121	liberty 447	madame 213	medium 394
know 120	license 500	magisterial 387	meed 267
	licit 500	magistracy 387	mega- 387
L.	lick 151	magistrate 387	megalosaurus 387
	ligament 130	magnanimous 387	
labial 438	light (n.) 80		megatherium 387
labiate 438	light (adj.) 146	magnitude 387	melancholy 162
labor (n.) 331	limit 442	majesty 387	mellifluous 390
labor (vb.) 331	limpid 282	major 387	melt 239
laborious 331	line 444	majority 387	memorable 391
lacerate 78	lineal 444	mal- 451	memorial 391
lachrymal 6	lineament 444	male- 451	memory 391
lactation 109	linear 444	malediction 451	mend 398
lacteal 109	linen 444	malefactor 451	mendacious 358
lag 128	linger 128	malevolent 451	mendicant 398
laggard 128	liniment 443	malice 451	menstrual 395
lake 78	lion 445	malign 451	mensurable 386
lamp 282	lip 438	malignant 451	mensuration 386
languid 127	liquid 500	maltreat 451	mental 358
languor 127	liquor 500	mania 358	mention 358
lantern 282	literal 443	maniac 358	mentor 358
lap (vb.) 438	literature 443	manifest 257	mercantile 392
lascivious 433	liturgy 436	maniple 304	mercenary 392
latitude 185	livid 293	manipulate 304	merchandise 392
laud 58	logarithm 440	mansion 358	merchant 392
laudable 58	logic 440	manual 386	meridian 394
lave 449	logomachy 440, 384	manufacture 386	meridional 394
lax 127		manumit 386	merit 392
league 130	-logy 440	manuscript 386	mete 386
lean (vb.) 57	long 128	martyr 391	metre 386
leave 500	longitude 128	master 387	metrical 386
lection 440	look 80	material 396	metropolis 311
lecture 440	loquacious 77	maternal 396	mid- 394
legal 130	lose 448	mathematical 358	middle 394
legible 440	lotion 449	mathematics 358	midst 394
legion 440	loud 58	matriculate 396	midge 401
legionary 440	lucid 80	matrimony 396	mild 389
legislate 130	lucrative 437	matron 396	milk 131
legitimate 130	lucre 437	matter 396	mill 402
leguminous 440	lugubrious 129	mayor 387	mimesis 386
-less 448	luminous 80	me 385	mimic 386
letter 443	lunar 80	meal 402	mince 398
levigate 441	lunatic 80	measure 386	mind (n.) 358
levity 146	lune 80	mean (vb.) 358	mind (vb.) 358
liable 130	lust 433	mediate 394	Minerva 358
libation 443	lustral 449	mediator 394	minim 398
liberal 447	lustrum 449	medical 358	minimum 398
liberality 447	lute 449	medicine 358	minister 398
liberate 447	luxate 442	mediocre 394	ministry 398
liberation 447	luxation 442	meditate 358	minor 398

ENGLISH INDEX OF COGNATE WORDS. 247

minstrel	398	muniment	380	nomenclature		obviate	147
mint	358	munition	380		28, 374	obvious	147
minus	398	mural	380	nominal	374	occult	29
mínute	398	murder	393	nominate	374	occultation	29
minúte	398	murmur	399	nominative	374	occupation	33
miracle	388	muscle	403	non-	365	occupy	33
miscellaneous		muscular	403	none	365	octave	86
	397	musquito	401	Nones	356	ocular	502
mix	397	mussel	403	normal	120	oculist	502
mixture	397	mutable	379	not	365	odious	268
mnemonic	358	mute	400	notation	120	odium	268
mob	379	mutiny	379	note	120	odor	240
mobile	379	mutter	400	notion	120	odorous	240
mobility	379	mutual	379	noun	374	of	274
mobilize	379	myope	400	nourish	370	off	274
mode	238	myops	400	novel	362	offend	257
model	238	myopy	400	November	356	offer	344
moderate	238	mystery	400	now	368	ogle	502
modern	238			noxious	83	oil	430
modest	238	**N.**		number	360	old	426
modify	238			numerate	360	oleaginous	430
modulate	238	nail	375	numerator	360	olfactory	240
molar	402	name	374	numerous	360	olive	430
moment	379	narrate	120	nuptials	335	omni-	333
momentary	379	nascent	112	nurse	370	omnibus	333
momentous	379	natal	112	nursery	370	on	352
momentum	379	nation	112	nutation	369	one	373
monarch	143	nature	112	nutriment	370	onomatopoeia	
monetary	358	nausea	359	nutritious	370		374
money	358	nautical	359	nutrition	370	ophthalmia	502
monitor	358	naval	359			ophthalmy	502
monster	358	navigate	359	**O.**		oppose	317
month	395	nay	365	oar	411	optic	502
monument	358	nebular	335	oats	233	optical	502
mood	238	nebulous	335	obedient	475	optician	502
moon	395	needle	364	object	493	optics	502
morals	386	nefarious	339	obligate	130	oracle	459
morbid	393	neglect	440	obligation	130	oral	459
morose	404	negligent	440	oblige	130	oration	459
mortal	393	nephew	284	oblique	442	orator	459
mortify	393	nepotism	284	obliterate	443	organ	123
mosquito	401	nerve	363	oblivion	293	orgies	123
mother	396	nervous	363	oblivious	293	oriental	414
motion	379	net	364	obloquy	77	orifice	459
mouse	403	neuralgia	363	obscure	101	original	414
movable	379	new	362	obsolete	426	orphan	336
move	379	nine	356	obstacle	175	orphaned	336
movement	379	night	84	obstetrical	175	osculation	459
mow	378	no	365	obstinate	175	osseous	172
municipal		noble	120	obstruct	185	ossify	172
	33, 380	nocturnal	84	obtain	188	ostensible	188
munificent	380	nod	369	obtuse	206	ostentation	188

248 ENGLISH INDEX OF COGNATE WORDS.

Word	Page	Word	Page	Word	Page	Word	Page
otter	246	pecuniary	285	physiognomy	348	potion	308
oval	486	pedagogue	322	physiology	348	poverty	292
ovary	486	pedal	242	picture	90	praetor	493
ovate	486	pedant	322	pigment	90	pre-	316
over	325	pedestrian	242	pinnacle	173	precentor	32
owl	453	pelt	294	pinnate	173	preceptor	33
oxide	2	pen	173	pinnated	173	precipice	52
oxygen	2	penal	310	pirate	296	precipitate	52
oxytone	2	penalty	310	pituite	318	precipitous	52
		penetrate	291	plagiarism	92	precise	244
P.		penitence	310	plagiarist	92	preclude	56
		penitent	310	plagiary	92	predatory	155
pacific	285	penury	295	plane	91	predetermine	316
pacify	285	people	304	plank	91	predicate	10
pact	285	perambulate	509	plebeians	304	predict	10
pagan	285	perceive	33	plenary	304	predominant	213
page	285	perception	33	pleonasm	312	preface	339
paint (v. and n.)		perdition	225	plumb	452	pregnant	112
	90	peregrinate	106	plumbago	452	prefer	344
pale	293	perennial	333	plumber	452	preference	344
pallid	293	perfidious	271	plural	312	prefix	136
palm	287	perforate	340	plus	312	prejudge	125
palmy	287	period	235	pneumatic	307	prejudicate	125
pan	174	perjure	125	pneumonia	307	prejudice	125
panorama	415	perjury	125	point	320	premeditate	358
papa	289	permanent	358	police	311	preoccupy	33
parboil	313	pernicious	83	policy	311	prepare	313
parent	313	perpetual	173	politic	311	preposition	317
parricide	289	persecute	497	political	311	prepositive	317
part	313	persist	175	politics	311	preposterous	316
partake	313	perspective	99	polity	311	prescribe	122
partial	313	persuade	209	pollute	449	present	459
participate	313	pertain	188	poly-	312	preside	234
participle	313	pertinacious	188	polysyllable	312	president	234
particle	313	perturb	208	popular	304	pretend	188
particular	313	petal	174	porch	296	pretext	194
partner	313	phaeton	339	porcupine	93	prevent	509
parturition	313	phantasm	339	pork	93	prevention	509
pastor	291	phantom	339	port	296	prevision	236
pastoral	291	phenomenon	339	portend	188	prey	155
pasture	291	phone	339	portico	296	prim	316
patent	174	phonetic	339	portion	313	primary	316
paternal	289	phonics	339	possess 317, 234		prime	316
patriarch	289	phonology	339	position	317	primer	316
patrimony	289	phonotype	339	positive	317	primitive	316
patriot	289	phonography	339	possible	314	principal	33, 316
paucity	292	photo-	339	postpone	317	prior	316
patron	289	photograph	339	postscript	122	priority	316
pauper	292	physic	348	potation	308	priory	316
pause	292	physical	348	potency	314	pristine	316
pavement	286	physician	348	potent	314	proclaim	28
peace	285	physics	348	potential	314	proclamation	28

ENGLISH INDEX OF COGNATE WORDS. 249

procreate	67	pullet	322	rape	275	refute	165
prodúce	12	pulmonary	307	rapid	275	regal	134
próduce	12	pulmonic	307	rapine	275	regenerate	112
product	12	pulverize	323	rapture	275	regent	134
production	12	punctilious	320	ravage	275	region	134
profane	339	punctual	320	raven	275	regular	134
profess	339	punctuate	320	ravenous	275	reiterate	490
profession	339	puncture	320	ravin	275	reject	493
professor	339	pungent	320	ravine	275	relax	127
proffer	344	punish	310	ravish	275	relic	500
proficient	256	pupil	322	re-act	104	relics	500
profound	273	puppet	322	reave	275	relict	500
profuse	165	pure	310	rebel	231	relieve	146
progenitor	112	purgation	310	recalcitrant	435	religion	440
progeny	112	purgatory	310	recalcitrate	435	relinquish	500
projéct	493	purge	310	recant	32	remain	358
próject	493	puritan	310	receipt	33	remedy	358
prolix	127	purity	310	receive	83	reminiscence	358
prolocutor	77	pursue	497	receptacle	33	remonstrate	358
promiscuous	397	purulent	319	reception	33	remunerate	380
prone	316	pus	319	reciprocal	316	render	225
propagate	285	pusillanimous		reclaim	28	rendition	225
proper	316		322	reclamation	28	renovate	362
propinquity	316	putrefy	319	recline	57	repair	313
propitiate	316	putrid	319	recluse	56	repeat	173
propitious	316	pyre	321	recognition	120	repent	310
propose	317			recognize	120	repentance	310
proposition	317	**Q.**		recondite	256	replenish	304
proscribe	122			rĕcreate	67	replete	304
prosecute	497	quadrant	517	re-create	67	replication	92
prospect	99	quadrate	517	rĕcreation	67	report	313
prospectus	99	quadruped		re-creation	67	repose	317
prostitute	175		517, 242	recusant	60	reprehend	155
prostrate	185	quality	506	red	253	reprehension	155
protect	135	quantity	506	redolent	240	represent	459
protuberance	205	quart	517	redound	247	reptile	281
proverb	412	quartan	517	reduce	12	repugnant	320
provide	236	quarter	517	reduction	12	reputable	310
providence	236	quartette	517	redundant	247	reputation	310
provident	236	quarto	517	refer	344	repute	310
provision	236	quick	512	referable	344	requiem	44
provocation	496	quiescent	44	reference	344	rescind	244
provoke	496	quiet	44	referrible	344	rescript	122
proximate	316	quotient	506	reflect	103	reside	234
proximity	316			reflux	345	resist	175
prudent	236	**R.**		refluent	345	resolute	448
puberty	322			refract	522	resolution	448
public	304	radical	419	refraction	522	resolve	448
publican	304	rag	78	refractory	522	respect	99
puerile	322	rap	275	refuge	142	respite	99
pugilist	329	rapacious	275	refulgent	140	restitution	175
pugnacious	320	rapacity	275	refuse	165	restrict	465

restriction	465	salient	523	segment	45	solar	528
resurrection	134	saliva	456	select	440	sole	235
retain	188	salt	524	selenography	528	solemn	333
reticulated	422	salubrious	454	semi-	382	solicit	54
reticule	422	salvage	454	seminary	463	solicitous	54
retort	508	salvation	454	senate	357	solid	527
retortion	508	salve	454	senator	357	solstice	175
retribution	204	salver	454	senile	357	solution	448
retroduce	12	sanctify	462	senior	357	solve	448
revere	415	sanction	462	separate	313	somniferous	324
reverence	415	sane	462	September	280	somnific	324
reverend	415	sanity	462	Septuagint	280	somnolent	324
reverent	415	sap	503	sequence	497	soporiferous	324
revise	236	sapient	503	sequester	497	soporific	324
revision	236	saponaceous	503	sequestrate	497	sow	467
revisit	236	Saturn	463	serene	528	species	99
revival	512	save	454	series	422	specimen	99
revive	512	savior	454	sermon	422	spectre	99
revocation	496	scale	96	serpent	281	speculate	99
revoke	496	scalpel	95	serrated	45	spew	318
revolt	429	scandal	96	servant	422	spit	318
revolution	429	scandalize	96	serve	422	spoil	101
revolve	429	scene	100	service	422	spue	318
revolver	429	schism	244	servile	422	spume	318
rhetoric	412	scholar	148	servitude	422	spur	323
rhetorical	412	school	148	session	234	spurious	323
rhinoceros	49	science	45	sesterce	382	spurn	323
rhythm	421	scissors	244	set	234	squalid	46
right	134	scope	99	settle	234	squalor	46
rival	443	scribe	122	seven	280	stability	175
river	443	scrofula	122	sew	466	stable	175
rivulet	443	seat	234	sex	45	stable (n.)	175
rob	275	secant	45	shaft	97	stamp	177
Rome	421	secern	69	similar	377	stand	175
root	419	seclude	56	similitude	377	star	167
rubric	253	second(adj.)	497	simple 488,	377	station	175
ruby	253	second (vb.)	497	simulate	377	statute	175
rudder	411	secondary	497	simultaneous	377	stay	175
ruddy	253	secret	69	singular	377	stead	175
ruin	421	secretary	69	single	377	steadfast	175
rule	134	secrete	69	sir	357	steady	175
rumor	425	sect.	45	sire	357	steer	191
rupture	283	section	45	sit	234	stellar	167
rust	253	secular	463	six	473	stellated	167
		secure	60	skew	94	stem	181
S.		sedate	234	smelt	239	stenography	178
		sedative	234	smile	388	sterile	180
sacerdotal	462	sedentary	234	soap	503	stick	183
sacrament	462	sedition	493	sociable	497	stigma	183
sacred	462	seduce	12	social	497	stile	152
safe	454	seduction	12	society	497	stimulate	183
salacious	523	sedulous	235	soil	235	stimulus	183

sting	183	subtlety	194	syllogism	440	thatch	135
stipend	181	succulent	503	syllogize	440	theatre	255
stipulate	181	suck	503	sylvan	458	theory	255
stirrup	152	sudorific	237	syncope	64	thermometer	
Stoic	186	suffer	344				386, 520
stolid	176	sufferance	344	**T.**		thesis	256
stomach	184	sufficient	256			thin	188
stone	182	suffix	136	tack	189	third	204
story	236	suffuse	165	tact	189	thou	192
strain	465	sue	497	tag	189	thread	198
strangle	465	suicide	489	take	189	three	204
stratum	185	suit	497	talent	195	threnode	262
straw	418	sum	325	tame	213	threnody	262
street	185	summit	325	tangent	189	throne	261
strew	185	superb	325	tax	189	through	197
strict	465	superficial	339	teat	254	throw	198
stricture	465	superficies	339	technical	194	thud	206
string	465	superfluous	345	telephone	339	thumb	205
stringent	465	superinduce	12	tempest	196	thump	207
strong	465	superinduction	12	temple	196	thunder	188
stub	207	superior	325	temporal	196	thyme	265
stubble	207	supernal	325	temporary	196	timber	219
stubborn	207	superpose	317	temporize	196	time	196
stump (n.)	187	superposition	317	tempt	188	tincture	193
stump (vb.)	207	superscribe	122	ten	8	tinge	193
stupefy	187	supersede	234	tenable	188	to	217
stupid	187	superstition	175	tenacious	188	tolerable	195
suasion	209	superstructure		tenant	188	tolerate	195
suavity	209		185	tend	188	tomb	205
subduce	12	supervene	509	tender	188	tone	188
subduct	12	supervention	509	tenement	188	tonic	188
subduction	12	supine	326	tenet	188	tonsorial	196
súbject	493	supplement	304	tenor	188	tonsure	196
subjéct	493	supplicate	92	tense	196	tooth	241
subjoin	125	supplication	92	tension	188	torment	508
subjugate	125	supply	304	tent	188	torrent	200
subjunctive	125	support	313	tentative	188	torsion	508
sublime	442	suppose	317	tenuity	188	tort	508
subscribe	122	suppurate	319	tenuous	188	tortoise	508
subsequent	497	supreme	325	tenure	188	tortuous	508
subside	234	sure	60	term	197	torture	508
subsidy	234	surface	339	terminate	197	touch	189
subsidiary	234	surge	134	terrace	200	toxicology	194
subsist	175	survive	512	terrestrial	200	tradition	225
substitute	175	susceptible	33	terrible	202	traduce	12
substratum	185	suspect	99	terrier	200	traduction	12
substructure	185	sustain	188	terrify	202	transact	104
subtend	188	sustentation	188	terror	202	transcend	96
subterfuge	142	suture	466	tertiary	204	transcribe	122
subterranean	200	sweat	237	testaceous	200	transfer	344
subtile	194	sweet	209	text	194	transfigure	126
subtle	194	swine	467	textile	194	transfix	136

transfuse	165	ulcerate	19	vest (vb.)	460	vomit	381
transient	493	ulceration	19	vest (n.)	460	voracious	514
transit	493	un-	351	vestige	152	voracity	514
transition	493	uncle	475	vestment	460		
transitive	493	under	355	vesture	460	**W.**	
transitory	493	undulate	247	veteran	169		
translucent	80	uni-	373	vex	147	wag	147
transmute	379	unicorn	49	vice	482	wagon	147
transom	197	union	373	vicinity	85	wain	147
transport	313	unique	373	vicissitude	14	walk	429
transpose	317	unit	373	victuals	512	warm	520
transposition	317	unite	373	vigil	138	water	247
treble	204	universal	373	vigilant	138	wave	147
tree	230	up	326	vigor	138	way	147
tremble	203	urge	124	vill	85	weave	338
tremendous	203			villa	85	web	338
tremor	203	**V.**		village	85	wedlock	248
tremulous	203			villain	85	weigh	147
tribe	204	valley	431	violate	481	well (vb.)	429
tribulation	198	van	476	violent	481	what	519
tribunal	204	vapid	35	violet	479	when	506
tribune	204	vapor	35	viper	313	where	506
tribute	204	vascular	460	virgin	133	whether	506
triennial	333	vegetable	138	virulent	480	which	519
triple	204	vegetate	138	virus	480	who	519
trite	198	vegetation	138	visible	236	whole	30
trivial	204	vehement	358	vision	236	-wich	85
trope	508	vehicle	147	visit	236	-wick	85
trophy	508	venal	376	visitation	236	will	525
tropic	508	vend	376, 225	vital	512	wind	476
tropical	508	vendee	376	vituperate	482	wine	483
trouble	208	vender	376	vivacious	512	with	171
tuber	205	vendor	376	vivacity	512	wolf	81
tumid	205	vendue	376	vivid	512	wool	413
tumor	205	ventilate	476	vocabulary	496	word	412
turbid	208	ventricle	110	vocal	496	work	123
turbulent	208	ventriloquist	110	vocation	496	wort	419
turn	198	verb	412	vociferate	496		
two	231	verbal	412	voice	496	**Y.**	
tympanum	207	verbose	412	volition	525		
		verdict	10	voluble	429	yard	159
U.		vernal	478	volume	429	yearn	158
		vesper	461	voluntary	525	yesterday	160
udder	269	vespers	461	volunteer	525	yoke	125
ulcer	19	vessel	460	voluptuous	277	young	224

www.ingramcontent.com/pod-product-compliance
Lightning Source LLC
Chambersburg PA
CBHW031955230426
43672CB00010B/2156